About Island Press

Island Press, a nonprofit organization, publishes, markets, and distributes the most advanced thinking on the conservation of our natural resources—books about soil, land, water, forests, wildlife, and hazardous and toxic wastes. These books are practical tools used by public officials, business and industry leaders, natural resource managers, and concerned citizens working to solve both local and global resource problems.

Founded in 1978, Island Press reorganized in 1984 to meet the increasing demand for substantive books on all resource-related issues. Island Press publishes and distributes under its own imprint and offers these services to other nonprofit organizations.

Support for Island Press is provided by The Geraldine R. Dodge Foundation, The Energy Foundation, The Charles Engelhard Foundation, The Ford Foundation, Glen Eagles Foundation, The George Gund Foundation, William and Flora Hewlett Foundation, The John D. and Catherine T. MacArthur Foundation, The Andrew W. Mellon Foundation, The Joyce Mertz-Gilmore Foundation, The New-Land Foundation, The J. N. Pew, Jr. Charitable Trust, Alida Rockefeller, The Rockefeller Brothers Fund, The Rockefeller Foundation, The Tides Foundation, and individual donors.

The
Wild and Scenic Rivers of America

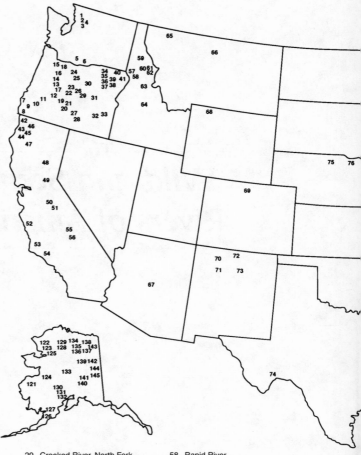

1. Skagit River
2. Cascade River
3. Sauk River
4. Suiattle River
5. White Salmon River
6. Klickitat River
7. Elk River
8. Chetco River
9. Illinois River
10. Rogue River
11. Umpqua River, North Fork
12. Willamette River, North Fork of Middle Fork
13. Quartzville Creek
14. Clackamas River
15. Sandy River
16. Roaring River
17. McKenzie River
18. Salmon River
19. Crescent Creek
20. Little Deschutes River
21. Big Marsh Creek
22. Squaw Creek
23. Metolius River
24. White River
25. Deschutes River
26. Crooked River
27. Sycan River
28. Sprague River, North Fork

29. Crooked River, North Fork
30. John Day River
31. Malheur River
32. Donner and Blitzen River
33. Owyhee River
34. Wenaha River
35. Grande Ronde River
36. Minam River
37. Powder River
38. Eagle Creek
39. Lostine River
40. Joseph Creek
41. Imnaha River
42. Smith River
43. Klamath River
44. Trinity River
45. Salmon River
46. Scott River
47. Eel River
48. Feather River, Middle Fork
49. American River
50. Tuolumne River
51. Merced River
52. Big Sur River
53. Sisquoc River
54. Sespe Creek
55. Kings River
56. Kern River
57. Snake River

58. Rapid River
59. Saint Joe River
60. Clearwater River, Middle Fork
61. Lochsa River
62. Selway River
63. Salmon River
64. Salmon River, Middle Fork
65. Flathead River
66. Missouri River
67. Verde River
68. Clarks Fork of the Yellowstone
69. Cache la Poudre River
70. Rio Chama
71. Jemez River, East Fork
72. Rio Grande
73. Pecos River
74. Rio Grande
75. Niobrara River
76. Missouri River
77. Eleven Point River
78. Cossatot River
79. Little Missouri River
80. Mulberry River
81. Buffalo River
82. Big Piney Creek
83. Hurricane Creek
84. Richland Creek
85. North Sylamore Creek
86. Saline Bayou

The National Wild and Scenic Rivers of America

1992

Many designated tributaries are not indicated.

87. Saint Croix River
88. Namekagon River
89. Wolf River
90. Vermilion River, Middle Fork
91. Black Creek
92. Sipsey Fork, West Fork River
93. Black River
94. Presque Isle River
95. Ontonagon River
96. Sturgeon River
97. Paint River
98. Yellow Dog River
99. Whitefish River
100. Sturgeon River
101. Indian River
102. Tahquamenon River, East Branch
103. Carp River
104. Pere Marquette River
105. Manistee River
106. Bear Creek

107. Pine River
108. Au Sable River
109. Obed River
110. Little Miami River
111. Little Beaver Creek
112. Chattooga River
113. Horsepasture River
114. New River, South Fork
115. Bluestone River
116. Loxahatchee River
117. Allegheny River
118. Delaware River
119. Wildcat Creek
120. Allagash River
121. Andreafsky River
122. Noatak River
123. Salmon River
124. Unalakleet River
125. Selawik River
126. Aniakchak River

127. Alagnak River
128. Kobuk River
129. Alatna River
130. Mulchatna River
131. Chilikadrotna River
132. Tlikakila River
133. Nowitna River
134. John River
135. Tinayguk River
136. Koyukuk River, North Fork
137. Wind River
138. Ivishak River
139. Beaver Creek
140. Gulkana River
141. Delta River
142. Birch Creek
143. Sheenjek River
144. Charley River
145. Fortymile River

Notes: Because many tributaries are not shown, the number of rivers listed here is not complete. See chapter 4 for further detail.

Rivers are numbered from west to east by state, followed by Alaska.

For the specific location of the rivers, refer to chapter 4, where rivers are listed alphabetically by state.

Rivers protected in programs related to the National Wild and Scenic Rivers System are not shown on the map, though they are included in chapter 4.

Also by Tim Palmer

The Environment of the Golden State
(editor and author of four chapters)

The Snake River: Window to the West

The Sierra Nevada: A Mountain Journey

Endangered Rivers and the Conservation Movement

Youghiogheny, Appalachian River

Stanislaus, the Struggle for a River

Rivers of Pennsylvania

The
Wild and Scenic
Rivers of America

Tim Palmer

ISLAND PRESS

Washington, D.C. ❑ *Covelo, California*

Library of Congress Cataloging-in-Publication Data

Palmer, Tim.
    The wild and scenic rivers of America / Tim Palmer.
       p.   cm.
    Includes bibliographical references and index.
    ISBN 1-55963-145-7 (alk. paper).—ISBN 1-55963-144-9 (pbk. :
alk. paper)
    1. Wild and scenic rivers—United States.   2. Stream conservation—
United States. I. Title.
QH76.P36 1993
333.91′62′0973—dc20   92-32660
                                            CIP

Printed on recycled, acid-free paper

Manufactured in the United States of America

10 9 8 7 6 5 4 3 2 1

Contents

A selection of photos follows page 96.

The
Wild and Scenic
Rivers of America

1

The Nation's Rivers

A RIVERINE TAPESTRY

From the arctic splendor of Alaska to the sandy flats of Florida, a collection of exceptional rivers has been protected and spared from biological wreckage. The National Wild and Scenic Rivers System includes many of our finest waterways and a rich American legacy.

Nothing comparable exists anywhere else in the world. Canada has named a small system of "heritage" rivers, and Costa Rica and some other countries have defended a few rivers in parklands, but no other nation has set out to keep a significant system of streams intact for the future.

Lying like short curls of thread thrown onto a map, the protected rivers remain strongholds of the free flow and refuges of the riparian Eden, of the mountain farmer and the rural landowner. The rivers are stretched-out green reserves overflowing with life, potential, and promise.

These rivers are home to trout, salmon, and sturgeon; steelhead, bass, and pike; squawfish, catfish, and carp. The eagle, heron, and kingfisher live here; also the otter, alligator, and beaver. And the rivers offer so much more, including people's favorite places, playgrounds, and living spaces. What an extraordinary system it is!

With the waters and shorelines and their inseparable valleys and canyons, the rivers represent perfection of the natural systems that constitute no less than life on earth. When we save a river, we save a major part of an ecosystem, and we save ourselves as well because of our dependence—physical, economic, and spiritual—on the water and its community of life.

The National Wild and Scenic Rivers System ranks among the major efforts of the federal government to protect natural areas, along with the national parks, wilderness areas, wildlife refuges, and forests. In contrast to those, the rivers program offers greater flexibility; it recognizes the coexistence of many uses on both public and private land. But despite its importance, the Wild and Scenic Rivers System remains distinctly smaller and less well known than other programs. Information can readily be unearthed about parks and wilderness, for example, but little has been written about the rivers. This is the new program, the uncharted one, unknown, really, yet fertile with possibilities.

In 1986 I wrote *Endangered Rivers and the Conservation Movement* as the history of river conservation, with a focus on protection from dams and water projects. *The Wild and Scenic Rivers of America* complements that book and presents an in-depth examination of the National Wild and Scenic Rivers System—the protection alternative to dams, diversions, canals, and leapfrogging land development. This volume consolidates information, thoughts, and analysis that were previously scattered and obscure, confined to the minds of a handful of experts, and that had not been described or probed much in public print until now. In addition, chapter 4 offers the first compendium of the nationally protected rivers.

How are these waterways protected? How was the system started, who stepped forward to initiate action, and what kind of struggles— political, physical, and rhetorical—have influenced the system's growth and lack of it? Which waterways were added, which were left out, and why? Where can the national rivers be seen? How can they be enjoyed? What is wrong with the system? Why the virulent opposition of some people? How are the rivers cared for after designation, and by whom? What dilemmas are faced today, what are the dimensions of the future, and how can protection be extended from the few rivers to the many? What should constitute a "system" of national rivers? What are the alternatives? Which streams should be added so that they remain wild and scenic for generations to come?

RIVERS OF NATURE, VICTIMS OF POLITICS

Congress passed the Wild and Scenic Rivers Act in 1968, and the system has grown in fits and starts from 12 rivers to 212 rivers as of August 1992, a number that includes large forks and branches of rivers but not small tributaries that are also named for protection under the act (see chapter 4 for important clarifications on the number of rivers). Including all named rivers and tributaries, 10,574.1 miles are designated. This book covers all the wild and scenic rivers plus 11 others in similar designations, such as "national rivers," "riverways," and "national recreation areas." Taken together, they form what this book often calls, simply, the "national rivers"—all being important nationally, all receiving federal protection, and in composite paralleling the national park system, though their administration and management are quite different.

These rivers are not just a collection of America's finest waterways, they are also victims of politics. A river of unexceptional value may be protected because political support exists for its protection, while an extraordinary stream may go unguarded because it lacks the votes. It is all a political resource in the end. The rivers system is based on turbulent contests of rhetoric, negotiation, leverage, influence, and plain luck, good and bad.

Having somehow made it over the hurdles of legislative consent, the national rivers shine as a showcase of life and natural wonders. In the Northeast, the Allagash churns darkly through the boggy wilds of Maine. The Obed in Tennessee and the Chattooga in Georgia burst white, green, and rocky from the Appalachians. In the deep south, Florida's Loxahatchee and Mississippi's Black Creek shelter an intricate abundance of life. The Eleven Point of the Ozarks riffles as a watery gem through the gentle lands of the Midwest. Dramatic in glowing light, the Rio Grande cuts through deep desert canyons of the Southwest. California—both abundantly blessed and severely stressed—is represented by the truly exceptional Kern, Merced, Tuolumne, American, and Feather rivers, along with four large river systems in the north, which form the greatest concentration of national rivers anywhere. In the Rockies, the Cache la Poudre in Colorado, the mosaic-bottomed Flathead in Montana, and a handful of Idaho rivers glimmer as they flow from great mountains. The Northwest, a land of rainfall and therefore a land of rivers, has the classic Rogue and a stunning collection of Oregon streams designated in one bold congressional bill. The Skagit and White Salmon flow from snowy Cascade peaks in Washington. In Alaska, where the wildness that once howled across the continent survives more or less intact, 33 national rivers drop from high country toward the sea in astonishing beauty.

A river lover's wish list, streams with wild and scenic protection include the Salmon, our longest river without a dam outside Alaska; the New, second-oldest river on earth; the Clarks Fork of the Yellowstone, arguably the wildest river in 49 states; the Selway, offering perhaps the preeminent wilderness river journey outside Alaska; the Klamath, the finest large stream for steelhead in the country; the Kings, whose upper reaches have the greatest undammed vertical drop on the continent; and the American and Delaware, backyard escapes for millions at each end of the country.

The system boasts variety, but it doesn't begin to represent a complete sampler of American rivers, important as that might be. Black waters of the Southeast are largely absent. Rivers of the Midwest, Northeast, and southern Rocky Mountains remain scarce. Few truly large rivers and few urban ones are included. Wild rivers as notable as the Colorado in the Grand Canyon and the Snake River in Grand Teton National Park lack the protection of national river status and suffer as a result.

The national rivers system includes 0.9 percent of the mileage of U.S. streams greater than five miles in length. If total stream mileage in the nation is counted, the national rivers account for only 0.3 percent—about 5 yards per mile. Meanwhile, dams block nearly every major river outside Alaska. More than 60,000 large dams and several hundred thousand smaller ones have been built. Considering also the development, channelization, and pollution that are so widespread, only 2 percent of the stream mileage outside Alaska having outstanding natural qualities remains unaffected by development or other changes. To protect this small percentage as national rivers would mean expanding the system to six times its present size—an enormous task, but one that talented, persistent, politically adept river advocates work toward.

Their work is urgent because the rivers of America face ongoing threats of five kinds, and national river designation can help to cope with some of these pressures. First, new dams are proposed. Although most large water projects fell victim to citizen opposition, fatal environmental reviews, and tight budgets, thousands of hydroelectric dams are on the drawing boards, and escalating oil prices would trigger construction of many. Second, channelization of rivers persists as a threat in some regions, especially the South and Midwest. Diversions from rivers in the West have devastated tens of thousands of miles of waterways and eliminated entire ecosystems. This depletion of water from rivers continues and worsens, though ample evidence along many streams shows that it is possible to have healthy rivers *and* supply irrigation and people's needs if we use water more efficiently. For municipal water supplies, the threat of diversions is increasing in the East. Third, although many rivers now run cleaner than they did 20 years ago, toxic wastes have worsened; nonpoint pollution from agriculture, logging, and urban storm runoff has scarcely been corrected at all; and advances in the past could be lost by rapid growth in some areas and by neglected funding for water quality. Fourth, land development along rivers—perhaps the most difficult problem— ranks as the foremost concern of citizens working to save streams nationwide. Fifth, poorly managed grazing, farming, logging, and mining ruin habitat and ecological integrity on a massive scale.

People's interest in protection has grown since John Muir initiated the idea at the Tuolumne River in Yosemite National Park in 1900 and since passage of the Wild and Scenic Rivers Act of 1968. Interest may accelerate in coming years for several reasons. First, river recreation has grown dramatically, bringing many people to a sense of the rivers' vitality and their role in the local economy. Fishing is one of the five most popular leisure activities in America. Where the occasional paddler used to drift down secluded waterways, canoeists along with rafters and kayakers now number in the hundreds of thousands. Trails and bikeways draw masses of people to riverfronts. Many of the people who walk, camp, watch birds, hunt, and otherwise have fun outdoors, or who simply sit down by the water's edge to relax, in fact depend on rivers and the pathways of greenery made possible by flowing water. A second, related reason for growing interest in river protection is the increased public concern for preservation of wildlife corridors and protection of watersheds for ecological integrity.

Third, the era of big dams has ended owing to exorbitant costs, shrewd opposition, and exhaustion of safe and suitable sites. Instead, people are slowly turning to the natural environment and to nonstructural approaches, such as flood plain management, rather than flood control dams; they are looking to water conservation, recycling, and reappropriation rather than to water-supply dams, and to solar energy rather than hydroelectric dams. At the same time, federal and state agencies have succeeded in reducing some water pollution, especially in urban areas, leading to new usability of and civic pride in the rivers.

Fourth, as the national parks and wilderness systems mature and Congress preserves the most important areas, more people will surely turn to river programs for protection of natural areas. Park and wilderness efforts will certainly continue for generations, but some of the emphasis placed on those efforts in the 1960s, 1970s, and 1980s may switch to rivers. River protection is a "frontier" in resource preservation and a type of program that doesn't depend on the controversial objectives of land acquisition, tight regulation, and highly specialized use.

Finally, protection programs will grow because rivers lie closer to people and are more central to community integrity and everyday life than perhaps any other feature of the landscape. Rivers are vastly more accessible than national parks, forests, wilderness, or wildlife refuges. More cities, towns, and villages have a river or stream than have mountains or, for that matter, woodlands. A waterway of some kind holds potential importance in virtually every community. That doesn't mean that national river designation will be appropriate for all streams—far from it—but it does mean that rivers could benefit from people's everyday concern for their local environment and neighborhood. Ironically, the universal appeal, presence, and use of rivers also make them difficult to protect.

Designation as a national wild and scenic river is the ultimate protection for a river, the clearest statement under law that we, as a people, have decided that this river should remain with its qualities intact. Enacted by Congress or by the secretary of the interior if requested by a governor, national river status does one thing for certain: it prohibits dams and other damaging water projects as decisively as a political system can.

A GREATER IDENTITY

The movement to protect rivers describes a grab bag of local efforts to save local rivers. All river politics is local politics. But a national movement also exists, bolstered by the Wild and Scenic Rivers Act and represented by the organization American Rivers, which since 1973 has spoken for river protection nationwide.

National support with broad backing and coalitions of groups with many concerns is essential for a truly national system of rivers to evolve and for the river protection movement to exceed the gains of the past. For this to happen, the rivers must have a greater identity as a group. Even now, a quarter century after passage of the Wild and Scenic Rivers Act, most Americans do not know of the system's existence. Without broad support in and out of government, a protection program will go nowhere. People's understanding must be accurate, based on facts, science, and history rather than on myth, rumor, and fear. Also, professionals involved with rivers can learn from history and from the accumulating body of experience based on rivers other than their own.

Finally, a celebration of the national rivers is in order. With a sense of pride, heritage, and accomplishment, people can look to these waterways as remarkable reminders of an idealized America that once was, and which still exists, though in fewer and fewer places. People can take pleasure in the rich tapestry of wild and scenic rivers that remain.

2

The Legacy of Protection

GENESIS IN AN ERA OF DAMS

The Wild and Scenic Rivers System appeared on a stage where untempered and frenetic development was taking place almost everywhere. Americans saw the Mississippi River as one string of dams and then nonstop levees, the Ohio River as back-to-back impoundments for all its 981 miles, the Tennessee River in continuous reservoirs built by the Tennessee Valley Authority, the Missouri River flooded for 250 miles at a time. In the Colorado River, dams blocked sublime canyons, and not a drop reached the sea anymore. The world's finest runs of salmon in the Columbia were reduced to a token few, and those that remain are either listed or destined for status as endangered species. Plugged in hundreds of places, the California rivers yielded water and power to fuel the permanent boom of agriculture and urban sprawl but fisheries, wild canyons, and wetlands were destroyed.

The developers making these decisions rarely concerned themselves with fish, wildlife, residents living along the rivers, recreation, or other uses of the free-flowing waters. People who cared accepted the losses as the price of progress or took comfort that other rivers remained. For a time, it seemed to be a large country.

Where dam-building agencies such as the Bureau of Reclamation and Army Corps of Engineers had not yet built dams, they proposed them: on the Colorado in the Grand Canyon, the Hudson in Adirondack Park, the Allagash and Saint John in Maine, the Delaware in Pennsylvania, the Potomac in Virginia, the Flint in Georgia, the Savannah in South Carolina, the Salmon in Idaho, the Klamath in California, the Illinois in Oregon, and on and on.

From John Muir's time at the turn of the century until the mid 1950s, conservationists directed protection at a few select rivers. Parklands motivated people to stop dams, much as they had attempted to do in 1910 at Hetch Hetchy in Yosemite, and as they had succeeded in doing in the 1940s at the Flathead River in Glacier National Park and in Kings Canyon. The Echo Park Dam controversy in 1955 launched a new era of nationwide attention, when coalitions of groups fought plans to dam the Green and Yampa rivers in Dinosaur National Monument. But saving a river because it was a river was not yet an accepted goal, so the Bureau of Reclamation dammed Glen Canyon of the Colorado River—the alternative to Echo Park—with little opposition.

From this genesis in park preservation, the story of river protection can be viewed as one of broadening concerns. Early in the history of river development in America—most of which occurred from 1900 to 1980—opposition to river destruction remained isolated and largely ineffective, yet gaining and maturing in strength. Following the early debates over national parks, people waged struggles in the 1960s to protect fish and wildlife, and landowners revolted against a government that aimed to buy them out. A new awareness of ecology, a booming interest in river recreation, and shrewd economic analysis followed, bringing a wider concern and a greater constituency for rivers.

Much as Hetch Hetchy had ignited political action to establish the National Park Service and institute better management of the parks, the Echo Park Dam fight sparked the wilderness movement, taking it from a simmering debate to a national campaign for the Wilderness Act of 1964—one of the most important pieces of natural areas legislation. Protection of rivers was thus the genesis of both the National Parks System and the Wilderness System.

After a proposal for dams in the Grand Canyon further escalated the fight for free-flowing streams, citizen opposition arose at scores of sites and in most states. Throughout the 1960s, citizens defended the

Allagash and Saint John in Maine, the Hudson in New York, the Red River in Kentucky, the Oklawaha in Florida, the Buffalo in Arkansas, the Kootenai and Flathead in Montana, the Kings and Middle Fork Eel in California, the Yukon in Alaska, and others.

Opposition to dams drove the river protection movement throughout the 1970s, until most of the remaining plans for large reservoirs had died, but many people had also become engaged in other aspects of waterways. Riverbed destruction through canals and channelization aroused the antagonism that dams had drawn, so that sites such as the Cross Florida Barge Canal, Trinity River Barge Canal in Texas, larger locks and dams in the Mississippi, and the Tennessee-Tombigbee Waterway in Mississippi and Alabama became national controversies, as did Soil Conservation Service channelization and draining of wetlands.

On another front, public action against water pollution had come in response to severe cholera epidemics in the nineteenth century, but the government accomplished only minimal precautions, such as construction of public water systems and the collection of sewage so it could be dumped into rivers instead of streets. In 1948 Congress passed the first act establishing a nationwide program dealing with pollution. Further interest in water quality for health and also for fishing, boating, and community pride grew in the 1950s and 1960s, resulting in important cleanups, such as that of the Potomac River in Washington, D.C. These efforts helped lay the foundations for the Federal Water Pollution Control Act of 1972.

Conservationists mostly excluded shoreline development from the river protection agenda, but a broader interest in open space protection grew in the 1960s. Land conservancies and planning programs tried to steer development away from flood plains, steep slopes, and prime farmland, which included river frontage, but the record of effectiveness along most waterways remained abysmal, as can be seen today in the rows and rows of houses and industrial plants pushed up against waterfronts. In the West, people became more aware of depleted streamflows resulting in dried-up riverbeds and elimination of riparian habitat.

Public interest and citizen action over dams, streambed destruction, water pollution, and shoreline development laid the foundation for different attitudes about the use and management of rivers. As isolated and uncoordinated battles to save certain rivers multiplied through the

1960s, new realizations crystallized: the United States was running out of natural rivers, costs of further development were escalating, alternatives to old-style exploitation could meet people's needs, scientific expertise supported conservation, the value of rivers could be somewhat quantified under the same economic systems that had justified the dams, and federal laws could allow conservation to compete more effectively with development.

Both attitudes and aesthetics changed. Concern over river protection spread from small groups striving to save a park or homeland to larger groups with wider aims. Interest in one river motivated people, but so did a wider awareness of rivers as the best part of nature, even as sacred places imbued with a spirituality earlier reserved for cathedrals, churches, and temples.

Beginning in the 1950s, a few people had realized that instead of constant opposition to development, a positive approach was needed. For antidam decisions to endure, society needed to recognize the value of rivers. Otherwise the builders would simply return when the political climate changed.

THE POSITIVE ALTERNATIVE

John and Frank Craighead grew up in the East, where their family vacationed at the West Virginia headwaters of the Potomac—an Appalachian garden of whitewater, green mountains, and wildlife. After studying wildlife biology, they settled in Montana and Wyoming, respectively, where they became the leading authorities on the grizzly bear, even seeking out the temperamental giants of the northern Rockies in their winter dens. The two scientists enjoyed rivers, and in Idaho they rafted upper Hells Canyon of the Snake, now dammed. They made films on the Middle Fork of the Salmon in which they first publicized the term *wild river*. Then came an experience that would change the course of river protection: they returned to the Appalachians.

"Years after we had moved west we went back and saw the Potomac," John Craighead said. "The water was polluted, it wasn't anything like what we had known." A homeland—the place of first impressions—may be a universal love, and seeing the loss of that special place has moved many people to act. "I realized that we still had wild rivers in the West, but we wouldn't for long if we didn't do something to save them."

Fighting the Army Corps of Engineers' Spruce Park Dam on the exquisitely wild Middle Fork of the Flathead in Montana, John Craighead wrote that conservationists should have a rivers program of their own instead of always acting on the defensive. In a 1957 issue of *Montana Wildlife* magazine he wrote, "Rivers and their watersheds are inseparable, and to maintain wild areas we must preserve the rivers that drain them." Wild rivers were a "species now close to extinction," needed "for recreation and education of future generations." With analysis of the rivers' potential for dams versus undeveloped use, Craighead believed that irreplaceable streams and landscapes could be saved while still meeting the needs for water.

At a Montana State University conference in 1957, John Craighead promoted his concept of river protection, writing later in *Naturalist* magazine that wild rivers were needed as "benchmarks" for comparison of environmental changes. Also in the *Naturalist*, Frank Craighead had described a system of river classification including *wild, semiwild, semiharnessed,* and *harnessed* rivers. He reasoned that once rivers were categorized, people would see the scarcity of quality streams and realize the need to protect them.

"I had worked on the wilderness legislation with Olaus Murie, Howard Zahniser, Stewart Brandborg, and others in the Wilderness Society," John Craighead recalled, "but they were not interested in rivers. They were most interested in specific areas of wilderness, many of them without rivers because the lands were at high elevations. The more I became involved, the clearer it became that we needed a national river preservation system based on the wilderness system but separate from it."

PROTOTYPICAL RIVERS

Like the Craighead brothers, Paul Bruce Dowling worked as a wildlife biologist and had spent part of his youth in the Appalachians of central Pennsylvania. He moved to Missouri, where dam proposals on the Current and Jacks Fork rivers were temporarily beaten in the 1940s, and the state government—progressive at the time in natural area preservation—supported protection of the two rivers in the 1950s.

The Current River Protective Association called for a river park with public ownership of recreation sites.

As secretary of the Missouri chapter of the Nature Conservancy in the mid 1950s, Dowling wrote to Senator Stuart Symington asking for a federal study of the Current and Jacks Fork. In 1983 Dowling recalled, "I had floated those rivers when I was a wildlife biologist with the state, and through a Nature Conservancy inventory we realized that many of the rare plant communities were along the streams of the Ozarks. Across the country we had national parks, and here I saw the potential for 'national rivers'—maybe ten or twenty of the unique gems, free-flowing streams representing the different physiographic regions."

In 1956 the National Park Service proposed a national recreation area along the Current and nearby Eleven Point River, where local people had also fought dams. The Park Service later recommended an Ozark Rivers National Monument, and held hearings on that proposal. Dowling testified that in 1957 the Missouri chapter of the Nature Conservancy had "introduced the idea of 'national rivers' as a designation appropriate to the Current River." This is perhaps the first official reference to *national rivers*.

Ted Swem, director of Park Service planning at the time, reflected, "We hoped that the Current River proposal would be prototypical, and that we could come forth with other river proposals." In 1959 the Park Service studied Montana's Missouri River below Fort Benton, but the river protection plan was shelved because of infighting among federal agencies. For Maine's Allagash, the Park Service proposed a national recreation area, but the state, fearing federal controls, vetoed the idea. Interior planners also studied the Suwannee in Florida and Georgia with no better results (in 1963, the Bureau of Outdoor Recreation added the Big South Fork of the Cumberland to this list of proposals, predating the Wild and Scenic Rivers Act by recommending a "wild river" where the Army Corps of Engineers was proposing a dam).

Not dissuaded, John Kauffmann and Stanford Young, planners in the Interior Department in the late 1950s, thought that a whole set of rivers should be protected and promoted this idea within the department. Swem recalled, "After studying the Current, the Allagash, and the Missouri, we began talking about the possibility of a system of rivers." In addition to Craighead and Dowling, Sigurd Olson in

Minnesota, Joe Penfold of the Izaak Walton League, Bud Jordahl in Wisconsin, and Leonard Hall in Missouri all spoke out for protection of rivers.

SHIFTING THE BALANCE OF THOUGHT

To thwart policies that President Eisenhower had instituted against federal dam projects ("creeping socialism," according to the president), the Senate formed a Select Committee on National Water Resources. It planned to retaliate with new dam proposals and move on with development. Ted Schad, director of the committee's staff, had served in a fascinating variety of jobs: as a Bureau of Reclamation budget director he had justified Echo Park and other dams, but at the same time he also served as a volunteer representing a Seattle hiking group on a Department of the Interior advisory committee. There he met Howard Zahniser of the Wilderness Society. "Zahniser convinced me that Echo Park should not be built," Schad recalled in 1983. After transferring to the Bureau of the Budget, Schad wrote Eisenhower's rivers and harbors veto messages.

At one of the committee's field hearings in 1959, the Craighead brothers called for a system of federally protected rivers. The Fish and Wildlife Service in the Interior Department meanwhile reported to the Select Committee that some rivers are most valuable if left unaltered, and in 1960 Interior officials wrote to the Committee on Interior and Insular Affairs: "There still remain in various sections of the country natural free-flowing streams whose integrity might be preserved in the face of the water-control onslaught if conscientious planning to this end were applied."

Armed with these recommendations, Schad proposed in the Senate Select Committee's report that certain streams be preserved in their free-flowing condition "because their natural scenic, scientific, aesthetic, and recreational values outweigh their value for water development and control purposes now and in the future." Examples were listed: the Allagash, Current, and Eleven Point, and the Rogue in Oregon. In retrospect, Schad thought that some senators on the Select Committee may not even have noticed the report's wild river recommendation—it was one of many in the document. The committee adopted the report without even discussing the river protection idea, and this became the federal government's first major proposal for a national rivers system.

In 1960 the National Park Service, responding to the Senate Select Committee, wrote, "Particularly in areas of dense population and in arid regions, clear, natural running water is now a rarity and under the pressure of anticipated future requirements may become nonexistent." As it turned out, most of the protection that later resulted was not in densely populated or arid regions.

Debates had been held about wilderness and how much of it was needed, leading to broader questions about recreation that no one could answer. As a result, Congress created the Outdoor Recreation Resources Review Commission to prepare the nation's first thorough study of recreation needs. Carrying forward the momentum for a rivers system, the commission's report *Outdoor Recreation for America* stated, "Certain rivers of unusual scientific, esthetic, and recreation value should be allowed to remain in their free-flowing state and natural setting without man-made alterations."

By 1961 the Craigheads' idea of classifying and protecting rivers had matured, and the idea of national rivers gained support. The Current River would be saved, and a growing collection of other river proposals was incorporated into government reports. Interior Department planners, enthusiastic about river protection, waited only for a secretary who was ready to act.

EVOLUTION OF A NATIONAL GOAL

"As a congressman in the 1960s I was prodam," Stewart Udall said during an interview in 1983. "I voted for the upper Colorado project that flooded Glen Canyon. I instinctively identified my values more with the Sierra Club than with dam building, except that I was from Arizona, and so you had to be for water. You couldn't go to Congress and be against dams."

On a field trip, rarely allowed by Interior committee chair Wayne Aspinall, Udall and his family were one of the last groups to float through Glen Canyon. "I got off the river with very mixed feelings. I didn't feel guilt-stricken, but I kept saying to myself that we hadn't done a very good job in the West of achieving balance. In deciding where to put dams we had made mistakes. So I began to have doubts."

In 1961 President Kennedy appointed Udall secretary of the interior. "Suddenly I had the national responsibility, and that put on my shoulders the burden of thinking for the nation and not just for Arizona, which is what a congressman would do when it comes to water. My thinking gradually changed in the early sixties at the same time that I was testifying for dams."

Udall personified the upheaval in water development philosophy. He had supported dams that were the epitome of river destruction and that rallied conservationists to the cause of river protection. But with the help of people who were working to save their rivers, by experiencing these waterways personally from a canoe or a raft, and with a statesman's regard for his job, Udall saw the need for balance and preservation. This man stood uniquely as a river developer and a river saver both, bearing the complications and compromises inherent in holding two opposite views at once.

"Three major things happened during my first year," Udall recalled. "Senator [Edmund] Muskie got a little floatplane and we went up to canoe the Allagash. He was anxious to leave the river alone, and it was threatened by the Rankin Rapids Dam. So the Allagash was identified as one of the finest wild rivers in the eastern part of the country, and the fact that people in Maine wanted to save it left an impression on me, particularly when I saw it, when I canoed it. I had never been canoeing, really; we didn't have that many rivers in Arizona. Senator Muskie knew that Maine couldn't afford to buy land, yet the state wanted to do the job itself, so we eventually matched their funds with federal funds. We preserved a river for about $3 million."

Udall, unequivocally a man of the Southwest, saw something new, something worth saving in the soggy bogs feeding this wild river of the far Northeast. "Then later that summer we were looking at new parks and seashores. It was an explosive period for that, and I made it a policy to go out and see the places in order to throw the spotlight on the proposals." On a Current River canoe trip Udall met George Hartzog, whom he later appointed director of the National Park Service.

"The third thing was even more of a catalyst. There was a big fight over an Idaho dam called Bruce's Eddy, now called Dworshak, on the Clearwater. The conservationists opposing it came to me and wanted me to help in the fight. I got involved, and it dramatized for me the flaws and misconceptions in the dam-building philosophy of the New

Deal. The values were changing, and if that dam were considered in 1964 it never would have been authorized. So for me, this is where the kernel of the idea for the wild and scenic rivers bill came from."

Udall sought an amendment banning additional Clearwater dams. This failed, but the concept would be resurrected for nothing less than an entire system of rivers where dams would be banned.

In *The Quiet Crisis* (1963), the secretary articulated his new view of river protection. "Generations to follow will judge us by our success in preserving in their natural state certain rivers having superior outdoor recreation values. The Allagash of Maine, the Suwannee of Florida, the Rogue of Oregon, the Salmon of Idaho, the Buffalo of Arkansas, and the Ozark Mountain rivers in the state of Missouri are some of the waterways that should be kept as clean, wild rivers—a part of a rich outdoor heritage."

Senator Gaylord Nelson of Wisconsin invited Udall to paddle the Saint Croix and, quite taken by these canoe trips, Udall paddled the Potomac and Shenandoah with Bob Harrigan, a boater who had pioneered many runs in the Appalachians.

"Big things under Kennedy were the national seashores, Canyonlands National Park, and the Ozark rivers, but the wilderness bill was the landmark legislation. As it came closer to law, my thinking began to turn more toward rivers legislation that would complement and be another kind of wilderness bill, and we started studies at Interior." Udall asked Frank Craighead, who worked for the U.S. Fish and Wildlife Service, to prepare a paper on river classification. Udall acted on the key recommendation of the Outdoor Recreation Resources Review Commission by creating the Bureau of Outdoor Recreation, and he wrote to Orville Freeman, secretary of the Department of Agriculture, to organize a wild and scenic rivers study team. In 1964 planners led by Stanford Young collected a list of 650 rivers for consideration, reduced it to about 70, then announced 22 rivers for detailed field study. Among the 70 rivers were the following:

Sacramento in California
Hoh, Methow, and Queets in Washington
Big Hole, Madison, Upper Missouri, and Yellowstone in Montana
Henry's Fork Snake and Teton in Idaho
Green in Wyoming
Colorado, Green, and San Juan in Utah

Animas and White in Colorado
Colorado and Salt in Arizona
Gila in New Mexico
Guadalupe in Texas
Big Fork in Minnesota
Wapsipinicon in Iowa
Gasconade in Missouri
Little Wabash in Illinois
Blue in Indiana
Buffalo in Tennessee
Cumberland in Kentucky
Black Warrior in Alabama
Tangipahoa in Louisiana and Mississippi
French Broad and Linville in North Carolina
James and Shenandoah in Virginia
Savannah in Georgia and South Carolina
Oklawaha, Suwannee, and Wacissa in Florida
Cheat, Cacapon, and Greenbrier in West Virginia
Potomac in Maryland, West Virginia, and Virginia
Susquehanna in New York and Pennsylvania
Youghiogheny in Pennsylvania and Maryland
Ausable, Hudson, and North Branch Susquehanna in New York
Mullica in New Jersey
Connecticut in New Hampshire
Penobscot, East and West branches in Maine

(An additional 21 rivers were listed that were eventually included in the Wild and Scenic Rivers System between 1968 and 1992.)

Critics who were against "locking up" resources attacked new national park proposals, so to sidestep political hazards, Interior officials sought innovative land protection. The federal recreation estate could be expanded by naming national recreation areas (most of the early ones surrounded large reservoirs), national seashores, lakeshores, and rivers without the restrictions of national park status that ignited the wrath of hunters and private landowners. Ted Swem said, "Although the national monument classification was justified for the Ozark rivers, it was obvious that the proposal would not be authorized if hunting was prohibited. So we suggested the national scenic riverways classification."

While planners within Interior explored the idea of a rivers system, the political support to protect the Current River had ripened. With Udall's recommendation, President Kennedy called for protection of the Current River in his conservation message to the Senate Select Committee on National Water Resources in 1961. At hearings in 1963 Udall testified, "It would be difficult to find an area where so much beauty and variety of natural features can be preserved by setting aside so little." Also in 1963 Senator Nelson introduced a bill to make the Saint Croix a national river (he had helped convince the Northern States Power company to sell and donate to the government 70 miles of frontage along both sides of the river where a power dam had been planned). The Ozark rivers bill passed the Senate but stalled in the House. Representative John Saylor went to work, and in 1964 the Ozark National Scenic Riverways were designated as the first national rivers, for "conserving and interpreting unique scenic and other natural values, including preservation of portions of Current River and Jacks Fork River as free-flowing streams." During the same year, Congress passed the Wilderness Act, requiring that certain public lands remain without development or logging. Conservation leaders, with political momentum on their side, looked to their next opportunity.

"John Craighead had left all this material on my desk," recalled Stewart Brandborg, then director of the Wilderness Society. "Howard Zahniser had talked about a system of 'wilderness rivers', and the idea of wild rivers was deep in the hearts of the old Wilderness Society leaders."

Comparing wilderness to river preservation, Udall said, "The wilderness concept began with Aldo Leopold and other foresters back in the twenties. The Wilderness Society was formed in the thirties. They said we needed a law, and wrestled around in the fifties, and the first bill was introduced in 1957. The wilderness concept had this 40-year gestation period. With wild and scenic rivers it was just a few years. It came on strong, even though there was no national constituency. The momentum of the wilderness bill had a tide moving, and sometimes you see two waves, and you jump on the second wave and ride it in. The timing was just perfect. President Johnson's chief of domestic affairs kept saying, 'Johnson wants new legislation,' and I told him about the wild and scenic rivers idea and he said, 'That sounds great, get it ready.'"

In 1964 the first wild and scenic rivers bill was called the Wild Rivers Act, focusing on the extraordinary rivers of the West, but Congress later broadened this to include "scenic" and "recreation" rivers. President Johnson called for a rivers bill in his 1965 State of the Union address: "We will continue to conserve the water and power for tomorrow's needs with well-planned reservoirs and power dams, but the time has also come to identify and preserve free-flowing stretches of our great rivers before growth and development have made the beauty of the unspoiled waterway a memory."

Udall vividly remembered his former committee chair's reaction. "After Johnson's message, Wayne Aspinall walked off the floor and told a reporter that wild rivers were the craziest idea he had ever heard of. He thought I was off my rocker by then on a lot of things. Since Senator Frank Church had been involved with the Clearwater [he supported the dam], he decided to take his life into his own hands and sponsor the wild and scenic rivers bill in the Senate. He was bold; he was from Idaho, and this was controversial. He was splitting from the other side. I remember going to John Saylor—he was in complete agreement with the rivers idea—and about Aspinall's comment Saylor said, 'We'll just wear him down.'

"In 1965 we got the bill passed overwhelmingly in the Senate, where Senators Church and Nelson were strong supporters. The Senate's vote said, 'The country wants wild and scenic rivers.' It left Aspinall with the question, Was he going to be arbitrary and obstruct the will of the country? Then Saylor started nagging him, 'Wayne, better get some hearings going or things are going to get mighty unpleasant around here.' "

Howard Zahniser was Saylor's personal friend, and he had stressed that the rivers idea paralleled the wilderness law but was broader because it included all types of rivers and could mobilize people nationwide. Brandborg remembered, "That's all you had to say to Saylor." The Rivers Act would be one of the Pennsylvania representative's greatest conservation accomplishments. Others included the Wilderness Act, the defeats of the Echo Park and Grand Canyon dams, the preservation of the Current and Jacks Fork, and the saving of Hells Canyon. A champion of new parks and traditional conservation, "Big John" Saylor was a master at congressional dealing and arm twisting in the old style.

Over a period of several years, congressional members introduced 16 different wild and scenic river bills. As forerunners to the Wild and Scenic Rivers System, House Report 1623 in 1968 credited the Ozark Scenic Riverways, designation of the Allagash as a "wilderness waterway" by the Maine legislature, land acquisition by Wisconsin along the Wolf River, and legislation calling for study of the Hudson and Connecticut rivers. The report also cited many laws whereby Congress had recognized the importance of commerce on rivers, along with flood control, pollution abatement, and fish and wildlife. It noted that "to date, however, the desirability of preserving some of our rivers simply for the sake of being able to enjoy them in their natural state or for their recreational value has not been noticed in any overall piece of Federal legislation." This recognition marked a turning point in America's attitudes toward rivers.

In 1967, after compromising the bill to eliminate threats to most water developments, Aspinall introduced the most complex legislation, reflecting compromises with various interest groups. What converted him? "He must have owed Saylor some real big favors," Brandborg said in 1983. In fact, Aspinall received support for five dams in Colorado that fit the classic description of a boondoggle, authorized in 1968 as part of the Central Arizona Project even though the Bureau of Reclamation did not recommend three of them.

The national rivers bill called for three classes of rivers: wild, scenic, and recreational. The wilderness idea of preserving the "glamour" rivers of the West was broadened; Secretary Udall said, "Rivers should be saved in all parts of the country." National conservation groups, canoe clubs, and dam fighters packed hearings in 1968. Breaking the myth that protected rivers were relevant only to wild expanses of the West, the Saint Croix, Eleven Point, and Little Miami, all in the Midwest, received the most support as citizens opposed dams once proposed on all three rivers. Stanford Young of the Interior Department said, "Mostly the motivation was against dams. The problems of riparian development were not yet perceived because they weren't dramatic." The bill included the Middle Fork of the Feather in California, though two dam sites proposed by the Richvale Irrigation District had been approved by the state.

The big water development agencies ensured that the act posed no threat to the dams they really wanted. They enjoyed a presumption that development was better than protection, a problem that persists in the 1990s. Tennessee Valley Authority chair Aubrey J. Wagner objected to protection of the French Broad River and the Little Tennessee, including the Tellico Dam site where the endangered snail darter was later found: "Planning and construction of water control and development projects have progressed to a point which would make it inappropriate to include these streams." The spectacular upper Green River in Wyoming was deleted because of an irrigation dam site at Kendall, also the site of a unique warm springs and an endangered fish. A Seattle City Light executive testified against the upper Skagit, where the municipal power company planned Copper Creek Dam to flood the river's only remaining whitewater (the rest of it—all the way into Canada—had already been buried by Ross Dam). The Tocks Island Regional Advisory Council supported Delaware River protection but only above the Tocks Island dam site (as testimony to the rapidly growing support for river protection, Tellico was the only dam among all these sites that was eventually built).

Residents shot down wild and scenic designation of Potomac tributaries in West Virginia, and landowners along the Shenandoah expressed fears that their property would be condemned—concerns that would be voiced more and more in the coming decades. The National Reclamation Association opposed the bills forthrightly: "The concept does not conform to the principles of multipurpose development."

The acting secretary of the army pursued a subtler strategy: "The Nation can well afford to forego the development of streams of unusual natural beauty. . . . But for very few of these have studies been made which provide an adequate basis for a wise decision." Because the bill would block dam proposals on the Salmon and Middle Fork of the Clearwater, several senators dissented from the Interior committee, and Len Jordan of Idaho said, "The combined runoff of the Salmon and Clearwater Rivers is greater than the total runoff of the Colorado River and the combined hydroelectric potential is greater than Grand Coulee or greater than all hydroelectric potential on the entire Colorado River."

From Udall's home state, Arizona representative Sam Steiger flatly said, "Under the guise of protecting scenic values, this legislation will stifle progress, inhibit economic development and incur a staggering expenditure."

But Stewart Udall knew what he was doing. "We had the momentum, and the dam people who didn't like it just weren't in a frame of
mind to fight it. I had been pretty good to them, giving them some of
the things they wanted, including dams. So I looked them in the eye
and said, 'We're going to balance things off.' "

LANDMARK LEGISLATION

As the conservation movement matured, the idea of river preservation
gained support. Contrasting those days to the 1980s, Robert Eastman,
who became director of the rivers program at the Department of the
Interior, said, "Back then, if you had a good idea you could put it to
work. The people were concerned about conservation. They wanted
to protect natural places. Secretaries Udall and Freeman wanted to
push programs, and Presidents Kennedy and Johnson were receptive.
There was money to do things without having to take it out of
someone else's program. Times were good and people didn't mind
spending funds on parks and rivers."

Reflecting on the parks and the new systems of wilderness, seashores, and national rivers, Ted Swem said of the 1960s, "I don't
know if we'll ever have a period like that again."

Because 1968 was an election year, Congress delayed action on the
rivers bill until many people thought it was too late. The House
refused to suspend rules to allow the bill to bypass committees and go
straight to the floor. The Interior committee quit meeting, but Aspinall, quite likely pushed by Saylor, agreed to poll his members, who
had dispersed across the states. On September 6 they agreed to release
the bill, and on September 12 the House voted 265–7 in favor of it. On
October 2, the Senate approved and President Johnson signed the
Wild and Scenic Rivers Act, designating parts of 12 rivers and identifying 27 others for study.

The act states

It is hereby declared to be the policy of the United States that certain
selected rivers of the Nation which, with their immediate environments, possess outstandingly remarkable scenic, recreational, geologic, fish and wildlife, historic, cultural, or other similar values,

shall be preserved in free-flowing condition, and that they and their immediate environments shall be protected for the benefit and enjoyment of present and future generations. The Congress declares that the established national policy of dams and other construction at appropriate sections of the rivers of the United States needs to be complemented by a policy that would preserve other selected rivers or sections thereof in their free-flowing condition to protect the water quality of such rivers and to fulfill other vital national conservation purposes.

Frank Craighead wrote that the Wild and Scenic Rivers Act was "as innovative as was the national park act."

The original "instant" rivers, a stunning collection, were the Middle Fork of the Clearwater and its large tributaries the Lochsa and the Selway for a total of 185 miles in Idaho, the Eleven Point for 44.4 miles in Missouri, the Middle Fork of the Feather in California (reduced in 1976 to 108 miles), the Rio Grande for 49 miles and its tributary Red River for 4 miles in New Mexico, the Rogue for 84.5 miles in Oregon, the Saint Croix and its major tributary the Namekagon for 200 miles in Wisconsin and Minnesota, the Middle Fork of the Salmon for 104 miles in Idaho, and the Wolf for 25 miles in Wisconsin. These are usually listed as 8 rivers, based on the legislative language that did not recognize tributaries, but in all, parts of 12 rivers were named.

Legislation earlier in 1968 had included two choice eastern rivers, West Virginia's Cacapon and Shenandoah, which were dropped because of landowner opposition. As a unified bloc, the Army Corps of Engineers, Bureau of Reclamation, Federal Power Commission, and Soil Conservation Service vigorously opposed protection for the upper Green River in Wyoming, the Feather, Middle Fork Salmon, and Rogue, but President Johnson included them anyway. Wyoming senators Simpson and McGee then succeeded in eliminating the upper Green, which remains unprotected.

Most of the designated rivers flowed through public land, and they represented the most outstanding wild rivers in the West. Private land bordered portions of the Eleven Point in Missouri, and the Wolf transected Indian land where the government and tribe failed in attempts at cooperative agreements for use of the river. The only other nonwestern rivers—the Saint Croix and Namekagon—owed their designation to Senator Nelson, who had worked to protect those streams since serving as governor of Wisconsin in 1959.

THE AMERICAN RIVERS CONSERVATION COUNCIL

As the Craigheads had envisioned 13 years before, river supporters now had a program of their own; with a positive alternative, they could take the initiative and did not have to posture "against" everything. Yet the movement had only begun. Rearguard battles preoccupied river supporters, who failed to get far enough ahead of the dam builders to launch long-term preservation efforts. At Interior secretary Walter Hickel's direction, the Bureau of Outdoor Recreation scrutinized controversial projects of the Army Corps of Engineers (but not of Interior's own Bureau of Reclamation) and helped to stop Salem Church Dam on Virginia's Rappahannock River, yet a recommendation to upgrade protection for that system to national river status went nowhere.

In the following two decades, the program grew and evolved with unpredictable twists, with disappointments and surprises, and with huge gulps of progress followed by entire congressional sessions of nothing.

In 1970 the Interior secretary added the Allagash at the request of the governor of Maine (a request that had originally stemmed from the work of Interior Department planners). In 1972 Congress amended the Rivers Act to add the lower Saint Croix, and then the secretary added the Little Miami at the request of Ohio's governor, but otherwise the system languished. Federal agencies completed few studies, which were essential for congressional action. The rivers program lacked the constituency enjoyed by the wilderness program, and in many ways saving rivers was a more difficult task. Stanford Young reflected, "Rivers are so much more controversial than blocks of land; many people are dependent upon the rivers." Unlike the western high country, rivers and their valleys appeal to a chorus of competing users. Bottomland timber is the best, and roads follow flood plains. Most streams are partly bordered by private land, and whether or not agencies proposed acquisition, residents feared condemnation of their property. The alternative—land use control—was likewise anathema, especially if coming from the state instead of the local level. Water developers with countless schemes desired the rivers for their own purposes. Because of implied water quality controls, towns upstream from potential designations, such as Wellsboro, Pennsylvania, situated above Pine Creek, opposed protection. State and local governments resented federal involvement even though the act allowed states to administer rivers without federal managers.

Rivers remained a secondary concern of the national environmental groups, busy with wilderness, parks, and wildlife, and the issues of air pollution and nuclear power. Michael McCloskey, executive director of the Sierra Club in 1981, said, "We're interested in saving substantial tracts of land that include rivers, but we're not enamored with the linear aspects. It's against the grain for us to be real happy with corridors. With wilderness, we get the whole package."

Gaylord Nelson, an environmental leader for 20 years in the Senate, initiator of Earth Day in 1970, and chairman of the Wilderness Society after 1982, said, "Much of the conservation activity has revolved around the issues of public lands, not rivers."

"The rivers have taken short shrift," added Brock Evans of the National Audubon Society. "The conservation groups budget their work on rivers within the category of public lands, and as a result, the rivers don't get the attention they deserve." "River people" formed state groups, such as Ohio's Rivers Unlimited in 1972, led by Mike Fremont, and California's Friends of the River in 1973, but no group adopted rivers nationwide or lobbied for the national system. In a 1972 article in the journal of the American Whitewater Affiliation, Jerry Meral, a whitewater canoeist and staff scientist for the Environmental Defense Fund in California, called for the formation of a national rivers organization to take responsibility for what was not yet being done.

In March 1973, 33 conservationists met in Denver at the invitation of Phil LaLena to form the American Rivers Conservation Council (ARCC). This group included Mike Fremont, founder of Rivers Unlimited in Ohio; Jerry Mallett of the Western River Guides Association in Colorado; Claude Terry, an outfitter and resource consultant from Georgia; Rafe Pomerance, later director of Friends of the Earth; Jerry Meral, founder of Friends of the River; David Foreman, later founder of Earth First!; and Chuck Clusen, who later worked for the Wilderness Society. Brent Blackwelder of the Environmental Policy

Center (later the Environmental Policy Institute) chaired the board for the next decade.

"We debated about what to do," Blackwelder recalled of that first meeting. "Should we fight dam proposals or support designations? We decided to work for scenic river protection, but some of the most logical choices were slated for damming, and if we didn't fight the developers, there would be no scenic rivers to protect. So we've always focused on getting rivers in the system and also on stopping dams, but scenic rivers were supposed to be the focus—nobody else was working on that." Other goals were to seek deauthorization of certain water projects, establish state river systems, increase interest rates charged for water projects, and eliminate fabricated recreation benefits justifying new dams without accounting for recreational losses on the rivers. The Salmon River in Idaho was one of few streams named for special action, though its protection would for years elude the group and much of the river remains unprotected.

One of the few founders still on the organization's board in 1992, Mike Fremont remembered, "Eventually we got to where we knew money was needed to kick this thing off, and Brent threw a hundred bucks down. Everybody pitched in and we had a few thousand dollars to start an operation." A director to be paid $400 a month was difficult to find, but eventually the board hired Bill Painter, who had worked on the original Environmental Teach-in at the University of Michigan in 1969.

Painter recalled the council's early days when he and Blackwelder shared a one-room, upstairs office packed full of paper and ringing telephones on a side street southeast of the Capitol. "Money was always a struggle, and I spent a lot of time learning the ropes on the Hill. I knew how to run a little ragtag outfit, but the lobbying—that I had to pick up from Brent. We got a newsletter rolling and I went to work trying to get more rivers in the national system.

"While I was trying to do that, Brent was in the thick of two dozen scrapes between the Environmental Policy Center and the Army Corps. That was before the tide was turned on bad projects—they were coming from everyplace. I could have done nothing but help Brent on each daily political crisis, but I saw that if ARCC was to have an identity, we had to get rivers in the national system."

The efforts of Painter and others paid off. In 1974 the Chattooga

River in Georgia, North Carolina, and South Carolina became the first river designated by Congress since the original act and the first to make it through the "study" process (see chapter 3). ARCC lobbied and helped to win a stronger federal flood insurance program to protect river frontage through flood plain zoning. In 1975, authorization for 29 river studies with the possibility of later designation passed Congress, more than doubling the original number of "study" rivers.

DOWN TO THE LAST MINUTE

On the final day of 1975 Congress passed the Hells Canyon National Recreation Area Act, adding the Snake in Idaho and Oregon and the Rapid River with its West Fork in Idaho to the national system and deauthorizing Asotin Dam, which had been planned for lower Hells Canyon. A milestone in river conservation, the Hells Canyon fight marked the first great success in the face of an imminent threat. Half the canyon and half the length of the 1,056-mile-long river had already been dammed. The remaining half of Hells Canyon was the second deepest canyon in the United States, one of the West's premier big whitewater runs, and a fishery for salmon, steelhead, and white sturgeon—the largest freshwater fish on the continent. A 1967 draft of the Wild and Scenic Rivers Act had deferred to the dam-building utility companies and excluded the endangered, final reach of Hells Canyon "in keeping with a balanced natural resource program."

In what had been simply a question of which dam among several power companies should be allowed to build, the Supreme Court ruled in 1967 that the Federal Power Commission must decide not just which dam should go up and who should reap the profits, but whether or not *any* dam should be built. This notable decision gave conservationists, led by the Hells Canyon Preservation Council of Idaho and by the Sierra Club, time to organize a campaign to add the Snake to the wild and scenic system.

The New River in North Carolina was the fledgling ARCC's most important case because, as in the case of Hells Canyon, the threat was immediate. Bill Painter recalled, "The national rivers system was mostly made up of rivers that no one else wanted for dams, but here was a case where we had to fight water developers on their own ground. The dam was already approved by the Federal Power Commission; national designation was the only way to save it. It seemed like a tough one to win, but the local people were organized." North Carolina residents, the state, and the Bureau of Outdoor Recreation had been working to save the river for several years, through court cases and intense political lobbying.

Painter developed a formula that later proved effective on other rivers. "We helped frame the campaign so it would sell in Congress. The local people were emphasizing the river, but I began to emphasize the Appalachian cultural history and the farmers who would have to move. We found out in the FPC [Federal Power Commission] files that there were alternate sites that would affect less land and fewer people. When the New was designated in 1976, it was a huge success. Conservationists had won a river that would otherwise have been dammed."

In 1976 Congress designated the extraordinarily scenic North, Middle, and South forks of Montana's Flathead, including the Glacier View dam site, which had been fought in the 1940s; the Spruce Park dam site on the Middle Fork, where the Craigheads had first advanced the idea of a protected rivers system; and the Smoky Range site on the North Fork, fought over in the 1960s. The Obed of Tennessee was included, where the Tennessee Valley Authority had studied a dam site, though the designated mileage was greatly reduced from the studied reach. Another section of the lower Saint Croix was added at the request of the governors of Wisconsin and Minnesota. Congress designated 149 miles of the upper Missouri, one of the initial rivers for which Interior Department planners had proposed national protection in the early 1960s. (Except for the Suwannee, this completed protection for the major prototype rivers recommended before the National Wild and Scenic Rivers System existed.) By 1977, 1,655 miles on 29 rivers (counting tributaries) were designated.

When Bill Painter left the ARCC, Howard Brown, who had analyzed water development for the Congressional Research Service, became the organization's second director. He brought to the job a knowledge of water policy that was important during the Carter administration and a steadfast, solid commitment to river conservation, in spite of the organization's limited financial resources to fight increasingly formidable problems.

MEETING THE RESISTANCE

Through the late 1970s, landowners fearing condemnation stalled many national river proposals in the East and Midwest. The government had exercised eminent domain in a few of the first designations, such as the Eleven Point, but by 1976 the thrust of protection was to avoid condemnation and focus instead on easements and zoning. Officials assured riverside landowners that they would not be evicted, but to no avail; the specter of a land grab could not be erased (see chapter 3).

Although ARCC's lobbying paid dividends, the rivers system failed to grow much, and a typical national river study required a tedious five to seven years to complete. Howard Brown explained, "The way the system has been set up makes it agonizingly slow, and the results are disappointing. A wilderness area or national park can go through Congress once, but wild and scenic rivers must make two trips—once for a study, then for designation." To speed protection, Brown supported incentives for state action and more emphasis on easements. Bills were introduced for generic reforms to the act, but none passed.

Overcoming the difficulties, Representative Phillip Burton of San Francisco, chair of the House Interior and Insular Affairs Subcommittee, led passage of the National Parks and Recreation Act of 1978, one of the most comprehensive natural area preservation laws ever written. After heavy lobbying by Howard Brown, who joined a blitz by the major national conservation groups, the act protected the section of the Delaware threatened by Tocks Island Dam and also designated the upper Delaware, lower Skagit, lower Rio Grande, upper North Fork American, Pere Marquette, middle Missouri, and Saint Joe rivers. The mileage in the national system increased by 689 miles or 43 percent, and 17 new study rivers were named. With other sections addressing national parks, wilderness, and recreation, Burton's bill approved 144 projects in 44 states and was dubbed "parks barrel" by both supporters and critics, who recognized its resemblance to pork barrel bills that had once authorized dams and canals all over the country.

The tenth anniversary of the National Wild and Scenic Rivers System at the end of 1978 showed growth from 12 rivers and 850 miles in 1968 to 43 rivers and 2,299 miles. This sounded like progress, and it was, but the curve of destruction was dramatically steeper: channel-ization alone destroyed 8,000 miles of streams in the same period.

ALASKA AND 1980

In 1980, 33 Alaska rivers (61 counting tributaries on 25 river systems named in the legislation) were designated by the Alaska National Interest Lands Conservation Act, adding 3,284 miles to the system. An initial screening of the state's rivers by federal agencies had come up with 166 waterways, which planners reduced to 69, then further reduced by political necessity to the 25 river systems that were designated. This Alaska Lands Act, which had brewed for a decade, increased the mileage of the national rivers system by 1.4 times its previous size.

Jack Hession, the Sierra Club's Alaska state representative since 1970, had kayaked on the northern rivers and was the primary and frequently the only advocate for the state's rivers. "Those streams were unlike any I had ever seen, untouched by modern times," Hession reflected in 1991. He made sure that rivers were added to the three natural area jurisdictions being withdrawn as part of the Alaska Lands Act. "The national parks, wilderness areas, and wildlife refuges were the main interest, but no one opposed inclusion of rivers; people seemed to think that wild and scenic rivers were a natural extension of the concept. By the end, I think rivers helped that system to fly." Bob Eastman, chief of the wild and scenic rivers program in the Bureau of Outdoor Recreation, likewise fought in a critical role within Interior to have rivers added to the legislation.

Chuck Clusen, chair of an Alaska coalition of environmental organizations at the time, credited Hession as "clearly the rivers' advocate in Alaska; if he hadn't been there, the rivers might have been dropped." The river conservation community, including ARCC, played only a minor role in the bill, leaving it to the mainstream environmental groups that were already committed to the Alaska debate. Clusen, working for the Wilderness Society, recognized the rivers' importance to the North. "People who know Alaska realize that it's nearly as arid as a desert, but with ribbons of life. The streams are the priority for biological values. Important struggles occur over valleys and lowlands, which are the most productive biologically but also the most developable." John Haubert, who ushered the rivers proposal through the Department of the Interior, emphasized that "one well-placed river with 50,000 acres might be more important than 500,000 acres of wilderness or national park on a glacier."

Alaska represented an effort to manage correctly what had been grossly mismanaged in other states, where large, fruitful rivers and valleys had been lost to dams and development, from the Ohio and Potomac to the Missouri and Columbia. Here was an opportunity to save some rivers in their entirety, rather than in disparate segments.

While other agencies were engrossed in the traditional land protection categories of parks, wilderness, and refuges in Alaska, the Bureau of Outdoor Recreation overcame its problem of lacking a clear mission by leading the river studies and guiding them through the legislative maze. But presumably by political necessity the bureau's study team gravitated to rivers already in the proposed parks, wilderness, or refuges. Hession recalled, "Outside these areas, the Forest Service told the rivers study team to get lost." The Forest Service apparently did some studies of its own, but its rivers were not recommended to Congress.

The disappointing aspect of the Alaska Lands Act was that only 7 of the rivers (plus 18 tributaries) were not already protected by a specialized designation of land. The river protection that counted most was at the Bureau of Land Management's Birch Creek and its Delta, Fortymile, Gulkana, and Unalakleet rivers, along with part of the National Park Service's Alagnak River, together accounting for only 27 percent of the designated mileage. The main reason that Birch Creek, the Unalakleet, and Beaver Creek were not casualties of cuts by the Alaska delegation was that environmental impact statements fortifying the case for protection had been completed by the Bureau of Outdoor Recreation—a statement on the value of what is sometimes viewed as mere procedural paperwork.

The disparity between the rivers that needed protection and those that got it is striking in view of what Jack Hession perceived as important. He wanted the Susitna because of huge dam proposals, but the site was considered too controversial. Interior officials and Congress demoted some rivers to study status, which proved effective in bypassing designation; the Alaska delegation intimidated federal agencies into burying the studies and silenced all efforts for additional river legislation after 1980.

Putting those shortcomings aside, the designated Alaska rivers are a wish list of northern beauty and biology. Included was the Noatak, the longest national river and one of the nation's finest examples of safeguarding not just a park or river but an entire ecosystem. The Lands Act also established the Yukon-Charley Rivers National Preserve, unique because it was established explicitly owing to river values.

Also in 1980, after years of rancorous debate, Congress added 125 miles of Idaho's Salmon River to the national rivers system. Before passage of the legislation, western senators had deleted 112 miles of the lower river that had been included in early versions of the original Wild and Scenic Rivers Act. Though compromised, protection for the shorter "River of No Return" reach secured one of the preeminent wild river journeys in the country and finally blocked old dam proposals of the Army Corps. The law allowed continued use of jet boats and backcountry air strips. Another 28 miles of the Little Miami were also added at the request of the governor of Ohio. Both the Alaska and Salmon River actions were pushed by President Carter and rode through Congress as parts of larger land protection bills.

CALIFORNIA'S REGION OF RIVERS

The last advance for rivers under President Carter's exemplary term was the federal protection of streams already in California's state rivers system. Among other reasons, this was important because of a dam proposed on the Middle Fork of the Eel.

To divert water southward, the Army Corps and Los Angeles in the 1960s had planned several versions of Dos Rios Dam, which would eliminate the state's largest summer steelhead run; drown the town of Covelo, which had a population of 2,000; bury much of the Round Valley Indian Reservation; and flood 30 miles of popular whitewater. A California state bill in 1972 had designated northern rivers, including the Eel, in a state scenic rivers system. This halted Dos Rios Dam but invited reconsideration in 1984.

Seeking better protection for the Eel and 4,000 miles of the state-protected rivers in all, Gov. Jerry Brown requested national designation from Interior secretary Cecil Andrus in 1980. Included in the proposal were the Smith, California's only major undammed river and one of the nation's outstanding scenic streams; the Klamath, the second largest river in California and the world's greatest producer of steelhead trout; the Scott, Salmon, and Wooley Creek, undeveloped Klamath tributaries; the Trinity and several of its forks; the Eel, with three forks running through a special beauty of grasslands, oak savannah, woodlands, and whitewater; and the lower American, one of the cleanest urban rivers in the nation, drawing 5.5 million visitors a year. Together the rivers represented 40 percent of California's runoff, vital to Indians, to sport anglers, and to the offshore commercial fishery.

Federal designation would make it more difficult for the powerful southern California and San Joaquin Valley political bloc of urban developers and corporate irrigators to rescind protection. It would also mean better management of logging on national forest river frontage, which had been immune to the strict waterfront requirements of the state's Forest Practices Act. Poor logging practices had already caused much silting of river gravel beds, essential to the spawning of salmon and thus to northern California's $13.4 million commercial fishing industry, which employed 7,000 people.

The U.S. Forest Service opposed designation, ostensibly to await completion of its own land management plans, but at the end of President Carter's term, even the shortest delay in administrative action would have left the question of wild river designation up to the incoming Reagan administration. James Watt became Reagan's secretary of the interior, and there is no doubt what he would have done with Governor Brown's request. The Forest Service went to the extent of trying to get the Wild and Scenic Rivers Act amended to disallow the protection request from the governor, but that rider, sponsored by Senator James McClure of Idaho, failed.

Interior secretary Andrus executed the designation of 19 rivers plus tributaries to the Smith River, totaling 1,238 miles. (Several thousand miles of small tributaries requested by Governor Brown were excluded because they were unimportant to salmon spawning.) Andrus signed the proclamation only hours before he left office on January 19, 1981. This single action increased by 18 percent the mileage of national rivers and protected four huge, adjacent river systems, establishing a wild and scenic rivers region of unprecedented and unrepeated significance. The Brown-Andrus designation could reasonably be termed the most significant ever for the National Wild and Scenic Rivers System because of the great mileage and large number of streams included, their extraordinary value, and the potential threats their designation averted. (Other great additions in mileage were the Alaska rivers, which were largely safeguarded anyway within protected land, and the Oregon rivers protected in 1988, which were generally less threatened.)

Determined to undo federal protection, southern California water agencies and northern timber companies sued, their arguments hinging on technicalities, such as the procedure used in issuing announcements of the environmental impact statement. More to the point, Earl Blaise, chair of the board of southern California's Metropolitan Water District, said, "Even though I do not feel there is any rush to develop the Eel, I always felt the option should be there if the state needed the water." The district lobbied for a bill to allow state legislatures to subtract rivers from the national system. Bills to rescind state protection of the Eel had been introduced in the state assembly, where the majority of southern Californians could open the way for Dos Rios Dam if the river lost its federal protection.

A federal judge in 1983 said that an environmental report's review period had been one day too short and declared Andrus's designation invalid, but a federal appeals court in 1984 found the objections to be "insignificant" and "trivial" and let Andrus's decision stand by restoring national status. The Supreme Court refused to hear a final appeal by water developers.

The California success confirmed Jimmy Carter as the greatest river protection president. With the Burton bill in 1978, the Alaska legislation, and the California designations, during his one-term presidency the system increased by over 5,000 miles or 300 percent. Further, in 1978 President Carter had also recommended designation of the Bruneau in Idaho, the Dolores in Colorado, the Mississippi in Minnesota, and the full 237 miles of the Salmon that had been studied in Idaho—all of which Congress failed to pass owing to opposition by local representatives.

The tragic loss in that otherwise brightening era for river conservation was the Stanislaus in the Sierra Nevada. More people floated through this deepest limestone canyon on the west coast than on any other whitewater in the West. New Melones Dam flooded a paradise of wildlife habitat, archaeological sites, and campsites on golden beaches shaded by towering gray cliffs, but only after the most concerted dam fight in U.S. history. A bill for national wild and scenic designation narrowly missed passing in the House subcommittee. River guide, activist, and educator Mark Dubois fought for the river with all means at his disposal, finally chaining himself to a rock at a hidden site in the canyon, forcing the Army Corps to either stop filling the reservoir or drown him (the corps stopped). The commitment and eloquence of Dubois and thousands of Friends of the River dramatized to the American public how passionately people could feel and act about rivers. Likewise, it showed the river conservation community the need to mobilize early and to wage sophisticated campaigns to counter the forces allied against them.

STRUGGLING TO SURVIVE

National politics of the 1980s brought new challenges and stern resistance to the national rivers movement, which was still a tentative, vulnerable component of conservation politics. The American Rivers Conservation Council lobbied for bills to protect 40 fishing rivers in 1980 and 8 Oregon rivers in 1982, and for incentives to encourage state programs in 1983, but lost in all these cases, a hint of rough times that lay ahead. Interior secretary James Watt—who once complained that a Grand Canyon raft trip was "tedious"—eliminated the Heritage, Conservation and Recreation Service (the former Bureau of Outdoor Recreation), which had been the agency responsible for the rivers program. Some of its functions were subsumed by the National Park Service. Rivers flowing through private land had rarely received approval by federal agencies, but previous administrations had occasionally recommended designations. Watt's directives, however, declared streams eligible but not "suitable" if private land lay within the boundaries or if developers of any kind objected. High officials in the Reagan administration mostly ignored Carter administration directives to protect rivers on public land, though the Forest Service incorporated river protection in management plans. The Federal Energy Regulatory Commission encouraged private permits for dams and attempted to streamline applications.

In the Department of Agriculture, Forest Service professionals recommended designation of eight streams for 505 miles—not much considering the mileage it had studied—but John Crowell, President

Reagan's assistant secretary of agriculture, sliced the list to 245 miles by cutting nearly all private land and even remotely possible dam sites.

In 1980, not only had Ronald Reagan and James Watt risen to power, but also the Senate had changed hands to a Republican majority for the first time in a generation. From 1980 to 1986, rivers legislation faced challenges from a skeptical Congress and also a formidable gantlet of hostility in the Senate, led by the chair and subcommittee chair of the key panels, James McClure of Idaho and Malcolm Wallop of Wyoming, respectively. Both were leaders of the "sagebrush rebellion" and found the rivers act a convenient whipping boy.

Fallout from designation of the upper Delaware River after 1978 further dampened the program in the early 1980s. Kevin Coyle, who had been chief of the studies division of the Bureau of Outdoor Recreation in the Northeast in the 1970s, blamed some of the problem on the agency's "top down" planning that stumbled fatally onto the path of irate landowners, for the Delaware was one of few national rivers with shorelines predominantly in private ownership. An original plan to acquire 36,000 acres of land or easements was reduced to 1,000 acres but nonetheless touched off a firestorm of opposition, requiring years of remedial action to salvage the program. Hiring consultants to plan and negotiate with the residents, the Park Service stepped back for a realistic view of the situation. Showing sensitivity to private landowners and an ability to handle hostility, Chuck Hoffman and his associates Keith Fletcher and Mike Presnitz set about crafting an acceptable program. Hundreds of thousands of dollars after designation, a plan was adopted by most towns and governing bodies, and the hostilities mostly died down, but this was not until the late 1980s, a decade after the river had been designated.

Worst of all, by 1982 the development moratorium for 11 key study rivers had expired because Congress failed to act on the river proposals within the allotted study period. Chris Brown, the new director of ARCC, sought a moratorium extension and testified that his organization "feels strongly that the fate of these rivers should not be decided by congressional default." Most important, the Tuolumne in California was slated to be dammed several times by the city of San Francisco and two irrigation districts that had applied for a Federal Energy Regulatory Commission (FERC) license. Hydropower proposals loomed over Oregon's Illinois and Colorado's Gunnison. A bill to extend protection failed, leaving FERC free to license the dams.

Even though the prospects for construction of large new dams by the federal government had subsided, hydroelectric threats increased with federal incentives to private power developers through the Public Utility Regulatory Policies Act of 1978. By monitoring permit requests in 1983, ARCC found nine applications that would affect designated national rivers in Washington and California alone. In violation of the Wild and Scenic Rivers Act, FERC issued a permit for a dam on the federally designated Suiattle River in Washington. ARCC appealed and stopped the project. Also in Washington, a nuclear power plant was exempted (but never built) in the study corridor of the Skagit River.

In Alaska, the state senate unanimously passed a resolution in 1983 asking Congress to delete Birch and Beaver creeks from the national system so miners could dredge gold without even the modicum of regulation that resulted from national river status. (Protection has not so far been rescinded for any of the national rivers, and only the Middle Fork of the Feather has been congressionally reduced after designation. In 1976 its headwaters were deleted where flows were low and braided, but perhaps more important, where the river passed through land owned by ranchers.) A Texas representative introduced legislation in the mid 1980s to rescind federal protection for the Rio Grande, raising questions of long-term security for the system. One act of Congress designated rivers; another could delete them. Would the national system deteriorate to a savings account of streams banked for future development? Working amid all these hazards and managing to garner public support for rivers in spite of the political hostility, Chris Brown answered, "Not if people keep supporting the rivers. We're sitting on a mountain of opportunity, but if we don't mobilize political support soon, some of our best streams will be lost to hydroelectric dams and other developments."

TURNING POINT ON THE TUOLUMNE

Flowing from Yosemite National Park, interrupted by O'Shaughnessy Dam—a monument to America's first dam fight in Hetch Hetchy Valley—and continuing through one of the finest whitewater runs in the West and a superb trout fishery, the Tuolumne represented everything good about a wild river. And it still provided prodigious water and power supplies for municipal and agricultural use. Two Central Valley irrigation districts, however, proposed yet more dams. The FERC issued a preliminary permit in 1982 and was prepared to license the project for construction. A campaign led by John Amodio of the Tuolumne River Preservation Trust gained the support of two-thirds of the state's 45-member House delegation. A two-year letter-writing campaign by Friends of the River involved river guides who enlisted their clients to deliver 12,000 pieces of mail to an uncommitted and reluctant Senator Pete Wilson, whose vote was needed. He eventually voted for designation, and the Tuolumne was protected as part of the 1984 California Wilderness Act. Chris Brown called the Tuolumne "the tide-turning success of the mid 1980s. Nothing had been designated in four years and nothing was going to be; this one broke the ice jam and kept the system alive."

Although most rivers had been designated without imminent threats of damming, the case of the Tuolumne was a classic last-minute save, much like those of the Snake River in Hells Canyon, the New, and the Delaware at Tocks Island. In the sense of urgent purposes fulfilled, these four rivers characterized the Wild and Scenic Rivers System at its finest: remarkable waterways rescued from otherwise certain destruction.

Also in 1984, other wilderness acts designated small parts of the Verde in Arizona, the Au Sable in Michigan, the Owhyee in eastern Oregon, and the Illinois in Oregon. The Illinois offers one of the most challenging and exciting whitewater wilderness runs in the West, with a 32 mile canyon of remarkable beauty. Congress likewise named four new study rivers.

DIFFICULT SUCCESS IN THE 1980s

Though the dramatic success of the Tuolumne campaign was not repeated, river conservationists continued to fight off regressive pressures in the 1980s and also scored a few important additions to the national rivers system. The National Park Service's technical assistance program for rivers and trails, which helped states and local groups to protect rivers, was cut from $3.6 million in 1981 to $1 million in 1985—not much of a budget considering that all federal agencies were spending $10 billion a year on water. At the same time the Army Corps and Bureau of Reclamation consumed a total of $4 billion a year on such ratholes as the foundation of Auburn Dam, where $250 million was spent to produce what looked like a strip mine before the project was stopped in the wake of earthquake dangers. William K. Reilly of the Conservation Foundation testified before the subcommittee on the interior in 1985 that the technical assistance program spurred local efforts and was cost-effective—virtues at any time but especially in the antifederal, anti-domestic-spending era of the 1980s. With nurturing by Bill Spitzer and Glenn Eugster of the National Park Service, who along with Chick Fagan had been the initiator of the innovative outreach program, and with lobbying by the American Rivers Conservation Council, the technical assistance budget stabilized, then grew in the late 1980s. The program continued to offer expert advice to states and local groups across the nation.

In 1985 the secretary of the interior designated a 7.5 mile segment of the Loxahatchee as Florida's first national wild and scenic river, nearly all of it already protected in a state park. In the same year, the Reagan administration recommended designation of only 174 miles out of 1,604 miles of rivers that had been studied and found eligible for protection. To add rivers to the national system—never an easy job—became increasingly difficult in the face of opposition by landowners, persistent interest by developers in hydroelectric dams, and neglect or outright hostility on the part of the federal administration. Chris Brown was moved to say, "We need to look harder at alternatives to national designation."

After years of agonizing debate and after lobbying by Chris Brown and a strong Colorado constituency, analysts found five of six proposed dams on the Cache la Poudre to be uneconomic. Supported by Representative (later Senator) Hank Brown, from a conservative district, the Poudre became Colorado's first national river in 1986.

The Penobscot, a premier fishing and rafting river flowing from Maine's Mount Katahdin, followed as a national priority of ARCC, which assisted local groups fighting a hydroelectric dam proposed by Great Northern Paper Company at Big Ambejackmockamus Falls. The company dropped the proposal. Even though the Interior Department had studied the river for national status, it remained unprotected owing to state and local fears of federal intervention.

In 1986 the Columbia Gorge National Scenic Area legislation included wild and scenic river status for parts of the Klickitat and White Salmon rivers of Washington, and a study requirement for upper sections of each. Congress passed short reaches of Black Creek in Mississippi and Saline Bayou in Louisiana as the first southern blackwater streams in the system. The Horsepasture River in North Carolina was designated for 4.2 miles, stopping a hydroelectric project at scenic waterfalls.

PROTECTED BY A DIFFERENT NAME

Similar in many ways to the wild and scenic rivers, another official designation, that of "national river," was established by Congress for the Buffalo River in Arkansas and the New River Gorge in West Virginia (below the wild and scenic reach already designated in North Carolina), somewhat on the model of the Current and Jacks Fork in Missouri that had been called the Ozark Scenic Waterways. Stanford Young of the Park Service wrote that the national rivers are "in effect, elongated national parks, centered on rivers," where the government acquires corridors of land.

A national river and national recreation area (NRA) on the Big South Fork of the Cumberland in Tennessee and Kentucky protected the river through a unique arrangement. After conservationists had defeated the Devil's Jump Dam proposal, Congress established the recreation area in a 1974 rivers and harbors bill—a form of legislation normally authorizing only dams and developments. The Army Corps bought land and built recreation facilities, which were later turned over to the National Park Service. The Chattahoochee River above Atlanta was likewise made an NRA, emphasizing the river's assets in that urban area.

Working on the Gauley River, ARCC helped to organize a local group in West Virginia, which fought an Army Corps hydroelectric scheme to divert water from three miles of one of the most challenging whitewater runs in the country. Attempts to designate the Gauley as a wild and scenic river were frustrated partly by outfitters who feared restrictions on commercial use, so Congress, after eight years of wrangling, made 26 miles of the river an NRA instead, plus 4.5 miles of the Meadow River, a tributary.

Representative John Siberling led NRA passage for the Cuyahoga River in Ohio in an attempt to realize urban recreation potential and reclaim a river whose lower reaches had been the butt of jokes after the trash-filled, oil-slicked waterway once actually burned in a stinking inferno.

California's Smith River (already a national wild and scenic river) was additionally designated an NRA in 1991 in an attempt to restrict logging and emphasize recreation use.

While the national rivers and NRAs have a somewhat higher recreational profile than the wild and scenic rivers, a lower profile was the objective in "damless" river legislation passed in the late 1980s for parts of the Kings in California, the Henry's Fork of the Snake in Idaho, the lower Salmon in Idaho, and a section of the Genessee River in New York. The Columbia Gorge National Scenic Area legislation likewise banned hydropower development on the entire Hood River for 67 miles in Oregon, the entire Wind River for 29 miles in Washington, and 18 miles of the Little White Salmon in Washington. In all these cases, new dams are banned, but the protection calls for nothing else.

THE GROWTH OF AMERICAN RIVERS

By the mid 1980s the American Rivers Conservation Council, although still a small organization, had grown as a leader of the rivers movement. The group lobbied for all of the wild and scenic designations and pushed to aid local and state programs through federal loans for open space acquisition and to protect state designated rivers from FERC hydroelectric licenses. Other activities included fighting dam proposals, pushing for water policy reform, and helping states to initiate rivers programs. The group lobbied for funding for the Park Service's technical assistance and study efforts, for land acquisition appropriations, and for water quality improvements.

Having worked effectively as ARCC's director from 1982 through 1986 even in a politically resistant era, Chris Brown counted the highlights as the Tuolumne designation and the revitalization of a faltering organization. "We've come a long way since then. At one point we had to take out a large bank loan secured by two board members so that the organization could survive." In the late 1970s and early 1980s, some staff members had gone many months without pay because the money just wasn't there. During Brown's tenure as director, with Rafe Pomerance as chair, the organization went from a deficit of $15,000 to a surplus of $115,000, which made important new advances possible.

Desiring to achieve the kind of growth experienced by some other national conservation groups, ARCC board members convened in 1984 and with the help of management consultant William Bryan initiated the "Great Leap Forward." An intensive program ensued to raise $325,000 for the first step of the "leap." Early in 1986 the board hired Kent W. Olson, former director of the Connecticut chapter of the Nature Conservancy, as executive director. Olson immediately changed the name of the group to American Rivers, Inc. With increased activity by staff and board members and with Olson's growth objectives, American Rivers grew from a staff of 10 and a budget of $300,000 in 1985 to a staff of 18 and a budget of $1.5 million in 1989. Membership increased from 7,000 to 18,000, with the largest contingents in California, New York, and Colorado. Pat Munoz, a mainstay of the organization since the mid 1970s, appealed to foundations and donors and secured great funding increases. A trademark of Olson's style was the documentation of organizational success shown in miles of rivers protected.

Doing a systematic search through its archives in 1986, the group found that since 1973 it had played a leading role in permanent protection of 1,284 miles of rivers with 376,392 acres of land, and a consulting role in protection of 8,628 miles of rivers and 6.2 million acres of land—together accounting for nearly 90 percent of the miles in the Wild and Scenic Rivers System. American Rivers's intervention had helped stop 59 destructive water projects at a savings of $4.8 billion in tax dollars. None of this denied the irreplaceable and frequently leading role of state groups, local river conservation communities, and other national organizations. In all, 269 local and state groups and 24 at the national level had been involved in the movement.

CALIFORNIA SHOWCASES

During one extraordinary month of lawmaking in 1987 that followed years of diligent work by local groups, Friends of the River, and

American Rivers, Congress designated three California streams and eight tributaries as wild and scenic. The Kings carves the deepest canyon in the United States, even deeper than the celebrated Hells Canyon. The Merced is the river of Yosemite Valley. The Kern is the longest river in the Sierra Nevada and offers the closest whitewater to America's third largest city, Los Angeles. The South Fork of the Kern displays abundant biological diversity where the Mojave Desert meets the Sierra Nevada. All three river systems have excellent trout fisheries and whitewater.

On the Kings—already dammed or depleted of flows for its entire length after leaving the Sierra Nevada—trout anglers had organized to defeat the Rogers Crossing Dam years before; they reorganized under the leadership of local fly fisherman Donn Furman in 1986 when faced with a serious threat. The Kings River Conservation District had invested hundreds of thousands of dollars in one of the worst new dam proposals that river conservationists had seen in many years. Heavily subsidized agribusiness giants of the San Joaquin Valley would benefit from the flooding of national forest land, a premier trout fishery, an outstanding whitewater run, and a canyon of spellbinding beauty with enormous oaks, grassland savannah, white churning rapids, and crystal-clear water. The information campaign of the committee to save the Kings cost $14,000 but proved more effective than the dam builder's investment of ten times that amount in the world's largest advertising agency. With staunch support by Representative Richard Lehman, a national river bill passed for the Kings' upper reaches and included "special management" provisions against damming the threatened section.

A hydropower developer had completed plans to dam the Merced at the boundary of Yosemite National Park and on the wild, picturesque South Fork and awaited what appeared to be only red-tape constraints. The Forest Service studied the river and supported designation in spite of the hydropower proposals. A three-year campaign led by Ron Stork of the Merced Canyon Committee fought off heavily vested interests and garnered the political support necessary for protection in another stellar victory over otherwise certain, heavy losses.

The statewide group, Friends of the River, battled for Kern River protection against hostile local opposition that degenerated into threats against the life of staff member Bea Cooley. The Forest Service had studied the Kern River forks and recommended designation.

Success in Friends of the River's "Three Rivers Campaign" for the Kings, Merced, and Kern marked a new plateau of effectiveness in the river conservation movement against real threats and amply funded opponents.

NATIONAL FOREST RIVERS AND THE OREGON PROTOTYPE

The California designations followed the time-tested model of intense lobbying and political action on a river-by-river basis. The real break-through of the late 1980s, however, occurred with rivers on national forest land. With its genesis in a directive by President Carter to protect streams in the Nationwide Rivers Inventory (see chapter 7), a directive from the office of the chief of the Forest Service in 1982 called on each forest supervisor to identify and evaluate rivers for the Wild and Scenic Rivers System while preparing the forest's land resource management plan. At least 500 rivers were to be evaluated on national forests—five times the number that had been congressionally authorized through the traditional study process. American Rivers and the Sierra Club Legal Defense Fund began reviewing the plans in 1986 and found that although some of the documents recognized wild and scenic river potential, others were inadequate. Based on Section 5(d) of the Wild and Scenic Rivers Act, which required agencies to consider rivers in their planning, a list of appeals resulted. By 1988 the agency had studied 700 rivers and found 460 eligible; by 1992 it had found 700 eligible rivers (see chapter 3).

Taking the concept of public-land river protection and running further with it, Oregon conservationists in 1988 successfully lobbied for a statewide omnibus bill that transfigured the Wild and Scenic Rivers System. Starting with Forest Service studies that identified potential wild and scenic rivers, the Oregon Rivers Council, founded and led by outfitter and conservationist Bob Doppelt, gained sponsorship from Senator Mark Hatfield, ranking minority member on the Energy and Natural Resources Committee. With support from Forest Service staff who prepared essential information on many of the rivers, Hatfield pushed legislation through with considerable force. The senator had spent a lifetime supporting the timber industry and water developers, but with the opportunity to create a "legacy" in one of his latter terms, he had decided to champion the cause of river conservation. Only one member of the state delegation opposed the bill, though his district included many of the rivers. The bill included some private land but not much as a percentage of total frontage.

While the rivers receiving designation without question deserved protection, six equally worthy rivers were rapidly jettisoned when landowners complained, and the upper Klamath, imminently threatened by a hydroelectric proposal, was removed from the bill. These omissions notwithstanding, Congress designated 44 rivers plus 9 small tributaries totaling 1,442 miles—the largest number of rivers and second largest mileage ever added to the national rivers program at one time. Chris Brown reflected, "By bringing dozens of rivers into protection at once, Hatfield's bill broke us out of the mold that only 100 or 200 rivers could be protected, instead encouraging a vision that some day the national rivers system might include a collection of rivers in every state."

River conservationists and some supportive Forest Service staff worked to develop statewide omnibus packages elsewhere, including in Washington where Doug North of the Northwest Rivers Council worked to have Forest Service and Bureau of Land Management rivers recommended, and in Michigan, Arkansas, West Virginia, Arizona, and California (see chapter 7). Also in 1988, a short reach of the Bluestone in West Virginia, the Sipsey Fork in Alabama, and the outstanding Rio Chama in New Mexico were added.

A NEW APPROACH

Paralleling American Rivers's success in working with the Forest Service on public land, the National Park Service conducted a new kind of river study at the Wildcat River in Jackson, New Hampshire. Flowing mostly through private land, the stream was the centerpiece of the picturesque New England town, where a hydroelectric entrepreneur planned to convert a scenic waterfall into pipes and turbines. Rather than just studying the river and recommending designation, a management plan was first devised with painstaking attention to local participation. The Park Service then announced that it would not recommend designation without local approval. All groups participated in a long process leading to agreement on local zoning changes, river restoration plans, and easements to protect scenery. The strength of this local commitment to protect the river convinced Congress that a federal presence was unnecessary, thus making designation palatable to the community. National Park Service study leader Rolf Diamant credited success in part to study legislation that was broad enough to allow for flexibility in cooperative agreements with local government. The river was designated in 1988.

During this fruitful era, American Rivers initiated the splashy publicity of its "most endangered rivers" list. In 1984, the Tuolumne had been recognized as the river of the year. In 1986 the Ripogenous Gorge area of the Penobscot was called the most endangered river, and when the Kings River debate roared to a crescendo in 1987 over Rogers Crossing Dam versus national designation, that river was declared the most endangered. The status proved to be an ingenious public relations ploy, so the group began annually to list ten rivers as the most endangered. (More accurately, the rivers are the most important endangered rivers, not always those facing the most immediate threats.) In 1988 the South Platte in Colorado, Klamath in Oregon, Little Big Horn in Wyoming, Greenbrier in West Virginia, Platte in Nebraska, Columbia in Washington, Susquehanna in Pennsylvania, American in California, Animas in Colorado, and Black in New York made up the list.

In spite of administrative and political roadblocks, and owing largely to the Oregon success, the number of designated rivers increased by nearly 50 percent during Reagan's eight years in office; it had increased by a factor of three during Carter's four years.

CELEBRATION AND PERSISTENCE

To celebrate the twentieth anniversary of the Wild and Scenic Rivers Act, American Rivers in 1988 hosted a conference in Washington, DC. It featured a banquet, attended by 600 people, at which masters of ceremonies Stewart Udall and Kent Olson honored dozens of people for their roles in saving rivers; speakers included John and Frank Craighead, Gaylord Nelson, and Dale Robertson, chief of the Forest Service. Robertson announced a goal of recommending 200 rivers on national forest land by 1993. Though his record held nothing of convincing value, President-Elect Bush sent a letter stating that as an environmentalist and fly fisherman he supported efforts to preserve natural rivers. The mood and the message were upbeat, showing confidence that a time for rivers had in fact arrived.

Though most proposals for new large dams had fallen under the weight of the river conservation lobby, tight budgets, and the exhaustion of good dam sites, two major proposals remained in the late 1980s: Two Forks Dam on the South Fork of the Platte in Colorado, and Auburn Dam on the American River in California. Conservationists tenaciously fought each at the state level. The federal Environmental Protection Agency halted Two Forks by denying a permit needed by the Denver Water Board, considered the most powerful political entity in Colorado. Momentum, however, fell short of securing protection in the national rivers system. Auburn persisted as an imminent threat to 48 miles of wild and spectacular canyons, heavily used for recreation, less than an hour's drive from Sacramento. The American is the only river to have appeared on the most endangered rivers list every year from 1988 to 1992.

THE 1990s

With no repetition of the growth resulting from the 1988 Oregon bill, and consistent with a congressional pattern of designating rivers mostly on even-numbered years (having to do with political campaigns), 1989 saw only the Middle Fork of the Vermilion designated at the Illinois governor's request by Secretary of Interior Manuel Lujan. In 1990, short reaches of the East Fork Jemez and Pecos in New Mexico were added, along with National Recreation Area designation for the Smith in California, adding six tributaries to that well-guarded system. A great success of 1990 was the long-awaited inclusion of 20 miles of the Clarks Fork of the Yellowstone, one of the wildest rivers in America. The Wyoming delegation finally allowed just this one of its many fine rivers to receive protection.

In 1990 American Rivers, the National Audubon Society, and the Sierra Club lobbied for designation of Nebraska's biological treasure, the Niobrara River, where dams had successfully been fought since 1976. As with the Penobscot, South Platte, and dozens of other rivers, the rearguard battles against dams were not extended to gain long-term security, and the time bombs of development just waited to go off again. In 1991 the Niobrara and 39 miles of the Missouri River were designated wild and scenic, but animosity of residents fearing the federal government posed a management challenge, and the Park Service prepared for a protracted planning effort not unlike the one that had evolved on the upper Delaware.

Oregon groups and American Rivers pushed to designate the upper Klamath River as FERC prepared to issue a federal license for a hydroelectric diversion that would remove 80 percent of the water from a 10 mile segment. National designation attempts failed, but in 1991 the state denied a water quality permit for the project, stopping it, though perhaps temporarily.

The Colorado River in the Grand Canyon suffered rapid degradation by the Bureau of Reclamation's management of Glen Canyon Dam, upstream. Flushes of water released for peaking power eroded sandy beaches, carrying trainloads of sand downstream daily. After massive nationwide lobbying by the Grand Canyon Trust, American Rivers, and Friends of the River to require an environmental impact statement on the hydropower flushing and an interim release schedule, temporary agreements were reached in 1991 to somewhat improve the flow regime for less damage. The case bodes well for the growing efforts to secure better management of dams, which have caused similar if less dramatic problems all over the country.

In a fight warming toward a political climax in the early 1990s, Alaska and British Columbia conservationists battled the development of a huge copper mine in the midst of wilderness as large, untouched, and rugged as any wilderness anywhere. Draining the 25 million acre region, the Tatshenshini and lower Alsek rivers offer world-class whitewater travel for 165 miles. Miners would bulldoze a road parallel to the Tatshenshini for 20 miles through the middle of the largest protected national park complex on earth, where unprotected land is surrounded by Glacier Bay and Wrangell–Saint Elias national parks in the United States and Kluane National Park in Canada's Yukon Territory. Opponents led by Peter Enticknap of Alaska and Ric Careless and Ethan Askey of British Columbia publicized the prospect of acid mine drainage sterilizing one of the world's premier salmon rivers and the likelihood of dam failures at tailings ponds holding toxic wastes in one of the most active seismic zones on earth. A shift in the provincial government in 1991 offered hope for saving these globally significant watersheds from the British Columbia mine.

In 1991 river conservationists strived for an omnibus rivers bill in Michigan to designate 520 miles primarily within national forest land, but their efforts were stymied that year by timber companies, fishing interests, and landowners. In 1992 the bill passed and became law, designating 24 rivers in 14 major river systems, most of them offering excellent fish habitat. The rivers are notable as national system members that have been restored from logging abuses of the past. The Michigan act was the most comprehensive action to designate rivers apart from the west coast and included the fourth largest group of rivers ever protected. In California, efforts to save the American River canyons from the Auburn flood control dam intensified, and designation was won in 1992 for the Big Sur and Sisquoc rivers and for Sespe Creek, a wild, Coast Range stream draining the habitat of the endangered California condor and the largest unprotected roadless area in the state.

Legislation introduced by the late senator John Heinz to designate 85 miles of the Allegheny River was supported by the entire Pennsylvania delegation, and passed in the banner year of 1992. After four years of studies and grass-roots work by the Forest Service and the state with local communities and landowners, Senator Dale Bumpers introduced the Arkansas Wild and Scenic Rivers Act, which designated eight Forest Service rivers, including parts of the Cossatot, Little Missouri, Mulberry, Buffalo, Big Piney Creek, Hurricane Creek, North Sylamore Creek, and Richland Creek, altogether 206.1 miles of streams. In an unusual arrangement, the Cossatot was to be administered by the Army Corps of Engineers.

To extend its reach, American Rivers set up temporary field offices in Florida, Connecticut, and Kentucky with part-time personnel, and one with a full-time staff in Arizona; it added a full-time director in Washington state in 1992. Former director Howard Brown had first tried to establish a field office in the northern Rockies in 1981, but lacked sufficient money. A Texas office operated for several years in the mid 1980s, but the 1991 effort showed a greater commitment and ability to support local staff.

The professionalism of American Rivers's staff also increased. After leading the group to conservation victories, a loftier profile, an impressive budget, and staff increases that required larger office space every other year, director Kent Olson stepped down in 1990 amid unfortunate conflict with the chair and several members of the board. Taking his place, Kevin Coyle brought to the job more river experience than any other American Rivers director, having worked for ten years in the Department of the Interior (including leadership on river studies) and for three years as American Rivers's director of conservation.

Organizations such as the New England Rivers Center and the Kentucky Rivers Coalition had grown and then disappeared, yet other state and regional efforts flourished in the early 1990s. The Oregon Rivers Council advanced from its great success in 1988 to push for watershed protection extending beyond limited reaches of rivers. Directed by Sandie Nelson and with effective work by lawyer and guidebook author Doug North, the Northwest Rivers Council and other Washington groups labored toward a bill to designate 1,000 miles in Washington, but they encountered immutable resistance awaiting the resolution of old-growth forest legislation. After winning state protection for the exquisite Payette River, Wendy Wilson and others formed Idaho Rivers United in 1990 to gain protection for a network of remarkable streams, including the middle Snake, Henry's Fork of the Snake, and the Boise.

The statewide groups demonstrate a formula for success: Where stable river protection organizations exist with at least one paid staff member working full time, rivers are saved.

REFLECTING ON THE MOVEMENT

Taking pause after this national rivers history of three decades, a simple look at the map raises some questions. A curious quirk of geography has a vast majority of U.S. river protection occurring in northern states, especially if northern California is counted. This trend is also apparent with state scenic rivers systems: the most effective programs lie in the North. To an even greater extent, the local, regional, and private river conservation efforts occur mostly in the northern tier (see chapter 6). Yet at an individual if not political level, southerners are fiercely devoted to their rivers; these states include conservationists as dedicated as any others. One obvious reason for widespread interest and political success in the North is that northern areas of the western states are wetter and have more rivers, and thus more fishing, canoeing, and water interest. Oregon, for example, fits this mold. Also, the North, with its harsher climate, has less development, so more river qualities survive, which motivates people toward protection, even if they are not residents. Alaska is one example, northern California another. Trout fishing, a cold-water pursuit, has motivated more conservation activity than warm-water fishing; the work of Trout Unlimited, founded in Michigan, has no parallel among major fishing groups. Yet there are good rivers in all regions of the country. Perhaps some of the regional discrepancy stems from an intangible factor—a philosophy of local caretaking that spread from New England, in which community integrity was based partly on religious pursuits rather than on purely exploitive goals. Some northern states have actually *attracted* conservationists; Vermont and Oregon have experienced a selective immigration of pilgrims with an environmental bent, as has northern California. Northern states (with a few exceptions, such as Alaska) tend to have a more liberal political background and thus make the step toward river conservation and other environmental concerns with greater ease. Several northern states have a deep heritage of general conservation, especially Vermont, New York, Michigan, Wisconsin, Minnesota, and Oregon. The South has typically followed later in social, educational, and environmental reforms, a cultural difference affecting public policy across the board. The Great Plains are an enormous gap in protection, owing to the combined factors of few natural rivers remaining, heavy stress on all water supplies, a tradition combining the conservative outlooks of both the South and the West, and an absence of the environmentally oriented immigrants who have tempered the radical conservatism of many western states.

This regionalism of river conservation suggests a few strategic thoughts. First, for success, focus on the North. Washington and Montana are perhaps the ripest areas for new or continuing work, as also Idaho, Minnesota, Wisconsin, and New England. Conversely, other regions of the country lag and harbor the greatest unmet needs. Arizona, Texas, Tennessee, Kentucky, North Carolina, and Florida stand out as states with good possibilities.

The twenty-fifth anniversary of the Wild and Scenic Rivers Act in 1993 invites reflection on the context, attitudes, and accomplishments of river conservation and of the national rivers program in particular. When the conservation pioneers started the system, society regarded rivers mainly as places to build dams and to develop water and shorelines. Even folksinger Woodie Guthrie promoted damming the Columbia (in his famous song "Roll On, Columbia"). The attitude was born in the seemingly unlimited vastness of landscape. Undeniably, real needs were at times met by efficient projects. Still, a storehouse of public programs to subsidize water development and a lack of appreciation of the ecological and recreational importance of natural rivers marked the times. A nearly religious conviction favoring untempered development reluctantly yielded to a view of "balance," at first a euphemism for setting aside token remnants of rivers—a bone to the Craigheads of the day. The 12 national rivers originally designated and all those that followed failed to constitute balance when compared to 60,000 large dams, even though balance was the founding principle of the Wild and Scenic Rivers Act.

Conservationists used "balance" as a deliberately understated goal to save pieces of rivers that had already been dammed 10 or 20 times each. More than a literal objective, the term was used to illustrate the gross *im*balance of development over preservation and was effective in fending off developers' common accusation that conservationists were extremists who wanted everything for themselves.

The much touted public awareness of environmental issues in the 1990s—the so-called "decade of the environment"—seems to have done little to elevate the national rivers system to protect shorelines along rivers flowing through private land. From a more general river conservation standpoint, however, the support for water quality and the opposition to proposed large dams have spread like storm waters through society and indeed mark a fundamental change in attitudes compared to the 1960s.

A rising awareness of the economic wastefulness of new water development schemes, knowledge of the benefits of free-flowing rivers, and the environmental awakening of 1970—renewed in the late 1980s and on Earth Day, 1990—established a whole new context in which to view rivers; natural qualities captured the public imagination and resolve.

The conservation movement had begun to integrate the interests of park supporters, fish and wildlife advocates, landowners threatened by dams, and river recreationists, and had honed persuasive arguments involving ecology, economics, and safety. Residual opposition to river conservation lay with the landowners, businesses, and developers that fought national river designations with traditional rhetoric touting individual rights and antigovernment outrage. In the early

1990s, opposition from "property rights" advocates was ominously on the rise. In the local arena, financial backing by blatantly vested interests in real estate development, logging, mining, and dam building detracted little from the persuasiveness of those opposing river protection. Public attitudes, deep in the American psyche, still favored a development orientation viewed as a baseline ideal—one that took precedence over environmental concerns when the choices were tough. America still has a long way to go toward the land and water ethic first articulated by Aldo Leopold in the 1920s.

In spite of all that, the Wild and Scenic Rivers Act was a milestone in public recognition of river values. The system has clearly saved many rivers, and through the discourse engendered by goals and proposals under the act, it has contributed to the change in public attitudes and thus to the protection of *all* rivers. The debates over individual streams have served to heighten awareness and delineate the arguments implicit in all river conservation. The national status and the efforts to designate rivers flowing through public land have pushed river conservation closer to the mainstream of U.S. political thinking on conservation, closer to par with wilderness and national park concerns that had ranked prominently for decades.

The national system led to the establishment of American Rivers, a group adopting not only the goal of river designation but also that of river conservation by whatever feasible means. By virtue of that fact alone, the Wild and Scenic Rivers Act was a catalyst for far broader conservation activity.

National river designation—the ultimate, most secure protective status under law—became a symbol and a standard for the protection of all rivers. If it seems unfortunate or disappointing that these efforts have not universally affected the fate of rivers everywhere, one might consider the national parks movement, which could just as well be criticized for not leading to a progressive policy of land use across the United States. In fact, the rivers program may have had a greater general effect on rivers than the Wilderness Act has had on wilderness beyond its corresponding, designated acreage. Many state river protection programs exist, while there are only a few for wilderness.

Long regarded as a stepchild to mainstream environmental concerns, the rivers program is now in a position to receive recognition of its contributions to the broader conservation movement. Near the top of this list, efforts to protect rivers have added greatly to a realization

that many approaches must be pursued, including those that are toler-
ant of dissident views by people such as private landowners. Much like
the "green line park" proposals that surfaced in the late 1970s at a few
places, such as the Santa Monica Mountains in California, but have yet
to be embraced or expanded across the land, river-saving strategies
must be complex and varied.

Even more important, the connected, linear nature of rivers and the
importance of riparian habitat have served as an effective half-step
toward ecosystem awareness, bridging the philosophic and practical
gaps between older style protection of specific places or species and
the goal of ecosystem management that embraces more than rivers but
includes them at the heart. Heartily advocated by conservation ideo-
logues but difficult to put into practice, ecosystem management may
benefit from the paths blazed by river preservation efforts.

Rivers, being everywhere important in natural areas and communities alike, constitute an inexhaustible frontier for environmental
action. Long after debates over national parks and wilderness have
simmered down, river protection will likely be going strong simply
because there are so many important streams. They are at both the
periphery of civilization and at its center, lending power, complexity,
and difficulty to this movement. The goal of protecting rivers may
become a prominent extension of other conservation agendas running
far into the future and touching virtually everyplace where water
flows.

The national rivers system is certainly not relevant to all the rivers
deserving protection, but as a symbol, as a forerunner of policy, and as
an illuminator of needs, the Wild and Scenic Rivers System has played
an important role in the evolution of the conservation movement and
in its direction toward the future.

Perhaps a simplified, condensed statement of effectiveness would be
this: The national rivers system has succeeded in protecting some
rivers from specific threats and has made important strides in reserving
nonthreatened public-land rivers, but it has only begun to come to
terms with the private-land issues and with the clash of two values,
both deeply ingrained in Americans—private property and land conservation. On private-land rivers, the program has usually succeeded
only when the most extreme threats were involved (see chapter 3).
Although the Wildcat River case in New Hampshire offers signs of
hope for broadening national river protection, this outcome is far

from certain and will in any event require extreme care and sensitivity in every case.

The history that this chapter has presented forms only a foundation for a probing and insightful analysis of national river protection. What, specifically, are the goals of river conservation and how are the proponents likely to get from here to there? How are priorities set? What are the unintended consequences of all this work? What are the barriers preventing more river conservation from occurring? Where do the greatest opportunities lie? What are the important tradeoffs between political expediency and a lasting, significant form of protection? These and other questions about the shaping of the Wild and Scenic Rivers System are explored in chapter 3.

A Malleable System

Intricate and complex, continent-wide, reflective of changes in times and politics, the National Wild and Scenic Rivers System represents not one response to the need for river protection but many. The program is continually being forged on its way to maturity.

Cautious and carefully compromised, the 1968 Wild and Scenic Rivers Act was also bold, an experiment maybe more advanced than anyone knew. Its implementation held many surprises. The system's various origins and its complexity can be blamed for failures but also credited for potential. A malleable system that can be adapted to meet the needs of individual rivers, this may be the most underrated of all natural areas programs, perhaps just the right approach in an era of limits.

A fascinating array of forces is now aligned for and against wild and scenic rivers, and understanding those forces will surely be a key to the future, if natural rivers are to *have* a bright future in America.

THE FUNDAMENTALS

Eliminating a threat of annihilation that galvanized river conservationists for many years, designation as a wild and scenic river prohibits dams and other federal projects destructive to the waterways. Federal agencies may not permit hydroelectric diversions or other damaging activities requiring a federal license. The program recognizes the importance of riverfront land protection, but instead of expensive and unpopular acquisition, the act encourages the use of easements— partial ownership including development rights—that allow residents to stay and keep their property but not to develop the land.

Management agencies have acquired land or easements sparingly or, on many rivers, not at all. Congress disallowed condemnation of land if more than half the corridor acreage is publicly owned, and it limited condemnation to 100 acres per river mile (320 acres if acquisition in both fee and easements is used, or roughly a quarter mile from each shore). Section 6(c) likewise bans condemnation on any land where a zoning ordinance that "conforms with the purposes of this Act" has been adopted.

The federal government cannot zone or regulate the use of private land. Irrespective of national river status, local, county, or state laws remain the sole method to regulate land use. States retain control of hunting and fishing.

An unquantified federal reserved water right is attached to wild and scenic designations to keep the resource intact. Though it has been supported by the courts, some western water users and politicians oppose this concept.

Wild and scenic status implies that water quality is a priority, but it does not impose special regulations or supply money for pollution control. (Further discussion of all these features as management concerns appears in chapter 5.)

Adding rivers to the system is no casual endeavor. Congress normally has to pass a law to designate a particular river, but first a study is often legislated under section 5(a) of the act. A federal agency—the National Park Service, Forest Service, or Bureau of Land Management—collects information, meets with people, decides if the river qualifies and how it should be classified, recommends an agency to manage it, writes a report, receives reviews, and holds hearings. While studies were standard procedure in the first decade of the act, 41 percent of the national rivers through 1991 passed without full studies, nearly all being streams flowing predominantly through public land.

Beginning in 1982, in the Reagan administration as a way of making designation harder to obtain, federal agencies have judged not only the eligibility of a river but its "suitability" as well. Considerations of suitability involve political controversy, local and state interest, feelings of private landowners, costs, and conflicting proposals, such as dams. Taken in the most positive sense, a suitability determination answers the question, Even if the stream is good enough to be a national river, is it in the public interest to designate it? But the agencies have frequently found rivers unsuitable if any conflicts existed at all.

To be eligible, the river segment (which can include creeks or streams), must be free-flowing and have one or more "outstandingly remarkable" features—scenic, recreational, geologic, fish and wildlife, historic, cultural, or other similar values. Congress has not found length to be a limiting concern; segments as short as 4 miles have been included as solely designated members, and tributaries as short as 1 mile have been included as part of a larger designation. Many rivers of even plausible worth have been found to hold at least one "outstandingly remarkable" value.

A semantically cumbersome part of the act classifies segments of rivers as wild, scenic, or recreational, depending on the amount of access and shoreline development. *Wild rivers* are "vestiges of primitive America," generally inaccessible by roads. *Scenic rivers* are mostly "primitive" with shorelines "largely undeveloped." *Recreational rivers* are "readily accessible by roads" and may have more development. The classification simply describes existing characteristics and is not a statement on difficulty of whitewater, quality of scenery, or appeal for recreation. The threefold classification, which conservationists pressed for because they thought the bill would be strengthened through management constraints after designation, introduced tedious complexity. Debates too often center on the semantics of classification, diverting attention from important questions, such as whether the river should be protected from dams. Perhaps the one value of the classification is that it defines the appropriate level of development and usually guides a management strategy to maintain the status quo (though that is the target in any event). On a wild river, for example, agencies presumably would not propose development of large access areas or encourage heavy recreation, though they may not do that on a recreational river either. It depends on a management plan, traditionally written after designation. One proposal for streamlining the act is to replace the three classifications with one—that of *national river*—and to relegate the management questions to a management plan, written before or after designation.

After the federal agency completes the wild and scenic river study, the document and agency recommendation proceed to the secretary of the department, the Office of Management and Budget, the president, and Congress. The two trips through Congress—first for study and then for designation—force river conservationists to embark on a political odyssey more fitting to a constitutional amendment than to saving Saline Bayou or White Clay Creek.

As an alternate route for designating a river, a governor can request the secretary of the interior to grant national designation of a state-legislated scenic river. This may require an environmental assessment but needs no congressional vote. Section 11 of the act calls for the federal agencies to help states protect rivers through their own systems and other alternatives, and to evaluate potential for additions to the system.

GREAT EXPECTATIONS

Congress intended to "balance" the nation's water development with the National Wild and Scenic Rivers System. What constitutes balance is a good question.

Total stream mileage in the United States is estimated at 3.6 million, mostly very small waterways. Roughly 10,000 streams run 25 miles or longer, totaling about 320,000 miles (a figure derived from National Park Service estimates based on U.S. Geological Survey and Water Resource Council data). The nation has about 1.1 million miles of streams of 5 miles or greater in length. Other estimates for these figures vary substantially. In this book I use data derived from the Park Service, but figures derived from *The Water Encyclopedia* (1990) indicate about 460,000 miles of streams greater than 5 miles in length, and a total of 3.2 million miles of streams in America. The Environmental Protection Agency in its *National Water Quality Inventory* (1988) stated that there are 1.8 million river miles, a figure that clearly excludes the smaller streams.

Some 60,000 to 80,000 dams over 25 feet high have been built; nearly every major river outside Alaska is dammed at least once. In the 1980s, dam builders proposed 6,000 new sites, most of them small.

No one has reliably counted the river miles buried beneath reservoirs, but the figure is in the hundreds of thousands of miles. For every river protected, canals and channelization have ruined tens of thousands of river miles; 200,000 miles were channelized by 1980. For barges alone, the government channelized or dammed 26,000 miles at a cost of billions of dollars. Furthermore, everything from PCBs (polychlorinated biphenyls) to sewage and mud pollutes additional hundreds of thousands of stream miles. A majority of shorelines in many areas of the country have been developed with cities, towns, roads, railroads, homesites, and vacation dwellings ranging from broken-down trailers to grand estates. Less obvious but perhaps as damaging, untended cattle cause erosion, siltation, dewatering, and a massive loss of riparian habitat on even more miles—a vast majority in the West. The point of all this is that the challenge of reaching "balance" is a substantial one, unachieved by just about any estimation.

Congress set no mileage goals for the Wild and Scenic Rivers System. Interior Department planners had begun with an inventory—though not a goal—of 650 rivers, 12 of which were designated in the initial act. As of August 1992, 223 rivers with 11,276.6 miles were in the National Wild and Scenic Rivers System and related national systems, constituting 0.3 percent of total stream miles or 1 percent of the mileage of streams over 5 miles in length. To one degree or another, states protect another 13,000 miles, bringing the total protected mileage to 0.7 percent of total stream mileage or 2 percent of the mileage of streams over 5 miles in length. Streams in national parks, refuges, and wilderness areas are largely protected, but the figures are unknown; also, federal agencies manage many rivers for protection, though these lack long-term or firm security.

Early advocates, such as Stewart Udall and John Craighead (see chapter 2), initially saw the national rivers system as limited to the unique "gems" here and there across the country. Udall said in 1983 that he was "very pleased" because "we really didn't know how successful the program would be." Yet in 1988 he noted that "the national rivers system is incomplete when compared to the national forests, parks, wildlife refuges, and BLM [Bureau of Land Management] lands." In an open letter to President Bush, he asked that river conservation be made a higher national priority.

Bob Eastman, director of the Interior Department's river programs in 1980, said, "I don't think the program ever really came into its own.

It was overshadowed in the early years by wilderness and was troubled in later years by political problems and budget cuts."

Many types of rivers, based on landscape or physiographic surroundings, lack protection. Few really long rivers and few of the biologically richest waterways are included in the system. Congress has not protected many of the finest and most interesting recreational rivers.

In the 1980s, a half dozen feature articles on wild and scenic rivers published in environmental magazines all bemoaned the system's lack of growth. The fine writer, photographer, and conservationist David Sumner, a champion of the Dolores and other Rocky Mountain rivers, wrote that the national system "consists of token remnants rather than a true system." More biting, the Wilderness Society in 1984 called the wild and scenic rivers "no more than a disarticulated skeleton of a system." Various articles by the veteran river writer, guide, and naturalist Verne Huser and by me likewise expressed disappointment.

The question is, How much river protection is enough? Bern Collins, who has worked on national rivers about as long as anybody in the federal government, suggested a goal of conserving as many freeflowing river miles as we have dammed or altered by construction. He reasoned that this would complement the national water quality goal "to make all rivers fishable and swimmable" and the proposed "no net loss" goal for wetlands, and it appeared reasonable in comparison. Collins recognized that with dammed and ruined miles numbering well into the hundreds of thousands, the Wild and Scenic Rivers System alone will not be adequate; other approaches must be taken.

When the American Rivers Conservation Council launched its growth era in the 1980s, it announced a goal of protecting 2 percent of the nation's total stream mileage, or 70,000 miles, by the year 2000, a figure based on a Park Service inventory of eligible mileage (see chapter 7). In 1987, American Rivers scaled back to a goal of protecting 10,000 miles during the next five years. This reflected a recommendation of the President's Commission on the American Outdoors—no coincidence, as Chris Brown of American Rivers provided effective testimony to the Commission. American Rivers ultimately wanted 5 percent or 170,000 of the nation's total stream miles protected.

These goals were later reconsidered in light of reality. Since its inception, the system has grown at about 460 miles per year, a rate requiring 152 years to protect 70,000 miles. "To protect 2 percent of the stream mileage of this nation is an awfully modest goal," said Kent Olson, director of the organization in 1990, "but it's also an unrealistic goal for the year 2000." The five-year period ending in 1991 saw designations increase to a rate of about 600 miles per year.

With targets of its own, the Wilderness Society in 1984 called for designation of at least 50 additional river segments on federal land and another 50 on nonfederal land. The Oregon Rivers Council and American Rivers nearly reached the first goal in 1988 alone; the latter will be a long time coming.

Rick Healy, staff director of the House interior subcommittee dealing with the system, envisioned that for each two-year session of Congress people might expect approval of one or two state omnibus bills, such as Oregon's, and designation of one or two rivers that are longer and complicated, such as the Tuolumne or Niobrara, possibly involving private land.

Kevin Coyle, director of American Rivers in 1992, said he hoped someday to see 1,000 or more river segments in the system, with more attention to whole rivers and to cultural and biological values. American Rivers announced a new goal of doubling the size of the national system by 1996 (adding roughly 10,000 miles) and securing some form of lesser protection to many additional miles, for a total of 70,000 river miles in the United States. Chapter 7 further addresses these questions of the unfinished agenda in river protection.

MATCHING UP

Despite progress in protecting rivers, an air of impatience has surrounded the growth of the rivers system. Is that attitude justified? The first national park was designated in 1872 (Yellowstone), and the system grew in 117 years to 354 units covering 80 million acres—an annual growth of 3 units per year. Even during the growth years of the 1960s, the system grew by only 9 units per year, many of them corner-lot attractions, such as the Johnstown Flood Memorial in Pennsylvania.

The National Wildlife Refuge System expanded from Pelican Island off the coast of Florida in 1903 to include 450 refuges and 90 million acres 87 years later—a rate of 5.2 units per year. From 1977 to 1985, a period when river protection grew rapidly, Congress added only 2 refuge units per year.

Wilderness designations increased rapidly from their inception in 1964, to reach 496 units covering 90 million acres in 1990—a growth rate of 19 units per year. The system began with 9 million acres, 10 percent of its current size. The rivers program was initiated with 850 miles, or about 8 percent of its size in 1992. In terms of political acceptance and success, Kevin Coyle believed that the rivers system in 1992 was about where the Wilderness System was in 1976.

The National Trails System, signed into law the same day as the rivers system, immediately incorporated 2,000 miles of the Appalachian Trail and 2,350 miles of the Pacific Crest Trail, and thus had quite a jump start. By 1990, 16 trails of 22,500 miles had been designated, though only about 6,750 of these miles actually existed as trail on the ground, the rest being designated but not constructed. This was an average growth rate of 0.7 trails and 307 miles per year, most of which came with the two backbone routes at the system's beginning. While the idea of national trails was relatively new, the concept of the Appalachian Trail had begun with planner Benton MacKaye in 1921, long before protected rivers were even a glimmer in a conservationist's eye.

Though some people grumble about the slow pace of river designation, the Wild and Scenic Rivers System (excluding related forms of designation) grew to 212 rivers of 10,574.1 miles in 24 years—a rate of 8.8 rivers and 440 miles per year. This figure can be compared to the national park's 3 units per year, the wildlife refuges' 5.2, and the wilderness system's 19. Far more dramatic is the comparison of recent years, for the Wild and Scenic Rivers System has grown rapidly since 1987, a period of less significant growth of parks and refuges.

National parks constitute 3.3 percent of the U.S. land area, national wildlife refuges 3.3 percent, and designated wilderness 3.7 percent; the rivers program has protected 1 percent of the mileage of streams over 5 miles in length in its first 24 years. Yet the expectation is that many more rivers should be protected. The stated goal of the rivers program was to balance development, but it's unlikely that anyone ever expected national parks, wilderness, or refuges to balance development on the rest of the American landscape.

The differences among all these systems are legion, a key one being that the rivers system allows for private property and various uses and involves only narrow corridors of land. Still, this brief analysis suggests that rivers have not fared badly relative to other programs. As the distinguished environmental historian Samuel Hays said, "The progress in protecting rivers has been rapid when you consider the larger picture of conservation and political change."

Clearly, the wilderness system has advanced faster. Steve Whitney of the Wilderness Society explains this by noting that "rivers do not fit nicely into an ongoing agenda." That has been a problem: The rivers program was not pushed by the mainstream environmental groups and has not enjoyed the high profile and public image of wilderness and parks. The wilderness movement gained much of its strength from hikers, people who used the wilderness. Rivers enjoy similar constituencies in people who fish and boat, but these individuals perhaps have been slower to become politically active.

Rivers are also much more complex. Wilderness involves only public land, while rivers involve private land as well. Rivers stretch up and down the landscape and affect water rights, bankrolled pork-barrel beneficiaries, and whole groups of opponents and controversies normally not encountered in the cases of wilderness, parks, and wildlife refuges. Steve Evans, who worked for both wilderness and river groups in California, said, "Though it's often untapped, I believe there's a wider constituency for rivers—anglers, rafters, and others. And river outfitters give more money for lobbying than backcountry outfitters. Some politicians know that saving rivers can show your concern without really locking anything up the way wilderness is thought to do. But it's tough where the controversies exist; water development is still regarded by many people as something that's good."

Rivers involve a potentially larger constituency because they touch so many people, places, and pastimes in a positive way, but that latent power has not fully materialized.

DEFINING A SYSTEM

Beyond the question of mileage and numbers of rivers is the issue of what should constitute a "system" of wild and scenic rivers.

"We should at least incorporate the crown jewels among America's rivers and at least one representative from each physiographic region of the nation," advised Dennis Canty, the National Park Service's river specialist in the Northwest in 1991. Many of those involved believe in rounding out protection with rivers representing the full range of biology and geography that America has to offer, much as an art museum might include pieces from each significant period and style.

The three main reasons for designating rivers are to halt damage from dams, channelization, and development; to better manage recreational uses of the rivers; and to recognize the truly great rivers as a unique legacy. Within this rationale, priorities have been set both by rigorous analysis and by hit-or-miss efforts. Surveys by federal planners in the 1960s, the Nationwide Rivers Inventory in 1982, and federal land management plans in the 1990s have systematically attempted to define what should be protected. Even more important, major threats to rivers have catalyzed political campaigns to designate them. Superseding all else, political opportunism is often the key factor in selection of a river for protection, for without local congressional support, efforts are difficult at best.

In spite of the system's troubles, which the rest of this chapter examines, knowledgeable people remain hopeful about the National Wild and Scenic Rivers System. Stanford Young, a 20-year veteran of rivers before his retirement from the Department of the Interior, said, "The program will have its ups and downs, but too many people care about rivers for them to be ignored. I predict that the system will grow just as parks and wilderness areas grew. It's only a matter of time." John Haubert of the Park Service said, "Rivers, trails, and wilderness are where the potential lies for new additions to the nation's protected lands." Tom Lennon of the Forest Service predicted growth in three areas: designation of inventoried rivers of high quality, cooperation with state and local governments to manage streams flowing through land of mixed ownership, and management of nondesignated waterways for recreation. But diverse and difficult obstacles stand in the way of these goals and expectations, beginning with the complexities of privately owned land.

RIVERS THROUGH PRIVATE LAND

Opposition by private landowners is the key reason many rivers go undesignated and is a roadblock to growth of the Wild and Scenic Rivers System. Ironically, landowners stand to gain a great deal in security and real estate values through protection from dams, destructive projects, and helter-skelter or ugly development, yet they frequently oppose river designations out of fear that their land will be condemned.

Because the 1968 act allows acquisition of land and permits eminent domain (condemnation) where less than 50 percent of the corridor is in public ownership, landowners assume the authority will be used. Fueling their fears are memories or tales of people elsewhere who were bought out, especially before safeguards for landowners were legislated and before groups organized into effective blocs for political influence. Concerned people can turn, for example, to the history of some national park for stories of landowners being forced to sell, or worse, to the record of the Army Corps of Engineers, which condemned whole landscapes for reservoirs. The knowledge of such heavy-handedness, however remote or secondhand, offers fertile grounds for fear and often leads to volatile opposition to protection efforts. More important, people who want to develop their land as large subdivisions or unfettered tourist enterprises instill fear in other people, who would normally oppose unbridled development, by leading them to believe that their homes are at stake. In the humid greenhouse of abiding distrust of government, the seeds of paranoia grow quite well. "Fear of condemnation is the most misconceived thing and probably the most detrimental to the Wild and Scenic Rivers System," said John Haubert.

Landowners' concern is not limited to rivers running through mostly private land. Individuals own from 5 percent to 50 percent of the property along national rivers in national forests, totaling 160,000 acres within the 1 million acres of Forest Service land in wild and scenic corridors in 1991. About 33 percent of the land involved in the Oregon act of 1988 was private; about 40 percent of the land covered in the Michigan bill in 1992 was private.

The strong opposition that formed in 1992 over the case of the upper Farmington in Massachusetts, for example, is nothing new. Landowners' fears date to the original hearings for the system, when a Shenandoah River native said, "I am made to feel that no longer does the right to ownership exist." Because of the concern, Congress in 1968 placed limits on the amount of acquisition and condemnation possible. River advocates argue that the whole purpose of the system is to maintain the status quo, so that landowners' fears are unjustified. In a question-and-answer brochure, the Park Service and Forest Service confirmed, "Wild and scenic rivers are established to maintain the existing conditions—including the natural resource values, the scenery, the recreational uses, the historical values, the local communities, and the existing land use within the river corridor."

"Wild and scenic rivers are one of the softest touches we have in natural areas conservation," said Rick Healey, staff director of the House interior subcommittee. "It's not like a park or wilderness. It's a flexible system that strives to maintain the status quo." Indeed, the system treats people and settlements as *part* of the designations. Yet convincing landowners of this is a daunting job.

Where acquisition does occur, the main intent is to stop big developments or to secure existing open space, not to relocate people. Congress stressed easements as a benign alternative to acquisition, whereby only the development rights are bought. This "softer" approach to open space preservation is embraced by most government planners today but did not come easily to some traditional Park Service managers, enamored of their "green maps" where all land was parkland. They showed little appetite for the intricate approaches of incomplete or mixed strategies that compose the reality of land protection in the late twentieth century. Even though easements had been recommended as early as 1963, when author William H. Whyte testified for national protection of the Current River, little was done. "The river managers and park superintendents always opposed easements," said Bob Eastman of the Park Service in 1980. "The first thing a new superintendent looks at is a map, and he wants to see a solid block of green—to own everything and to keep the job simple—but we can't afford to do that today." Eastman's own perspective seems dated in the 1990s, when the issues go beyond questions of affordability. Park Service planners see that the slightest threat of condemnation is likely to kill a protection attempt on private-land rivers.

Unnecessary aggravation stems even from the management guidelines for the act, which state that "scenic" river areas are to undergo "no unharmonious improvements and few habitations permitted." Had the guideline been prefaced by "on public land," it would pose no problem, but to implicate private land is at best insensitive and in fact ludicrous, since the federal government has no authority to regulate land use. Part of the reason local residents became confused about the rivers system was that the agency staff were themselves confused. Entrenched in careers of managing public land, some administrators had no sensitivity to other concerns and different views. In the 1990s, the political and practical realities have changed, and many of the staff who were unwilling to change have retired. Those who remain have had to evolve with the times.

Some conservationists also fell prey to unrealistic expectations. Kevin Coyle explained, "People who had campaigned for wilderness were used to asking for a thousand acres in order to get a hundred. When they worked on rivers they did the same thing: to get 20 miles they asked for 50. But the problem with rivers is that when you extend the lengths that much you pick up more and more private property and pretty soon the whole proposal is lost." Meaningful public involvement, negotiation, compromise, and recognition of local views ranked paramount with all river protection involving private land.

The government has rarely exercised eminent domain in the Wild and Scenic Rivers System. The only condemnation by the Forest Service for fee title was along the Eleven Point River. Easements were condemned, involving no displacement of people, for 751 acres along the Rogue, Clearwater, and Flathead, with many of those actions uncontested except to set a price. Ironically, because the Forest Service holds authority to condemn any land within a forest proclamation boundary, involving vast amounts of private property, the wild and scenic program often grants inholders *more* protection against condemnation, not less.

The Bureau of Land Management has condemned land for wild and scenic rivers—44 acres along the Rogue in Oregon—and acquired 577 acres of easements along the Rio Grande and Rogue under eminent domain, the last condemnation occurring in 1985. The National Park Service condemned 70 out of 1,973 tracts acquired for wild and scenic rivers, most of it early in the system's history, and all of it at two rivers, the Saint Croix and Obed. (In the 1960s and early 1970s the Park Service pursued protection for the Current River in Missouri and Buffalo in Arkansas on the model of linear national parks and did condemn land, but those rivers are not in the Wild and Scenic Rivers System.)

A large percentage of the condemnations do not involve a landowner's refusal to sell but are simply served to "quiet" title to the land where deeds are not entirely clear—a common situation in many rural areas. Other condemnations result from a landowner's desire for a court rather than a federal agency to set the price; landowners are likely to get more money when they refuse to sell "willingly."

"Condemnation is a last resort," said Ken Myers, assistant director of lands for the Forest Service in Washington, DC. "Where it occurs in the Forest Service system, it's usually not because of refusal to sell but a result of disagreement over price whereby the court decides on the value." John Haubert confirmed, "Condemnation is absolutely a last resort, to be used if a new development would seriously degrade the river."

Regardless of the record and of the best intentioned government planner who repeats and repeats explanations about both the limits of the law and the comforting history of river administration, landowners often respond with singular defiance. Ed Pembleton of the National Audubon Society recalled, "At the Niobrara, no one ever intended to displace a single ranching family or affect their lifestyle with government regulations, but it became very difficult to convince local people of that."

The wild and scenic rivers program has aroused more fear of condemnation than have the hydroelectric developers that *are* allowed to condemn private land when the Federal Energy Regulatory Commission permits a power dam (even state parkland can be condemned in this relatively critic-free windfall to private entrepreneurs). The degree of concern for the essentially harmless rivers system is also curious when compared to the concern for highway projects. According to D. R. Neuzil of the Institute of Transportation and Traffic Engineering at the University of California, nearly 100,000 people a year have been relocated for road projects. Though many of the highway projects may have justifications eminently vulnerable to challenge, there appears to be a greater acceptance of social sacrifice for the sake of traffic than there is for protecting ecosystems.

All the facts aside, the ambiguities of the wild and scenic rivers law and the similarities to other government programs where land in fact has been condemned are sufficient to allow one or two staunch opponents to create mass hysteria just about anywhere. The National Inholders Association travels to rivers being considered for wild and scenic status and heightens concerns by meeting with landowners and talking about condemnation elsewhere. Charles Cushman, a Los Angeles–area insurance salesman whose private cabin in Yosemite National Park was once sought for acquisition by the Park Service, founded and directs the group. The Inholders' newspaper called the designation of Oregon rivers in 1988 the "mass Federalization of 40 river valleys," even though the majority of the land had been national forest property since the turn of the century. The Inholders Association strongly opposed the National Park Service across the country and asserted that wild and scenic rivers were a "feeder group" for new parks, though no wild and scenic rivers have ever been converted to national parks. In fact, no serious proposals for conversions had been made until legislation (opposed by the Park Service) designating the Niobrara River in 1991 called for study of a potential park.

Myron Ebell, the Washington, DC, lobbyist for the Inholders Association, claimed that the wild and scenic rivers program "in effect has almost unlimited condemnation authority." He described the river corridors as a "one-half mile wide strip giving authority to harass people and threaten condemnation if people don't do exactly what the park ranger tells them. If a park ranger doesn't like the color of your eyes he can give you a problem, and they do." Vast numbers of people believe these things when told by outside "experts." Fully aware that very few acres have ever been condemned under the rivers act, Ebell maintained that "the threat is the problem."

Ebell argued not only against condemnation but also against government purchases from people who want to sell and who perhaps have a rare opportunity to do that without turning their land over to a developer's bulldozer. "Federal acquisition destroys the fabric of rural life. Local economics depend on cattle raising. It gets into the problem of the common interest. To sell to the government may be in the interest of the individual owner but against the sum of the individuals' interest. It's against the interest of landowners but that's not seen for awhile."

Ebell argued that landowners are the best conservationists, a point that is certainly true some of the time but overlooks the many streams degraded by private development from the East River in New York to the Los Angeles River in California. "On the Niobrara, ranchers have been taking care of their property." Regarding the proposed Norden Dam, a serious threat to the Niobrara through the 1970s, he said, "That's dead. There are no threats to that river at all. The way the Park Service works is that if you take good care of your land they'll reward you by condemning it." Though people can stay and continue existing land uses after selling easements to the government, the Inholders Association regarded easements with the same disdain as condemnation of land in fee.

If the Inholders Association views the rivers program as one that should be prolandowner and is not antigovernment simply for anti-government's sake, it has agreement from virtually everybody. Fair treatment of landowners, protection of homes and farms by river designations, and the minimization if not elimination of condemnation for fee-simple purchase are a long-standing goal of the river conservation community as well as government spokespeople.

When the facts are disregarded, wild and scenic river proposals become antigovernment punching bags for people to vent frustrations about everything from the Internal Revenue Service to welfare, and to express antibureaucracy resentment that has frequently been smoldering for a lifetime. What Kevin Coyle of American Rivers called "the politics of human fear" pervades the private-land issue.

Opposition thrives on that aspect of human nature that makes it easier to oppose something than to support something, that resists minor changes now even if their purpose is to avoid major and distasteful changes later, that distrusts anybody and anything that questions the status quo, that fails to see incremental losses if they are incurred in normal activities, and that embraces one-line articles of faith that seek to simplify life rather than recognize the complexity of it.

Examples of these social dynamics are plentiful. On Pine Creek in Pennsylvania, one of the original study rivers, resistance to designation was based on people's fear of condemnation. Just when the federal study process, with a people-oriented staff from the federal Bureau of Outdoor Recreation, had allayed much of the concern, officials of the state Bureau of Forestry announced in an unrelated action that it "intended" to buy private land in the remote Pine Creek Canyon, a statement that incited all the other landowners to a new plateau of opposition. Other early study rivers—the Penobscot in Maine and the Shepaug and Housatonic in Connecticut—failed to gain designation because of landowners' fear of federal control. Congress halved the length of the Obed River designation because of landowner opposition. On the Greenbrier in West Virginia, 70 miles of private land and a flood control proposal stopped a wild and scenic bill for one of the longest free-flowing rivers in the East. The Forest Service dropped parts of rivers with private land as "unsuitable" on the North Branch of the Au Sable in Michigan and the Saint Joe in Idaho. For the same reason, it dropped the whole study reach of the Cahaba in Alabama, though the Heritage, Conservation and Recreation staff disagreed. Even along rivers with minuscule areas of private land, agencies and Congress balk or delete private sections. The spectacular Snake River in Wyoming is an unfortunate example of this practice.

The federal response to private-land rivers is changing, with the upper Delaware as the benchmark case. This was one of the original study rivers, designated in 1978 in part to stop Tocks Island Dam. Unfortunately, the Army Corps of Engineers had already condemned land and evicted residents before the Park Service inherited the river following the dam's defeat by a broad coalition of local residents and conservationists. For the upper Delaware, above the Tocks Island reach, Park Service planners wrote a management plan and revised it to address citizen concerns, finally recommending zoning by local townships and acquisition of 20 sites for public recreation, including a modest 1,000 acres along the 75 mile reach of river. Nonetheless, the valley exploded in controversy. Incapacitated by "Park Service go home" belligerence, the agency hired outside consultants to rewrite the plan, and Chuck Hoffman, an expert with a convincing, populist style, moved to the river with a commitment that endured threats of death and of lawsuits, shouting matches that canceled hearings, and 18 successive drafts of a plan. When asked about a substantial constituency that indeed cared for the river, Hoffman replied, "The opposition was so ugly that other people didn't even come out to look." With Glenn Eugster ushering the new approach through the Park Service bureaucracy in Philadelphia, most towns, two states, the Delaware River Basin Commission, and the Park Service agreed on a plan in 1988. Through a conference of local governments, municipalities zone for some degree of riverfront protection or are subject to the Park Service's authority to condemn land if irreconcilable conflicts arise. With the likelihood of condemnation close to nil and acquisition of any kind only an unlikely possibility, opposition evaporated. Real estate agents now advertise proudly about federal protection. The cost of the planning process totaled a whopping $1.2 million. "But you shouldn't have to spend nearly that much," Hoffman said. "Two-thirds of it was damage control—things you should never have to do but were needed because the situation had simply gotten out of hand."

The plan provided for a variety of protections. Most relevant is a land-use regulation for building setbacks of 100 feet from the river, which does not sound like much considering the amount of time, effort, and money spent in the process. But the cost of buying ease-ments for the 100 foot zone would certainly have been far more than $1.2 million, even in the unlikely event that it would be politically thinkable.

Lessons of the Delaware were to establish partnerships of local, state, and federal agencies early in the process; to involve people fully; and to write a management plan before trouble arises, even before designation. "We learned about bottom-up planning the hard way," said Glenn Eugster. Government planners had once regarded "public participation" as a matter of holding a series of meetings and talking with local officials; now they realized that formal committees, citizen initiative in management decisions, and years of effort are required, and that the agency staff involved must have the right attitude. It is clear, simply by observation, that the Park Service planners on more recent studies in New England are skilled professionals, knowledge-able about their program, and acutely aware of their challenges. These are great advantages over some staff of the 1970s, who were rotated in and out of studies far too quickly and who may not have been per-sonally interested in either rivers or public involvement.

The Park Service used the lessons of the Delaware at the Wildcat River in New Hampshire, designated for study in 1984. People there wanted designation to stop a hydroelectric project urgently threaten-ing the river. This was unlike the social dynamic on the upper Dela-ware, where many people saw no need for protection, but federal planners nonetheless used great care and skill in public information and planning, involving local people the whole way. Led by planner Rolf Diamant, the staff acted as consultants to a local process and not at all as federal managers. The wild and scenic study was not under-taken solely as a precursor to designation but with the aim of establish-ing a local conservation plan regardless of whether or not the river would ultimately be designated. The plan provided a summary of private, local, and state actions taken during the study to protect the Wildcat. This built a credible case that federal intervention other than the legal safeguard of simply being in the system was not necessary or desirable, and in effect became the management plan, executed before rather than after designation. By creating and implementing the plan, people knew exactly what they were getting. Wildcat became one of the smallest members of the national rivers system in 1988 but did so with unanimous support of the local people.

The final planning cost totaled $200,000 to protect 7 miles of privately owned riverfront and preclude the otherwise certain loss of a scenic waterfall—the town's centerpiece—to a private hydroelectric developer. The plan resulted in effective private and local action, including easement donations of 650 acres by 1988, estimated at $600,000 in value. In some cases citizen organizations or local governments could presumably take the initiative to plan and organize entirely from within the community to gain the political strength needed for wild and scenic designation without such federal planning expenses.

Park Service planner Phil Huffman in the early 1990s expanded the Wildcat model to a larger and more complex river, the Farmington in Massachusetts and Connecticut, which has seven townships and 1,000 landowners within the study area. Believing that success there could pave the way for other private-land rivers, Kevin Coyle of American Rivers called Huffman "the most important individual in the wild and scenic rivers program today."

The Farmington study cost $500,000. Even so, only the lower portion, explicitly threatened by a diversion for Hartford's waterworks, is likely to have the local mandate needed for designation. Support for the upper river was eroded by the familiar antigovernment response in spite of legislation that would ban both condemnation and even a benign federal presence.

At the Allegheny, a much larger river, the new tone in studies was repeated with an encouraging response. Considered for protection for a decade, the river finally received support from the Pennsylvania delegation in 1992, owing much to effective work by Forest Service personnel, who were directly responsible for only short mileages but took an admirable interest in a longer reach of the river. Strong support was developed with county commissioners and local leaders.

Counter to all the troublesome cases, the lower White Salmon in Washington, flowing entirely through private land, was designated with support of local people and without the elaborate planning process. The river had been the site of six hydroelectric proposals, tenaciously fought for years by residents, many of whom welcomed the certainty of national river protection and refused to buy into the paranoid approach.

The only national rivers with mostly private land are the Allegheny, Delaware, Wildcat, New, Little Beaver, Little Miami, Ontonagon, Wolf, lower Saint Croix, Namekagon, lower Missouri,

Niobrara, John Day, Imnaha, Eel, Van Duzen, White Salmon, Klickitat, and Skagit. About one-third of the land in the corridors of all designated rivers lies in private hands, and 16 percent of the corridor land along Forest Service rivers is private. The percentage of private land is likely to decrease with a focus on adding Forest Service and Bureau of Land Management rivers, yet many private-land rivers deserve protection.

Even though the existing program offers safeguards and has exercised little condemnation authority, the obstacles of misinformation and fear remain formidable. To designate a short reach of the Farmington may take as much work as it took to designate 44 rivers predominantly on federal land in Oregon.

Some people advocate a total elimination of condemnation authority under the act, claiming that the rare "necessity" is too rare—indeed, virtually nonexistent—and undeniably blocks progress on the whole system. It can be argued that the cumulative benefits of using condemnation throughout the history of the National Wild and Scenic Rivers System are exceeded by the costs of failing to designate even one river—and not one but many rivers have failed to be protected because of the condemnation threat.

But Rick Healy of the congressional staff opposed a stripping of condemnation authority. "If an awful development were going to happen, buying the land is the only way the federal government has to avoid the problem." Deen Lundeen of the Forest Service likened the eminent domain threat to a "speed limit" that is enforced only when necessary but is important nonetheless. Chuck Hoffman, who has borne the brunt of the backlash as much as anyone, also opposed rescinding the authority. But Iowa and Pennsylvania have both relinquished condemnation in their state scenic rivers systems and report better progress without it. The Farmington study proposed to eliminate the eminent domain threat. "We'd get nowhere if it were even a vague possibility," said Jamie Williams, a Park Service planner for the study. Also opposing authority for condemnation, Jerry Meral, long-time river activist and director of the California Planning and Conservation League, pointed out that his state's Wildlife Conservation Board has the authority but has never used it through 45 years and tens of thousands of acres of acquisition. To do so would be suicidal, he believed.

One logical compromise would be to ban condemnation of homes or farms that would displace residents—the real heartfelt issue—and to continue to allow, as a last resort, eminent domain for easements or open space acquisition that seeks only to prevent damaging development. This generic amendment, to be applied systemwide, could be accomplished as a one-sentence rider on any wild and scenic bill and could go far toward satisfying the concerns of landowners who are told by federal planners that the government is unlikely to condemn homes but receive no legal assurance of it.

The planners on the Farmington study likewise proposed no "boundaries." Drawing these lines on a map is usually the first requirement of the administering agency and is a more onerous task than it sounds. The lines enclose a half-mile-wide corridor, on average, centered on the river, or a corridor from rim to rim if a canyon is involved. Obviously useful for public-land rivers, the boundaries show where management requirements would apply. With private land, the boundaries show the maximum extent of government interest in protection, which is fine, but the inevitable, though incorrect implication is that *all* land within the boundaries will be "controlled" or acquired. This is an unrealistic fear on any modern-day, private-land river. Any acquisition is now likely to be opportunistic and limited to minor acreage. To eliminate the fear aroused by the dreaded boundary lines, they should no longer be required on private-land rivers. Protection techniques should be governed by simple criteria regarding river frontage, flood plains, steep slopes, and other critical areas addressed in any responsible local zoning ordinance. If boundaries must be drawn, they could be limited to areas of public ownership and to zones of open space already agreed upon by local government.

Whenever acquisition is needed and appropriate, a better approach might be for private, nonprofit land trusts to do the job and, when appropriate, to resell the land at cost to government agencies that will manage it. Along the Wildcat River, the Society for the Protection of New Hampshire Forests acted in concert with the town of Jackson to secure donations of easements to 600 acres of riparian property. A similar approach was used on the Pemigawasset and Merrimack, two rivers under study in New England. Citizens have formed land trusts in many regions, and the River Network in Portland, Oregon, specializes in riverfront acquisition, exchange, and preservation in many regions of the country. Riverfront conservancies could become commonplace along many streams, whether or not they are national rivers, as a local approach to reimburse willing sellers, secure protection, and eliminate the strife and ill-will of government acquisition. Public expense can sometimes be saved, though many conservancies must resell the protected land to the government in order to recoup costs. The Nature Conservancy acquired 54,000 acres of vital frontage along the biologically rich Niobrara in Nebraska, something the federal government could not have done. The Idaho chapter of the Nature Conservancy preserved cottonwood forests along the upper Snake River, the Trust for Public Land purchased much of the Gauley River Gorge in West Virginia, and the River Network bought important tracts in Hells Canyon of the Snake River and along Icicle Creek in Washington.

The Wild and Scenic Rivers Act clearly recognized the importance of rivers through private land and anticipated mixed ownership. Although there has always been a distinction between public-land and private-land rivers, Kevin Coyle said, "the system is dividing in two and the difference is becoming more profound. The public-land rivers are moving successfully toward protection. The private-land rivers are not."

Coyle did not give up, and American Rivers has continued to articulate the benefits of designation to landowners and residents. First, property value increases. Evidence shows that market values of land along protected rivers increase more than real estate values elsewhere. On the New River, land cost $250 an acre before designation in 1976; with promotion for second homes in a protected area, subdividers got $10,000 an acre in 1991. Land along the Rogue River showed a modest increase in value of 0.4 percent per year while values outside the corridor decreased. Second, designation and river recreation together can strengthen the local economy. A 1984 survey at the Kern River in California found that whitewater boating produced $10 million each year and 169 jobs. Along the Klamath, recreation generated $2.5 million annually. Recreation dollars have transfused West Virginia's economy, which was badly in need of diversification from coal and chemicals.

Some people are more convinced by the argument that designation improves the ability of federal, state, or local agencies to manage public use and to prevent trespassing, litter, and vandalism. Wild and scenic status can enhance fishing because habitat improvement becomes a priority, and it strengthens the local way of life, as it did by stopping a hydroelectric project on the Wildcat River.

Thousands of rivers with private land deserve protection, and many landowners agree with this. Second-home owners in particular have formed a constituency for protection in many regions, such as Lake Tahoe, California, and Jackson Hole, Wyoming.

"People living along rivers support the status quo," Kent Olson of American Rivers said in 1990. "The challenge to the conservation community is to communicate to people that the concerns of landowners and conservationists are often the same." But without the explicit threat of a dam or some other project, usually proposed by people from elsewhere and thereby considered an alien intrusion, the case for protection is difficult to make. Barry Beasley, director of South Carolina's state rivers program, said, "It's difficult to go to a group of people and say, 'We need to protect your river.' They ask, 'Why?' If no crisis is happening, we're hard pressed to give a satisfying answer."

State and local alternatives to national designation frequently make the best and only approach for private-land rivers and have succeeded on the Blackfoot River in Montana, the Edisto in South Carolina, the upper Mississippi in Minnesota, and elsewhere. State river systems have likewise proliferated, particularly in the East (see chapter 6).

Whether through wild and scenic designation or alternatives, protection of private-land rivers promises to be critical to the future of the rivers of America. With the demise of the dam-building era, land development poses the main threat to many natural waterways, and private land is where the development occurs.

Perhaps the best case for persistence in protecting rivers flowing through private land is simply that the frontier era has ended, and the nation has been settled. It's time to protect places where people live. Through much of the history of conservation, a premium has been placed on the spectacular and the unique, but the rivers movement has also recognized the importance of ordinary landscapes—valleys that River Network director Phil Wallin once affectionately called "outstandingly common."

RIVERS THROUGH PUBLIC LAND

The genesis of the National Wild and Scenic Rivers System lay in the undeveloped rivers with publicly owned shorelines, and with those networks of waterways the movement had its brightest success in the early 1990s.

It was always known that the glamour rivers receiving protection—the Selway, Salmon, Rogue, Snake, Tuolumne, and Chattooga—were only a few of those on the list of quality rivers running through land of the Forest Service and Bureau of Land Management, involving tens of thousands of miles, most of it without the complications of private ownership or development. Many of these rivers, excellent in water quality and wildness, are popular for recreation.

The Department of the Interior's Nationwide Rivers Inventory listed some of the public-land rivers as eligible for wild and scenic designation (see chapter 7). In 1979 President Carter directed that federal agencies protect rivers on the inventory and consider their inclusion in the wild and scenic system as a part of the planning process for federal land. In 1982 deputy chief R. M. Housley of the Forest Service ordered that the Nationwide Rivers Inventory be addressed in forest plans. Guidelines further called for protection of eligible rivers as if they were designated until plans dictated otherwise, but the agency process for carrying out this direction and the expertise of forest planning teams was inadequate.

While controversy raged over similar requirements for wild lands and led to the RARE II (the second Roadless Area Review and Evaluation) study of potential wilderness areas, only a few people recognized the possibilities for river protection through forest planning—a virtual RARE II for waterways. Forest Service staff developed procedures for addressing river protection based on Section 5(d) of the Wild and Scenic Rivers Act, which directed agencies to consider river protection when planning land use. These were sent to field offices on a trial basis in 1983 and made final in 1987. In 1986, after about half of the forest plans were written, Chris Brown of American Rivers met with Bob Dreher of the Sierra Club Legal Defense Fund and devised a strategy to appeal the plans lacking adequate river protection. Dreher and Kevin Coyle, as American Rivers's conservation director, then systematically appealed 53 of 120 national forest plans for their failure to address wild and scenic eligibility, classification, management, and other aspects.

"The biggest hurdle," Dreher recalled, "seemed to be that some Forest Service people would look at a river, and if it wasn't as good as the Salmon with a mile-deep canyon and raging whitewater, they didn't think it qualified." Tom Cassidy, who was hired by American Rivers to work full time on the public-land questions, added, "We once went out to a small river with Forest Service staff in North Carolina. They asked, 'Is this a river?' Well, yes, it was a river, and one that had some unique features. Planning for the rivers has changed the Forest Service's image of what they have, with the realization that rivers are valuable." A shift in agency orientation occurred.

"From the top down, the policy is now to look at rivers," said Deen Lundeen, the agency's wild and scenic rivers program manager in Washington, DC, adding, "We're now looking at wild and scenic candidates, and also at protection needs and alternatives for all the rivers." Chief Dale Robertson announced that through the land-planning process the Forest Service would recommend 200 rivers for designation by 1993, a statement that won him American Rivers's conservationist of the year award in 1989. Why 200 rivers? "The field staff had identified about 400 eligible rivers and we estimated conservatively that half of them would be suitable for wild and scenic recommendations," Lundeen explained. Later, the agency found that far more than 400 rivers were eligible out of over 1,500 evaluated in the forest plans.

In Alaska's Tongass National Forest—the nation's largest, covering 17 million acres, the size of West Virginia—the Forest Service originally planned to study 8 of 860 rivers. American Rivers complained, and 112 rivers were found eligible with 24 considered "suitable" in the draft plan.

Unlike the adversarial relations that existed between the Forest Service and wilderness advocates, the agency's relationship with American Rivers—including the appeals process—was founded on cooperation. "They've been more willing to negotiate than most conservation groups," Lundeen said, "and the progress we've made in river conservation is remarkable."

Chief Dale Robertson said, "There's now a lot of acceptance that rivers should be protected, acceptance throughout the agency. Rivers hold a special place in everybody's heart. People like to fish and boat and swim, and rivers are scenic and valuable habitat. Rivers are at the heart of conservation."

The Forest Service had taken a landmark step by planning to recommend hundreds of new rivers for wild and scenic protection, but one thing was wrong: the agency included few rivers where there was any hint of a conflict. A hydroelectric project on the Little Bighorn in Wyoming had no license and was only a remote possibility, but the Forest Service did not recommend that the river segment be protected (the Wyoming congressional delegation had pressured the chief of the Forest Service to change the regional forester's study recommendation). The Cosumnes in California survived as one of two remaining Sierra Nevada rivers without any dams, but the Forest Service omitted it from recommendations because it flowed through middle elevations of the mountains that served as the agency's breadbasket of cuttable timber. It did not recommend the North Fork of the Illinois Bayou in the Ozarks because a downstream town wanted a reservoir (the project was later abandoned, making the river available for reconsideration). Even at the Kings, one of the superlative wild and scenic rivers in the nation by any standard, authorities at the Sequoia National Forest refused to say that the river so much as qualified for the system, all because big agribusiness had proposed a dam, a proposal that was repeatedly found to be uneconomic but was nonetheless sought by corporate farming's political machine (once the river was congressionally protected, the Forest Service found the previously vulnerable reach "eligible").

Even if the Forest Service is justified in passing the buck regarding development proposals, such as Rogers Crossing Dam on the Kings, the agency is criticized for regarding many developments as serious proposals when in fact they are only remote possibilities. "The largest factor in these decisions," explained Lundeen straightforwardly, "is lack of local public support and the position of the state congressional delegation." Chief Robertson elaborated, "Our support will be reasonable and balanced. Where there are conflicts, we take a double and triple look. We consider the tradeoffs, and obviously there are fewer of those rivers recommended for designation." How important is designation of the unthreatened national forest rivers? "Over the long term," Robertson answered, "I think many designations will make a difference. Many rivers not threatened today will be tomorrow."

The Forest Service position on rivers points out a fascinating evolution in the agency. Severely criticized through the 1980s by the conservation community because of the commodity fixation of the forest-planning process, the official rhetoric in 1991 stressed river protection and land management reforms. "The balance is changing rather significantly," Robertson said. "We're trying to look at the forest in terms of the total spectrum of values, to manage an ecosystem, and to manage special areas, such as rivers. It's coming out significantly different than a few years back. It takes time, but the values have changed. I believe the Forest Service sees where people are going and is changing about as fast as it ought to be changing. We're not siding with any interest group but recognizing all legitimate groups."

With encouragement by American Rivers, the Bureau of Land Management (BLM) followed the new federal agency standard set by the Forest Service and in 1988 announced studies of 100 rivers throughout the agency's 272 million acre domain. Gary Marsh, a river specialist in Washington, DC, pointed out that BLM had been involved in river management as long as any agency, with responsibility for 35 major rivers in the national system and another 50 to 80 segments specially managed for recreation use. He said, "Wilderness studies were the focus after 1978, winding down in 1987. Now we can look at the rivers." Some outstanding, undesignated streams in the BLM domain include Westwater Canyon of the Colorado River, the Snake River below Palisades Dam, the Bruneau and Jarbidge in Idaho, and the Squirrel in Alaska.

Taking a lesson in rhetoric from the Forest Service, BLM director Cy Jamison in 1989 announced the bureau's new priorities as protection of riparian habitat, wildlife, and recreation. He said, "Either we're going to become truly multiple use for all American people or we're in deep trouble." What this agency—historically dominated by ranchers and miners—will deliver is anyone's guess. Even when supporting protection in the past, as at the Stanislaus River in California, BLM professionals have been routed by the more powerful Bureau of Reclamation within the Interior Department. Wild and scenic river designations, however, have given the agency the directives and backbone essential in dealing with other agencies and with the conflicting forces of traditional commodity extraction.

River eligibility studies were started in Alaska, where BLM oversees a multitude of exceptional streams. In south-central Alaska alone, 290 rivers cross BLM land, and bureau staff found 13 eligible for wild and scenic status. Some argued that this was an inadequate share of the pie when virtually all the rivers qualify for national designation, but that dissatisfaction was rapidly eclipsed. In 1990 the agency abruptly terminated all river studies after overt intervention by the Alaska congressional delegation. Director Jamison wrote to his state director, "Until the State has formally provided us with their thoughts and concerns relating to wild and scenic rivers . . . it is not proper to move forward with any studies." The decision was ostensibly based on a phrase in the Alaska Lands Act limiting further consideration of land protection. The BLM director left the question to Governor Walter Hickel, and it was clear that the state had no time to provide "thoughts and concerns" about rivers because it was busy proposing a pipeline to ship water to California, new railroads to serve unknown shippers, new pipelines to serve unproven oil fields, and new roads to remote ends of the state. The BLM director's decision disgusted conservationists and stirred dissent among the ranks of BLM staff. "How can we be pro-active on rivers and drop Alaska?" one official asked. American Rivers appealed the decision and argued for the river evaluations.

The Fish and Wildlife Service supported the rivers system during the Alaska Lands Act debates, and the designations of 1980 prevent oil and gas drilling in corridors that might otherwise be opened even within refuges. Still, the agency has not launched any studies for new designations. Director John Turner in 1991 supported conservation in theory: "I've been a personal advocate of wilderness designation and wild and scenic rivers, and some of our rivers fit very well. We now have to be more concerned about outside developers affecting the refuges. In the past, we didn't foresee a problem of shortages of water flowing into the refuges. Wild and scenic rivers will certainly be one of the appropriate long-range tools. The problem is that the Fish and Wildlife Service is probably the most underfunded land resources agency in the United States. A refuge manager might be lucky to just look at all his land twice a year, let alone review rivers for the Wild and Scenic Rivers System."

The National Park Service launched a survey of its rivers in 1991. Though 108 dams have been built in the parks, most are small and old, and eligibility can be argued for almost all park rivers. Park status alone has protected most streams since the early precedents denying major dams. Jack Hession, the Sierra Club Alaska staff member who has worked on river conservation since 1970, said, "Designation of park rivers is unnecessary duplication, but the worst thing is that the other side uses it against you. Whenever you go in with a proposal for a river that really needs protection, they say, look, you've already got all those rivers. You people want the whole world." Other critics argue that working for designation on national park rivers steals valuable time from streams that really need help.

"In a strictly legal sense, not much is to be gained by designating a national park river," said Chuck Clusen, chair of American Rivers in 1991, "but I can see a value if the designation extends out beyond the park." This is the "magnet" argument, which holds that the exceptional qualities of a river in a park will bolster the case for protection with momentum to extend it farther downstream to where it counts. A Merced River dam just outside Yosemite, for example, would have affected park wildlife but is now banned.

Tom Cassidy, general counsel for American Rivers, supported designation of national park waterways. "The system should represent the best rivers in the country; many of those have their origins in national parks but continue through unprotected areas." Even in parks, he argued, streams will benefit. "If the Merced had been designated earlier, Yosemite Valley would look fundamentally different than it does today. Many of the 'protected' rivers really aren't. People think the Colorado in the Grand Canyon is preserved, which is a sad misrepresentation. It's not being managed for natural and ecological values but for hydropower." Cassidy believed that designation inside the parks would add leverage against developments outside them. Designation of Alaska's Alsek could sharpen the contrast between Glacier Bay National Park and British Columbia's portion of the basin where a copper mine is planned. Within national parks, wild and scenic status also confers additional water rights protection. None of these arguments, however, refutes Hession's point that opponents will hold up designated mileage and argue that a "fair quota" has been met.

The large number of public-land rivers raises additional questions. While river supporters will certainly work for a larger system, will the system be "diluted" by the additions of hundreds of streams that might possess reasonably common values? This concern was once the rationale for not designating any river that was not on a par with the Salmon or Rogue. It is now assumed by many that diverse and numerous rivers do deserve protection, but with a plethora of new waterways—on the Oregon model, for example—will national river management really be any different from the management of undesignated streams? Will watersheds be protected any better if to do so means a significant change in other resource programs? Will available funds, presumably spread thinner, make any appreciable difference? These questions are pursued in chapter 5, but with the exception of rivers that are already protected by other means, it appears that the designations do benefit the rivers and do not jeopardize the system.

With action of varying degrees by the federal agencies, hundreds of land managers and planners strived to protect rivers in the 1990s where in earlier years only a few people had worked. Many of those people, especially in the middle and lower levels of the federal agencies, personally supported river preservation. The simple power of bureaucracy finally augmented river conservation rather than resisted it. The program had earlier been seen as one that conflicted with traditional priorities, diverted staff time from ongoing commitments, cost money, and attracted opposition from commodity-based professionals, local residents, and business-backed politicians. All that remains true, but in the 1990s river protection found better acceptance.

Commitments of the Forest Service and BLM leadership called for designation of 300 or more new river segments within five years; by 1992 planners had found 700 rivers eligible on those federal lands and the number was climbing. Even with the substantial shortcomings, such as exclusion of threatened rivers, the combined effects of the federal agencies constituted the largest joint action ever initiated to protect rivers across the United States. The difficult part is to gain congressional backing. Dale Robertson assured, "There is administration support. We will be aggressive in pressing for action in Congress." He argued that the "flexibility" of the rivers program was a great advantage. "You're not arguing absolutes the way you are with wilderness." Kevin Coyle added, "The challenge here will be to get support on a scale we never imagined six years ago."

STAFF ENTHUSIASM AND A POINT OF RESPONSIBILITY

Unlike the response to some other government programs, staff within the Bureau of Outdoor Recreation, Forest Service, Park Service, and Bureau of Land Management who worked on wild and scenic river proposals often acted with great dedication toward the intent and not just the narrower requirements of their jobs. Many pursued their tasks with a determination to save rivers. Planners and managers quickly became attached to the streams they were studying and were often disappointed with the lack of initiative or support at higher levels in the government and in local communities. Staff members were responsible for advancing the program through hard work, consensus building, and consistent though frequently subtle support for designations. Their personal feelings of support were not necessarily recognized in the recommendations that eventually emanated from the office of the department secretary or from the president.

Undermining individuals' enthusiasm, no single agency shouldered responsibility for the Wild and Scenic Rivers System. Until the late 1980s, the Forest Service often argued that special protection was not needed; the agency preferred to use its open-ended mandates under the National Forest Management Act in managing the rivers and shorelines. The Park Service said it had already protected its rivers. The BLM opposed new river designations as it did any measures perceived to interfere with grazing and mining. The only government advocate was a planning agency, the Bureau of Outdoor Recreation, later renamed the Heritage, Conservation and Recreation Service and then disbanded during the Reagan administration, though partially absorbed under the Park Service.

Agency responses changed in the 1990s but still no office is fully responsible for the program. Rivers thus lack a powerful constituency within the government itself, so that there is a void of institutional incentive to properly care for the system. John Haubert of the Park Service said, "River designation is mostly ignored in the Park Service. We don't expect another Saint Croix or Delaware, and we're not sure we want one. But in the Forest Service and Bureau of Land Management I think we'll see more involvement on federal land, and we'll see quite a few new recommendations." Haubert's view was reflected in the agency's opposition to Niobrara River legislation in 1991. The Park Service argued that not enough public participation work had been done, but the designation was passed anyway, putting the Park Service once again in the hot seat on a private-land river.

As a minimum, various organizations and commissions have called for better coordination of federal actions affecting rivers to avoid absurdities, such as the Soil Conservation Service draining wetlands while the Fish and Wildlife Service tries to create them, and the Army Corps spending millions to bulldoze out the meanders of the Kissimmee River in Florida one year and considering their more costly replacement a few decades later. Up to 15 different agencies at the federal, state, and local levels at once can be making decisions regarding a particular river.

An executive mandate similar but more extensive than President Carter's directive in 1979 could unify diverse programs in a cohesive package with the understanding that the federal government values its natural rivers, yet the Bush administration has shown no such inclination. Though crippled along the way by administration policies, directives requiring federal consistency for wetlands pose something of a model. The Coastal Zone Management Act might indicate the type of direction and coordination necessary to really protect rivers. That program seeks to have planning guidelines met by state and local agencies for development along oceans and bays.

ECOSYSTEM MANAGEMENT

The Wild and Scenic Rivers System ignores most lowland rivers with outstanding wildlife habitat. The Platte in Nebraska, the Snake in Idaho, the Susquehanna in Pennsylvania, the blackwaters in the Southeast, and many other waterways are typically considered too developed and too affected by people's uses to be national rivers, yet wildlife abounds along these lowland lifelines.

As if the other problems weren't enough, an ecosystem approach raises even more encompassing difficulties to river protection and management. Diversions and grazing, for example, have caused the loss of 95 percent of Arizona's riparian habitat. Because of agriculture and urbanization, California lost 90 percent of its riparian zone. In the spectacular eastern Sierra, diversions affect 85 percent of the stream miles. Water quality problems plaguing eastern and midwestern streams spill from abundant sources, few of them affected by considerations of wild and scenic value.

Ed Pembleton of the National Audubon Society saw the inability to deal with ecosystems as a major shortcoming of the wild and scenic program. "We support the system but generally seek protection in other ways." On the Platte River for example, the complex workings of hydrology and habitat depend on a bevy of water projects in several states. System-wide problems attract more opposition—consider the listing of salmon as an endangered species in the Snake River—but the support for river protection also broadens with broader issues. "Imagine how much larger the constituency would be for a whole river system as opposed to the support for fishing or rafting," said Beth Norcross, American Rivers's lobbyist.

"American Rivers's focus is changing with the changing threats," Kevin Coyle said. "We now have to deal with hydropower, land use, and instream flow problems. The breadth of interest is increasing. As of 1991, river conservation is probably the closest we've come to a national policy to actually protect ecosystems."

American Rivers broadened its official mission statement from "to preserve the nation's outstanding rivers and their landscapes" to "to preserve and restore America's river systems and to foster a river stewardship ethic." With the recognition that river-dependent species decline even faster than terrestrial ones, a new program embraces the protection of endangered aquatic and riparian species. Related to this, the group adopted water quality as a new goal, with a focus on protection of pristine waterways and the restoration of biological integrity in river ecosystems. American Rivers likewise targeted western water allocation and instream flows for increased attention.

URBAN RIVERS

Yet another set of rivers is the urban ones, actual or potential centerpieces to many towns and cities in America. As early as 1978, analysts in the Department of the Interior criticized river protection programs for excluding recreational, urban, or cultural rivers. Greenway plans capitalizing on local, state, or federal cooperation and benefiting both local business and real estate can emphasize open space protection and recreational opportunities for residents on thousands of rivers. The American River in Sacramento, Boise in the capital of Idaho, Schuylkill in Philadelphia, Potomac in Washington, DC, and Spokane in the city of Spokane, Washington, stand out as successful urban waterfront projects, with new and struggling efforts being made along the Jordan in Salt Lake City, the San Joaquin in Fresno, and in other cities. New federal funding for greenway programs is likely in the early 1990s.

THE ANTICIPATORY CONFLICT

The idea of river designation is to maintain the status quo and protect river values, yet many people assume that much more will happen. Landowners fear condemnation of property, loggers fear bans on cutting, and outfitters fear reductions in the number of allowable boats. "There's more misinformation on wild and scenic rivers than with any other kind of natural areas designation," said Beth Norcross. If *any* controversy on any issue surfaces or even might surface, federal agencies and Congress will likely abandon the river in what Kevin Coyle called the *anticipatory conflict*. "It's conceivable that an individual could block a designation in some states by simply drawing a circle on a map and declaring an intent to build a water project someday." Coyle recommended better criteria in determining "suitability" for designation. In a deck stacked to favor development, officials automatically upgrade remotely possible schemes to "foreseeable conflicts."

Another way agencies sidestep conflict is *segmentation*. The river is broken into segments, some of which are recommended for protection and some not. On Sespe Creek in California, a dam proposal midway in the already short river was segmented and left out by the Forest Service. On the Kings River, wild and scenic designation included spectacular sections but only as far as a proposed dam site, though the entire purpose of the national river campaign had been to stop the dam. Representative Richard Lehman banned it, but through a "special management area" lacking wild and scenic status. Worse, an important mile-long section at the bottom of the threatened reach was given no designation so as to allow possible raising of the existing Pine Flat Reservoir. Seeking to pacify all river opponents, segmentation erodes the integrity for which protection was sought in the first place.

The anticipatory conflict and segmentation eliminate most rivers for which designation would really count—where it would save mileage that would otherwise be damaged. For a river burdened by conflicts to be adopted, a major, prolonged, expensive campaign at the state and national level is usually required.

THE FUTURE FOR RIVERS

With a thoroughly professional view of the problems, Chris Brown of the National Park Service said, "We can save any river if we devote enough time and energy to it. Look at Two Forks Dam on the South Platte. What could be more powerful than the Denver Water Board saying it needs more water? Yet a resourceful, broad-based coalition beat it."

"As we go into the 1990s," said John Turner, director of the Fish and Wildlife Service, "resources are under unprecedented siege. At the same time, we have the opportunity to do bold new things."

How can people pursue the goal of protecting a whole system of the nation's outstanding rivers? Leaders in the field call for an integrated approach using a variety of tools, including national and state river programs, water quality laws, fisheries enhancement, flood plain and land use management, wetlands regulations, and erosion control.

Should river conservationists pursue a few important rivers or seek protection of many nonthreatened streams on public land? Should private land be ignored because of divisive problems? Should protection seek only to stop dams rather than to deal with land use? Because thousands of rivers are worthy, the key question is, How can more rivers be protected faster?

"I believe that all rivers are important and that we should seek appropriate conservation levels for most rivers rather than just a few that are 'worthy'," said Bern Collins of the Park Service. Recognizing that the Wild and Scenic Rivers System will never be large enough, he proposed a hierarchy for conservation: national watersheds with basinwide protection; the wild and scenic rivers; national recreation rivers, including the popular reaches and urban waterways; state and local river systems; and a national damless rivers system. Affording less protection than a wild and scenic river, this final category would grant congressional protection only against the threat of dams or other federal projects; it would altogether avoid the issue of land use.

Kent Olson agreed: "Such a designation would eliminate immediate threats to the flow and would assure riparian owners that their land would remain private. Think of the value that would be created for property. You'd send a message all the way up and down that river,

'This place has value.' Protection would be an ideal springboard for local communities to take their own initiative to consider land use along the banks." Making it easier to secure rivers from the blatant threats of dams, supporters of a damless rivers program argued that many more miles could be protected. Damless protection in fact resulted on the Henry's Fork, lower Snake, and lower Salmon in Idaho as a compromise by Senator James McClure, who was hostile to the Wild and Scenic Rivers Act but somewhat responsive to constituents who were avid anglers. "McClure, of all people, handed us a tool that we've done nothing with," Olson said.

A similar approach but involving even less protection could be a national register of rivers modeled after the national Register of Historic Landmarks. Congress would give the Park Service authority to list rivers on the register, which would require special consultation before dams or other federal permits could be allowed. The program would put river protection on more equal footing with hydroelectric development; FERC now permits dams without congressional approval. Pope Barrow of the American Whitewater Affiliation summarized the problem: "To protect a river, we have to go to Congress, but to dam a river the developers only have to go to a prodevelopment agency." He argued that listing rivers under a registry would be relatively easy to do, and since it would afford only limited protection, this option wouldn't steal attention from the Wild and Scenic Rivers System, something he fears might happen if a damless rivers act were passed.

Other people believe that the rivers act should at least be amended to eliminate the condemnation threat.

Skeptics to all these ideas argue that without protecting a river from poor land use, one cannot protect a river; that land use conflicts are indeed the major problem; that the wild and scenic system should be left alone; and that conflicts with local residents should be dealt with as they are at present—by avoiding landowners on the public-land rivers and by careful citizen involvement elsewhere. They argue that if a ban on dams is otherwise enacted, there will be little interest in adding new rivers to the wild and scenic system.

A counterpoint to all this is the view that rivers are essential to ecosystems, and that more protection, not less, is required. Not just the river but the whole watershed needs support. Bern Collins's idea of national watersheds would represent the most effective approach.

While a few national rivers, such as the Smith, represent good watershed protection, most politically acceptable basins will likely be too small to qualify as much of an ecosystem, though interest in this topic is growing as a result of frustrating efforts to save endangered species.

These may all be good ideas, but in 1992 many people including House committee chair Bruce Vento opposed tampering with the Wild and Scenic Rivers Act. "Once you open the Act you'd spend all your time fighting regressive actions," warned Chris Brown.

Kevin Coyle believed that the Wild and Scenic Rivers System will remain the main tool for protection of the nationally significant rivers, but that new legislation may be needed to address conservation, not just on the outstanding rivers, but on all of them. He projected a future in which the system will grow greatly with public-land rivers, both the act and the skills of agency staff will be improved to more effectively protect private-land rivers, and a registry of some kind will be devised for streams that are not so nationally significant and for cases where land use controversies would otherwise kill protection.

While history has proven that local support is critical to river designations, many of the great advances resulted because the rivers were seen in a national context—the New, Delaware, Snake, and Kings, for example. Though many rivers and regions of rivers remain unprotected in spite of nationwide importance, it has become harder to make the national case. Nationalizing the issue may still be important in Alaska and Idaho, and for unique biological waterways of various regions, but Beth Norcross of American Rivers cautioned, "It's very difficult to make another state into an Alaska, and even there, the delegation always had a huge influence. With any area where lines appear on a map, the state delegation is going to call the shots."

Beyond the other political problems, both the House and Senate in 1992 lacked effective spokespeople for river conservation. Bruce Vento expertly shepherded viable proposals on the House subcommittee, but few members could be counted on to support rivers as a broad issue the way John Saylor, Frank Church, or Gaylord Nelson had done. "My goal," said Norcross, "is to find more river champions."

Tuolumne River below Clavey Falls, California

Merced River in Yosemite Valley, California

Kings River, Middle Fork in Tehipite Valley, California

Kings River, South Fork below Kings Canyon National Park, California

American River, North Fork near Iowa Hill Bridge, California

Kern River, North Fork below Forks of the Kern, California

Eel River, Middle Fork near Dos Rios, California

Salmon River near Klamath River, California

Smith River at Jedediah Smith Redwoods State Park, California

Feather River, Middle Fork below Milsap Bar, California

Klamath River below Weitchpec, California

Trinity River north of Willow Creek, California

*American River in
Sacramento,
California*

*Merced River, South
Fork at Hite's Cove,
California*

Grande Ronde River below Wallowa River, Oregon

Illinois River, Green Wall Rapid, Oregon

Imnaha River above Snake River, Oregon

Metolius River below Camp Sherman, Oregon

Deschutes River below Mack's Canyon, Oregon

Rogue River below Grave Creek, Oregon

Elk River near Sunshine Campground, Oregon

Skagit River below Marblemount, Washington

Klickitat River above Columbia River, Washington

White Salmon River below Trout Lake, Washington

Delta River at Richardson Highway, Alaska

Sheenjek River near Table Mountain, Alaska

Flathead River, North Fork near Big Creek, Montana

Missouri River near Loma, Montana

Flathead River, Middle Fork at Spruce Park, Montana

Snake River, Hells Canyon, Wild Sheep Rapid, Idaho and Oregon

Clearwater River, Middle Fork below Lowell, Idaho

Selway River at Selway Falls, Idaho

Salmon River, Middle Fork at Sheep Creek confluence, Idaho

Salmon River below Shoup, Idaho

Saint Joe River above Spruce Tree Campground, Idaho

Clarks Fork of the Yellowstone River near Thief Creek, Wyoming

Verde River above its confluence with the Salt River, Arizona

Niobrara River above Norden, Nebraska

Saint Croix River below Namekagon River, Wisconsin and Minnesota

Namekagon River above Saint Croix River, Wisconsin

Current River above Van Buren, Missouri

Jacks Fork River below Highway 71, Missouri

Eleven Point River near Greer, Missouri

Little Miami River above Cincinnati, Ohio

Chattooga River near Bull Sluice Rapid, Georgia and South Carolina

New River, South Fork below Highway 221, North Carolina

Little Beaver Creek at Fredericktown, Ohio

Delaware River above Shohola, Pennsylvania and New York

Pemigawasset River, a wild and scenic study river, New Hampshire

Suwannee River, White Shoals Rapids, a wild and scenic study river, Florida

Youghiogheny River, Railroad Rapid, a wild and scenic study river, Pennsylvania

Green River, Desolation Canyon, a wild and scenic study river, Utah

The Cast of Rivers

AN ACCOUNTING OF THE RIVERS

Each of the national rivers shines with its own qualities and character, biological and cultural importance, and appeal for recreation, escape, and a way of life. This chapter presents a summary description of the rivers and information on how to see and enjoy them. The system was not conceived as a promotional enterprise, and that is not the spirit of this chapter. Still, unless people grasp the scope of what has been protected, realize the success and popularity of the system, and begin to see and experience these rivers for themselves, interest in river protection will surely fade. Instead, public interest must increase if more rivers are to be safeguarded, or if we are to keep the ones we have.

The "official" number of rivers in the National Wild and Scenic Rivers System was 151 in August 1992, taken from the various legislative titles and designations by the secretary of the interior but often reflecting a "short title" and not itemizing designated tributaries, even ones as significant as the Selway and Lochsa. For example, the East Fork of the Andreafsky, one of the longer rivers in the system at 137 miles, is longer than the Andreafsky's main stem but is not counted as a "river," while the Yellow Dog River, only 4 miles long, is counted.

Conversely, the traditional list counts several rivers twice, and the Saint Croix three times, only because of a separate legislative history. Thus, the 151 figure does not count many waterways and counts some others more than once. It does not include similar programs, such as river-based national recreation areas. Virtually all written accounts of the system to date have used the numbers based on the legislative titles. This book does not; rather, it relies on specific counting.

A total of 314 rivers and named tributaries were included in the National Wild and Scenic Rivers System as of August 1992, and another 11 were included in related designations, for a total of 325 nationally protected streams. "Rivers" account for 223 of these. A *river* is defined here as any waterway named a *river, fork,* or *branch,* regardless of length, plus creeks if they are the only waterway named in the legislation. Creeks are not reflected in the numbers when listed as tributaries of a designated river, nor are forks of forks.

The following figures summarize what has been protected:

Designated rivers and tributaries: 325, for a total of 11,276.6 miles
Designated rivers: 223
Designated rivers in the Wild and Scenic Rivers System, not counting related programs: 212, for a total of 10,574.1 miles (several rivers have reaches in both categories)
Designated rivers in legislative titles (the commonly used number in other literature): 151, for a total of 10,574.1 miles
Rivers designated by the secretary of the interior rather than by Congress: 28 rivers, plus 45 tributary creeks to the Smith River, for a total of 1,495.3 miles (includes one river with reaches also designated by Congress)

Counting the wild and scenic and related systems of protection, Oregon has the largest number of designated rivers, followed by California, then Alaska. (Counting small tributaries, however, California has the most.) Alaska has by far the most mileage in the system, followed by California, which in turn is closely followed by Oregon. Idaho ranks as the fourth highest state in mileage, Michigan, with 26 rivers, ranks fourth in number of designated streams, followed by Montana, Idaho, and Washington. As a region, northern California comes the closest to having all of its rivers protected. The west coast, including Alaska, plus Idaho, has 7,983 miles or 71 percent of the national river mileage.

Alaska's abundance of protected mileage was all born in the Alaska Lands Act of 1980, legislation that dealt mainly with land issues. Many of the designations are less important compared to other protected rivers because 2,413 miles on 24 rivers—73 percent of the designated mileage—is doubly protected by being in national parks, preserves, wilderness, refuges, or other safeguarded areas.

The California rivers are an eclectic blend of great quality. Much of the plentiful mileage at the north coast flows through national forest land and was designated at Governor Jerry Brown's request by Interior Secretary Cecil Andrus in 1981. Unlike the cases of Alaska and Oregon, which involved less controversial rivers, mostly designated by single pieces of legislation owing to extraordinary political events or personalities, California's Sierra Nevada designations are a result of long-term, sophisticated lobbying and public information efforts over truly endangered rivers conducted by a statewide organization with a paid staff of a dozen people.

Most of the Oregon mileage was enacted in the Oregon Omnibus Rivers Act of 1988, and most of the shorelines are national forest and BLM land, though only 161 miles were already in wilderness areas before the rivers act was passed. Although few immediate threats existed on the Oregon rivers that were designated, these lands were not guarded from future harmful uses until the 1988 law. The Idaho rivers were designated earlier and represent the classic wild rivers— large streams of landmark quality and great popularity for fishing and whitewater boating, mostly located in national forests. Most of the Michigan and all of the Arkansas rivers were designated in omnibus bills in 1992.

Montana, Washington, and New Mexico have several national rivers each. Twenty-four states have one, two, or three rivers, but most have only one, and usually short ones at that. No national rivers have been designated in Vermont, Massachusetts, Rhode Island, Connecticut, Delaware, Maryland, Virginia, Indiana, Iowa, Oklahoma, Kansas, North Dakota, Utah, Nevada, or Hawaii. A few states have many quality rivers but little nationally protected mileage, including Maine, New York, West Virginia, North Carolina, Florida, Kentucky, Minnesota, Colorado, and Wyoming.

Regionally, Alaska has 29 percent of the mileage; the Pacific Northwest, 19 percent; California, 17 percent; the Rockies, 11 percent; the Midwest, 15 percent; the Southwest, including Texas, 3 percent; the Northeast, 3 percent; and the Southeast, 3 percent.

The most complete coverage of a watershed by the national rivers system is the Smith in California, where all major branches are designated from source to mouth, plus many tributaries, for about 338 miles in all. Much of the Fortymile system in Alaska is likewise protected: the entire main stem to Canada, 3 forks, and 13 smaller tributaries, for a total of 396 miles—the most miles in any one river system that is nationally designated. The Eel in California has 346 miles protected on its main stem and major forks.

The longest designated river is the Noatak in Alaska, at 330 miles. The only other river with more than 200 miles of designated length (not counting tributaries) is Alaska's Nowitna at 225. The Salmon in Idaho has 237 miles if the "damless" section is added to the national river reach of 125 miles; the Middle Fork Salmon and Salmon total 286 continuous miles of protected river, 174 of them in the National Wild and Scenic Rivers System. A hundred miles or more are designated on 27 rivers, 11 of them in Alaska.

The Yellow Dog River in Michigan, designated for 4 miles, is the shortest river legislated by itself and not flowing continuously with another designated tributary.

It is often said that these rivers are protected, but in most cases only segments are protected, often amounting to a tiny percentage of the whole river. With headwaters protected as wilderness above its designated reach, the Middle Fork Eel–main stem Eel combination is the longest river protected from source to mouth. This prestigious list of rivers includes the Middle Fork Salmon at 104 miles (though its "source" is not the origin of its flow but the confluence of two streams), the Charley at 104, Middle Fork Flathead at 101, the Wind in Alaska at 98, and the Selway at 94. Altogether, 47 rivers are designated from source to mouth, not counting tributary creeks, of which 46 are so protected.

About 3,040 miles on 48 rivers were already protected in other ways, such as by national park, wilderness, wildlife refuge, or national conservation area status. All but about 360 of these miles are in Alaska and Oregon. Outside Alaska, the highest mileage in wilderness is the Middle Fork of the Salmon with all of 104 miles included, the Middle

Fork of the Flathead (50 of 101 miles), and the Minam in Oregon with all of 39 miles in wilderness. Along the Rio Grande in Texas, 67 miles on one side of the river were already protected in Big Bend National Park. Portions of California's Tuolumne, Merced, Kings, and Kern were also already in parks. A summary of national rivers by state is presented in the table.

NUMBERS, MILES, AND DESIGNATIONS OF PROTECTED RIVERS, BY STATE

State	Number of Rivers	Number of Rivers & Tributaries	Total Designated Miles	Rivers & Miles Designated by Sec. of Interior Rather Than by Congress[a]	Rivers & Miles in Alternate Designations[b]
AL	1	10	61.4		
AK	33	61	3,284		
AZ	1	1	40.5		
AR	8	9	342.3	1/10.7	1/132
CA	38	84	1,908.8	19/1,238	1/11
CO	2	2	75		
FL	1	1	7.5	1/7.5	
GA	3	3	104.9		1/48
ID	10	10	746.6		2/173
IL	1	1	17.1	1/17.1	
KY	1 (dup)	1	20		1/20 (most in TN)
LA	1	1	10		
ME	1	1	95	1/95	
MI	26	26	624.8		
MN	1	1	155 (sh. WI)		
MS	1	1	21		
MO	3	3	178.4		2/134
MT	4	4	368		
NE	2	3	208		
NH	1	4	14.5		
NJ	1	1	35 (sh. PA)		
NM	5	5	108.9		
NY	1	1	73.4 (sh. PA)		
NC	4	4	40.7 (incl. Chattooga, which fl. GA)		

NUMBERS, MILES, AND DESIGNATIONS OF PROTECTED RIVERS,
BY STATE (*continued*)

State	Number of Rivers	Number of Rivers & Tributaries	Total Designated Miles	Rivers & Miles Designated by Sec. of Interior Rather Than by Congress[a]	Rivers & Miles in Alternate Designations[b]
OH	6	7	149	5/127	1/22
OR	49	58	1,820.1 (incl. 66.5 mi. Snake, sh. ID, & North Fork Smith, which fl. CA)		
PA	2	2	193.4		
SC	1	1	40 (sh. GA)		
SD	1	1	98 (sh. NB)		
TN	3	7	98		1/53
TX	1	1	191.2		
WA	10	10	223.5		2/47
WV	4	4	93		3/82.5
WI	3	3	277		
WY	1	1	20.5		
Total[c]	223	325	11,276.6	28/1,495.3	14/702.5

Abbreviations: fl. = flows into; *incl.* = includes; *sh.* = shared with.

[a] Figures are included in lefthand columns.

[b] Includes national rivers, river-centered national recreation areas, and legislated dam prohibitions.

[c] Does not double-count rivers or mileage shared between two states.

SEEING THE RIVERS

Visitors to the national rivers should be aware of permit requirements for overnight boating trips on some of the waterways; check the descriptions, and write to the administering agency. On every river, visitors should respect the place, its wildlife, local residents, and other people. Avoid private property or first ask permission to cross it, pack out trash, and give anglers as wide a berth as possible when boating. Remember that extra care needs to be taken on these exceptional streams. As use increases, the impact on wildlife by people simply *being there* grows worse. A great blue heron, for example, will likely leave its feeding site whenever a boater passes by. If a boater passes once every ten minutes, the heron cannot hunt and eat. It's no wonder that little wildlife is seen on heavily used rivers. Remember also that there is no other place for that wildlife to go, since suitable habitat elsewhere is likely filled up. In wildlife-rich areas, visitors should stay off the rivers in the prime feeding times of early morning and evening, and also in the spring when young waterfowl and other birds are most vulnerable. When boating, avoid stopping at nesting areas, and don't harass wildlife by trying to take pictures from too close a position.

The recreation information given in this chapter is based partly on my own experience but mostly on the best available written sources, including government reports and guidebooks, and on agency reviews. The description of each river was sent to the administering agency, and most of them did review the text, but not even that can guarantee total accuracy. Some data, especially regarding small designated tributaries, were not available from written documents or agency personnel.

Whitewater difficulty listed here should be regarded only as a general guide and is best considered cautiously. Anyone planning a trip should seek out detailed sources of boating information. The administering agency can often provide this. Once they arrive, boaters should confirm the difficulty of larger rapids by scouting them. When sources conflicted, I listed the more conservative whitewater ratings. These ratings, however, assume relatively low water; *virtually everything is more dangerous at high water.* Classes of rapids conform to the international scale:

Class I is easily run whitewater, consisting of moving water with riffles and small waves. Passages are clear with few or no obstructions, and little maneuvering is required.

Class II consists of rapids of moderate difficulty with waves up to three feet. The river channel has wide, clear passages and occasional obstructions requiring some maneuvering. Scouting usually is not required.

Class III is difficult whitewater, containing numerous high and irregular waves. Channels with narrow passages and numerous obstructions (rocks and eddies), may require complex maneuvering. Scouting is usually needed.

Class IV is very difficult whitewater, typically consisting of long, continuous rapids with powerful and irregular waves. The river channel is obstructed with dangerous rocks and boiling eddies and passages are constricted, requiring powerful and precise maneuvering. Scouting is mandatory.

Class V rapids are extremely difficult whitewater, consisting of very long and violent rapids following each other almost without interruption. The channel is highly obstructed with big drops, rocks, and large, chaotic waves, requiring very precise maneuvering. Scouting and close study are essential but often difficult, and the consequences of an unsuccessful run may be severe.

U.S. Geological Survey (USGS) maps are available for every river but are not listed in this text except for Alaska. An index is available from USGS, Box 25286, Federal Center, Denver, CO 80225. I have frequently listed maps of larger scale, less expense, and better local availability. Forest Service (USFS) and BLM maps are good for finding the way to a river. American Automobile Association (AAA) regional maps are good for locating highways. Access information given here is not always detailed enough for recreational use but will help in locating sites on a state road map or in pursuing more information on maps or on the ground. NPS indicates National Park Service.

A recreation narrative for each river usually addresses boating and fishing and sometimes hiking and camping as well. Nearly every river presents opportunities for other activities: picnicking, walking, nature study, wildlife watching, photography, biking along riverfront roads, and swimming. I do not repeat these opportunities under each river description. Beyond its utility to canoeists, rafters, and other boaters, information on river running is covered here because it conveys an important description of the character of the river. Each stream has a fascinating history, which I have rarely touched upon.

The rivers are listed alphabetically by state. Rivers shared by two states are covered under the state with the most mileage. Under the heading for each state, the number of rivers is followed by the combined number of rivers and designated tributaries.

Some sources for other information are itemized, the most important ones being listed at the beginning of the section for each state. Wild and scenic river studies or reports have been written for most rivers by the administering agency and are not listed here. Fishing guides can often be found locally.

ALABAMA
1 river, 10 rivers and tributary creeks, 61.4 mi

Sipsey Fork of West Fork River, north-central Alabama, designated in 1988; 22.2 mi, source to Sandy Creek.

Classification: wild, 8.2 mi, source to Sipsey Wilderness boundary; scenic, 14 mi, wilderness boundary to Sandy Creek.

Designated tributaries: 28.2 mi wild classification, 11 mi scenic, including the following streams:

Hubbard Creek, forest road 210 to mouth, wild classification.

Thompson Creek, source to mouth, wild.

Tedford Creek, upper reaches to Thompson Creek, wild.

Mattox Creek, upper reaches to Thompson Creek, wild.

Borden Creek, Sipsey Wilderness, wild; scenic below.

Montgomery Creek, upper reaches to Borden Creek, scenic.

Flannigan Creek, Sipsey Wilderness, wild; wilderness to Borden Creek, scenic.

Braziel Creek, upper reaches to Borden Creek, wild.

Hogood Creek, upper reaches to Braziel Creek, wild.

Total mileage: 61.4, including 36.4 mi wild, 25 mi scenic.

Administered by: Bankhead National Forest, P.O. Box 278, Double Springs, AL 35553.

Access: Hwy. 33, Payne Creek Rd., Cranal Rd.

River difficulty: Class I, II.

Maps: Bankhead National Forest.

Other information: John Foshee, *Alabama Canoe Rides and Float Trips* (1986).

The Sipsey Fork flows through sandstone bluffs and thick forests from the Sipsey Wilderness—an uncommonly protected wilderness river of the South. Old-growth trees remain below the bluff line.

Water levels rapidly rise and fall depending on rainfall in a karst topography with plentiful limestone, sinkholes, small caves, and scenic bluffs that rise 30–100 ft. Native fishes are self-sustaining without stocking. The rare flattened musk turtle lives here. Appalachian plant life mixes with that of the coastal plain, creating interesting diversity. Two-thirds of the watershed lies in the Bankhead National Forest.

The upper river above Cranal Road is floatable for 20–60 days a year; Cranal Road to Hwy. 33, with one Class II rapid, can be canoed most of the time.

ALASKA
33 rivers, 61 rivers and tributary creeks, 3,284 mi

Alaska rivers constitute one of the showcase collections in America. Most of the wild and scenic rivers are protected in other ways; only 7 rivers (25 including tributaries) are outside national parks or preserves, wildlife refuges, wilderness areas, national recreation areas, or national conservation areas. These otherwise unprotected streams total 847 mi, 27 percent of the national river mileage in Alaska. The rivers lacking additional land protection are the Delta, Fortymile, Gulkana, and Unalakleet, plus portions of the Alagnak, Nowitna, and Birch Creek.

Virtually all the designated rivers offer excellent wildlife habitat. Grizzly bears, black bears, moose, coyotes, foxes, lynxes, wolves, beavers, minks, muskrats, and wolverines thrive along many of the rivers. Mosquitoes and biting insects plague people from June to mid August, except for some of the southern rivers. For more information on all the Alaskan national rivers, see Nancy Lange Simmerman, *Alaska's Parklands* (1984), an important source for any touring of this state. For many rivers, see Jack Mosby and David Dapkuz, Alaska Paddling Guide (1986). Access to many of the rivers is limited to airplanes, making the use of inflatable or collapsible boats much more practical than use of rigid craft.

Mileage figures for protected reaches come from field offices for the rivers; mileage of float trips comes from the agencies or from Simmerman's excellent guide. However, visitors should carefully check all figures on topo maps when planning the details of a trip.

Alagnak River, southwestern Alaska, designated in 1980; 56 mi, source to 20 mi above Kvichak River.
Classification: wild.
Administered by: Katmai National Park and Preserve, P.O. Box 7, King Salmon, AK 99613.
Access: floatplane to Kukaklek Lake. Fly out from lower river or Naknek.
River difficulty: Class III.
Maps: USGS, Iliamna A-7, A-8; Dillingham A-1, A-2, A-3.

Exceptional for its red (sockeye) salmon spawning areas, the 80 mi long Alagnak is part of the Kvichak River system, reported as the largest producer of red salmon in the world.

Beginning at Kukaklek Lake, the upper one-third of this clearwater river flows through a canyon, then through the lake-dotted Iliamna lowlands and coastal plain surrounded by tundra and scattered spruce. For about 20 mi the river runs through the Katmai National Preserve. Rainbow trout, Dolly Varden, grayling, and lake trout are found, and the river is important to all five salmon species in Bristol Bay and to bald eagles. Grizzly bears feed at the river during the salmon runs.

Superb sport fishing supports several commercial lodges operating on the lower river. A tremendous volume of flow cuts through small canyons with a 5–8 mph current. Class I rapids predominate, with one set of III–IV, a hazard appearing around a corner without warning where canyon walls make portaging nearly impossible. Rafts are recommended. A braided river and slower current then flow to the Kvichak River. Trips of 74 mi are run, including the lower 20 mi of the Alagnak, which is used by power boats. Take-out is recommended 10 mi above the river's mouth to avoid upriver winds and tidal influence on the Kvichak. The village of Naknek lies 25 mi farther down the Kvichak River. Avoid use of private Native land along the lower river. Cool, wet summers and strong winds can be expected.

Alatna River, north-central Alaska, designated in 1980; 83 mi, source to
  Gates of the Arctic National Park boundary.
Classification: wild.
Administered by: Gates of the Arctic National Park and Preserve, P.O. Box
  74680, Fairbanks, AK 99707.
Access: floatplane to headwaters lakes or Circle Lake. Fly out from Malamute
  Fork or Allakaket.
River difficulty: Class I and II, with 1 Class III rapid in upper reaches.
Maps: USGS, Survey Pass, Hughes, Bettles.

A clearwater river through the heart of the central Brooks Range, the Alatna ranks as an extraordinary stream geologically. At the headwaters, the Arrigetch Peaks soar 7,000 ft including smooth granite walls sweeping upward 3,000 ft. Snowcapped mountains make a scenic backdrop for half the river's length, with scattered bluffs.

The entire designated reach is in Gates of the Arctic National Park. Tundra vegetation in upper reaches gives way to white spruce, paper birch, and aspen. A migration route for the Arctic caribou herd, the valley provides excellent habitat for many species. The fishery consists of chum salmon, grayling, burbot, northern pike, and sheefish (a species found in only a few arctic and subarctic drainages in the world).

Excellent fishing, canoeing, and hiking can be enjoyed in upper reaches. Float trips run from headwater lakes to the village of Allakaket on the Koyukuk River—260 mi with no serious obstacles, though lining may be required above the Unakserak River. Swarms of biting insects are inevitable, June–August.

Andreafsky River, west-central Alaska, designated in 1980; 125 mi, source to about Yukon Delta National Wildlife Refuge boundary.
Classification: wild.
Designated tributaries: all headwaters, unknown mileage.
Administered by: Yukon Delta National Wildlife Refuge, P.O. Box 346, Bethel, AK 99559.
Access: airplane to lakes or the river. Fly out from Saint Marys at the Yukon River.
River difficulty: Class I, II.
Maps: USGS, Unalakleet A-6; St. Michael A-1; Kwiguk D-1, C-1, B-2, A-4.

Entirely within the Yukon Delta National Wildlife Refuge and Andreafsky Wilderness, the Andreafsky River is considered one of the top three king salmon spawning rivers and one of the best chum salmon rivers in the Yukon basin. Grizzly bears congregate during the July and August salmon runs. Here is the world's only known nesting area of the bristly-thighed curlew.

The clearwater river begins in tundra and winds past balsam poplar and white spruce. Low mountains and the Nulato Hills border the river. Grayling and arctic char thrive along with the salmon. The river is exceptional for easy boating and for fishing.

Andreafsky River, East Fork, west-central Alaska, designated in 1980; 137 mi, source to Yukon Delta National Wildlife Refuge.
Administered by: Yukon Delta National Wildlife Refuge, P.O. Box 346, Bethel, AK 99559.
Access: airplane to lakes or the river. Fly out from lower river or village of Saint Marys.
River difficulty: Class I, II.
Maps: USGS, Unalakleet A-6; Holy Cross D-6, C-6; Kwiguk C-1, B-1, B-2, A-2, A-3.

The East Fork Andreafsky is an exceptional king and chum salmon spawning stream. A 100 mi river trip is possible without difficult whitewater. Grizzly bears feed at the river during the July and August salmon runs.

Aniakchak River, southwest Alaska, designated in 1980; 27 mi, source to mouth at Pacific Ocean.
Classification: wild.
Designated tributaries:
  Hidden Creek, 8 mi.
  Albert Johnson Creek, 8 mi.
  Mystery Creek, 4 mi.
Total mileage: 47.

Administered by: Aniakchak National Monument and Preserve, P.O. Box 7, King Salmon, AK 99613.

Access: floatplane to Surprise Lake. Fly out from Aniakchak Bay.

River difficulty: Class IV.

Maps: USGS, Chignik D-1; Sutwik Island D-6, D-5.

The Aniakchak is the only national river flowing from an active volcano crater, beginning in a very large caldera, 6 mi in diameter. Cinder cones, lava plugs, and hot springs form the spectacular headwaters within the caldera. A 3,300 ft high cone, which erupted in 1931, rises within the larger volcano, scoured by glaciers. The river flows from the turquoise waters of Surprise Lake and then exits the caldera through the Gates—rock faces rising 2,000 ft. Nine different beach lines have been eroded where the river meets the Pacific Ocean. This is one of few rivers designated from source to sea, and all of it is in the national monument and preserve.

Eruptions have denuded the headwaters area, but the lower valley supports abundant shrub thickets and tundra grasslands near the ocean. Wildlife includes grizzly bears, moose, caribou, bald eagles, red foxes, and offshore seals, sea lions, otters, and whales. Because of remoteness and miserable weather, Aniakchak National Monument and Preserve is one of the least visited units in the National Park System.

Severe weather is a hazard to be taken to heart. Winds can be extreme, especially near the Gates. Cold rain can be counted on with hypothermia frequently a danger. Scientific trips have been canceled even after arrival at Surprise Lake. Rough seas often delay air pickup. Upper reaches have Class III and IV whitewater and lower reaches have Class I.

Aniakchak River, North Fork, southwest Alaska, designated in 1980; 9 mi, source to mouth.

Classification: wild.

Administered by: Aniakchak National Monument and Preserve, P.O. Box 7, King Salmon, AK 99613.

This tributary to the Aniakchak Wild River is seldom visited.

Beaver Creek, east-central Alaska, designated in 1980; 127 mi, Bear Creek to Victoria Creek.

Classification: wild.

Administered by: BLM, 1150 University Ave., Fairbanks, AK 99709 (111 mi); Yukon Flats National Wildlife Refuge, 101 12th Ave., Box 14, Fairbanks, AK 99709 (16 mi).

Access: Steese Hwy. northeast of Fairbanks to mi 57 and down Nome Creek Rd. 11 mi; or fly in. Fly out from Victoria Creek, or paddle down the Yukon River to the Dalton Hwy. bridge, another 270 mi.

River difficulty: Class I.
Maps: USGS, Livengood B-1, B-2, C-2, C-1, D-1; Circle C-6, D-6, D-5.

With gently flowing clearwater, this river curves through boreal forests and offers an excellent canoe trip for boaters without much experience, though access is difficult.

The river flows within the White Mountains National Recreation Area and the Yukon Flats National Wildlife Refuge, with rich wildlife habitat and grayling fishing. Limestone peaks of the White Mountains, 4,000 ft high, form a continuous backdrop to the forested shores and gravel bars. Warm springs at Big Bend keep a section of river ice-free all winter. While steep slopes climb 1,000 ft from the shores in upper reaches, the river below Victoria Creek meanders through the Yukon Flats Wildlife Refuge, where water is darkened from bogs and where pike and whitefish do well.

Boaters can embark on a 130 mi trip from Nome Creek to Victoria Creek, excellent for canoeing and fishing, with a swift current of 5 mph but no rapids. Mosquitoes and biting insects are troublesome throughout the summer, which is warm and dry. Nome Creek is most easily floated after summer rains, and boaters can fly to a put-in below the creek, though the first 15 mi may still involve a lot of boat dragging at low flows. Enjoyable hiking trips can be taken from the river to the White Mountains.

Birch Creek, east-central Alaska, designated in 1980; 126 mi, south side of
　　Steese Hwy. to Jump-Off Creek.
Classification: wild.
Administered by: BLM, 1150 University Ave., Fairbanks, AK 99709.
Access: Steese Hwy. west of Fairbanks, mi 94. Take-out at Steese Hwy.
　　bridge, mi 147.
River difficulty: Class I–III.
Maps: USGS, Circle B-4, B-3, B-2, B-1, C-1.

Upper reaches of about 80 mi lie within the Steese National Conservation Area. One of the more popular canoeing rivers in Alaska, Birch Creek is road-accessible at both put-in and take-out but offers 125 mi of wilderness in between.

Swift headwaters flow through boreal forests of the Tanana Uplands with excellent wildlife habitat and rolling mountains; the lower 35 mi meander through the Yukon Flats. Large outcrops of schist highlight the geology, and the endangered peregrine falcon nests above the river.

Popular because of its qualities and accessibility, the river includes Class III rapids, which can be portaged below Coulombas Fork. Summer weather is warm and dry with many biting insects. At low water, the upper

8 mi may require dragging. Below the Steese Highway bridge, paddlers can continue 300 mi on flatwater to the Yukon and then to the Dalton Highway bridge.

A wilderness in other respects, Birch Creek has suffered heavy siltation from gold-mine dredging at the headwaters and on tributaries. Though the first 12 mi remain affected by mining silt, the situation has improved since the late 1980s, and below Harrington Fork, the stream has been relatively clear.

Charley River, east-central Alaska, designated in 1980; 104 mi, source to mouth.
Classification: wild.
Designated tributaries:
  Copper Creek, 28 mi.
  Bonanza Creek, 11 mi.
  Hosford Creek, 14 mi.
  Derwent Creek, 17 mi.
  Flat-Orthmer Creek, 20 mi.
  Crescent Creek, 31 mi.
  Moraine Creek, 4 mi.
  Unnamed tributary, 22 mi.
Total mileage: 251.
Administered by: Yukon-Charley Rivers National Preserve, P.O. Box 64, Eagle, AK 99738.
Access: airplane to upper Charley airstrip, 20 mi above Crescent Creek. Fly out from Circle, 63 mi down the Yukon River from the mouth of the Charley, or continue down the Yukon to the Dalton Hwy. bridge.
River difficulty: Class I–IV, mostly Class II.
Maps: USGS, Eagle D-5, D-6; Charley River A-5, A-4, B-4, B-5, B-6, C-6; Circle C-1, D-1.
Other information: NPS, *Yukon-Charley Rivers* (brochure).
  Considered one of the most beautiful rivers in Alaska and with the clearest water, the Charley makes an excellent trip by raft or inflatable kayak for the experienced paddler. This is one of the longest rivers designated from source to mouth. Along with the Yukon, the Charley is one of few rivers explicitly named to justify the establishment of a national park (the Yukon-Charley National Preserve). About 130 mi of the Yukon River from 15 mi below Eagle to 15 mi above Circle are also included in the preserve.

The entire Charley River and its tributaries lie in the national preserve. The upper 60 mi cross the Yukon Tanana Uplands with current and rapids; lower sections wind gently through the Yukon River valley. Dall sheep graze just above the banks, unique to this river. The Fortymile caribou herd winters and calves here. The water owes its cleanness to the fact that little gold was found here.

The Charley's Class IV rapids above Crescent Creek can be portaged, but difficult rapids extend for many miles in the middle section. Average gradient is a steep 31 ft per mile. Canoeing is uncommon because it is difficult to carry canoes on aircraft to the put-in. Summers are warm and fairly dry with light winds. The Park Service recommends a maximum group size of ten people.

During 1991 a fire burned 32,000 acres on both sides of the river between Highland Creek and Erickson Creek. Low-flying military aircraft are thought to have caused the fire; visitors who spot low-flying military planes should report them to the Park Service.

Chilikadrotna River, southwest Alaska, designated in 1980; 11 mi.
Classification: wild.
Administered by: Lake Clark National Park and Preserve, 4230 University
   Dr., Suite 311, Anchorage, AK 99508.
Access: airplane to Twin Lakes. Fly out from Dummy Creek area of
   Mulchatna River or from New Stuyahok on the Nushagak River.
River difficulty: Class I–III.
Maps: USGS, Lake Clark C-3, C-4, C-5, C-6, C-7.

The national river reach of the Chilikadrotna lies entirely within Lake Clark National Park. A longer reach forms one of the outstanding white-water rivers in Alaska, with swift water, long rapids, excellent scenery, fish, and wildlife.

Lowland forest and alpine tundra meet, and both moose and caribou graze by the river. All five species of Pacific salmon spawn here, along with abundant grayling, rainbow trout, and Dolly Varden.

The river offers excellent rafting, kayaking, and fishing, with hiking in alpine tundra at Twin Lakes. By combining the Chilikadrotna with the Mulchatna and Nushagak, it is possible to float the three rivers for 200 mi to New Stuyahok. Class II and III rapids are found in the 5 mi below Twin Lakes and about 5 mi below the Little Mulchatna River, with logjams possible on the upper reaches. Summer weather is cool and overcast. The designated mileage was cut from a proposed 60 mi to 11 mi.

Delta River, south-central Alaska, designated in 1980; 62 mi, Tangle Lakes
   to Black Rapids Glacier.
Classification: wild, 20 mi; scenic, 24 mi; recreational, 18 mi.

Administered by: BLM, P.O. Box 147, Glennallen, AK 99588.
Access: Denali Hwy. at Tangle Lakes. Take-out on Richardson Hwy., mi 212.
River difficulty: Class I–III with one portage.
Maps: USGS, Mount Hayes A-4, B-4.
Other information: BLM, *Delta National Wild and Scenic River* (brochure).

Cutting through the snowcapped Alaska Range, this exceptionally scenic river is road-accessible at both ends and runnable by experienced canoeists.

The upper 24 mi of the designated section consist of Tangle Lakes. The river then runs 38 mi through the Alaska Range, where mountains rise to glacial heights of 9,000 ft. Lake trout, grayling, wildlife, and waterfowl thrive. Clear water grows silty with Eureka Creek's glacial runoff. Archaeological sites date back 10,000 years. A waterfall requiring portage occurs at the Denali Fault, one of the longest fault zones in Alaska, which extends to the summit of Mount McKinley.

A 2–4 day canoe trip, the Delta has become one of Alaska's popular paddling rivers, even with its mandatory portage and Class II–III water. Tundra slopes are fine for hiking. Insects can be expected in summer; weather is cool and often wet.

Fortymile River, east-central Alaska, designated in 1980; 40 mi, source to Canada.
Classification: scenic.
Designated tributaries:
   Napoleon Creek, 7 mi, source to mouth, scenic classification.
   Franklin Creek, 6 mi, source to mouth, scenic.
   Uhler Creek, 8 mi, source to mouth, scenic.
   Wade Creek, 10 mi, source to mouth, recreational.
   Champion Creek, 29 mi, wild.
   O'Brien Creek, 27 mi, source to mouth.
Total mileage: 127.
Total designated mileage of entire Fortymile system: 396.
Administered by: BLM, 1150 University Ave., Fairbanks, AK 99709.
Access: Taylor Hwy. at Mosquito Fork bridge, South Fork bridge, or Fortymile bridge at O'Brien Creek (mi 112). Take-out at Clinton Creek in Canada or Eagle on the Yukon River.
River difficulty: Class I, II, with 1 or 2 Class III rapids and 1 or 2 Class III–IV rapids in Canada.
Maps: USGS, O'Brien Creek to Eagle: Eagle B-1, A-1, C-1, D-1. Canadian maps (Dept. of Energy, Mines, and Resources, Ottawa): Dawson 116 C/7, 116 C/8, 116 C/9, 116 C/10. Above O'Brien Creek: see descriptions of Fortymile forks.

Other information: BLM, *Fortymile National Wild and Scenic River* (brochure).

The largest designated network of a river and its tributaries in the National Wild and Scenic Rivers System, the Fortymile offers excellent canoeing and fishing.

The river flows mainly through forests but also through muskeg marshes. Many rapids on middle and lower reaches cut through wooded canyons. Sheefish live in upper sections; king salmon, chum salmon, northern pike, and whitefish in lower reaches; grayling, burbot, and round whitefish are found throughout.

A trip of about 100 mi can be paddled from O'Brien Creek to Eagle on the Yukon River. Biting insects are common in summer when weather is warm and mostly dry.

The Fortymile's water has been seriously polluted with siltation from gold mining in the past, but water quality has improved with tighter regulation following the national river designation.

Fortymile River, Middle Fork, east-central Alaska, designated in 1980; 42 mi, Joseph Creek to mouth at North Fork confluence.
Classification: wild.
Designated tributaries: Joseph Creek, 23 mi, source to mouth, wild classification.
Total mileage: 65.
Access: airplane to Joseph. Take-out at the Fortymile bridge on Taylor Hwy., with longer trips possible.
River difficulty: Class I–II, with 1 Class III rapid and one Class V portage.
Maps: USGS, Eagle B-5, B-4, B-3, B-2, A-2, B-1.

The Middle Fork is inaccessible by road. A trip from Joseph Creek, down the Middle Fork and then down the North Fork to the Fortymile bridge on the main stem is about 88 mi. For the most complete Fortymile trip, fly to Joseph and float on the clear waters through beautiful scenery down the Middle Fork, North Fork, and main stem through Canada to the Yukon River, taking out at Eagle, Alaska.

Fortymile River, North Fork, east-central Alaska, designated in 1980; 58 mi, source to mouth.
Classification: wild.
Designated tributaries: Hutchison Creek, 19 mi, source to mouth, scenic.
Total mileage: 77.

Access: fly in to the Joseph bush airfield along the Middle Fork. Take-out at Fortymile bridge on Taylor Hwy., with longer trips possible.

River difficulty: Class II with 1 Class III rapid below the mouth of the Middle Fork and a Class IV–V rapid below Hutchinson Creek.

The North Fork system is inaccessible by road and is usually reached by flying to Joseph, on the Middle Fork, and floating down to the North Fork confluence.

Fortymile River, South Fork, east-central Alaska, designated in 1980; 28 mi, source to mouth.

Classification: scenic.

Designated tributaries:

Mosquito Fork, 38 mi, Kechumstuk to mouth, wild.

Dennison Fork, 19 mi, West Fork of Dennison Fork to mouth, scenic.

West Fork of Dennison Fork, 13 mi, Logging Cabin Creek to mouth.

Logging Cabin Creek, 17 mi, source to mouth at West Fork Dennison Fork.

Walker Fork, 12 mi, Liberty Creek to mouth, scenic.

Total mileage: 127.

Access: Taylor Hwy. at West Fork bridge, Mosquito Fork bridge, or South Fork bridge (mi 75 on Taylor Hwy.). Take-out at Taylor Hwy. at Fortymile bridge (longer trips are possible).

River difficulty: Class I, II.

Maps: USGS, Tanacross D-3, D-2; Eagle A-2, B-2, B-1. Dennison Fork maps: Tanacross D-3, D-2; Eagle A-2, B-2, B-1.

A 69 mi trip can be run from mi 49 on Taylor Highway at the West Fork bridge to the Fortymile bridge. The West Fork of the Dennison Fork at the West Fork bridge, the Walker Fork at the Walker Fork bridge, and the Mosquito Fork at the Mosquito Fork bridge can be floated only on high water of springtime.

Gulkana River, south-central Alaska, designated in 1980; 47 mi, Paxson Lake to Sourdough.

Classification: wild.

Administered by: BLM, P.O. Box 147 Glennallen, AK 99588.

Access: Paxson Lake Campground. Take-out at Sourdough Campground at mi 147 on Richardson Hwy.

River difficulty: Class I–IV.

Maps: USGS, Gulkana D-4, C-4.

Other information: BLM, *Gulkana National Wild and Scenic River* (brochure).

With sections of rapids and easy water, the Gulkana flows through wild country with distant views of the Wrangell Mountains. An important king and red salmon spawning stream, the Gulkana ranks among the state's most popular sport-fishing rivers, accessible at both ends by roads.

Low hills, bluffs, and spruce-hardwood forests create good wildlife habitat and furnish many bald eagle nesting sites. Grayling, rainbow trout, steelhead, and salmon populate the clearwater stream.

Rafters, kayakers, canoeists, and anglers all enjoy this river, often run as a 3–5 day trip. Class III rapids occur for 3 mi below Paxson Lake. The "Canyon Rapids" include a Class IV drop, which can be portaged, and 8 mi of Class II and III water. The Meiers Lake Trail, at mi 169 of the Richardson Highway, is a 7 mi long path for hikers to the Middle Fork and Gulkana confluence. The Haggard Creek Trail, also 7 mi long, begins at mi 161 on the highway and goes to Canyon Rapids.

Gulkana River, Middle Fork, south-central Alaska, designated in 1980; 32 mi, source at Dickey Lake to mouth.
Classification: wild.
Access: Tangle River Campground, mi 22, Denali Hwy. Take-out at Sourdough Campground, Richardson Hwy.
River difficulty: Class I–IV.
Maps: USGS, Mount Hayes A-5; Gulkana D-5, D-4, C-4.

The Middle Fork flows through a series of glacial moraines and bedrock areas as it leaves the base of the Alaska Range and flows through rolling uplands.

Three portages between lakes lead to the Middle Fork headwaters at Dickey Lake; the longest portage is 1 mi. Lining may be necessary in upper reaches, and log jams can be expected on the 84 mi run from Tangle Lake to Sourdough, a 4–7 day trip. The 10 mi long Swede Lake Trail, at mi 16 on the Denali Highway, crosses the Middle Fork.

Gulkana River, West Fork, south-central Alaska, designated in 1980; 79 mi, source to mouth.
Classification: wild.
Designated tributaries:
   South Branch of West Fork, 24 mi, from an unnamed lake to mouth at North Branch, wild classification.
   North Branch of West Fork, 30 mi, from unnamed lakes to mouth at South Branch, wild.
Total mileage: 133.
Access: drive to Lake Louise, or take floatplane to lakes at headwaters of

North Branch or South Branch. Take-out at Sourdough Campground, Richardson Hwy., on the Gulkana River.

River difficulty: Class II.

Maps: USGS, Gulkana D-6, C-6, C-5, C-4.

The West Fork flows through rolling hills of the Copper River lowlands. The South Branch is reached via four portages from Tyrone River and between lakes. The river riffles and meanders and may include logjams in the 100 mi run to Sourdough, often a 10 day trip.

Ivishak River, northeast Alaska, designated in 1980; 60 mi, source to Flood Creek.

Classification: wild.

Designated tributaries: unnamed headwater streams, 20 mi.

Total mileage: 80.

Administered by: Arctic National Wildlife Refuge, 101 12th St., P.O. Box 20, Fairbanks, AK 99701.

Access: fly to tundra benches along the upper river, or fly to Porcupine Lake (not advisable for floaters). Fly out from gravel bars along the lower Ivishak, or float 55 mi down the Sagavanirktok River to Deadhorse and fly out.

River difficulty: Class I.

Maps: USGS, Arctic C-5, D-5; Philip Smith Mountains C-1, D-1; Sagavanirktok A-1, A-2, B-2, B-3. Sagavanirktok River continuation: C-3, D-3; Beechy Point A-3.

Beginning high in the Brooks Range, the swiftly flowing Ivishak is fed by hanging glaciers.

The entire designated reach lies within the Arctic National Wildlife Refuge. Mountains rise to 7,000 ft from the upper valley, offering stark views of glaciated limestone. The tumbling glacial current braids into a 1 mi wide valley and traverses a treeless tundra. Overflow ice near perennial springs can persist late into the summer. Arctic char and grayling thrive in the river.

Boating from Porcupine Lake is not advised because the outlet is shallow. Lower on the river, braiding can make channels difficult to find, and passages through overflow ice may not appear until mid June. Excellent hikes can be taken throughout, but especially in the upper reaches with good viewing of caribou, raptors, and other wildlife.

John River, north-central Alaska, designated in 1980; 52 mi, source to lower boundary of Gates of the Arctic National Park.

Classification: wild.

Administered by: Gates of the Arctic National Park and Preserve, P.O. Box 74680, Fairbanks, AK 99707.

Access: airplane to Hunt Fork Lake. Fly out from Old Bettles at mouth of the John or from Bettles after lining 5 mi up the Koyukuk River.

River difficulty: Class I, II.

Maps: USGS, Chandler Lake; Wiseman D-5, C-5, B-5, B-4, A-4; Bettles D-4.

This spectacular river flows beneath 6,000 ft mountains and through a glacially carved valley.

Entirely within Gates of the Arctic National Park and Preserve, the designated reach of this clearwater river includes gravel bars, high cliffs, and vegetation from alpine headwaters to forested lowlands. Because it originates in the lowest pass of the Brooks Range, the river's route is also that of the Arctic caribou herd.

An excellent stream for easy paddling, the John flows quickly but without major obstacles for about 100 mi from Hunt Fork to Bettles with scenic hiking in upper reaches.

Kobuk River, north-central Alaska, designated in 1980; 110 mi, source to lower boundary of Gates of the Arctic National Park.

Administered by: Gates of the Arctic National Park and Preserve, P.O. Box 74680, Fairbanks, AK 99707.

Access: airplane to Walker Lake. Fly out at Kobuk or downstream villages.

River difficulty: Class I with two sections of II–IV.

Maps: USGS, Survey Pass, Hughes, Shungnak, Shungnak D-2.

The Kobuk parallels the Brooks Range, offers scenery of mountains and forest, and supports Alaska's largest sheefish.

The designated reach is entirely within Gates of the Arctic National Park, where a wide valley offers sweeping vistas of low mountains. Stands of spruce constitute the longest continuous forests in the Brooks Range. Bluffs rise 200 ft. Below the wild river reach, archaeologists discovered a significant archaeological find at Onion Portage.

From Willow Lake, a 140 mi float on mostly Class I water can be run to the village of Kobuk, with two canyons and Class III whitewater that can be portaged. Private land lines much of the Kobuk below the designated reach.

Koyukuk River, North Fork, north-central Alaska, designated in 1980; 102 mi, source to Middle Fork Koyukuk.

Classification: wild.

Administered by: Gates of the Arctic National Park and Preserve, P.O. Box 74680, Fairbanks, AK 99707.
Access: airplane to Gates of the Arctic or Bombardment Creek for hiking. Boats can be flown in to Gates of the Arctic. Fly out from Bettles.
River difficulty: Class I, II.
Maps: USGS, Chandler Lake A-1; Wiseman C-2, C-3, B-2, A-2, A-3, D-1, D-2; Bettles D-3, D-4.

The North Fork Koyukuk begins near the famed Gates of the Arctic, a photogenic valley surrounded by peaks. The entire river flows within Gates of the Arctic National Park.

A clearwater river, the North Fork runs through broad, glacially carved valleys that constitute the major migration route of the Arctic caribou herd, the largest in Alaska. Vegetation evolves from alpine tundra to spruce-hardwood forest along most of the river.

Experienced boaters can fly to Redstar Lakes below Gates of the Arctic and paddle about 100 mi to Bettles, 25 mi below the North and Middle Fork confluence. Backpacking is superb in the headwaters area.

Mulchatna River, southwest Alaska, designated in 1980; 24 mi, source to Lake Clark National Park boundary.
Classification: wild.
Administered by: Lake Clark National Park and Preserve, 4230 University Dr., Suite 311, Anchorage, AK 99508.
Access: airplane to Turquoise Lake or to lakes below Bonanza Hills. Fly out from the river 12 mi or more below the Chilikadrotna confluence, or from the village of New Stuyahok.
River difficulty: Class I–III.
Maps: USGS, Lake Clark D-3, D-4, C-4, D-5, D-6, C-6, C-7, B-7, B-8; Taylor Mountains B-1, A-1, A-2; Dillingham D-2, D-3, C-3, C-4, B-4.

Especially scenic in upper reaches, the Mulchatna flows out of the jewellike Turquoise Lake; the glacier-covered Chigmit Mountains lie to the east.

A shallow, rocky river beneath high peaks for 22 mi, the Mulchatna broadens to gentle water through spruce-hardwood forests below the Bonanza Hills. The Mulchatna caribou herd calves at the headwaters. Sport fishing is popular for grayling, rainbow trout, and Dolly Varden, and the river provides an important king and chum salmon spawning area.

Though floated by rafters, the river is less dramatic than its tributary, the Chilikadrotna. Rapids between Turquoise Lake and Bonanza Hills are often shallow in summer. After a Class III drop above Bonanza Creek, the Mulchatna meanders for 70 mi to the Chilikadrotna confluence, where speed increases and the river braids through a forested plain to the Nushagak River.

A trip of about 230 mi can be run from Lake Turquoise to New Stuyahok. The Turquoise Lake area offers excellent hiking terrain.

Noatak River, northwest Alaska, designated in 1980; 330 mi, source to Kelly River confluence, 33 mi above Noatak village.
Classification: wild.
Administered by: Gates of the Arctic National Park and Preserve, P.O. Box 74680, Fairbanks, AK 99707; Noatak National Preserve, P.O. Box 1029, Kotzebue, AK 99752.
Access: airplane to Lake Matcharak or gravel bars. Fly out from the lower river or Noatak Village.
River difficulty: Class I, II.
Maps: USGS, Survey Pass, Ambler River; Howard Pass; Misheguk Mountain; Misheguk Mountain A-3, A-4, A-5; Baird Mountains D-3, D-4, D-5, D-6; Noatak D-1, D-2, C-2, C-3, B-3, B-2, A-2, A-1.

The Noatak is the longest designated wild and scenic river in the United States and drains the nation's largest mountain-ringed river basin that is virtually unaffected by human activities. This is also the longest river in a national park, and nearly the entire basin is designated wilderness—the largest protected watershed in the country.

Beginning high in the Brooks Range, the narrow glacial valley beneath snowcapped peaks broadens to a tundra wilderness with a mountainous background. The northwesternmost boreal forest on the continent and a lake-covered landscape are followed by the Noatak Canyon, a 5 mi long gorge with 400 ft cliffs. Game fish and wildlife are plentiful and include 17 species of raptors.

The most popular river in the Brooks Range for floating, the reach from Lake Matcharak to Noatak village runs about 350 mi. Upper areas offer excellent hiking.

Nonvianuk River, southwest Alaska, designated in 1980; 11 mi, source at Nonvianuk Lake to mouth at Alagnak River.
Classification: wild.
Administered by: Katmai National Park and Preserve, P.O. Box 7, King Salmon, AK 99613.
Access: floatplane to Nonvianuk Lake. Fly out from Alagnak River or Hallersville.
River difficulty: Class I, possibly II.
Maps: USGS, Iliamna A-7, A-8; Dillingham A-1, A-2, A-3.

A tributary to the Alagnak National Wild River, the Nonvianuk includes a superb sport fishery with spawning areas for salmon of the rich Bristol Bay fishery.

Recreational boating for rafts, canoes, and kayaks is good on the entire river, which is mostly Class I with a possible Class II rapid 4 mi from Nonvianuk Lake. Combined with the Alagnak, a Class I trip of 66 mi runs to the lower Alagnak. The Battle Lake Wilderness Lodge, a concession in the park, rents cabins at Nonvianuk Lake.

Nowitna River, west-central Alaska, designated in 1980; 225 mi, Nowitna National Wildlife Refuge to mouth at Yukon River.
Classification: wild.
Administered by: Nowitna National Wildlife Refuge, P.O. Box 287, Galena, AK 99714.
Access: airplane to Clearwater Creek. Fly out from Ruby, 41 mi down the Yukon River from the Nowitna.
River difficulty: Class I.
Maps: USGS, Medfra D-4; Ruby A-4, A-3, A-2, B-2, B-3, C-3, C-4, D-3.

This second longest of the national rivers flows from rolling uplands to flats blanketed by large white spruce.

The river shows all species of trees of the Alaska interior, and gravel bars hold garnets, petrified wood, chalcedony, and agates. Sheefish and northern pike thrive. During an average year, the Nowitna Refuge produces 15,000 ducklings and 76 trumpeter swans, and an additional 5,000 adult ducks use the refuge. Most of the designated section flows through the Nowitna National Wildlife Refuge. The current is slow for the entire reach.

Salmon River, northwest Alaska, designated in 1980; 70 mi, source to mouth.
Classification: wild.
Administered by: Kobuk Valley National Park, P.O. Box 1029, Kotzebue, AK 99752.
Access: airplane to Anaktok or Sheep Creek areas. Fly out from Kotzebue or village of Kiana on the Kobuk River.
River difficulty: Class I, II.
Maps: USGS, Baird Mountains; Baird Mountains A-2, A-1, A-3; Selawik D-3.

A small Brooks Range river named for healthy runs of chum and pink salmon, this stream offers exceptional beauty in the form of deep pools, rock outcrops, clearwater, and unusual blue-green gravels.

The entire river lies within Kobuk Valley National Park. A narrow, steep-sided valley widens to rolling hills while the river alternates in pools and riffles. Lower sections course through flats of spruce and treeless bogs.

The 90 mi run from Anaktok Creek to Kiana includes low water in upper reaches, then riffles and small rapids. Fishing for chum salmon, pink salmon, and grayling is excellent, and grizzly bears come to the river during the salmon runs. Tundra of the upper river makes good hiking country.

Selawik River, northwest Alaska, designated in 1980; 168 mi, source to Kugarak River.
Classification: wild.
Administered by: Fish and Wildlife Service, Selawik National Wildlife Refuge, P.O. Box 270, Kotzebue, AK 99752.
Access: floatplane to lakes near Shiniliaok Creek. Fly out from Kotzebue or the villages of Ambler or Galena.
River difficulty: Class I.
Maps: USGS, Shungnak, Selawik.

The designated reach of this gentle river flows entirely within the Selawik National Wildlife Refuge, nesting habitat for thousands of migratory waterfowl, waterbirds, and shorebirds.

The river rises in arctic tundra and small spruce forests and flows through open tundra, narrow spruce forests, and willows. Canada geese and harlequin ducks nest along the upper river, and many waterfowl species use lower reaches. Tundra swans and sandhill cranes are common along lower sections. The river contains large numbers of grayling, northern pike, and sheefish; moose and caribou are common.

Fallen spruce trees across many channels can be a hazard. The lower 25 mi have deep water, a slow current, and headwinds, which may generate waves up to 2 ft high. June is the best month to float to assure adequate water in upper-reach riffles and to avoid the insects of July. Emergency assistance is available at the Fish and Wildlife Service cabin 3 mi downstream of the confluence of the Kugarak River. From Shiniliaok Creek to the village of Selawik is about 230 mi.

The lower 60 mi pass through public and private land, and private Native allotments are scattered along the entire river, including the wild river reach. To respect private property, campers should avoid areas with orange engineer's tape and any signs of development, such as tent frames and fish-drying racks.

Sheenjek River, northeast Alaska, designated in 1980; 155 mi, source to Arctic National Wildlife Refuge southern boundary with one 28 mi exclusion.

Administered by: Arctic National Wildlife Refuge, 101 12th Ave., P.O. Box 20, Fairbanks, AK 99701.

Access: airplane to Last Lake or gravel bars of the upper river. Fly out from the lower river or from Fort Yukon near the Porcupine and Yukon confluence.

River difficulty: Class I, II.

Maps: USGS, Table Mountain A-4, A-5, B-4, B-5, C-5, D-5; Coleen D-5, D-6, C-6; Christian A-1, B-1, C-1; Fort Yukon C-2, C-3, D-1, D-2.

Beginning with glaciers in the highest part of the Brooks Range, the Sheenjek offers extraordinary high country boating and a variety of wildlife and fishery habitat on one of the longer protected rivers in America.

Glaciers dramatically scoured upper reaches, which are now spectacular with barren limestone peaks above the broad valley. A braided river deepens, crosses vast expanses of tundra-covered hills, and eventually leaves the mountains to cross the Yukon Flats, one of the most important waterfowl nesting areas in North America. As the river flows south, silty, glacial waters become transparent due to settling of silt and possibly filtration of the water through expansive gravel deposits. Caribou of the Porcupine herd are common along the upper river; grizzly bears and wolves track the beaches throughout. The grayling fishery is good, and the lower river is important to chum salmon and northern pike. The entire designated reach lies within the Arctic National Wildlife Refuge.

Overflow ice may completely block sections of the upper river and require portage even in August. Some rapids are found near Table Mountain. To take out at Fort Yukon, boaters should use the Sucker Creek access on the left shore about 4 mi above the mouth of the Porcupine and difficult to find. An alternate take-out, near the Porcupine and Yukon confluence, requires motorboat shuttle for 1 mi up the Yukon.

The designation of the upper river is limited to the protected wilderness area. A 28 mi section was excluded because the state proposed a natural gas pipeline. The Alaska Lands Act called for consideration of the rest of the Sheenjek as a national river, but studies have not been completed. If the remaining reach is designated, the Sheenjek will be the longest national river from source to mouth.

Tinayguk River, northeast Alaska, designated in 1980; 44 mi, source to mouth.

Classification: wild.

Administered by: Gates of the Arctic National Park and Preserve, P.O. Box 74680, Fairbanks, AK 99707.

Access: airplane to gravel bars near Savioyok Creek. Fly out at Bettles.
River difficulty: Class I, II.
Maps: USGS, Waiseman D-4, D-3, C-3 (see North Fork Koyukuk for continuation).

This small river, remote and seldom visited, lies entirely within the Gates of the Arctic National Park and Preserve. Clearwater flows through a broad glacial valley bordered by Brooks Range peaks. The tundra-covered valley holds only a few scattered stands of spruce.

Rapids are shallow in upper reaches. From Savioyok Creek to Bettles is about 120 mi, 35 of them on the Tinaguk and the rest on the North Fork of the Koyukuk, also a national wild river. Mosquitoes plague visitors until August. Hiking is excellent at the upper river.

Tlikakila River, south-central Alaska, designated in 1980; 51 mi, source to mouth at Lake Clark.
Classification: wild.
Administered by: Lake Clark National Park and Preserve, 4230 University Dr., Suite 311, Anchorage, AK 99508.
Access: airplane to Summit Lake. Fly out from Lake Clark or the village of Port Alsworth, 23 mi down Lake Clark from the river's mouth.
River difficulty: Class I–IV.
Maps: USGS, Kenai D-8, C-8; Lake Clark C-1, C-2, B-2, B-3, B-4, A-4.

One of the most spectacular mountainous and glacial river areas in North America, the Tlikakila is flanked by 6,000 ft peaks of rock and snow, glaciated and sculpted in waterfalls and cirques.

The entire river flows within Lake Clark National Park. The swift, small river affords excellent views of glaciers and then drops through a broad valley and crosses three different vegetation zones on its way to the turquoise depths of Lake Clark.

Excellent for rafting, the Tlikakila includes fast water. Below the North Fork, a short Class III or IV rapids can be portaged. At high flows, rapids continue for 3 mi. From Summit Lake to Lake Clark the river offers a 70 mi float trip. Good hiking can be found at the upper river.

Unalakleet River, west-central Alaska, designated in 1980; 80 mi, source to Chiroskey River.
Classification: wild.
Administered by: BLM, 6881 Abbott Loop Rd., Anchorage, AK 99507.
Access: airplane to the village of Unalakleet, then by chartered motorboat upriver to Tenmile Creek. Fly out from Unalakleet.
River difficulty: Class I, II.

Maps: USGS, Norton Bay A-2; Unalakleet D-2, D-3, D-4.

An excellent fishery for grayling and char, and king, silver, pink, and chum salmon, the Unalakleet River formed an important prehistoric and Russian-era trade route.

The tea-colored waters flow through a broad, forested valley to tundra at the Bering Sea. The river and its shores remain vital for subsistence by local Innuit at the lower reaches of the river below the Chirosky River. Plentiful waterfowl summer in the river, and grizzly and black bears populate the valley during the mid June to mid July salmon runs.

From Tenmile Creek to Unalakleet is a 70 mi float trip. The Kaltag Trail often lies within 1 mi of the river on its south side—a link in the historic, 1,000 mi Iditarod Trail between Nome and Anchorage.

Wind River, northeast Alaska, designated in 1980; 98 mi, source to mouth at East Fork Chandalar River.

Classification: wild.

Designated tributaries: headwaters and one unnamed tributary, 42 mi.

Total mileage: 140.

Administered by: Arctic National Wildlife Refuge, 101 12th Ave., P.O. Box 20, Fairbanks, AK 99701.

Access: airplane to lake near Center Mountain, other lakes downriver, or gravel bars. Fly out from the village of Venetie on the Chandalar River, 80 mi downstream from the mouth of the Wind River.

River difficulty: Class I–III.

Maps: USGS, Philip Smith Mountains A-1, B-1, B-2, C-1; Arctic A-5; Christian D-5, D-6; Chandalar D-1. Chandalar River continuation to Venetie: Chandalar A-1, B-1; Christian A-5, A-6, B-5, B-6, C-5.

A scenic river from a glacial valley of the Brooks Range, the Wind is one of the longer national rivers from source to mouth and offers exciting white-water and wilderness.

Entirely within the Arctic National Wildlife Refuge, the river is bordered by steep mountains rising 3,000 ft above the wide, tundra-covered valley. Overflow ice can block the water's flow for short distances. Forested hills, lakes, and meadows characterize the lower river.

Water levels may require lining of some rapids or may drop too low in upper sections during dry years. Good hiking opportunities lie in the headwater areas.

ARIZONA
1 river, 40.5 mi

Verde River, central Arizona, designated in 1984; 40.5 mi, Beasley Flats below Camp Verde to Red Creek.
Classification: wild, 18.5 mi; scenic, 22 mi.
Administered by: Prescott National Forest, P.O. Box 2549, Prescott, AZ 86302.
River difficulty: not normally run.
Maps: Prescott, Tonto, and Coconino national forests.

A desert river flowing through varied and scenic landscapes, the Verde offers views of peaks and a canyon of vivid colors. Threatened and endangered plant and fish populations include the desert-nesting bald eagle.

The river supports riparian habitat otherwise rare in the Sonoran Desert setting, and 21 wildlife and fish species are threatened, endangered, or of special interest to wildlife agencies. An estimated 19 plants were proposed for listing as threatened or endangered in 1980, and 25 species of fish are found in the river. Several roadless areas adjoin the corridor.

Whitewater boaters use the river during the high flows of March and April, but rapids and fallen trees pose dangers. Fishing for bass, bluegill, sunfish, and especially catfish is popular. Swimming holes and the Verde Hot Springs are visited by local residents.

Cottonwood trees, essential to the health of the riparian system and to bald eagles, ceased regerminating about 100 years ago, probably because of cattle, which continue to graze, though the Forest Service has attempted to protect critical areas. Nearly 100 percent of the corridor is public land. Only about half of the Verde's eligible mileage was designated in the national rivers system.

ARKANSAS
8 rivers, 9 rivers and tributaries, 342.3 mi. 132 mi of the Buffalo is not in the National Wild and Scenic Rivers System

Big Piney Creek, northwest Arkansas, designated in 1992; 45.2 miles, source to Ozark National Forest boundary.
Classification: scenic.
Administered by: Ozark–St. Francis National Forest, 605 W. Main St., P.O. Box 1008, Russellville, AR 72801.

Access: F.R. 1005B and 1485 near Walnut, 1404 at Limestone, 1802 near Trace Creek, 1804 off Hwy. 164, Hwy. 123 at Fort Douglas.
River difficulty: Class I–II with several Class III rapids.
Maps: Ozark National Forest.

This scenic river is considered one of the finer smallmouth bass streams in the state, excellent for water quality, popular for recreation, and supporting bald eagles during their migration season.

Big Piney Creek winds through a narrow valley with steep slopes, flat-topped ridges, and sandstone bluffs. Waterfalls and rapids alternate with pools. Oak, hickory, and pine are interspersed with pastures. Two state-listed endangered plant species are found here.

The river is heavily used for camping, swimming, fishing, and canoeing. Long Pool Recreation Area offers developed facilities. Hunting for deer, turkeys, bears, and small game is popular. The river is floatable for 125 days in the spring. Sixty-two percent of the corridor is in National Forest owner-ship.

The river is listed as an "extraordinary resource water" by the state and is subject to an antidegradation policy.

Buffalo River, northern Arkansas, 132 mi designated in 1972, but not in the Wild and Scenic Rivers System, 15.8 mi designated in the system in 1992; 147.8 mi, 15.8 mi from source to Ozark National Forest boundary; 132 mi from above Hwy. 21 to confluence with the White River.
Classification: national river for 132 mi; wild, 9.4 mi; scenic, 6.4 mi.
Administered by: NPS, Buffalo National River, P.O. Box 1173, Harrison, AR 72602 (National River reach); Ozark–St. Francis National Forest, 605 W. Main St., P.O. Box 1008, Russellville, AR 72801.
Access: many points, including Hwys. 21, 74, 7, 123, 65, and 14, and Hwy. 126 on the White River just above the Buffalo; F.R. 1463 in upper reaches.
River difficulty: Class I, II below Hwy. 21; sections with Class I only.
Maps: NPS, Buffalo River; Ozark–St. Francis National Forest.
Other information: The Ozark Society, *Buffalo National River Canoeing Guide* (The Ozark Society, P.O. Box 2914, Little Rock, AR 72203).

One of only a few "national rivers" (most of the reach is not officially a part of the National Wild and Scenic Rivers System), the Buffalo offers fishing, canoeing that many people consider the finest in the Midwest, and an environment of biological diversity and geological interest.

A showcase of the Ozark Mountains, the river has remained wild even in the Midwest. The region's streams support 13 unique species of clearwater fish that never dispersed into surrounding muddy rivers and 160 species of fish in all. Plant life of the eastern woodlands and Great Plains meet, and glaciers deposited northern species but stopped their southward advance here. Up to 1,000 flowering plant species can be found. Bluffs of 500 ft are the tallest in the Ozarks, and a 175 ft tributary waterfall is the highest between the Appalachians and Rockies.

Canoeing trips of various lengths can be run from Ponca to the White River (125 mi). Wildernesslike conditions are found from Highway 123 to Woolum and below Highway 14. Between Ponca and Kyles the river flows through a designated wilderness of 10 mi. Below Highway 65 the lower river is usually floatable all year and safe for beginners except at high water. Class II whitewater is found from Highway 74 (Ponca) to Highway 7, floatable only in winter and spring. Class III and IV rapids are found above the national river reach, with a 14 mi run from Forest Road 1463 at Dixon Ford to Highway 21 after heavy winter and spring rains. Anglers fish for bass, catfish, and panfish. Trails follow the river from Ponca to Highway 7 and from Woolum to Highway 65. Motors of less than 10 hp are allowed below Erbie Ford—that is, on most of the river.

Protection of the Buffalo resulted from opposition to dams proposed by the Army Corps of Engineers. The National Park Service in 1963 reported that the river was nationally significant, one of the first recommendations for national protection of a river. Unlike wild and scenic rivers, the national river was viewed as an elongated national park, and most private land along the waterfront was acquired.

Cossatot River, west-central Arkansas, designated in 1992; 26.1 mi, below Mine Creek and from Hwy. 4 to Duchett's Ford.
Classification: scenic, 21.9 mi; recreational, 4.2 mi (10.4 mi were designated by the secretary of agriculture).
Designated tributaries: Brushy Creek, 5 mi, scenic classification.
Total mileage: 31.1.
Administered by: Ouachita National Forest, P.O. Box 1270, Federal Bldg., Hot Springs, AR 71902.
Access: Hwys. 246 and 4 cross the river, F.R. 31 and 140 parallel and cross the river, all north of Gillham Reservoir.
River difficulty: Class II, III, with 1 Class IV or V rapid.
Maps: Ouachita National Forest.

Congress designated 15.7 mi of the Cossatot and 4.4 mi of Brushy Creek; another 10.4 mi of the Cossatot and 0.3 mi of Brushy Creek in Cossatot River State Park were added by the secretary of agriculture in 1992.

Also a state-designated scenic river, the Cossatot is considered one of the finest whitewater canoeing rivers in Arkansas, has exceptional water quality, and may support the threatened leopard darter.

With nearby mountains rising 2,000 ft, the Cossatot flows past rocky bluffs and hillsides of pine, oak, and hickory forest. Alder, sweetgum, sycamore, and river birch grow along the water. Spotted bass, smallmouth bass, brim, and goggleye are found. Part of the reach flows through the Caney Creek Wilderness.

The river is popular for camping, fishing, hunting, and canoeing, with outstanding Class II and III whitewater from the F.R. 31 bridge to Hwy. 4 from December through June. Cossatot Falls, a Class IV–V drop, was recently acquired by the state, and Cossatot River State Park, with facilities under construction, will serve many visitors.

The reach is classified as extraordinary resource water by the state and lies above Gillham Dam, unsuccessfully opposed by river conservationists in 1970 through the first National Environmental Policy Act lawsuit intended to stop a dam.

Hurricane Creek, north-central Arkansas, designated in 1992; 15.5 mi, source to Big Piney Creek.
Classification: wild, 2.4 mi; scenic, 13.1 mi.
Administered by: Ozark–St. Francis National Forest, 605 W. Main St., P.O. Box 1008, Russellville, AR 72801.
Access: F.R. 1209 above the Hurricane Creek Wilderness, F.R. 1209c, cty. rd. between F.R. 1209 and Sexton Cemetery.
River difficulty: not frequently run.
Maps: Ozark–St. Francis National Forest.

Hurricane Creek flows through rugged terrain with rock outcrops and cliffs, and one segment passes through the Hurricane Creek Wilderness. Smallmouth bass, largemouth bass, catfish, and sunfish are found. The bristle-fern, threatened in Arkansas, grows here. Bald eagles migrate through in winter. The stream is designated as an extraordinary resource water by the state, and 89 percent of the corridor is national forest land.

The river is only lightly used for recreation, owing to limited access and little recreational development, but does see some camping, fishing, and canoeing. The Ozark Highlands Trail and a natural arch attract visitors.

Little Missouri River, west-central Arkansas, designated in 1992; 15.7 mi, source and downstream.
Classification: wild, 4.4 mi; scenic, 11.3 mi.
Administered by: Ouachita National Forest, P.O. Box 1270, Federal Bldg., Hot Springs, AR 71902.
Access: F.R. 539 at Little Missouri River Recreation Area; F.R. 25, 912, 73, and others at the upper river; F.R. 914 at the Albert Pike Recreation Area; F.R. 73, 512, 914, 106, and 220, all northwest of Langley.
River difficulty: Class I–IV.
Maps: Ouachita National Forest.

With some of the best whitewater in Arkansas, the Little Missouri offers fine scenery and archaeological sites including rock shelters. Eagles winter along the river.

A narrow waterway in upper reaches, the river grows to flow through a broad channel with large pools and riffles, bordered in places by rocky bluffs. Classified as extraordinary resource water by the state, the Little Missouri supports rainbow trout, smallmouth bass, channel catfish, and many non-game species, including the brook silverside, orangebelly darter, and yellow bullhead. The caldo madtom is a candidate for federal listing as a threatened or endangered species.

The Albert Pike Recreation Area offers developed facilities. Canoeing is excellent but limited to late winter and spring following heavy rains. An 8.5 mi run from Albert Pike Recreation Area to Hwy. 84 drops 25 ft per mi with Class IV rapids during high water.

Mulberry River, northwest Arkansas, designated in 1992; 56 mi, source to Ozark National Forest boundary.
Classification: scenic, 19.4 mi; recreational, 36.6 mi.
Administered by: Ozark–St. Francis National Forest, 605 W. Main St., P.O. Box 1008, Russellville, AR 72801.
Access: Hwy. 215, Hwy. 103 near Oark, Wolf Pen Campground, Redding Campground, High Bank, Campbell Cemetery, and Hwy. 23.
River difficulty: possibly Class I–III in some sections.
Maps: Ozark National Forest.

Canoeing is very popular on this scenic stream and accounts for 11,440 visitors a year. The Mulberry is also one of the better smallmouth bass streams in the state, and bald eagles feed here during migration. Woodlands and many private structures are located along the river. The outstanding sport fishery includes smallmouth and spotted bass. The river is classified as extraordinary resource water by the state.

The Mulberry is heavily used by campers, anglers, and hunters. Floatable 98 days a year, February–May, this is one of the best whitewater streams in Arkansas.

North Sylamore Creek, north-central Arkansas, designated in 1992; 14.5 mi, Barkshed Campground to White River.
Classification: scenic.
Administered by: Ozark–St. Francis National Forest, 605 W. Main St., P.O. Box 1008, Russellville, AR 72801.
Access: F.R. 91055C in Slick Rock Hollow, 91054B in Petrie Cave Hollow, 1102 at Gunnar Pool, and 1112 at Barkshed.

River difficulty: not normally run.
Maps: Ozark National Forest.

North Sylamore Creek has a high diversity of fish species and is also used by bald eagles during migration. The endangered Indiana bat and gray bat live here.

Bordered by oak, hickory, and pine forests, the creek also flows by pastureland, but 96 percent of the corridor is National Forest. The creek is popular for camping, swimming, and hiking, with use concentrated at the Blanchard Springs Recreation Complex, Barkshed Recreation Area, and Gunnar Pool Recreation Area. The North Sylamore Hiking Trail parallels the river from Barkshed to the creek's mouth. Canoeing is light because the river is floatable only at very high flows.

Richland Creek, north-central Arkansas, designated in 1992; 16.5 mi, source and downstream.
Classification: wild, 5.3 mi; scenic, 11.2 mi.
Administered by: Ozark–St. Francis National Forest, 605 W. Main St., P.O. Box 1008, Russellville, AR 72801.
Access: F.R. 1200 parallels the river; also F.R. 1205 at Richland Creek Campground, 1203 near Meeks Hollow.
River difficulty: Class III–IV.
Maps: Ozark National Forest.

With interesting geology, an important upland swamp, and bald eagle habitat during migration, Richland Creek is also popular for recreation.

This is one of the better smallmouth bass streams in the state, also supporting largemouth bass, catfish, and sunfish. With some wilderness frontage, 88 percent of the corridor is national forest. The state classified the stream as extraordinary resource water.

Camping, swimming, and fishing are popular, with developed facilities at the Richland Creek Recreation Area. Boating use is light, with adequate flows only about 20 days a year.

CALIFORNIA

38 rivers (14 counting only main stems), 84 rivers and tributaries, 1,900.8 mi, including 11 mi on part of 1 river not in the National Wild and Scenic Rivers System, and including 19 rivers and 1,328 mi designated by the secretary of the interior

The north coast rivers are legally administered by the California Resources Agency, the U.S. Forest Service (USFS), and BLM, but in most cases USFS is the most involved. The *Northern California Atlas and Gazetteer* published by DeLorne is a good map source for all of northern and central California.

American River, central California, designated in 1981; 23 mi, Nimbus Dam to mouth at Sacramento River.

Classification: recreational.

Administered by: Sacramento County Department of Parks and Recreation, 3711 Branch Center Rd., Sacramento, CA 95827; California Resources Agency, 1416 9th St., Sacramento, CA 95814.

Access: many streets and recreation sites in Sacramento, including Sunrise Blvd., Watt Ave., Howe Ave., Glen Hall Park (Carlson Dr.), Discovery Park at the mouth of the river, and a bike trail along the entire length.

River difficulty: Class I with 2 Class II rapids.

Maps: Sacramento County Parks and Recreation Dept., American River; Dept. of Boating and Waterways, California Resources Agency, "A Boating Trail Guide to the American River Parkway."

The lower American is one of the most used urban rivers in the nation and the most used national river. Clear water, urban parks, bikeways, footpaths, and equestrian trails, along with swimming, fishing, and boating opportunities, make this a model for urban rivers.

Though the river is confined between levees, a riparian corridor lines the shores with plant life. Deer, beavers, muskrats, river otters, and a variety of birds are seen within the city.

Dozens of picnicking and nondesignated swimming areas are heavily used along this Central Valley waterway, where summer temperatures often exceed 100 degrees. The bikeway paralleling the river is the longest bicycle trail in the national rivers system. The entire reach, but especially Nimbus Dam to Watt Avenue, is used by many thousands of canoeists, rafters, and tubers each year. San Juan Rapid, below Sunrise Boulevard, is a favorite spot for local kayakers. Fishing use is heavy throughout, especially during steelhead season. The river is critical to surviving but dwindling runs of king salmon and is rated as the fifth most important salmon spawning stream in the state.

The lower American was designated in the California scenic rivers system in 1972 and in the federal system by Interior Secretary Cecil Andrus at the request of Gov. Jerry Brown in 1981 and is the finest example of an urban river in the national rivers system. Administration is officially shared by the state and county governments, with the County Parks and Recreation Department carrying out most responsibilities. The river is chronically threatened by proposals to divert upstream water for irrigation if Auburn Dam and new distribution canals are built.

American River, North Fork, east-central California, designated in 1978; 38.3 mi, The Cedars to Colfax–Iowa Hill Bridge.
Classification: wild.
Administered by: Tahoe National Forest, P.O. Box 6003, Nevada City, CA 95959, 26.3 mi; BLM, 2800 Cottage Way, Sacramento, CA 95825, 12 mi.
Access: I-80 to Colfax exit to Colfax–Iowa Hill Bridge, Norden exit to The Cedars via unimproved road.
River difficulty: Class IV–V.
Maps: Tahoe National Forest.
Other information: A Guide to the American River Canyons (available from Friends of the River, 909 12th St., Sacramento, CA 95814); James Cassady and Fryar Calhoun, *California White Water* (1984).

This spectacularly rugged canyon extends from the heart of the Sierra Nevada near Donner Pass to the foothills and includes remote wilderness, extreme whitewater, and a state-designated wild trout fishery of 36 mi.

Below The Cedars, reached by a rough dirt road, the river plunges through the nearly impassable Royal Gorge and then through the 3,500 ft deep Giant Gap with canyon walls and a gradient of 180 ft per mile, prime nesting habitat for the endangered peregrine falcon and the golden eagle. Trails provide for dramatic day hikes and wilderness backpacking, the easiest trail extending upriver from the Colfax–Iowa Hill Bridge. Upper reaches offer excellent backcountry skiing in winter. The Giant Gap run is one of the preeminent Class V kayak descents in the United States.

In 1972, 48 mi of the North Fork were designated in the state scenic rivers system, halting plans for a dam at Giant Gap. Even though the river is superb for many miles downstream through reaches that have greater recreational activity, the designation stops at the highwater mark of the proposed Auburn Dam.

Big Sur River, southwest California, designated in 1992; 7.4 mi, source at North and South forks confluence to Ventana Wilderness boundary.
Classification: wild.
Designated tributaries:
   Big Sur River, South Fork, source to mouth at Big Sur River.
   Big Sur River, North Fork, source to mouth at Big Sur River.
Total designated mileage of system: 19.5.
Administered by: Los Padres National Forest, 6144 Calle Real, Goleta, CA 93117.
Access: Ventana Wilderness trails, Pfeiffer Big Sur State Park.
River difficulty: Class II from Pfeiffer Big Sur State Park Campground to mouth, below the designated reach.
Maps: Los Padres National Forest.

The Big Sur was the only national rivers system candidate in the southern ranges of the coast redwood. The rivers wind through groves of redwoods and diverse plant life of the coast range. Foggy river bottoms contrast frequently with dry slopes of grass and chaparral; rapids alternate with pools and waterfalls. Three hot sulfur springs are found in this canyon offering year-round hiking, camping, and swimming. A rainbow trout fishery remains excellent because of limited access. All of the designated reach flows through the Ventana Wilderness.

Eel River, northwest California, designated in 1981; 157 mi, Van Arsdale Dam to mouth at Pacific Ocean.
Classification: wild, 12 mi; scenic, 6 mi; recreational, 139 mi.
Total mileage, Eel River system: 346 (see description of forks).
Administered by: California Resources Agency, 1416 9th St., Sacramento, CA 95814.
Access: upper river via Laytonville–Dos Rios Rd., Hwy. 162, Alderpoint Rd.; Hwy. 101 parallels the lower river, and a county road reaches the mouth.
River difficulty: Class I–IV in various sections.
Other information: Thomas Harris, *Down the Wild Rivers* (1973); James Cassady and Fryar Calhoun, *California White Water* (1984); Lars Holbek and Chuck Stanley, *A Guide to the Best Whitewater in the State of California* (1984).

A diverse, accessible, large river, the Eel has excellent fishery values and whitewater. It may carry more silt than any other river of its size in the United States. The Eel is one of four national rivers (main stems) designated to the ocean and is the fifth longest national river outside Alaska and the fourth longest in unbroken mileage.

The Eel passes over wide gravel bars and into deep canyons, but most characteristically it flows through grasslands and oak savannah in a pristine and unusual setting. In a wide valley, the lower river passes redwood groves, farms, and small communities until—bordered by pastures and marshes—it meets the Pacific. After enormous winter and springtime flows the river drops suddenly and yields only 1 percent of its water in the summer.

A premier fishery for coho and chinook salmon, the Eel is also important for American shad and Pacific lamprey, and with tributaries it carries California's largest spring run of steelhead. The river provides habitat for the endangered bald eagle, peregrine falcon, and brown pelican. The town of Scotia, along the river, is one of the last company-owned lumber-mill towns in the West.

A variety of excellent whitewater and float trips can be taken on the Eel in the winter and spring; May is exceptionally beautiful. Scott Dam to Buckwell

Creek is a 5.7 mi Class III–IV run. Dos Rios to Alderpoint is a superb 46 mi trip, Class II–III. Long sections on the lower river offer Class I paddling. Fishing on all reaches is popular.

The Eel is unusual in the national rivers system in being a long, large river (averaging 7,600 cfs) with 80 percent private ownership in the corridor. Scott and Cape Horn dams near the headwaters have contributed to declines in salmon populations; a private utility diverts water from Cape Horn Dam to the East Fork of the Russian River and reduces Eel River flows radically beginning in April. When logging increased substantially between 1938 and 1975, chinook salmon, coho salmon, and steelhead declined by 59 percent, 83 percent, and 78 percent, respectively.

Eel River, Middle Fork, northwest California, designated in 1981; 54 mi, south boundary of Middle Eel–Yolla Bolly Wilderness to mouth.

Classification: wild, 46.5 mi; recreational, 7.5 mi.

Administered by: Mendocino National Forest, 420 E. Laurel St., Willows, CA 95988; California Resources Agency, 1416 9th St., Sacramento, CA 95825.

Access: Eel River Ranger Station near national forest boundary (10 mi east of Covelo), Dos Rios Road near the mouth.

River difficulty: Class II–IV, 1 portage.

Other information: James Cassady and Fryar Calhoun, *California White Water* (1984).

One of California's finest long whitewater runs, the Middle Fork of the Eel provides a picturesque blend of conifer and oak forests with vast sweeps of grassland in steep terrain. With the headwaters that are protected as wilderness, the Middle Fork Eel–main stem Eel combination is the longest stream protected in the national rivers system from source to mouth and from source to the ocean.

The upper 6 mi of the designated reach are within the Yolla Bolly Wilderness, and the upper 23.5 mi are in national forest land. Most of the river runs through a deep canyon opening occasionally to mountain views. Rapids, sandbars, and deep pools are plentiful. Unstable soils result in huge landslides; silt loads at peak flows reach 15 times those of the Mississippi per unit of water. Offering excellent habitat for summer steelhead, the river also supports winter-run steelhead, winter- and spring-run chinook salmon, and rainbow trout. Bald eagles winter here, and peregrine falcons have nested in the canyon. Archaeological sites are plentiful, and the river borders the Round Valley Indian Reservation.

In the national forest reach, several trails touch the river. On lower reaches, three trails lead to the river, which is popular for fishing, with catch-and-release regulations on summer steelhead. The 30 mi whitewater run from

Black Butte River to Dos Rios is popular in the spring. Coal Mine Falls is nearly unrunnable for rafts and difficult to portage.

The subject of one of the major dam fights in California, the Middle Fork was to be impounded by Dos Rios Dam and the water diverted south. Protection in the state scenic rivers system in 1972 temporarily preempted the dam, and national designation later banned the project. The uppermost 14.5 mi of the river, undesignated, are in the Yolla Bolly Wilderness.

Eel River, North Fork, northwest California, designated in 1981; 34 mi, Old Gilman Ranch to mouth.
Classification: wild, 32 mi; recreational, 2 mi.
Administered by: Six Rivers National Forest, 1330 Bayshore Way, Eureka, CA 95501; California Resources Agency, 1416 9th St., Sacramento, CA 95814.
Access: the gravel Hulls Creek and Mina roads cross the river near Covelo.
River difficulty: Class III.
Maps: Six Rivers National Forest.
Other information: James Cassady and Fryar Calhoun, *California White Water* (1984).

A small, remote river, the North Fork of the Eel flows through rugged terrain and a spectacular gorge with a waterfall at Split Rock—a monolithic formation rising 600 ft above the river. Flowing through a mixed conifer forest in upper reaches and then through oaks below, the river supports an important winter-run steelhead and native rainbow trout fishery.

The Hulls Creek–Mina Road reach of 8.4 mi is a seldom kayaked but scenic Class III run in December–April. Respect private and Indian land at the put-in. Lower reaches are largely unrunnable. Fishing is limited by difficult access and private or tribal land.

Eel River, South Fork, northwest California, designated in 1981; 101 mi, confluence with Section Four Creek near Branscomb to mouth at the Eel River.
Classification: wild, 7 mi; recreational, 94 mi.
Administered by: California Resources Agency, 1416 9th St., Sacramento, CA 95814.
Access: Branscomb Rd. in upper reaches, many sites along Hwy. 101 below.
River difficulty: Class I–V with long reaches of Class I.
Other information: James Cassady and Fryar Calhoun, *California White Water* (1984).

With shorelines including some of the finest old-growth forests anywhere, the South Fork of the Eel is a river of the redwoods.

Flowing from a canyon in upper reaches, the stream broadens to gentle riffles through 32 mi of Humbolt Redwoods State Park. This is the leading producer of chinook and coho salmon in the Eel River system; South Fork steelhead are known for their large size. Bald eagles have nested along the river.

A Class IV–V reach runs for 16 mi from Branscomb to Tenmile Creek in winter and spring. A 66 mi run from the Hermitage to the mouth is punctuated by three Class III rapids but is mostly Class I with redwood scenery, runnable before mid June. Excellent hiking trails lead to the river in Humbolt Redwoods State Park.

Feather River, Middle Fork, northeast California, designated in 1968; 108 mi, railroad bridge near Beckwourth to Oroville Reservoir.

Classification: wild, 32.9 mi including Nelson Point area; scenic, 9.7 mi above Nelson Point area and Milsap Bar area; recreational, 65.4 mi, Beckwourth to 3 mi below Sloat.

Administered by: Plumas National Forest, P.O. Box 11500, Quincy, CA 95971.

Access: Hwy. 70 parallels the upper river; Sloat Bridge, Grayeagle Bridge, LaPorte Rd., unimproved Milsap Bar Rd.

River difficulty: Class III–V.

Maps: Plumas National Forest.

Other information: James Cassady and Fryar Calhoun, *California White Water* (1984).

Among the first wild and scenic rivers designated, the Feather's Middle Fork is considered by Charles Martin, author of *Sierra Whitewater*, to be the most beautiful river in California.

Exquisite, clear water is bordered by white gravel bars, rich green forests, and canyon walls. Lower reaches are secluded and can be seen only after strenuous hiking. Bald Rock gorge includes granite walls of 2,000 ft and waterfalls. Feather Falls, 640 ft high on a tributary near the river, is the sixth highest waterfall in the nation.

The Middle Feather is one of the finest wild trout fisheries in California. Several trails provide access to the river. From Sloat to Nelson Point on the upper river is an excellent 8 mi Class II and III whitewater run in the spring. Below there, 34 mi constitute an extremely difficult but spectacular whitewater descent, a barrage of Class V rapids in a remote canyon, for experts only.

A hydroelectric developer has proposed diversions affecting Feather Falls. Industrial-scale mining on the upper river led to appeals, and Forest Service approvals were overturned. In 1976, under pressure from upstream ranchers, Congress amended the Wild and Scenic Rivers Act to delete Middle Fork mileage that meandered through private land above Beckwourth—the only deletion ever made to the national rivers system. The remaining upper recreational section includes private land.

Kern River, North Fork, southeast California, designated in 1987; 78.5 mi, source to Tulare-Kern county boundary.

Classification: wild, 61.2 mi; recreational, 17.3 mi.

Administered by: Sequoia National Forest, 900 W. Grand Ave., Porterville, CA 93257; Sequoia National Park, Three Rivers, CA 93271.

Access: Johnsondale-Kernville Rd. parallels the lower river for 20 mi; trails along the upper river.

River difficulty: Class III–V.

Maps: Sequoia National Forest, Sequoia National Park.

Other information: James Cassady and Fryar Calhoun, *California White Water* (1984).

With the runoff of Mount Whitney—the highest peak in 49 states—the North Fork of the Kern drops through stunning wilderness and offers one of the premier multiday, difficult runs in the United States and the closest whitewater to Los Angeles.

The river begins as an exquisite stream of the high Sierra, flowing over vast slabs of granite. The 4,000 ft deep canyon follows a remarkably straight fault line for nearly 30 mi. For 48 mi the river transects Sequoia National Park and the Golden Trout Wilderness. Then it flows through national forest with granite cliffs and domes and shorelines of pine and fir, unlike most of the boatable California canyons, which are found at lower elevations. The extraordinary variation in elevation has resulted in 15 different plant communities along the river and habitat for at least 6 endangered or rare species.

The river is an excellent trout fishery and offers superb backpacking from Johnsondale to the source. Boating is not allowed in Sequoia National Park. Through Sequoia National Forest, the Forks of the Kern is a 17 mi raft and kayak run through pristine wilderness, 6 Class V rapids, and 80 significant rapids in all. *California White Water* calls this "one of the finest stretches of expert whitewater on earth." The put-in at the Little Kern confluence is reached by a 2 mi trail. A Forest Service permit is required, and low quotas guarantee that visitors will see few other parties. The lower river below Johnsondale is intensively used for fishing, camping, and rafting, with various lengths of runs, most involving Class V water where a Forest Service permit is needed. A lower section includes 2 mi of Class II and III water.

Legislation exempts the existing Fairview Dam and its diversion by Southern California Edison from any effects of the designation and permits reconstruction of the hydropower project to its existing size.

Kern River, South Fork, southeast California, designated in 1987; 72.5 mi, source to south boundary of Dome Land Wilderness.

Classification: wild, 61.9 mi; scenic, 10.6 mi.

Administered by: Sequoia National Forest, 900 W. Grand Ave., Porterville, CA 93257.
Access: Hwy. 395 to Hwy. J41 to Kennedy Meadows.
River difficulty: not run.
Maps: Sequoia National Forest.

In a pivotal setting between high and low elevations and between mountains and desert, the Kern's South Fork supports exceptionally diverse plant communities and wilderness and is home to the rare golden trout, the official state fish. The river cuts through deep gorges with granite outcroppings and domes interspersed with meadows.

The South Fork is little used for recreation except at the road-accessible Kennedy Meadows. The Pacific Crest Trail follows near the river for 9 mi, including a section through Kennedy Meadows. The native trout fishery is excellent, reached in places only by tortuous off-trail hiking.

Kings River, east-central California, designated in 1987; 17 mi, source at Middle and South forks confluence to 1 mi above Pine Flat Reservoir; only the upper 6 mi of the main stem are in the Wild and Scenic Rivers System.
Classification: wild, 6 mi; special management area, 11 mi.
Total designated mileage, Kings River system: 92.5 mi (see Middle and South forks), 37 mi administered by USFS, 55.5 mi by NPS.
Administered by: Sequoia National Park, Three Rivers, CA 93271; Sierra National Forest, 1600 Tollhouse Rd., Clovis, CA 93612.
Access: Garnet Dike Rd. (gravel) above Pine Flat Reservoir; the Yucca Point Trail reaches the upper section from Cedar Grove Rd.
River difficulty: Class III–V in 2 sections.
Maps: Kings Canyon National Park, Sierra National Forest.
Other information: James Cassady and Fryar Calhoun, *California White Water* (1984).

The Kings and its forks have carved the deepest canyon in the United States—8,300 ft from Spanish Peak to the river—and this river flows over the greatest undammed vertical drop of any river on the continent, 13,291 ft from headwaters to where the river flows into Pine Flat Reservoir. This is one of the most extraordinary of all national rivers.

The river is one of the largest of California's designated wild trout fisheries and one of the cleanest rivers of its size anywhere, owing to national park and wilderness protection and the river's granite basin. A wealth of wildlife, plant life, archaeological sites, caves, and tributary waterfalls is found, with Garlic Falls dropping hundreds of feet into the river.

One of the finest large trout fisheries in the state, the Kings draws thousands of anglers each year. The Kings River National Trail follows the river for 3 mi and is planned for 10 mi to the Middle and South forks confluence. A wilderness river with extreme hazards, the Kings above Spring Creek is considered one of the ultimate expert kayaking runs in America.

The Kings was designated as a result of a concerted campaign to stop the proposed Rogers Crossing Dam, but national river status unfortunately excluded the threatened section (immediately downstream from the wild and scenic reach), which was named a Special Management Area where no dams may be built "without specific authority of the Congress." This includes 11 mi of superb river, immensely popular for fishing, and one of California's favorite rafting runs—Class III and sometimes IV water used by 20,000 people a year. After the dam threat was past, the Forest Service declared this section eligible for wild and scenic designation.

Kings River, Middle Fork, east-central California, designated in 1987; 35 mi, source to mouth at South Fork Kings.
Classification: wild.
Administered by: Kings Canyon National Park, Three Rivers, CA 93271 (27 mi); Sierra National Forest, 1600 Tollhouse Rd., Clovis, CA 93612 (8 mi).
Access: a hike of 1 or 2 days is required to reach the river at Tehipite Valley or in upper reaches.
River difficulty: not run.
Maps: Kings Canyon National Park.

Beginning on 14,000 ft peaks, waters of the Middle Fork flow through some of the most spectacular high country in the United States. Canyon walls rise to peaks 7,000 ft above the river on both sides, a canyon depth that is unmatched on the continent.

Hundreds of waterfalls and deep pools alternate with tumultuous rapids beneath granite walls thousands of feet high. The river is the centerpiece of the wilderness site of Tehipite Valley—the closest thing the nation has to another Yosemite.

The Middle Fork basin is one of the premier backpacking regions in America. Excellent native trout fisheries and wildlife habitat are found.

Kings River, South Fork, east-central California, designated in 1987; 40.5 mi, source to mouth at Middle Fork Kings.
Classification: wild, 25 mi; recreational, 15.5 mi.
Administered by: Kings Canyon National Park, Three Rivers, CA 93271 (28.5 mi); Sierra National Forest, 1600 Tollhouse Rd., Clovis, CA 93612 (12 mi).
Access: Cedar Grove Rd., trails at the headwaters.
River difficulty: boating is not allowed in the national park; Class IV–V below park.
Maps: Kings Canyon National Park.

With many similarities to the Middle Fork, the South Fork Kings offers exceptional backcountry of high peaks, granite canyons, and some of the southernmost glaciers in America.

Trails parallel sections of the river and penetrate much of the high country. A popular hike of 4 mi leads to Mist Falls. The river is the centerpiece of Cedar Grove, a recreation center of campgrounds and visitor facilities in one of the most exquisite valleys in the Sierra. The Cedar Grove Road offers spectacular views of the South Fork canyon.

Klamath River, northern California, designated in 1981; 188 mi, Iron Gate Dam to mouth at the Pacific Ocean.

Classification: scenic, 13 mi; recreational, 175 mi.

Administered by: Klamath National Forest, 1312 Fairlane Rd., Yreka, CA 96097; California Resources Agency, 1416 9th St., Sacramento, CA 95814.

Access: Hwys. 96 and 169 parallel the river for 150 mi; Hwy. 101 and I-5 cross the river.

River difficulty: long sections of Class I–II, some sections of Class III–IV.

Maps: Klamath National Forest, Six Rivers National Forest.

Other information: James Cassady and Fryar Calhoun, *California White Water* (1984).

One of the finest steelhead rivers in the nation, the Klamath is the second longest and second largest river in California, the third longest designated national river outside Alaska, and the second longest free-flowing reach on the West Coast. This is one of four rivers designated to the ocean, though not from its headwaters.

From Iron Gate Dam to the Pacific, the Klamath crosses the Siskiyou, Marble, and Salmon mountain ranges, with a splendid diversity of plant life linking interior California to the coast. The waterway flows through Redwood National Park near the ocean, and is a major producer of coho and chinook salmon. Several reaches remain as sacred sites to the Karok Indians.

The river is popular for trout, steelhead, and salmon fishing, and access sites are plentiful. From Iron Gate to Sarah Totten Campground, a 48 mi reach of Class I–II rapids flows through drier canyons than the middle river. From there to Weitchpec, 100 mi of scenic Class I–IV water abounds. Ishi Pishi Falls, near Somes Bar, should not be run. The Class IV Ikes rapids lie below Somes Bar. Weitchpec to the ocean is slow and winding, through Indian land where visitors are not always welcome.

Merced River, east-central California, designated in 1987; 52 mi, source to Halls Gulch below Briceburg.

Classification: wild, 16 mi; scenic, 14 mi; recreational, 22 mi.

Total designated mileage, Merced River system: 114, 78 mi administered by

NPS, 29 by USFS, 3 by NPS and USFS combined, and 4 by BLM. See Merced River forks.

Administered by: Yosemite National Park, P.O. Box 577, Yosemite, CA 95389; Sierra National Forest, 1600 Tollhouse Rd., Clovis, CA 93612; BLM, 800 Truxtun Ave., Bakersfield, CA 93301.

Access: trails upstream from Yosemite Valley; Hwy. 140 parallels the river from Briceburg to Yosemite; gravel road from Briceburg downstream to Railroad Flat.

River difficulty: Class I–V, upper sections unrunnable.

Maps: Yosemite National Park, Sierra National Forest.

Other information: The Merced River Canyon (brochure, California Department of Water Resources, 1416 9th St., Sacramento, CA 95814); James Cassady and Fryar Calhoun, *California White Water* (1984).

The Merced is the famed river of Yosemite Valley, including some of the more spectacular waterfalls in America, the most idyllic glaciated valleys, and fine whitewater in lower stretches.

Beginning beneath Yosemite's highest peak, Mount Lyell, the Merced has forks and upper reaches extraordinary in glaciated scenery, pools, falls, and long cascades. Vernal Falls may be the most visited, trail-accessible waterfall in the United States. In Yosemite Valley the Merced winds through meadows and forests with the backdrop of Half Dome and El Capitan—granite monoliths up to 5,000 ft high—and is the centerpiece of one of America's favorite national parks. Below Yosemite, the river slices for 25 mi through the Sierra foothills.

Upper reaches offer some of the country's finest backpacking. Day hikes from Yosemite Valley lead to Vernal and Nevada falls, among the most spectacular anywhere. Other trails allow easy strolling in what many people consider the most beautiful valley in America. Below the park, several reaches offer Class III, IV, and V boating until July. Fishing is popular on all reaches.

A hydroelectric proposal with a dam and diversion just below the Yosemite Park boundary was halted by the designation. A lower reach of 8 mi from Halls Gulch to Maclure Reservoir was perennially proposed for damming, but was being considered for wild and scenic designation in 1992. The Merced includes one of few dams on a national river and also in a national park. Hydroelectric generation at the site has been discontinued, and the Park Service hopes to eventually dismantle the small dam.

Merced River Headwaters Forks, east-central California, designated in 1987.

Lyell Fork, 6 mi, source to mouth, wild classification.

Triple Peak Fork, 4 mi, source to mouth, wild.

Merced Peak Fork, 5 mi, source to mouth, wild.
Red Peak Fork, 4 mi, source to mouth, wild.
Total mileage of Headwaters Forks: 19.
Administered by: Yosemite National Park, P.O. Box 577, Yosemite, CA 95389.
See Merced River description.

Merced River, South Fork, east-central California, designated in 1987; 43 mi, source to mouth at Merced River.
Classification: wild, 37.5 mi; scenic, 5 mi; recreational, 0.5 mi.
Administered by: Yosemite National Park, P.O. Box 577, Yosemite, CA 95389 (22 mi); Sierra National Forest, 1600 Tollhouse Rd., Clovis, CA 93612 (21 mi).
Access: Hwy. 140 at the mouth; Hwy. 41 crosses the upper river at Wawona.
River difficulty: Class IV.
Maps: Yosemite National Park, Sierra National Forest.
Other information: Lars Holbek and Chuck Stanley, *A Guide to the Best Whitewater in the State of California* (1984).

One of the more significant complete rivers in the National Wild and Scenic Rivers System, the South Fork Merced features rugged wild canyons, clearwater with precipitous rapids, and stunning springtime wildflower displays.

Beginning in the Sierra Nevada high country of southern Yosemite National Park, the river winds through forested glades and inaccessible canyons. Lower sections feature brilliant fields of wildflowers. Yosemite deer herds migrate down the canyon and are important to the rare cougar.

A trail leads up the South Fork from Highway 140 for 4 mi to Hite's Cove. Expert kayakers can put in by carrying boats 3 mi down a trail reached by the Hite's Cove dirt road. An excellent fishery, the South Fork is one of few remaining pristine Sierra streams with self-sustaining rainbow, brook, and brown trout.

A hydroelectric project proposed for lower reaches of the river was banned by the wild and scenic designation.

Salmon River, northwest California, designated in 1981; 21 mi, source at North and South forks confluence to mouth at Klamath River.
Classification: scenic, 8 mi; recreational, 13 mi.
Designated tributaries: Wooley Creek, 8 mi, Marble Mountain Wilderness Area to mouth, wild classification.
Total mileage: 29.
Administered by: Klamath National Forest, 1312 Fairlane Road, Yreka, CA 96097.

Access: Cecilville Rd. parallels the river upstream from its mouth at Hwy. 96.
River difficulty: Class III–V.
Maps: Klamath National Forest.
Other information: James Cassady and Fryar Calhoun, *California White Water* (1984).

One of the finer expert whitewater runs in the country, the Salmon includes steep rapids, verdant shorelines, a rugged mountain setting, and excellent steelhead and salmon habitat. It is protected from its source at the North Fork headwaters where the river designation joins a wilderness area. Counting continuous mileage from the headwaters wilderness, the North Fork Salmon–Salmon–Klamath—a continuous reach of about 100 mi—constitutes the second longest river that is protected from source to sea (the Middle Fork Eel–Eel is the longest).

Beginning with the only glacier in the Coast Range, green and white waters plunge through gorge-bound rapids interspersed at low flows with dark green pools. Lush vegetation thrives on 80 in of rain a year. Silver salmon, steelhead, and trout are important species, with Wooley Creek especially critical to spring-run salmon and steelhead. Sturgeon have also been found. King salmon spawning areas are vital for sport fishing, for commercial catches in the ocean, and for subsistence at the Hoopa Valley Reservation. Nearly 100 percent of the watershed lies in national forest land.

This is a superb river for trout, steelhead, and salmon fishing and also one of the prized whitewater rivers for expert paddlers. A 19 mi trip beginning at Forks of Salmon includes three Class V and eight Class IV rapids, runnable in winter and spring. Class III runs are possible in the upper 4.3 mi and the lower 5 mi.

Salmon River, North Fork, northwest California, designated in 1981; 25
    mi, Marble Mountain Wilderness Area to mouth.
Classification: wild, 3 mi; recreational, 22 mi.
Administered by: Klamath National Forest, 1312 Fairlane Road, Yreka, CA
    96097.
Access: Etna Rd. parallels the river to Idlewild Campground.
River difficulty: Class IV.
Maps: Klamath National Forest.
Other information: Lars Holbek and Chuck Stanley, *A Guide to the Best Whitewater in the State of California* (1984).

An exceptionally clear, steep, beautiful river, the North Fork retains wilderness character even though a road lends access to it.

Rising in rugged wilderness of the Salmon Mountains and the Marble Mountain Wilderness, the river offers a challenging Class IV run of 19 mi in winter and spring. Fishing for silver salmon, steelhead, and trout is excellent.

Salmon River, South Fork, northwest California, designated in 1981; 17 mi, Cecilville to mouth.
Classification: scenic, 6 mi; recreational, 11 mi.
See Salmon River description.

Scott River, northwest California, designated in 1981; 24 mi, Shackleford Creek west of Fort Jones to mouth at Klamath River.
Classification: scenic, 6 mi; recreational, 18 mi.
Administered by: Klamath National Forest, 1312 Fairlane Road, Yreka, CA 96097.
Access: Hwy. 96 to Scott River Rd., which parallels the river.
River difficulty: Class II–IV.
Maps: Klamath National Forest.
Other information: James Cassady and Fryar Calhoun, *California White Water* (1984).
The Scott flows through a rugged canyon with difficult whitewater and with steelhead, king salmon, and silver salmon runs.
A 68 mi long tributary to the Klamath, only the lower 24 mi are designated, mostly through national forest land. Headwaters drain both the Marble Mountains and Trinity Alps. After 30 mi of gentler water in Scott Valley, the river enters the designated section and cuts through an 18 mi precipitous canyon. The endangered modest rock cress (*Arabis modesta*) is found on rocky walls and bluffs. Salmon and steelhead declined in the 1970s, probably due to irrigation diversions in Scott Valley.
From sites above the Kelsey Bridge to the Klamath, the Scott offers 22 mi of expert whitewater and Class III rapids at the lower 3 mi.

Sespe Creek, southwest California, designated in 1992; 31.5 mi, Trout Creek confluence and downstream for 27.5 mi; confluence with Rock Creek and Howard Creek downstream to Trout Creek (4 mi), excluding a reach with private land and a potential dam site.
Classification: wild, 27.5 mi; scenic, 4 mi.
Administered by: Los Padres National Forest, 6411 Calle Real, Goleta, CA 93117.
Access: Hwy. 33 at the upper river.
River difficulty: Class IV+, but not normally run.
Maps: Los Padres National Forest.
Sespe Creek is the last remaining undammed river in southern California, running through one of the nation's largest roadless and wilderness areas near a metropolitan region. The California condor, nearly extinct, has been reintroduced in the area following a captive-breeding program.
Twenty-five mi are designated a Wild Trout Stream by the California

Department of Fish and Game, and the Sespe is considered the finest trout stream between Monterey and Mexico. It is one of few streams in southern California with potential for restoring steelhead, whose migration is blocked by diversions below the national forest.

Sandstone cliffs rise 500 ft above the river, and prehistoric settlements and rock art sites can be seen. Eight miles flow through the Sespe Condor Sanctuary. Flows vary from 70,000 cfs to lows of 1.5 cfs in summer months. Sediment, naturally carried to the ocean by the river, is essential to prevent further coastal beach erosion south of Point Mugu.

Heavily used by backpackers, campers, horseback riders, mountain bikers, and anglers, the stream is also noted as an extreme whitewater run for expert kayakers. Only a few hours' drive from Los Angeles, the small river received 60,000 visitors in 1990, primarily near Lion Campground along the upper river.

The lower 8 mi of the creek, to its confluence with the Santa Clara River, are not designated. Wild and scenic status precludes two potential dams but allows for study of a reservoir at Cold Springs on the upper river between Chorro Grade Canyon and Bear Canyon.

Sisquoc River, southwest California, designated in 1992; 33 mi, source to
    Los Padres National Forest boundary.
Classification: wild.
Administered by: Los Padres National Forest, 6144 Calle Real, Goleta, CA
    93117.
Access: trails northeast of Hwy. 154, south of Santa Maria.
River difficulty: not normally run.
Maps: Los Padres National Forest.

Flowing through choice habitat for the California condor, the Sisquoc includes pools, waterfalls, and many archaeological sites.

The narrow channel, punctuated by waterfalls, broadens to a flood plain with terraces beneath steep, chaparral-covered slopes and oak-shaded grasslands. Live oak, valley oak, and blue oak are all found, with western sycamore along the river. Black bears and mountain lions live here. The entire reach flows through national forest land, and all but 2 mi are in the San Rafael Wilderness.

Within a few hours of Los Angeles, the river is used for hiking, horseback riding, fishing, and swimming, especially during March through June when the water is up and wildflowers are abundant.

Smith River, northwest California, designated in 1981; 16 mi, source at
    Middle Fork confluence to mouth at the Pacific Ocean.

Classification: recreational. Much of the Smith River system was also designated a national recreation area in 1990.

Designated tributaries (source to mouth unless noted; information from the state was not available for reaches under California jurisdiction):

Rowdy Creek, Oregon state line to mouth, recreational classification.

Dominie Creek, recreational.

Savoy Creek, recreational.

Little Mill Creek, recreational.

Mill Creek, West Branch.

Mill Creek, East Fork.

Bummer Lake Creek.

Total mileage: about 39.

Total mileage of the designated Smith River system (see description of forks), including 13 mi of the North Fork in Oregon: 338 mi.

Administered by: Six Rivers National Forest, 1330 Bayshore Way, Eureka, CA 95501; California Resources Agency, 1416 9th St., Sacramento, CA 95814.

Access: Hwy. 199 parallels the main stem, with easy access at Jedediah Smith Redwoods State Park; forest roads and trails reach many tributaries.

River difficulty: Class I, II.

Maps: Six Rivers National Forest.

Other information: James Cassady and Fryar Calhoun, *California White Water* (1984).

The Smith is the only major basin remaining in California with no dams, and it is one of the most substantial undammed rivers in the nation. It is a fine example of a nearly pristine river in a forest environment, and the preeminent river of old-growth forests as it flows through Jedediah Smith Redwoods State Park. With 3 major forks and 45 smaller tributaries also designated, the Smith is the nation's best example of a national wild and scenic watershed.

Heavily forested, the many tributaries of the Smith drop through shaded canyons and verdant mountainsides where 100 in of rain a year create one of California's wettest watersheds (the Mattloe is even wetter). Crystal-clear water in all but times of flood and all but logged areas is a bonus attraction. The Smith is an excellent trout, steelhead, and salmon river and important to the salmon's survival in California. Roadless areas exist on about 130,000 acres—one-third of the basin—where 27 rare or endangered plants still grow.

Jedediah Smith Redwoods State Park offers excellent riverfront recreation in one of the foremost redwood groves, with miles of trails. Trout, salmon, and steelhead fishing is popular along most of the river. The lower Smith through the state park makes a fine Class I and II canoe trip of 10 mi.

Threatened by timber sales through the 1980s, forks of the Smith had already seen some sedimentation and fishery declines due to logging on erodible soils. Estimates of the decline of chinook salmon are 60 percent or more. A cobalt mine and related dam were proposed at Hardscrabble Creek and could become threats again.

With anadromous fisheries as the main criterion, only 12 percent of the Smith River system mileage that had been included in the California state scenic rivers system was added to the national system.

Smith River, Middle Fork, northwest California, designated in 1981; 32 mi, source to mouth.
Classification: wild, scenic, and recreational.
Designated tributaries (source to mouth; these USFS figures exclude any private land that might lie along the streams):
Smith River, Siskiyou Fork, wild classification, 4.5 mi; recreational, 3.5 mi, total, 8 mi.
South Siskiyou Fork, 4.75 mi, wild.
Packsaddle Creek, 3.5 mi, scenic.
Griffin Creek, 3.5 mi, recreational.
Knopki Creek, 4.75 mi, recreational.
Patrick Creek, 3.25 mi, recreational.
Patrick Creek, East Fork, 4 mi, recreational.
Patrick Creek, West Fork, 2.75 mi, recreational.
Kelly Creek, 3.25 mi, scenic.
Shelly Creek, 8.75 mi, recreational.
Monkey Creek, 7.25 mi, recreational.
Little Jones Creek, 3.5 mi, recreational, designated in 1990.
Hardscrabble Creek, 6.25 mi, recreational, designated in 1990.
Myrtle Creek, 2.5 mi, wild; 3.5 mi, scenic; total, 6 mi.
Total mileage: 101.5.
Access: Hwy. 199 parallels much of the river and Griffin Creek; forest roads and trails reach some tributaries.
River difficulty: Class IV, V.
Maps: Six Rivers National Forest.
Other information: Lars Holbek and Chuck Stanley, *A Guide to the Best Whitewater in the State of California* (1984); James Cassady and Fryar Calhoun, *California White Water* (1984).

The Smith's Middle Fork includes steep rapids, wilderness tributaries, and road-accessible frontage. With continuous mileage on the main stem of the Smith, this river is protected from source to sea.

From Patrick Creek at the base of a Class V gorge, 8.4 mi of Class IV whitewater extend to Gasquet and the North Fork confluence. Below there, 6 mi of Class III water lead to the Thunderous Oregon Hole Gorge, a 1 mi long descent in Class IV and V water.

Erosion from road cuts has affected the Middle Fork more than other sections of the Smith basin.

Smith River, North Fork, northwest California, designated in 1981; 13.5 mi, Oregon border to mouth at Middle Fork Smith; another 13 mi in Oregon were designated in 1988.
Classification: wild, 11.5 mi; scenic, 1 mi; recreational, 1 mi. In Oregon, an additional 8.5 mi are classified wild and 4.5 are scenic.
Designated tributaries (source to mouth unless noted):
  Diamond Creek, 2 mi, scenic; 5.5 mi, recreational; total, 7.5 mi.
  Diamond Creek, North Fork, 1.5 mi, recreational.
  Bear Creek, 2.5 mi, scenic.
  High Plateau Creek, 2.5 mi, scenic.
  Still Creek, 2.75 mi, scenic.
  Peridotite Creek, 5 mi, wild, designated in 1990.
  Stoney Creek, 5.75 mi, scenic, designated in 1990.
Total mileage: 41, plus 13 mi in Oregon.
Access: gravel roads north of Gasquet; Hwy. 199 crosses near the mouth.
River difficulty: Class IV.
Maps: Six Rivers National Forest.
Other information: James Cassady and Fryar Calhoun, *California White Water* (1984).

The North Fork of the Smith is considered one of the most beautiful whitewater and wilderness rivers in the nation, rarely visited because access is difficult and summer flows are low. Combined with the main stem of the Smith, the North Fork is designated from source to sea.

Draining the Kalmiopsis Wilderness in southern Oregon, this tributary to the Middle Fork penetrates forests never cut because the trees are stunted owing to deficient trace elements in the soil. The river roars through small gorges and a dark wilderness forest for most of its length.

Outstanding Class III and IV rapids make a 14 mi wilderness run from beginning to end. The fishery is closed above Stoney Creek during salmon and steelhead season.

Smith River, South Fork, northwest California, designated in 1981; 38 mi, source to mouth.
Classification: wild, 17 mi; scenic, 3 mi; recreational, 18 mi.
Designated tributaries (source to mouth unless noted; these Forest Service figures exclude private land):
  Prescott Fork, 6 mi, wild.
  Craigs Creek, 9.25 mi, recreational.
  Coon Creek, 9.25 mi, recreational.

Rock Creek, 1 mi, recreational.

Gordon Creek, 6.5 mi, recreational.

Canthook Creek, 2.5 mi, recreational.

Hurdygurdy Creek, 14.25 mi, recreational.

Goose Creek, 15 mi, recreational.

Goose Creek, East Fork, 6.5 mi, recreational.

Jones Creek, 11.5 mi, recreational.

Muzzleloader Creek, 2.75 mi, recreational.

Blackhawk Creek, 2 mi, recreational, designated in 1990.

Buck Creek, 1.75 mi, wild from source to Lower Bucks Creek; 5 mi, scenic; total, 6.75 mi.

Quartz Creek, 7.25 mi, recreational.

Eightmile Creek, 6.75 mi, wild.

Williams Creek, 4.5 mi, wild.

Harrington Creek, 6.5 mi, wild, designated in 1990.

Total mileage: 156.5.

Administered by: Six Rivers National Forest, 1330 Bayshore Way, Eureka, CA 95501; California Resources Agency, 1416 9th St., Sacramento, CA 95814.

Access: Hwy. 99 to South Fork Rd., which parallels the lower river; forest roads to some upper reaches and tributaries.

River difficulty: Class III–V.

Maps: Six Rivers National Forest.

Other information: James Cassady and Fryar Calhoun, *California White Water* (1984).

This longest of the Smith River tributaries is crystal-clear in wild headwaters for many miles. The river combines scenery of the Siskiyou Crest's granite outcrops and steep mountains, deep and diverse conifer forests, and cascading tributaries. With continuous mileage of the main stem of the Smith, this is one of the longest rivers protected from source to sea.

The South Fork Trail offers excellent hiking along many miles of roadless river frontage. An exciting Class III whitewater run in the winter and spring extends from the South Fork bridge to an unmarked take-out above the South Fork Gorge, which is a 1 mi long Class V flume.

Headwaters have been threatened by new logging proposals and the Gasquet-Orleans Road, which would connect the Smith and Klamath drainages by opening up wilderness country.

Trinity River, northwest California, designated in 1981; 111 mi, Lewiston Dam to mouth at Klamath River.

Classification: scenic, 13.5 mi; recreational, 97.5 mi.

Administered by: Shasta-Trinity National Forest, 2400 Washington Ave.,

Redding, CA 96001; Six Rivers National Forest, 507 F St., Eureka, CA 95501; BLM, 2800 Cottage Way, Sacramento, CA 95814; California Resources Agency, 1416 9th St., Sacramento, CA 95814; Hoopa Valley Indian Reservation, P.O. Box 817, Hoopa, CA 95546.

Access: Hwy. 96 parallels lower sections, and 299 follows upper reaches.

River difficulty: Class II–IV in various reaches.

Maps: Shasta-Trinity National Forest, Six Rivers National Forest.

Other information: James Cassady and Fryar Calhoun, *California White Water* (1984); Thomas Harris, *Down the Wild Rivers* (1973).

This largest Klamath River tributary, 170 miles in total length, offers extended rugged canyons and the longest section of canoeing water in mountainous areas of California. The Trinity River supports trout, salmon, steelhead, and white sturgeon in lower reaches. The designated tributaries, combined with the continuous mileage of the main stem below the confluences, are among the few rivers protected from source to sea.

From Lewiston to the North Fork at Helena the river runs for 32 mi in riffles and Class II and possibly III rapids, followed by Class III water from the North Fork to Big Flat, with boating possible well into the summer. Big Flat to Cedar Flat is Class II with higher flows than in the upper sections. Cedar Flat to Hawkins Bar constitutes an 8.5 mi run of screaming Class V and VI water in the isolated Burnt Ranch Gorge, inaccessible except by boat, one of the premier expert runs in California during late spring and early summer flows. From Hawkins Bar to Weitchpec is 39 mi of mostly Class II with perhaps a few Class III rapids and with remote canyons and choice scenery. The lower 17 mi from Willow Creek to Weitchpec are one of the finest canoe runs in California but include a Class IV drop, portageable near the end of the run. Respect Indian property in this lower reach through the Hoopa Valley Reservation.

Upper sections of the river were heavily silted by gold mining, which affected the Trinity more than any other north coast river in California. Trinity Dam, forming California's third largest reservoir, and Lewiston Dam allow diversion of most of the upper river's water through a tunnel to the Sacramento basin, reducing rich runs of salmon and steelhead by 90 percent. Interior Secretary Cecil Andrus in 1981 ordered release of at least 300 cfs year-round. Conditions improved but did not approach restoration of the great fishery that once existed. Efforts continue to restore the fishery of the Trinity basin.

Trinity River, New Fork (New River), northwest California, designated in 1981; 20 mi, Salmon-Trinity Primitive Area to mouth.

Classification: wild, 10 mi; scenic, 3.5 mi; recreational, 6.5 mi.

Access: Hwy. 299 to roads near Denny.

River difficulty: Class IV, V.
Maps: Six Rivers National Forest.
Other information: Lars Holbek and Chuck Stanley, *A Guide to the Best Whitewater in the State of California* (1984).
This seldom visited Trinity tributary has intense springtime whitewater in a remote setting.

Trinity River, North Fork, northwest California, designated in 1981; 14 mi, Salmon-Trinity Primitive Area to mouth.
Classification: wild, 12 mi; recreational, 2 mi.
Administered by: Shasta-Trinity National Forest, 2400 Washington Ave., Redding, CA 96001.
Access: Hwy. 299 east of Big Bar to North Trinity Rd., Hobo Gulch Rd.
River difficulty: Class V.
Maps: Shasta-Trinity National Forest.
Other information: Lars Holbek and Chuck Stanley, *A Guide to the Best Whitewater in the State of California* (1984).
This supremely rugged canyon is the home of one rock-choked rapid after another, considered by guidebook authors Holbek and Stanley to be the steepest and most difficult kayak run in the north coast region. Many portages are required. A steep trail reaches portions of the river.

Trinity River, South Fork, northwest California, designated in 1981; 55 mi, Hwy. 36 bridge to mouth.
Classification: wild, 23 mi; scenic, 21 mi; recreational, 11 mi.
Access: Hwy. 96 parallels the lower river; Hwy. 36 crosses west of Hayfork.
River difficulty: Class II–IV.
Maps: Six Rivers National Forest.
Other information: James Cassady and Fryar Calhoun, *California White Water* (1984.)
This scenic river has extremely difficult and remote whitewater in upper canyons and a beautiful Class I–II section at the bottom.
The river rises beneath the Yolla Bolly Mountains, snow-covered into summer months. Much of the stream slices through nearly impassable canyons with falls and boulder-strewn rapids. The lower 8 mi feature gravel bars for camping and a prime day trip by canoe, mostly run during spring runoff.

Tuolumne River, east-central California, designated in 1984; 83 mi, source to New Don Pedro Reservoir excepting Hetch Hetchy Reservoir.
Classification: wild, 47 mi; scenic, 23 mi; recreational, 13 mi.
Administered by: Yosemite National Park, P.O. Box 577, Yosemite, CA

95389 (54 mi); Stanislaus National Forest, 19777 Greenley Rd., Sonora, CA 95370 (29 mi).

Access: Hwy. 120 at Tuolumne Meadows and the upper river, Hetch Hetchy Road, Wards Ferry and Lumsden roads north of Groveland.

River difficulty: Class IV with impassable upper sections.

Maps: Yosemite National Park, Stanislaus National Forest.

Other information: James Cassady and Fryar Calhoun, *California White Water* (1984); Terry Wright, *Rocks and Rapids of the Tuolumne* (1983).

Beginning in the brilliant Sierra high country of Yosemite National Park, the Tuolumne River drops through the stunning Grand Canyon of the Tuolumne and later churns through one of the premier whitewater runs in America. This is one of the most exquisite high mountain rivers anywhere, and its trout fishery is among California's finest.

Snow and granite of the upper river mix with forested pockets and majestic domes until the backwaters of Hetch Hetchy Reservoir are reached. Below O'Shaughnessy Dam, the transparently clear water plunges through a 2,000 ft deep canyon of cliffs, ponderosa pine, oak savannah, and chaparral.

Upper reaches offer extraordinary backpacking and hiking; trout fishing is excellent throughout. The lower 18 mi are heavily used for 1–3 day raft and kayak trips, with many Class IV rapids and one classic drop, Clavey Falls. Forest Service permits are required for this run, which was floated by 5,600 people in 1990.

Hetch Hetchy Valley was considered the twin of Yosemite, and John Muir's fight to preserve it marked the beginning of river and wilderness preservation efforts in America. That struggle was lost and the valley is now buried under flatwater. The fight to protect the lower canyons was a landmark of river conservation following an intense political battle between river conservationists and hydroelectric developers.

Van Duzen River, northwest California, designated in 1981; 48 mi, Dinsmores Bridge to mouth at Eel River.

Classification: scenic, 14 mi; recreational, 34 mi.

Administered by: California Resources Agency, 1416 9th St., Sacramento, CA 95825; Six Rivers National Forest, 1330 Bayshore Way, Eureka, CA 95501.

Access: Hwy. 36 parallels much of the river; Van Duzen River Rd. leads to upper sections.

River difficulty: mostly Class I and II in lower reaches, not normally run.

Maps: Six Rivers National Forest.

The Van Duzen has one of the highest proportions of private land in the wild and scenic system (83 percent), though the basin is sparsely populated. Because of unstable soils, this river and the Eel to which it flows have one of the highest erosion rates in the country.

Pine and fir forests at the upper reaches of the mountainous basin yield to drier, grassy slopes with oaks, where unstable soils often slide. Steep sections at the headwaters flatten to meanders with broad gravel bars, and redwood stands shade some lower reaches. Steelhead, silver salmon, and chinook salmon are important fish species.

COLORADO
2 rivers, 75 mi

Cache la Poudre, north-central Colorado, designated in 1986; 56 mi, Poudre Lake and downstream, with some sections omitted.
Classification: wild, 18 mi; recreational, 38 mi.
Total designated mileage in Cache la Poudre system: 75, including 30 mi wild classification, 45 mi recreational.
Administered by: Arapaho and Roosevelt National Forests, 240 W. Prospect, Fort Collins, CO 80526.
Access: Hwy. 14 parallels much of the river.
River difficulty: Class IV, V, 1 short Class II reach.
Maps: Arapaho and Roosevelt national forests.
Other information: Doug Wheat, *A Floater's Guide to Colorado* (1984).

The Poudre with its South Fork is one of few large rivers in Colorado that has not been changed extensively by dams. It is also an extremely popular fishing stream, the only river in the Front Range of such quality, and Colorado's only river system with wild and scenic status as of 1992.

Beginning on wilderness peaks of the Front Range, and with 10.5 mi in Rocky Mountain National Park, the river later cuts through steep-walled granite canyons 1,000 ft deep and into narrow valleys. The stream opens to a U-shaped, glaciated canyon with slower water in a pastoral landscape. Homes and tourist facilities have been built along some sections. Fish and wildlife are more abundant in this canyon than in others on the east slope of the Rockies. The threatened or endangered greenback cutthroat trout is one of 15 fish species. Large mammals along the river include elk, bighorn sheep, and cougars.

During a fluctuating season of about six weeks, kayakers and rafters flock to whitewater in some sections of this expert-level stream. Between the headgate dam above Ted's Place and the mouth of the canyon, seven or more sections are run, all expert-grade except for one 3 mi reach. This is one of the most fished rivers in Colorado. Upper reaches draw many hikers and backpackers; campgrounds and picnic areas are dotted along road-accessible sections.

The natural flow is augmented by eight transbasin diversions into the Cache la Poudre for use on the east side of the Rockies after storage in downstream reservoirs. Water agencies considered four additional dams or diversions that would have affected much of the river's length. Most of the proposed dams are now precluded, but some threats persist.

Cache la Poudre, South Fork, north-central Colorado, designated in 1986; 19 mi, source and downstream in 2 sections.
Classification: wild, 12 mi; recreational, 7 mi.
River difficulty: not run.

Four miles of this designated reach flow in the Cache la Poudre Wilderness Area, and 3.5 mi are in Rocky Mountain National Park. The middle section is paralleled by national forest roads. In its lower 10 mi, the South Fork drops 1,350 ft with many logjams. The wild, forested canyon holds many hazards and is not considered runnable.

FLORIDA
1 river, 7.5 mi.

Loxahatchee River, Northwest Fork, southeast Florida, designated in 1985; 7.5 mi in Jonathan Dickinson State Park.
Classification: wild, 1.5 mi; scenic, 5.5 mi; recreational, 0.5 mi.
Administered by: Florida Dept. of Natural Resources, Florida Park Service, 3900 Commonwealth Blvd., Tallahassee, FL 32303.
Access: Riverbend Park at Indiantown Rd., Jonathan Dickinson State Park.
River difficulty: Class I.

One of few subtropical rivers in the National Wild and Scenic Rivers System and the only Florida river as of 1992, the Loxahatchee is also one of the shortest designated streams. All but 0.5 miles of the reach flow in Jonathan Dickinson State Park.

The river winds sinuously through a closed canopy swamp, largely pristine for 3.5 mi with 500-year-old bald cypress. At the park's Trapper Nelson Interpretive Site the stream widens, the cypress have been killed because of saltwater intrusion, and mangroves dominate. The park contains 78 federal and state endangered and potentially endangered plant and wildlife species, and the entire river is critical habitat for the West Indian manatee. Largemouth bass, tarpon, snook, mullet, bluegill, and shellcracker are just a few of the fish found in this blend of freshwater and saltwater.

A 7.5 mi canoe trip can be taken starting at Riverbend County Park west of the town of Jupiter, with a take-out at the boat ramp in Jonathan Dickinson

State Park. Fishing is popular, and the Trapper Nelson Interpretive Site is an early homestead reached by canoe or by the *Loxahatchee Queen*, a park concession tour boat.

The river's surroundings—variously ditched, drained, and farmed—face growing urban pressures that are changing the flow conditions and natural drainage patterns. Canals and dikes at the headwaters have altered water quality and quantity in the river. The improved Jupiter Inlet has caused upstream intrusion of Atlantic Ocean saltwater into the state park. The river was designated by the secretary of the interior at the governor's request.

GEORGIA
3 rivers, 104.9 mi, including 39.6 mi shared with South Carolina and 48 mi not in the Wild and Scenic Rivers System

Chattahoochee River, north-central Georgia, designated in 1978; not in the Wild and Scenic Rivers System; 48 mi, Buford Dam to Peachtree Creek in Atlanta.
Classification: national recreation area.
Administered by: NPS, 1978 Island Ford Pkwy., Dunwoody, GA 30350.
Access: many sites upstream of Atlanta, including access facilities at Buford Dam, Abbott's Bridge on Hwy. 120, Medlock Bridge on Hwy. 141, Jones Bridge west of Hwy. 141, Chattahoochee River Park below Hwy. 9, Morgan Falls Dam below Hwy. 9, Powers Island west of I-285, and Paces Mill below I-75.
River difficulty: Class I–III and possibly IV.

Flowing rapidly through the incised Appalachian foothills, the Chattahoochee above Atlanta is one of America's finest scenic streams within an urban area and one of the most used rivers for recreation.

The river shows miles of wooded shorelines, islands, riffles, rapids, farmland, Civil War ruins, Indian rock shelters occupied 8,000 years ago, and modern home sites. The Palisades section from I-75 to I-285 features high bluffs accessible by mass transit only 30 minutes from downtown Atlanta.

Whitewater boating, tubing, fishing, hiking, and picnicking attract crowds along undeveloped sections and in community parks. Many sections can be boated for 2–13 mi or longer reaches, usually Class I and II but some with larger rapids. The Great Chattahoochee Raft Race was listed in the *Guinness Book of Records* as the world's largest participation sporting event. Near Paces Mill, Island Fork, and Jones Bridge, trails lead to the river with views of islands and whitewater shoals. Fish species include trout, bream, and catfish.

After several local and regional planning attempts and unsuccessful appeals for state protection, development pressures intensified along the urbanizing river, and the national recreation area was established to acquire and manage riverfront land. Over 3,000 acres were bought, but fragile lands have still been developed.

Chattooga River, northeast Georgia, designated in 1974, including 39.6 mi shared with South Carolina; 39.6 mi, North Carolina state line to Tugaloo Reservoir; another 10 mi reach lies upstream in North Carolina, beginning 0.8 mi below Cashiers Lake.

Total mileage: 49.6.

Total designated mileage, Chattooga system: 56.9, including wild classification, 39.8 mi; scenic, 2.5 mi; recreational, 14.6 mi (includes West Fork and 10 mi in North Carolina).

Administered by: Chattahoochee National Forest, 508 Oak St., Gainsville, GA 30501; Nantahala National Forest, P.O. Box 2750, Asheville, NC 28802; Sumpter National Forest, P.O. Box 2227, Columbia, SC 20202.

Access: Hwys. 1107 and 1178 in North Carolina; Hwys. 646, 28, 76, 511, and others in Georgia and South Carolina.

River difficulty: Class II–V in 4 sections.

Maps: USFS, "Chattooga National Wild and Scenic River."

Other information: Gene Able and Jack Horan, *Paddling South Carolina* (1986).

Flowing through a wild Appalachian gorge, the Chattooga ranks as a preeminent whitewater river of the East, one of the longest and largest undeveloped streams in the Southeast, and the longest national river in the South.

The waterway flows through steep, wooded gorges with many rocky shores. Brown trout and some rainbow trout live in upper reaches, and redeye bass are found below. Deer, wild turkeys, quail, grouse, and small mammals are plentiful.

The Highway 28 bridge to Earl's Ford ("section II") offers a 7 mi Class II canoe trip with one Class III rapid. Earl's Ford to Highway 76 includes steep gorges and Class IV rapids with Bull Sluice as a climax, seen from half a mile above Highway 76. From there to Tugaloo Reservoir involves 7 mi of difficult Class IV rapids. Trout fishing is good above Highway 28. Fifty miles of hiking trails lie near the river, excellent for backpacking.

Among rivers originally studied for a wild and scenic rivers program in 1963, the Chattooga scored among the highest. This was the first river to be congressionally designated after the original Wild and Scenic Rivers Act of 1968. Designation prevented a dam and resulted in public acquisition from willing sellers. Vandalism of visitors' cars has occasionally been a problem.

Chattooga River, West Fork, northeast Georgia, designated in 1974; 7.3 mi above Chattooga River.

Classification: wild, 3.3 mi; recreational, 4 mi.
Administered by: Chattahoochee National Forest, 508 Oak Street, Gainsville, GA 30501.
Access: Hwys. 86, 28.
River difficulty: Class I, II.

The West Fork above Highway 86 offers good fishing for native trout. The 4 mi below the bridge are suitable for canoeing, with a take-out along Highway 28 on the main stem. A trail leads from Highway 86 to the headwaters.

IDAHO
10 rivers, 746.6 mi, including 2 rivers and 173 mi not in the
Wild and Scenic Rivers System

For more information on most rivers see Greg Moore and Don McClaran, *Idaho Whitewater* (1989); and Grant Amaral, *Idaho, The Whitewater State* (1989).

Clearwater River, Middle Fork, northeast Idaho, designated in 1968; 22 mi, source at Selway and Lochsa confluence to Kooskia.
Classification: recreational.
Administered by: Clearwater National Forest, 12730 Hwy. 12, Orofino, ID 83544; Nez Perce National Forest, Rt. 2, Box 475, Grangeville, ID 83530.
Access: Hwy. 12 parallels the river.
River difficulty: Class II.
Maps: Clearwater National Forest.

One of the original wild and scenic rivers, the Middle Fork Clearwater is a premium steelhead stream and one of the larger, mostly undeveloped rivers of the greater Northwest.

This river drifts westward with green shorelines and forested mountain views. With higher flows than any other tributary to the Snake River, this remains one of the strongholds of steelhead and salmon in that enormous and vital basin.

Highway 12 offers many views of the river and access to riverfront camping. The entire reach makes an excellent canoe trip, runnable all summer. Fishing is popular from shore, drift boats, and rafts.

The wild and scenic designation prevented construction of a dam that would also have flooded the lower reaches of the Lochsa and Selway rivers.

Lochsa River, northeast Idaho, designated in 1968; 69 mi, Powell Ranger Station to mouth at Middle Fork Clearwater.

Classification: recreational.
Administered by: Clearwater National Forest, Rt. 4, Orofino, ID 83544.
River difficulty: Class III–IV.
Maps: Clearwater National Forest.

As part of the Middle Fork Clearwater, the Lochsa was among the first national rivers and offers some of the finest river and mountain scenery reached by road.

Beginning near Lolo Pass, the river runs westward in an extraordinary display of transparent water, deeply forested shorelines, and heartily challenging rapids. Lewis and Clark faced their greatest trials on their westward route via the Lolo Trail just north of the river.

An exciting and beautiful Class III and sometimes IV whitewater run extends 20 mi to Split Creek Pack Bridge, and 15 mi of Class II and III run to the mouth, all boatable through early summer and constituting some of the nation's finest difficult whitewater that is road-accessible. Cutthroat trout fishing is popular throughout and on tributaries, though the river is closed to fishing during salmon and steelhead seasons. Wilderness Gateway Campground, the Lochsa Historical Ranger Station, and the Bernard DeVoto Memorial Cedar Grove make fine stops for travelers.

Rapid River, west-central Idaho, designated in 1975; 18 mi, source to fish hatchery 2 mi upstream from mouth.
Classification: wild.
Administered by: Hells Canyon National Recreation Area, Wallowa-Whitman National Forest, P.O. Box 832, Riggins, ID 83549.
Access: road to fish hatchery off of Hwy. 95, 5 mi south of Riggins.
River difficulty: not run.
Maps: Hells Canyon National Recreation Area.

This small river remains entirely wild from its source in the Seven Devils Mountains to a salmon hatchery. The relatively undisturbed basin has high quality water. A trail follows the stream and offers choice backpacking.

Rapid River, West Fork, west-central Idaho, designated in 1975; 8.8 mi, source to mouth at Rapid River.
Classification: wild.

Flowing beneath the highest peaks of the Seven Devils Range, the West Fork drops from the 8,956 ft Monument Peak and flows for 3 mi through the Hells Canyon Wilderness. A trail follows the stream for most of its length.

Saint Joe River, northeast Idaho, designated in 1978; 66.3 mi.
Classification: wild, 26.6 mi; recreational, 39.7 mi.

Administered by: Idaho Panhandle National Forests, 1201 Ironwood Dr.,
   Coeur d'Alene, ID 83814.
Access: Saint Joe River Rd. parallels part of the river.
River difficulty: Class III, IV.
Maps: Idaho Panhandle National Forests.

From Saint Joe Lake in the Bitterroot Mountains, the Saint Joe River flows
with fine fishery, wildlife, and whitewater qualities.

Upper reaches cut through a canyon with forested slopes rising 3,000 ft and
then on to 6,000 ft peaks; below Marble Creek the valley widens. Cutthroat
trout migrate in some abundance from Coeur d'Alene Lake, but populations
have been reduced under competition from introduced species and degradation of the lake. Many deer, elk, and black bears attract hunters. An occasional cougar, mountain goat, and moose might be seen, and grizzly bears
may survive in some remote areas. Six national forest roadless areas adjoin the
river corridor. The lower river, not designated, is part of the largest osprey
breeding grounds in the West.

A 17 mi Class IV kayak run extends through a roadless section from the
Heller Creek Campground to Spruce Tree Campground, also paralleled by a
hiking trail. A 7 mi section from Gold Creek to Bluff Creek offers Class III
and IV rapids in the spring. Fishing is popular at all accessible sites; the
drainage upstream from Prospector Creek is catch-and-release, except for
mountain lakes.

Salmon River, central Idaho, designated in 1980; 237 mi, North Fork to
   mouth, including 112 mi not in the Wild and Scenic Rivers System; wild
   and scenic designation, 125 mi, North Fork to Long Tom Bar.
Classification: wild, 79 mi; scenic, 46 mi.
Dam prohibition classification: 112 mi, Long Tom Bar to mouth at the Snake
   River.
Administered by: Salmon National Forest, Box 180, North Fork, ID 83466;
   lower river below Long Tom Bar by BLM, Rt. 3, Box 181, Cottonwood,
   ID 83522.
Access: Salmon River Rd. west of North Fork and east of Riggins; Hwy. 95
   parallels the river for 25 mi below Riggins.
River difficulty: Class III, IV.
Maps: Salmon National Forest; BLM.
Other information: John Garren, *Idaho River Tours* (1987); Johnny Carrey
   and Cort Conley, *River of No Return* (1978); (lower river) BLM, *Lower
   Salmon River Guide* (1983).

The Salmon is America's longest river outside Alaska with no major dam.
The wild and scenic section appeals to many people as one of the finest week-
long river trips with whitewater, wilderness, wildlife, fisheries, and campsites.

Called the River of No Return, the wild and scenic middle reaches of the Salmon cut across mountain ranges that constitute the granitic batholith of central Idaho. This large river flows clear and green all summer through one of the nation's most rugged long canyons amid mountainsides rising 6,000 ft. Ponderosa pine and Douglas fir cover most slopes, while others are open with grasses. This constitutes one of the most important winter ranges for wildlife in Idaho, providing sustenance for bighorn sheep, deer, mountain goats, bears, cougars, and bald eagles. The spring and summer chinook salmon and steelhead are critical to the survival of wild anadromous fish in the Columbia basin; 98 percent of the chinook salmon in Idaho spawn in the Salmon River basin. Forty major rapids grace the 79 mi long roadless reach.

From the North Fork to Corn Creek, 45 mi are road accessible with Class II and III rapids. At Corn Creek, Forest Service permits are required for the 80 mi trip to Vinegar Creek, including many Class III rapids with Class IV at higher flows. The entire river, from the Sawtooth Mountains above Stanley to the Snake River, is 420 mi long. Many trails reach points on the river or parallel it. Steelhead and trout anglers flock to this river, also heavily used by hunters. A number of riverfront dude ranches provide tourist facilities.

The Forest Service recommended 237 mi of the Salmon for wild and scenic status; about half was designated in 1980. Jet boats and many preexisting air strips are allowed.

From Long Tom Bar to the mouth, the 112 mi long lower Salmon River is protected from hydroelectric projects by legislation in 1988 banning dams but not conferring wild and scenic status. The lower river has big Class III and IV whitewater in remote desert reaches and includes the third deepest canyon in America as the Salmon nears its mouth in Hells Canyon. In addition to excellent winter range for wildlife and a vital anadromous fishery, there are four canyons in the lower reach that have archaeological sites 8,000 years old.

The Bureau of Land Management manages the lower river for recreation and has administratively avoided approving new mines for a 20 year period. About 83 percent of the lower Salmon corridor is public land. National river designation, considered in 1992, would add security to the lower end of one of America's preeminent wild and scenic rivers and would make this the second longest waterway in the National Wild and Scenic Rivers System.

Salmon River, Middle Fork, central Idaho, designated in 1968; 104 mi, source at confluence of Marsh and Bear Valley creeks to mouth.
Classification: wild, 103 mi; scenic, 1 mi.
Administered by: Challis National Forest, Box 750, Challis, ID 83226.
Access: Hwy. 21 to Dagger Falls Rd., Salmon River Rd. to mouth of Middle Fork west of Shoup, airplane to Indian Creek.

River difficulty: Class III, IV.

Maps: Challis National Forest.

Other information: USFS, *The Middle Fork of the Salmon: A Wild and Scenic River* (booklet).

The Middle Fork of the Salmon is widely regarded as the ultimate wild and scenic river in America. This is the pristine stronghold of the surviving Snake River basin salmon, a major river almost entirely in wilderness, and a canyon 6,000 ft deep with rapids and hot springs, sublime campsites, cascading tributaries, and abundant and diverse wildlife. This is one of the longest national rivers designated from source to mouth.

The Middle Fork cuts across the Salmon River Range, first through dark woods of Douglas fir, Englemann spruce, and lodgepole pine, then past towering ponderosa pine and sun-baked slopes of mountain mahogany and bitterbrush. Sections of the canyon rise as sheer cliffs for hundreds of feet; other areas offer expansive sand bars and luxuriant forests. Elk, mule deer, bighorn sheep, mountain goats, cougars, black bears, coyotes, and bobcats live here. It is a vital river to threatened runs of salmon; nearly one-third of the chinook in the Salmon River basin spawn here. Steelhead, Dolly Varden, and rainbow trout thrive in these pure waters.

The Middle Fork is one of the most sought-after and prized river runs in the country. The Forest Service has required permits since 1973 for the 96 mi trip of up to eight days. In 1991, 10,166 people went down the river. By August, low water makes floating in the upper river difficult, and boaters fly to Indian Creek. Fishing from drift boats and rafts has drawn anglers for 50 years. Several trails reach the river and serve backpackers in the Frank Church River of No Return Wilderness that surrounds the river—America's largest designated wilderness outside Alaska at 3.2 million acres, and probably the largest wilderness in the temperate zones of earth. About 97 percent of the land in the corridor is national forest. The Middle Fork is one of the most intensely managed wild rivers in the United States.

Selway River, northeast Idaho, designated in 1968; 94 mi, source to mouth at the Middle Fork Clearwater.

Classification: wild, source to Magruder Ranger Station and Paradise launch site to Race Creek; recreational, Magruder Ranger Station to Paradise launch site and Race Creek to mouth.

Administered by: Bitterroot National Forest, 316 N. 3rd St., Hamilton, MT. 59840; Clearwater National Forest, Rt. 4, Orofino, ID 83544.

Access: Hwy. 93 to gravel Nez Perce Trail Rd. to Paradise launch site, Selway Falls Rd. east of Lowell.

River difficulty: Class IV.

Maps: USFS, "Selway River Guide."
Other information: John Garren, *Idaho River Tours* (1987).

The Selway is spoken of in near mythic tones by avid wild-river runners. Major Class IV rapids are combined with a wilderness setting and permit restrictions that allow only one group per day on the river, a good guarantee of solitude. This is one of the longest national rivers designated from source to mouth.

The forests of the western Bitterroot Mountains grow vivid and lush with hemlock, grand fir, and western red cedar. The water runs transparently clear, studded with boulders and rocky rapids. For 47 mi the Selway churns through the Selway-Bitterroot Wilderness Area, one of the largest in the country at 1.8 million acres and separated by only one dirt road from the 3.2 million acre River of No Return Wilderness.

Above the usual rafting put-in at Paradise, an 11 mi Class IV section of the river is boatable in early summer. Paradise to Race Creek makes a stunning 48 mi trip of three to five days. Permits, required here by the Forest Service, are among the hardest to get anywhere, issued by lottery with odds of 1 in 32 in any year. The Selway is the only river managed for such a quality wilderness experience. Fishing is excellent (catch and release), and a trail follows the river for the entire length, one of the finest river-backpacking opportunities in the country. Selway Falls, a tourist attraction, can be reached by road at the lower end of the river. A fine Class II day trip extends from the falls to the mouth at Lowell.

Snake River, west-central Idaho, designated in 1975 (also in Oregon); 66.5 mi, Hells Canyon Dam to 4 mi upriver from the Oregon-Washington border.

Classification: wild, 32.3 mi; scenic, 34.2 mi.

Administered by: Hells Canyon National Recreation Area, Wallowa-Whitman National Forest, 2535 Riverside Dr., P.O. Box 699, Clarkston, WA 99403.

Access: Hells Canyon Dam northwest of Cambridge, unimproved road from White Bird to Pittsburgh Landing, Heller Bar (south of Asotin, Washington).

River difficulty: Class II–IV.

Maps: USFS, "The Wild and Scenic Snake River."

Other information: John Garren, *Idaho River Tours* (1987); Tim Palmer, *The Snake River, Window to the West* (1991).

One of the premier big-water runs, the Snake River cuts through Hells Canyon, the second deepest canyon on the continent (Kings Canyon in California is deeper).

Below Hells Canyon Dam the Snake runs without reservoirs for 100 mi to Asotin. Massive in scale, the river averages 13,000 cfs in low flows of August in an enormous breadth and depth of canyon with mountains rising up to 8,000 ft above the water. Upper reaches are a blend of ponderosa pine, fir, and grasslands; lower sections are rocky and arid. The fishery is intricately varied, with bass, trout, salmon, steelhead, and white sturgeon, the largest freshwater fish in North America. Tributary streams, such as the Imnaha, are brilliant, and rapids are powerful. Indian pictographs decorate sheltered rock faces.

This is one of the classic rafting trips in the West, and permits are required by the Forest Service. A trip of five days may be adequate, but more time allows for exploration of this fascinating canyon. Trails lead to the river and follow it for many miles in some sections, but summertime temperatures reach 110 degrees. Jet boats cruise the canyon regularly, with heavy traffic below Pittsburgh Landing.

The Hells Canyon designation was one of the most dramatic examples of the Wild and Scenic Rivers System being used to save a unique resource from otherwise certain damming. National river study status in 1988 for the lower reach below Heller Bar terminated a series of hydroelectric schemes dating to authorized Army Corps plans and to a more recent application by a firm in Connecticut. If built, Asotin Dam would tip remaining anadromous fish runs to extinction. With easy access and gentler water, a lower reach below Heller Bar is a favorite recreational spot demanding a concerted management program. This section was also studied for national river status in the 1970s but was not designated.

Snake River, Henry's Fork, east-central Idaho, designated in 1988; not in the Wild and Scenic Rivers System; 61 mi, Big Springs to Ashton Bridge.
Classification: hydroelectric dam prohibition.
Administered by: Targhee National Forest, P.O. Box 20, Island Park, ID 83429.
Access: Hwy. 20, Big Springs Rd., Harriman State Park, forest roads.
River difficulty: Class I–IV and impassable.
Maps: Targhee National Forest.

Many trout anglers credit the Henry's Fork as the premier dry fly stream in the nation. Trumpeter swans depend on the river in winter, and Upper and Lower Mesa Falls are among the most spectacular in the West.

The upper Henry's Fork is the closest thing the nation possesses to another Yellowstone: it was formed by nearly identical geologic processes with volcanism and calderas. Near the source, Big Springs provides a bountiful flow of crystal-clear water where people casually watch 2 ft long trout (fishing is banned from the spring to Henry's Lake outlet, 1.5 mi downstream). Mirrored waters at Harriman State Park constitute legendary trout water, followed by shorelines of leaning lodgepoles over gentle currents, then waterfalls including the 114 ft Upper Mesa.

A mecca for serious anglers, the river also provides sightseeing stops along roads at Upper and Lower Mesa Falls. A Class I canoe trip of 6 mi runs from the Big Springs boat launch (1 mi below Big Springs) to the Highway 20 bridge all summer long. Another 6 mi section below the bridge includes Coffeepot Rapids, a long Class III drop with frequent obstructions where the Forest Service recommends portaging. Below Lower Mesa Falls, 13 mi of Class II and some Class III water can be run all summer to the Highway 20 bridge near Ashton.

Efforts to designate the river wild and scenic failed under the opposition of Sen. James McClure, but he agreed to ban hydroelectric dams that had been serious threats at the two falls. Controversy abounds over additional hydroelectric dams proposed on tributaries, including the Fall River. Below the Bureau of Reclamation's Island Park Reservoir, water is needed for trumpeter swans but has been cut below levels necessary to keep the river from freezing and eliminating the swans' food source. The Henry's Fork was nearly designated a state scenic river in 1992, and it is being evaluated for wild and scenic eligibility by the Forest Service.

ILLINOIS
1 river, 17.1 mi

Vermilion River, Middle Fork, east-central Illinois, designated in 1989; 17.1 mi, Kinny's Ford to Kickapoo State Park.
Classification: scenic.
Administered by: Illinois Dept. of Conservation, Streams Program, P.O. Box 149, Aledo, IL 61231.
Access: Kinny's Ford east of Collison, Kickapoo State Park north of I-74, Higginsville Bridge east of Collison, Bunker Hill about 1.5 mi south and 3 mi east of Collison.
River difficulty: Class I.
Other information: Larry Rice, "The Middle Fork of the Vermilion," *Canoe* (March 1989).

Considered a highlight of Illinois rivers, the Middle Fork Vermilion is a remnant of the state's prairie heritage. Fourteen endangered and three threatened bird species on the state list are found along the corridor, plus one endangered amphibian, several uncommon mussels, and rare fishes, including the endangered bluebreast darter.

This small tributary to the Wabash River offers clear water, a rich diversity of plant life, and undeveloped shores. Banks are shaded by sycamore, walnut, and silver maple. Vestiges of native prairie grasses and wildflowers survive on bluffs. Most frontage is publicly owned. Scenic easements for 2 mi of frontage were donated to the government by Illinois Power Company.

From March to June, canoeists run a 12.8 mi reach from Kinny's Ford to Kickapoo State Park. This is also a good smallmouth bass stream.

A dam for Danville's water supply was planned and land acquired in the 1970s, but in view of alternate sources and citizen opposition, the plan was dropped, and the Vermilion was designated a state protected river. Interior Secretary Donald Hodel declined to honor Gov. James Thompson's request for national river designation—the only case where an interior secretary has not complied with a governor's request. A second attempt by Governor Thompson and local political support persuaded Interior Secretary Manuel Lujan to designate the river.

KENTUCKY
1 river, 20 mi

See Tennessee, Big South Fork Cumberland River. Not in the Wild and Scenic Rivers System.

LOUISIANA
1 river, 10 mi

Saline Bayou, northwest Louisiana, designated in 1986; 10 mi, Saline Lake to lower boundary of Kisatchie National Forest.
Classification: recreational.
Administered by: Kisatchie National Forest, 2500 Shreveport Hwy., Pineville, LA 71360.
Access: Hwy. 126 bridge, F.R. 513 and 507, Hwy. 156 bridge above Saline Lake.
River difficulty: Class I.
Maps: Kisatchie National Forest.

Saline Bayou was the first southern blackwater river designated in the National Wild and Scenic Rivers System.

Its calm water shaded black by tannic acid in swamps and wetlands, the Saline Bayou hosts abundant animal and bird life and thick vegetation. Wood ducks, pileated woodpeckers, minks, alligators, snakes, and snapping turtles of up to 150 lb can be seen. Over 70 species of fish live here. Forests range from upland pines to cypress tupelo swamp and include water oak, blackgum, ironwood, swamp chestnut, sweetgum, hickory, ash, loblolly pine, post oak, willow, mayhaw, red maple, wild pecan, white oak, American holly, southern magnolia, river birch, and catalpa. One 70 acre area holds nine plant species considered rare in Louisiana. Lower reaches show moss-laden bald cypress.

The waterway is ideal for quiet canoeing and fishing. High flows can be dangerous, and low flows of late summer can involve dragging. The 7.5 mi section from Forest Road 507 to Highway 156 offers the dark, wet, mysterious character many people associate with Louisiana swamps. No motorboats are allowed above the Highway 126 bridge; 25 hp maximum is allowed between Highway 126 and 156; motors are unrestricted below Highway 156. The Cloud Crossing Recreation Area includes camping facilities at Forest Road 513.

MAINE
1 river, 95 mi

Allagash River, north-central Maine, designated in 1970; 95 mi, upper reaches to East Twin Brook.
Classification: wild.
Administered by: Maine Dept. of Conservation, Allagash Wilderness Waterway, P.O. Box 939, Millinocket, ME 04462.
Access: Private roads open to the public to Telos Lake or Umsaskis, originating in Millinocket, Greenville, Ashland, or Alagash Village. Take-out at West Twin Brook or the Saint John River, reached by a road west of Fort Kent.
River difficulty: Class I–III with 1 portage.
Maps: Dept. of Conservation, "Allagash Wilderness Waterway."

Perhaps the finest long wilderness river in the East, the Allagash offers a classic canoe trip through the woods of Maine. The region may be the largest primitive area east of the Mississippi.

Starting with a chain of lakes controlled by unobtrusive dams, the river drops northward through an undeveloped expanse of forest.

A canoe trip of eight days and 92 mi alternates between lakes and current and features a 9 mi whitewater challenge of Class II with some Class III water at Chase Rapids above Umsaskis Lake and a portage of 40 ft high Allagash Falls. Levels permit boating all summer and fall. Ice doesn't break up until mid May, black flies plague people through June, and then canoeists flock to the river until September. Brook trout, togue, and lake whitefish do well. Group size for float trips is limited to 12 people.

Early river conservationists defeated the proposed Cross Rock Dam on the Saint John River, which would have flooded the lower Allagash in the 1950s. The National Park Service recommended an Allagash National Recreation Area in 1960, one of the pilot studies in river conservation. In 1963 the Bureau of Outdoor Recreation issued a report calling for an Allagash National Riverway, predating the National Wild and Scenic Rivers System. The state enacted legislation in 1965 for an Allagash Wilderness Waterway, and in 1970 the river was the first to be included in the Wild and Scenic Rivers System by the secretary of interior at the request of a governor. This was also the first national river to be administered by a state and the first to be added to the system after the original designations of 1968. A Maine bond act approved $1.5 million for land acquisition, matched by the federal government.

MICHIGAN
26 rivers, 624.8 mi

For many Michigan rivers, see *Canoeing Michigan Rivers: A Comprehensive Guide to 45 Rivers* (1986).

Au Sable River, northeast Michigan, designated in 1984; 23 mi, 1 mi below Mio Pond to 1 mi above Alcona Pond.
Classification: scenic.
Administered by: Huron-Manistee National Forest, Mio District, 401 Court St., Mio, MI 48647.
Access: local roads to Mio Dam, Comins Flats, and other sites.
River difficulty: Class I.
Maps: Huron-Manistee National Forest.

A small portion of this 240 mi river—one of the Midwest's finest for trout fishing and canoeing—has been protected.

A mix of woodland and wetlands bordering the river hosts an abundance of plant species and wildlife, including wood ducks, bald eagles, otters, beavers, and minks. After heavy abuse by logging, qualities of the river are returning. Rainbow trout are stocked. Brown and rainbow trout in this section are affected by warm water releases at Mio Dam.

Many people canoe this reach, especially the upper 9 mi to Comins Flats; liveries account for 86 percent of the traffic. Though not as popular as other sections of the Au Sable, this reach is fished and managed for trophy-size trout, and artificial lures are required for 13 mi from Mio to McKinley Bridge.

About 88 percent of the corridor is public land. The Forest Service had recommended 74 mi for designation, but 51 were deleted because of private landowner opposition. The state manages the entire Au Sable and tributaries as a designated natural river with state wild and scenic classification.

Bear Creek, west-central Michigan, designated in 1992; 6.5 mi, Coates
  Hwy. to Manistee River.
Classification: scenic.
Administered by: Huron-Manistee National Forest, 421 S. Mitchell St.,
  Cadillac, MI 49601.
Access: local roads near Brethren.
River difficulty: not normally run.
Maps: Huron-Manistee National Forest.

This is a small tributary to the Manistee River, entering on the north side near the Manistee State Game Area. A fine fishery, the creek is bordered by northern hardwoods and includes good wildlife habitat.

Black River, northern Michigan, designated in 1992; 14 mi, Ottawa National
  Forest boundary to Lake Superior.
Classification: scenic.
Administered by: Ottawa National Forest, 2100 E. Cloverland Dr., Iron-
  wood, MI 49938.
Access: Cty. Rd. 513 parallels part of the river, north of Bessemer.
River difficulty: Class I, II, with unrunnable sections.
Maps: Ottawa National Forest.

This is one of only four national rivers with a designation extending to one of the Great Lakes and the only protected river running to Lake Superior. The Black includes diverse fisheries, old-growth timber, and waterfalls.

Upper sections flow through flat terrain, then drop 500 ft through a gorge with six waterfalls between Copper Peak and Lake Superior. Northern hardwoods and conifers crowd the shores and include old-growth maples, birch, basswood, hemlock, and white pine. Water quality is excellent, colored brown by organic acids from wetlands. Good habitat for waterfowl, eagles, osprey, otters, mink, deer, and bears can be found. Below Rainbow Falls a lake-run anadromous fishery includes trout, coho salmon, chinook salmon, and steelhead, with resident brown trout, brook trout, and walleye above the falls. Fifty-seven percent of the corridor is national forest land.

Fishing throughout the river and kayaking on the upper reaches in springtime are popular. The North Country National Scenic Trail parallels lower reaches; other trails lead to waterfalls. Six recreational sites are developed along the river. The total length of the river is 33 mi, beginning on the northern continental divide in Wisconsin.

Carp River, northern Michigan, designated in 1992; 27.8 mi, upstream of Lake Huron.
Classification: wild, 12.4 mi; scenic, 9.3 mi; recreational, 6.1 mi.
Administered by: Hiawatha National Forest, 2727 N. Lincoln Rd., Escanaba, MI 49829.
Access: Hwy. 123; many forest roads; F.R. 3308 parallels the river in one section; Carp River Campground off F.R. 3445: a Forest Service recreation area at the mouth at Lake Huron; all north of Moran.
River difficulty: Class I in most sections.
Maps: Huron National Forest.
  This is the only national river designated into Lake Huron. Osprey and eagles use the river year round, and the fishery includes brown trout, brook trout, chinook salmon, pink salmon, and steelhead. All but 1 mi of the river flows through public land, and 7.5 mi flow through the Mackinac Wilderness.
  Fishing for salmon and steelhead is popular. Canoeing on gentle water is possible in some sections throughout the summer; swift water runs above McDonald Rapids, and Rock Rapids forms a small waterfall.
  Logging in the early 1900s damaged the river, causing bank erosion and a continuing bedload movement of sand, but restoration work since 1980 has begun to correct some of the problems.

Indian River, northern Michigan, designated in 1992; 51 mi, Hovey Lake to Indian Lake.
Classification: scenic, 12 mi; recreational, 39 mi.
Administered by: Hiawatha National Forest, 2727 N. Lincoln Rd., Escanaba, MI 49829.
Access: F.R. 2257 parallels the river for 5 mi; Cty. Rd. 437 follows the river near Steuben; Hwy. M-94 leads to Indian River Campground; Cty. Rd. 449 crosses the river.
River difficulty: Class I, II, with some unrunnable sections because of shallows.
Maps: Huron National Forest.
  The Indian River is unusual in its mixture of lakes connected by narrow river channels and is considered an excellent example of a lake-and-marsh riverine system. Bald eagles nest here and lake sturgeon—a threatened species in Michigan—spawn in the river.
  The blend of marshlands and river channels in this highly glaciated area offers a wide variety of vegetation and habitat; other sections have steep

banks. Lower reaches are isolated from development and have shallow, mazelike channels. The river produced an excellent trout fishery in the past; restoration work is improving habitat. The brown trout and brook trout fishing is good in upper reaches.

Though the river is not heavily used by canoeists, canoeing is possible in some sections with tight bends and also with open channels and high banks. Below Bar Lake, canoeing is popular, with a put-in at Widewaters Campground. The Brunos Run trail lies near the river.

Manistee River, west-central Michigan, designated in 1992; 26 mi, below Tippy Dam to Hwy. 55 bridge.
Classification: recreational.
Administered by: Huron-Manistee National Forest, 421 S. Mitchell St., Cadillac, MI 49601.
Access: various roads and four public access areas east of Parkdale.
River difficulty: Class I in sections, not often boated.
Maps: Huron-Manistee National Forest.

The Manistee River is an excellent fishing stream for steelhead and salmon that attracts many anglers, but it is heavily affected by flushing flows from an upstream hydroelectric dam. Eagles nest along the river.

With banks as high as 100 ft, the scenic river corridor is heavily wooded by lowland forests of northern white cedar, hemlock, tamarack, and hardwoods. Porous aquifers release groundwater for a reliable flow all year. Along with the spring and fall runs of salmon and steelhead, the river provides habitat for brown trout, bass, and pike. The lower river flows through a state waterfowl refuge. Eighty-six percent of the corridor is public land.

Four public and four private launch areas provide boating and fishing access. The section below Tippy Dam is popular; anadromous fish are concentrated there because they can't get past the dam. The river is lightly used for boating because of fluctuating water levels.

The Tippy hydroelectric dam, just upstream of the designated reach, releases flows that fluctuate as much as 4 vertical ft twice daily—a change that can be seen 10 mi downstream, causes bank erosion, and impacts the resident fishery. Out of this 182 mi long river, 144 mi qualify for wild and scenic river status, and the Forest Service recommended 51 mi.

Ontonagon River, Cisco Branch, northern Michigan, designated in 1992; 37 mi, source at Cisco Lake Dam to Ten-Mile Creek south of Ewen.
Classification: scenic, 27 mi; recreational, 10 mi.
Administered by: Ottawa National Forest, 2100 E. Cloverland Dr., Ironwood, MI 49938.

Access: Cisco Lake Cty. Rd., Hwy. 2, various county and forest roads.
River difficulty: Class I, II in some sections.
Maps: Ottawa National Forest.

Known for its brook trout fishery, the Cisco Branch Ontonagon is one of few national rivers whose corridor is predominantly in private ownership, with only 39 percent as national forest land.

A dam at Cisco Lake—the river's source—controls the stream flow. The small river runs north, drops over several waterfalls including Kakabika and Wolverine, and then enters the South Branch of the Ontonagon. The river corridor provides valuable winter deer range, and northern hardwoods offer habitat for bears, beavers, fishers, mink, and other wildlife.

Anglers fish for native brook trout, and canoeists can run sections from F.R. 6930 north.

Ontonagon River, East Branch, northern Michigan, designated in 1992; 46 mi, source at Spring Lake to Ottawa National Forest boundary.
Classification: wild, 25.5 mi; recreational, 20.5 mi.
Administered by: Ottawa National Forest, 2100 E. Cloverland Dr., Ironwood, MI 49938.
Access: S. Sidnaw Rd.; F.R. 139; Lake Thirteen Rd.; Hwy. 28; F.R. 138, 1100, and 207; all south of Mass City.
River difficulty: not frequently run.
Maps: Ottawa National Forest.

With gorges, rapids, and waterfalls, the East Branch Ontonagon is an excellent fishery and includes bald eagle habitat.

Bordered by wetlands, the channel meanders in upper reaches; lower sections cut through a gorge with rapids and spruce forests. The fishery includes trout, salmon, and steelhead; among the wildlife are osprey, bears, beavers, otters, and other species. National forest land constitutes 75 percent of the corridor. Small dams at Upper Dam Lake, Lower Dam Lake, and the town of Kenton lie within the designated reach.

Fishing for native brook trout, Lake Superior run steelhead, salmon, and brown trout is the most popular recreation along this river. Whitewater canoeists occasionally paddle on lower reaches from Kenton north, especially in springtime when water is high and covers logjams. Campgrounds are found at Sparrow Rapids and Lower Dam Lake.

Ontonagon River, Middle Branch, northern Michigan, designated in 1992; 59.4 mi, source at Crooked Lake to northern boundary of Ottawa National Forest.
Classification: wild, 17.4 mi; scenic, 14 mi; recreational, 28 mi.

Administered by: Ottawa National Forest, 2100 E. Cloverland Dr., Iron-
wood, MI 49938.
Access: many local roads; Hwys. 2, 45, and 28; all south of Mass City.
River difficulty: Class I, II in some sections.
Maps: Ottawa National Forest.

The Middle Branch Ontonagon has an excellent fishery, scenic views
especially during the time of autumn colors, and good summer canoeing.
Four bald eagle nests allow a good opportunity to see this endangered species
from the river.

Though known for its native brook trout fishery, the upper river is affected
by past logging and a resulting bedload movement of sand. Stream habitat
projects have improved upper sections. Brown trout, smallmouth bass, walleye, and muskellunge are found.

Canoeing and fishing are popular on upper segments. Below Agate Falls,
canoeing is blocked by low flows and logjams. Fishing for Lake Superior run
steelhead is popular below Agate Falls.

A dam at Bond Falls results in diversions and lower stream flows. The
public owns only 36 percent of the corridor, making this one of few national
rivers predominantly in private ownership.

Ontonagon River, West Branch, northern Michigan, designated in 1992; 15
mi, Cascade Falls to Victoria Reservoir.
Classification: recreational.
Administered by: Ottawa National Forest, 2100 E. Cloverland Dr., Iron-
wood, MI 49938.
Access: Hwy. 28 and Norwich Road, both east of Bergland.
River difficulty: Class I, II in lower reaches.
Maps: Ottawa National Forest.

The Ontonagon River has one gorge section, a bald eagle nest, and adequate flows in lower reaches for summer canoeing. A dam at the river's
source of Lake Gogebic controls releases and results in low and unpredictable
water levels, though a walleye fishery is able to exist. Eighteen percent of the
corridor is national forest land.

Recreational use is light, with some canoeing possible in lower reaches.
Mediocre fishing owes partly to low summer releases from the Upper Peninsula Power Company dam at Lake Gogebic.

Paint River, northern Michigan, designated in 1992; 6 mi, confluence of
North and South branches to Ottawa National Forest boundary.
Classification: recreational.
Total designated mileage of Paint River system: 51.

Administered by: Ottawa National Forest, 2100 E. Cloverland Dr., Iron-
wood, MI 49938.
Access: Cty. Rd. 137, F.R. 2180 to Block House Campground, F.R. 3485, all
near Gibbs City.
River difficulty: Class I.
Maps: Ottawa National Forest.

The wide, deep Paint River provides for trout fishing and canoeing
throughout the summer. Though this reach is only 6 mi long, the designated
section of the North Branch adjoins the main stem. The river is rated top
quality for brook, brown, and rainbow trout. Wildlife includes bald eagles,
osprey, bears, otters, fishers, and other species. A reliable year-long flow
makes summer canoeing possible.

Paint River, North Branch, northern Michigan, designated in 1992; 17 mi,
source at Mallard Lake to mouth at Paint River.
Classification: recreational.
Administered by: Ottawa National Forest, 2100 E. Cloverland Dr., Iron-
wood, MI 49938.
Access: several forest roads, Cty. Rd. 657, Winslow Lake Rd., all north of
Gibbs City.
River difficulty: not normally run.
Maps: Ottawa National Forest.

Log drives in the past and low flows cause the North Branch Paint to be a
wide, shallow river. Water quality is excellent but low through much of the
year. Three low head dams block the river between Mallard Lake and F.R.
16. Forests include aspen, jack pine, red pine, black spruce, balsam fir, and
northern hardwoods in this corridor that is 74 percent national forest land.
Fishing is good only briefly in the spring.

Paint River, South Branch, northern Michigan, designated in 1992; 28 mi,
source at Paint River Springs to mouth at North Branch Paint River.
Classification: recreational.
Administered by: Ottawa National Forest, 2100 E. Cloverland Dr., Iron-
wood, MI 49938.
Access: Hwy. 2, many forest roads, all west of Gibbs City.
River difficulty: not normally run.
Maps: Ottawa National Forest.

This is one of few rivers in the East designated from source to mouth. A
Michigan Blue Ribbon Trout Stream, the South Branch Paint shows great
resiliency, as it was once used for log drives and had five dams that no longer
impound water.

Upper reaches pass through wet areas of cedar and mixed swamp conifers.

Below F.R. 16 the stream deepens and widens and includes rocky rapids, meadows, and low hills. Many springs feed this excellent native brook trout fishery with year-round flows. Bald eagles, osprey, bears, otters, fishers, and other wildlife live here. National forest land constitutes 68 percent of the corridor.

Fishing is very good. Overhanging vegetation makes canoeing nearly impossible.

Pere Marquette River, west-central Michigan, designated in 1978; 66.4 mi, confluence of Middle and Little South branches near Baldwin to old Hwy. 31 bridge.
Classification: scenic.
Administered by: Huron-Manistee National Forest, 421 S. Mitchell St., Cadillac, MI 49601.
Access: public sites off Hwy. M-37 and U.S. 10.
River difficulty: Class I, II.
Maps: Huron-Manistee National Forest.

One of Michigan's fine fishing streams, the Pere Marquette is known nationwide for large brown trout and steelhead.

Hardwood forests, rolling hills, and lakes surround the swift moving, clear river. Alkaline water, rarely above 70 degrees, with a gravel bottom, defines this as ideal trout habitat. No other major river in lower Michigan flows without any dams.

From Baldwin to the mouth can be canoed, with Rainbow Rapids posing the only possible challenge to beginners. Several launch sites can be used. Steelhead fishing is good from November to April. Fishery managers chose the Pere Marquette as one of two Michigan rivers for introduction of Atlantic salmon, which migrate up the river in September. A number of campgrounds are sited along the shores.

Fifty million people live within a day's drive and cause intense recreational and developmental pressures along the river. Designation allowed for the construction of a dam or electric barrier near the river's mouth to control the upriver movement of lamprey eels, which have invaded through the Saint Lawrence Seaway and prey on sport fish.

Pine River, west-central Michigan, designated in 1992; 25 mi, Lincoln Bridge and downstream.
Classification: scenic.
Administered by: Huron-Manistee National Forest, 421 S. Mitchell St., Cadillac, MI 49601.
Access: Hwy. 37, many local roads east of Wellston.

River difficulty: Class I, II in some sections.
Maps: Huron-Manistee National Forest.

This fine trout stream is one of the Midwest's most popular canoeing rivers, easily accessible from Detroit, Grand Rapids, and other cities.

Swift currents and clear waters rush beneath banks as high as 100 ft, and porous aquifers provide a source of water year round. Cold water temperatures, a sand and gravel bottom, and shoreline vegetation make the Pine River an excellent fishery for rainbow, brown, and brook trout, though a bedload movement of sand harms the fishery by filling in pools and covering spawning beds. The river is not heavily fished, perhaps due to canoeing activity. The corridor is forested by oaks, other hardwoods, and conifers. Ninety percent of the corridor is publicly owned.

This is probably the most canoed river in Michigan, resulting in some controls to limit the number of boaters. Camping is so popular that the Forest Service has restricted it within one-quarter of a mile from the water. Three campgrounds are sited along the river.

The Forest Service recommended designation of 38 mi of the 50 mi long river. If Tippy Dam (downstream on the Manistee River) and Stronach Dam were removed, the river would be opened to anadromous coho salmon, chinook salmon, and steelhead.

Presque Isle River, northern Michigan, designated in 1992; 23 mi, source at confluence of East and West branches to Minnewawa Falls.
Classification: scenic, 6 mi; recreational, 17 mi.
Total designated mileage of Presque Isle River system: 57.
Administered by: Ottawa National Forest, 2100 E. Cloverland Dr., Ironwood, MI 49938.
Access: Hwy. 64, Hwy. 2, Hwy. 28 at Tula, many local roads.
River difficulty: Class I–IV with waterfalls.
Maps: Ottawa National Forest.

In a rugged gorge with waterfalls and rapids, the Presque Isle River offers perhaps the most challenging whitewater paddling in Michigan, if not the Midwest. *Canoe* magazine in July 1981 listed the Presque Isle among a group of rivers "that define the outer edge of contemporary white water paddling."

The river begins at the confluence of the East and West branches with a gorgelike setting that is distinctive above Hwy. 28. White oak, burr oak, and silver maple, uncommon on the Upper Peninsula of Michigan, grow along the river. A heron rookery and eagle nest can be seen. Forty-five percent of the corridor is national forest land. A trophy brook trout fishery can be found north of Hwy. 2, primarily fished in the springtime at deep holes and spring-fed reaches.

Canoeists and kayakers paddle most reaches in the spring and fall, but low water prevents boating between Hwy. 2 and M-28 during summer.

Presque Isle River, East Branch, northern Michigan, designated in 1992; 14 mi, Ottawa National Forest boundary to mouth at Presque Isle River.
Classification: recreational.
Access: F.R. 322 leads to a canoe-launching site; other forest roads south of Marenisco.
River difficulty: Class I, not often run.
Maps: Ottawa National Forest.

The East Branch Presque Isle is a narrow, slow-moving stream that meanders over a flat plain, has excellent water quality, and provides a cold- and warm-water fishery. Red pine plantations border the river in upper reaches with alder and hardwoods below. Ninety percent of the corridor is national forest land, only lightly used for recreation.

Presque Isle River, South Branch, northern Michigan, designated in 1992; 7 mi, from Ottawa National Forest boundary to mouth at Presque Isle River.
Classification: recreational.
Access: Hwy. 64, the Mallard canoe landing off F.R. 8100.
River difficulty: Class I.
Maps: Ottawa National Forest.

A slow-moving stream and a good warm-water fishery for northern pike, the South Branch Presque Isle also offers habitat for waterfowl, otters, and muskrats. An eagle nest is located near the mouth. Ninety-three percent of the corridor is national forest land.

The river is lightly used for recreation, including some fishing, canoeing, and duck hunting. Lower reaches remain canoeable during summer.

Presque Isle River, West Branch, northern Michigan, designated in 1992; 13 mi, Ottawa National Forest boundary to mouth at Presque Isle River.
Classification: scenic.
Access: canoe landings at Hwy. 8100 and F.R. 8300, Hwy. 64, F.R. 83, all west of Marenisco.
Maps: Ottawa National Forest.

Flowing slowly through lowland terrain and wetlands, the West Branch Presque Isle provides good habitat for eagles, black terns, waterfowl, marsh birds, otters, and muskrats. A dam was built for the maintenance of a wetlands area known as the Presque Isle River Flooding near Hwy. 64. Large brook trout may be seen, but warm-water fish predominate. Ninety-one percent of the corridor is national forest land.

Duck hunters and trappers come here. Some fishing is done, with small amounts of canoeing in lower, spring-fed reaches.

Sturgeon River, Hiawatha National Forest, northern Michigan, designated in 1992; 43.9 mi, above Lake Michigan.
Classification: scenic, 21.7 mi; recreational, 22.2 mi.
Administered by: Hiawatha National Forest, 2727 N. Lincoln Rd., Escanaba, MI 49829.
Access: Cty. Rd. 497 parallels the river from the mouth to Hwy. 2; Hwy. 2; F.R. 13; other local roads; all north of Nahma.
River difficulty: Class I.
Maps: Hiawatha National Forest.

The Sturgeon is one of only two rivers designated to its mouth at Lake Michigan and one of only four extending to the Great Lakes. With a mild microclimate caused by the river, the riparian zone features a southern flood plain forest with species atypical to the area.

The slow-moving river has many meanders and sloughs, with up to 18 oxbows per mi. Marshes, conifer swamps, and meadows border the waterway. One pair of eagles nests here, along with osprey. Bobcats, bears, fishers, martens, beavers, otters, and other wildlife thrive. Archaeological sites are plentiful.

The Flowing Well Campground lies north of Hwy. 2. Fishing is poor to good for brown trout, brook trout, and northern pike. Salmon and steelhead spawn in fall and spring. Canoeists can paddle upper reaches only in spring. The lower 10 mi grow deep and swift and can be boated from May to November, though several portages may be necessary.

Sturgeon River, Ottawa National Forest, northern Michigan, designated in 1992; 25 mi.
Classification: wild, 16.5 mi; scenic, 8.5 mi.
Administered by: Ottawa National Forest, 2100 E. Cloverland Dr., Ironwood, MI 49938.
Access: F.R. 2200, 2270, both southwest of Baraga.
River difficulty: Class I, II, and possibly greater.
Maps: Ottawa National Forest.

Entirely separate from the Sturgeon River in Hiawatha National Forest, this stream flows through a gorge with depths of 200–300 ft. Sturgeon Falls lies in a protected wilderness area. A natural area with virgin balsam fir and other trees can be seen along the upper river. Habitat for the state-endangered lake sturgeon occurs below Prickett Dam where the water meanders slowly through wetlands. Steelhead run from the mouth to Prickett Dam; trophy brook trout are found above the dam. The river and its old-growth forests form habitat for bald eagles, otters, bears, and other wildlife. Seventy-four percent of the corridor is national forest land.

Trails lead to Sturgeon Falls, and a short section of the North Country Trail follows the northern bank. Recreational use remains light, with some fishing and with springtime whitewater canoeing below the Sturgeon River Campground.

Prickett Dam, operated by the Upper Peninsula Power Company, lies within the designated reaches of this 98 mi long river and causes erratic flows.

Tahquamenon River, East Branch, northern Michigan, designated in 1992; 13.2 mi, source to Hiawatha National Forest boundary.
Classification: wild, 3.2 mi; recreational, 10 mi.
Administered by: Hiawatha National Forest, 2727 N. Lincoln Rd., Escanaba, MI 49829.
Access: F.R. 3356, Hwy. 28 east of Strongs Corners, Hwy. 123, Salt Point Rd., old hatchery site at Echerman.
River difficulty: not normally run.
Maps: Hiawatha National Forest.

The East Branch Tahquamenon ranks as one of the finest brook trout fisheries in the Upper Peninsula. National forest land constitutes 80 percent of the corridor. Fishing for brook trout is popular near the towns of Strongs and Eckerman.

The Nationwide Rivers Inventory recommended 54 mi of the river for national river study; most of this mileage involved private land and was avoided in the designation. Omitted sections include Upper and Lower Falls of the Tahquamenon within Tahquamenon State Park, listed as a "potential" hydropower site by the Federal Energy Regulatory Commission.

Whitefish River, northern Michigan, designated in 1992; 11.1 mi, confluence of East and West branches to Lake Michigan.
Classification: scenic, 9 mi; recreational, 2.1 mi.
Designated tributaries:
Whitefish River, East Branch, 15 mi, Cty. Rd. 003 to mouth at Whitefish River, scenic classification.
Whitefish River, West Branch, 7.5 mi, Cty. Rd. 444 to mouth at Whitefish River, scenic classification.
Total designated mileage in Whitefish River system: 33.6.
Administered by: Hiawatha National Forest, 2727 N. Lincoln Rd., Escanaba, MI 49829.

Access: Hwys. 2, 41, both north of Rapid River.
River difficulty: Class I, II in some reaches.

One of only two rivers designated to its mouth in Lake Michigan, the Whitefish supports one of the better runs of chinook salmon and steelhead in the Upper Peninsula.

The river supports a walleye run in spring, and the East and West branches sustain good populations of brook trout. The West Branch offers the best steelhead spawning grounds. A pair of bald eagles nests here, and habitat remains good for otters, mink, and other species of wildlife, while the river bottom provides a critical wintering area for deer. Important archaeological sites lie at the mouth of the river on private land. Like many of the designated Michigan rivers, the Whitefish has partially recovered from damaging log drives at the turn of the century.

Anglers come here for a variety of species and in springtime canoeists enjoy sections with some whitewater, then slow current in lower reaches. Water flows more swiftly in the East and West branches, which are not normally boated.

Yellow Dog River, northern Michigan, designated in 1992; 4 mi, Bulldog Lake Dam to Ottawa National Forest boundary.
Classification: wild.
Administered by: Ottawa National Forest, 2100 E. Cloverland Dr., Iron-wood, MI 49938.
Access: forest roads leading to the McCormick Wilderness southwest of Big Bay.
River difficulty: not normally run.
Maps: Ottawa National Forest.

One of few eastern rivers classified wild, this segment of the 28 mi long Yellow Dog River flows within the McCormick Wilderness and the McCormick Research Natural Area. Discounting tributaries of designated streams, this ranks as the shortest river in the wild and scenic system.

The upper reach flows through wetlands, then drops 240 ft over cascades. Old-growth forests include hemlock, sugar maple, northern red oak, and other species. The river provides a good brook trout fishery, and moose have been reintroduced. An upstream dam at Bulldog Lake, operated by the Forest Service, controls river flows. Recreational use is low but includes hiking at East Falls.

MINNESOTA
1 river, 155 mi of the Saint Croix River shared with Wisconsin

MISSISSIPPI
1 river, 21 mi

Black Creek, southeast Mississippi, designated in 1986; 21 mi, Moody's Landing on Hwy. 301 (5 mi downstream from Brooklyn), to Fairley Bridge Landing on Hwy. 318.
Classification: Scenic.
Administered by: DeSoto National Forest, 100 W. Capitol St., Jackson, MS 36269.
Access: Big Creek Landing at Hwy. 335-E west of Brooklyn (above the designated reach), Moody's Landing on Hwy. 301, Janice Landing on Hwy. 29, Cypress Creek Landing on Hwy. 305-B, and Fairley Bridge Landing on Hwy. 318 northwest of Wiggins.
River difficulty: Class I.
Maps: DeSoto National Forest.

With deep blackwater and wide, white sand bars, Black Creek is considered one of the most scenic streams in Mississippi. The waterway meanders through the coastal plain, a gently rolling terrain of loblolly, longleaf, and slash pine forest with rich bottomlands of southern hardwoods: sweetgum, willow oak, bald cypress, sweetbay, and red maple. Almost totally denuded early in this century, the area has recovered with second-growth forest. The creek winds through the 5,052 acre Black Creek Wilderness between Janice Landing and Cypress Creek.

The creek is popular for canoeing, fishing, and backpacking in a rare wilderness setting of the Deep South. A canoe trip of 40 mi is possible with quiet water and a current of 1 mi per hour except after heavy rains, when the level can rise rapidly to treacherous levels, submerging logs and snags. All five of the access areas have picnic sites and boat-launching facilities. The Black Creek National Trail extends 40 mi from Big Creek Landing to Fairley Bridge Landing, 10 mi of it in the Black Creek Wilderness.

MISSOURI
3 rivers, 178.4 mi, including 2 rivers and 134 mi not in the
Wild and Scenic Rivers System

Current River, southeast Missouri, designated in 1964; 94 mi, Montauk State Park at Hwy. 119 to Hawes Campground (east of Grandin) or to Ripley County line.

Classification: Ozark National Scenic Riverways (134 mi including Jacks Fork).

Administered by: NPS, Ozark National Scenic Riverways, P.O. Box 490, Van Buren, MO 63965.

Access: Hwys. 60, 19, 106, and many park access areas.

River difficulty: Class I, II.

Maps: NPS, "Ozark Riverways."

Other information: Tom Kennon, *Ozark Whitewater* (1989).

With protection predating the National Wild and Scenic Rivers System, the Current and Jacks Fork offer some of the nation's finer gentle water canoeing with fascinating springs and caves.

Cutting narrow passages through limestone bluffs, the river is lucidly clear with riffles, expansive gravel bars, and densely wooded flood plains. Springs feeding the Current are among the largest in the United States: one is 300 ft deep, another discharges 270 million gallons a day. More than 100 caves—some of them immense—drop into dark depths of the karst topography. Many archaeological sites reflect an ancient way of life. The plant life and wildlife are the most diverse in the state. Smallmouth bass and rock bass are the favorite game fish, while the upper river boasts a trophy trout fishery. An amazing 26 species of snakes live here.

This is one of the most canoed rivers in the nation, with 300,000 people a year on the Current and Jacks Fork. The upper river has faster water and more use than lower sections. Steady spring flows allow canoeing all year. People fishing often prefer John boats and use the river throughout. Swimming, tubing, and hiking are also popular activities.

The national scenic riverways designation resulted from a wish to protect the rivers and riparian land but to also allow hunting. The end result was essentially an elongated national park centered on the rivers, and the government acquired private frontage. The riverways preceded the National Wild and Scenic Rivers System by four years.

Eleven Point River, southeast Missouri, designated in 1968; 44.4 mi, Thomasville to Hwy. 142.

Classification: scenic.

Administered by: Mark Twain National Forest, 401 Fairgrounds Rd., Rolla, MO 65401.

Access: Hwys. 99 at Thomasville, 19 at Greer, 160 at Riverton, and 142.

River difficulty: Class I, II.

Maps: Mark Twain National Forest.

Distinguished among the first wild and scenic rivers, the Eleven Point is an outstanding canoeing stream with some of the nation's largest springs.

Flowing through a landscape of rolling hills and karst topography with cliffs 300 ft high, the river is fed by over 30 springs. Greer Spring, the second largest in Missouri, more than doubles the flow of the river. Few buildings or developments are seen along the entire reach, half of which is in public ownership. Bald eagles and osprey winter here. Archaeological sites include the Pigman Mound, an outstanding mound site.

Canoeists can begin as high as Thomasville, though midsummer flows may be too low until reaching Greer Spring near Highway 19, followed by a 19 mi float to Highway 160, heavily used in summer. Campsites at access areas and on gravel bars are plentiful and spaced out over the reach. Class II rapids are found at Mary Decker and Halls Bay. Fishing for stocked trout is popular; a trophy trout area lies down river from Greer for 5 mi.

The designation stemmed from opposition to a proposed Army Corps dam that would have flooded 20 mi of river. Designated early in the history of the National Wild and Scenic Rivers System, this is one of few rivers where any land was condemned.

Jacks Fork River, southeast Missouri, designated in 1964; not in the Wild
  and Scenic Rivers System; 40 mi, 3 mi above Hwy. 17 to mouth at the
  Current River.
Classification: Ozark National Scenic Riverways.
Access: Hwys. 17, E, 19, V, and NPS access areas.
River difficulty: Class I, II.
Maps: NPS, "Ozark Riverways."
The Jacks Fork, a tributary to the Current River, offers splendid scenery of natural Ozark landscapes from a small, clear, twisting river.

Caves, dolomite bluffs, sandbars, and miniature rapids highlight this exquisite river. Popular for canoeing and fishing, this river can be combined for paddling trips with the lower Current, for a voyage of nearly 100 mi, most of it through public land.

MONTANA
4 rivers, 368 mi

For other information on Montana rivers, see Hank Fischer, *The Floater's Guide to Montana* (1986).

Flathead River, Middle Fork, northwest Montana, designated in 1976; 101
  mi, source at Trail Creek to mouth at North Fork confluence.
Classification: wild, 46.8 mi; recreational, 54.2 mi.
Access: airplane to Schaefer Meadows; Hwy. 2 parallels the middle river from
  Bear Creek to West Glacier; Blankenship Bridge at the mouth.

River difficulty: Class II–IV.
Maps: Flathead National Forest.
Other information: USFS, *Three Forks of the Flathead River.*

Sometimes called Montana's wildest river, the Middle Fork Flathead combines exceptional Rocky Mountain wilderness with difficult rapids, pristine water quality, wildlife, and a fine trout fishery. This is the fourth longest river protected from source to mouth.

Beginning between the glaciated peaks of the Bob Marshall Wilderness, the Middle Fork plunges for 50 mi through the Great Bear Wilderness with cliff faces, boulder-riddled rapids, and prime grizzly bear habitat. Highway 2 and the Burlington-Northern Railroad parallel middle sections, also the border of Glacier National Park. Critical to one of the larger undisturbed ecosystems in the temperate zones of the earth, the Middle Fork watershed is wilderness habitat for many wildlife species. The endangered Montana west slope cutthroat lives here, and kokanee spawn in the river. At Bear Creek, mountain goats congregate on cliffs; this is the only place where goats can regularly be seen along a large river.

The upper river can be run only by packing or flying to Schaefer Meadows, beginning a 25 mi Class III and IV wilderness trip from June to mid July. Highway 2 then follows the river for 35 mi to West Glacier, offering a variety of Class II and III reaches. Grizzly bears might be seen throughout. A half day of Class I and II water drops from West Glacier to Blankenship Bridge. The Middle Fork fishery is good, reached by road, trail, or raft. Trails reaching to headwater sections above Schaefer Meadows make the Middle Fork one of the premier backpacking rivers.

It was at the Spruce Park dam site, above Big Creek, that Frank and John Craighead conceived the idea of a national system of wild and scenic rivers.

Flathead River, North Fork, northwest Montana, designated in 1976; 58 mi, Canadian border to mouth at the South Fork Flathead confluence.
Classification: scenic, 40.5 mi; recreational, 17.5 mi.
Administered by: Flathead National Forest, P.O. Box 147, Kalispell, MT 59901.
Access: gravel Polebridge Rd. parallels the river.
River difficulty: Class II, III.
Maps: Flathead National Forest.
Other information: USFS, *Three Forks of the Flathead River.*

A superb canoeing river of extraordinary beauty, the North Fork of the Flathead has some of the clearest water and most brilliantly colored river rocks anywhere. This reach displays the Northern Rockies at their finest.

The river riffles past nearly untouched shorelines with spacious gravel bars, then swirls into green pools. Groves of pine and cottonwood shade the shores, and views extend to the peaks of Glacier National Park, whose western boundary is the river. The route is scarcely affected by the gravel road on the west side, making a wild river experience possible where access in fact exists. The area offers rich wildlife habitat for moose, cougars, otters, and bald eagles. Visitors should take precautions for grizzly bears, especially on the east shore. Being a glacial stream and lacking nutrients, the fishery is not inordinately productive, though cutthroat trout populate many pools. Dolly Varden, once plentiful in Montana, are found in substantial numbers only in the Flathead basin and may qualify as an endangered species. The Montana west slope cutthroat, living here, is listed as endangered. Kokanee salmon migrate from Flathead Lake to spawn in the river.

Boaters can run from the Canadian border early in the summer, and at lower flows from Ford River. Other access is at Polebridge, Big Creek, and Glacier Rim, with a take-out at Blankenship Bridge. To Polebridge, the river is fast and logjams are a possibility. From there to Big Creek is the easiest Class II float. Big Creek to Glacier Rim involves the Class III Fool Hen Rapids above Canyon Creek.

The Glacier View and Smoky Range dam sites were important controversies in the 1940s and 1950s and marked some early successes in river conservation. Coal deposits in Canada's headwaters linger as perennial threats to the Flathead's pellucid water quality, while oil and gas drilling in the Flathead National Forest poses threats even closer to the river. Efforts to improve and pave the road for tourism and logging have thus far been defeated by landowners and conservationists. About 87 percent of the Flathead River forks pass through public land.

Flathead River, South Fork, northwest Montana, designated in 1976; 60 mi, source at Youngs Creek to Hungry Horse Reservoir.
Classification: wild, 51.2 mi; recreational, 8.8 mi.
Access: a gravel road along Hungry Horse Reservoir continues upriver beyond the reservoir for 10 mi to Cedar Flats.
River difficulty: Class IV.
Maps: Flathead National Forest.
Other information: USFS, *Three Forks of the Flathead River.*

With the elephantine exception of Hungry Horse Reservoir at the river's lower end, the South Fork of the Flathead is one of Montana's most pristine rivers, winding through an unroaded valley of 45 mi, all but about 17 mi of it in the Bob Marshall Wilderness.

The remarkably wild shores of untouched forests, mountains, and gorges of the Northern Rockies flow over green, red, black, and white gravels and through one cleft that can be stepped across. Another gorge is incised 150 ft deep in bedrock. The river feeds an excellent cutthroat trout fishery, and grizzly bears roam the valley.

In early summer, rafters pack gear for 27 mi on foot or horseback via Holland Lake and Gordon Creek to Big Prairie, though the upper river can be too low by July. The run includes a possible portage, logjams, and Class IV rapids. A road-accessible 10 mi float can be taken from Cedar Flats to the reservoir. The South Fork offers good fishing and excellent backpacking.

Hungry Horse Dam, built before an effective river conservation movement was under way, buried what some people considered to be the finest of all the Flathead drainage.

Missouri River, north-central Montana, designated in 1976 (see also Nebraska, Missouri River); 149 mi, Fort Benton to Hwy. 191 (Fred Robinson Bridge).
Classification: wild, 63.5 mi; scenic, 25.5 mi; recreational, 60 mi.
Administered by: BLM, Lewistown District, Airport Rd., Lewistown, MT 59457.
Access: Fort Benton, Coal Banks Landing east of Virgelle, Judith Landing northwest of Winifred, McClelland Ferry north of Winifred, Hwy. 191.
River difficulty: Class I.
Maps: BLM, Lewistown District.

This one section of the 2,500 mi long Missouri—one of the most important routes of western expansion in the nation—still exists much as it did when Lewis and Clark navigated it in 1804. Gentle water, undeveloped shorelines, and the historic sites of Lewis and Clark campsites make "Big Muddy" a unique member of the national rivers system. This is the fourth longest national river outside Alaska.

Private lands and low hills border the upper 42 mi from Fort Benton to Coal Banks Landing. Isolated bends with white or tan cliffs, bizarre rock formations, and cottonwood groves extend for the next 46 mi, followed by the Missouri breaks—a maze of ravines and sharply eroded badlands. Below Cow Island the valley broadens with cottonwood stands. The river is a rare example of remaining prairie wildness and has a heritage of exploration, fur traders, steamboats, and settlement. This reach is the foremost part of the Lewis and Clark National Historic Trail and is intersected by the Nez Perce National Historic Trail at Cow Island. The river is home to 49 species of fish and the largest of only 6 remaining populations of paddlefish in the United States.

Runnable from mid spring through mid fall, the Missouri receives heavy use by canoeists—3,000 people a year. Trips of one to ten days are taken on these wide waters that have no major rapids but do have heavy headwinds that can produce breaking waves. Motorboats are allowed but are restricted from extended upriver travel and are subject to a "no whitewater wake" requirement.

Most other reaches of the Missouri have been dammed, as the Army Corps proposed to do in this section. The Missouri was one of four prototype studies in the early 1960s leading to the National Wild and Scenic Rivers System. The National Park Service had first proposed a Lewis and Clark National Wilderness Waterway, and in 1968 the Bureau of Outdoor Recreation proposed a Missouri Breaks National River. Even after designation, cattle overran much of the protected reach in 1990, denuding and trampling native plant life, dominating campsites, and virtually eliminating the succession of the picturesque cottonwood forests, vital to the whole riparian ecosystem. The legislation provides that grazing be allowed to continue, but management plans dictate that livestock be fenced at recreation areas. Recent efforts have been made by the Bureau of Land Management to control the cattle.

NEBRASKA
2 rivers, 3 rivers and tributaries, 208 mi, including 98 mi
shared with South Dakota

Missouri River, two sections: upper reach in northeast Nebraska, designated
in 1991; lower reach designated in 1978. Both sections are shared with
South Dakota (see also Montana, Missouri River). Upper reach: 39 mi,
Fort Randall Dam to Lewis and Clark Reservoir; lower reach: 59 mi,
Gavins Point Dam near Yankton, South Dakota, to Ponca State Park.
Classification: recreational.
Total mileage: 98.
Administered by: NPS, Niobrara/Missouri National Scenic Riverways,
O'Neill, NE 68763.
Access: upper reach, Hwy. 14 north of Verdigre, Ridge Rd. northwest of
Verdel; lower reach, Gavins Point Dam, Hwy. 81, Cedar County Park
north of Saint Helena, Cedar County access north of Obert, recreation
sites near Vermilion and south of Burbank, Ponca State Park.
River difficulty: Class I.
Maps: NPS, "The Missouri National Recreation River."
One of the largest national rivers in volume of flow, these sections of the
Missouri are among few that remain undammed and were the historic route
of Lewis and Clark. Only one-third of this river remains unchannelized and
undammed.

The upper reach is one of few sections of this once vast ecosystem that remains in a relatively natural state. Wide, meandering channels include many shifting sandbars, islands, and sloughs. Sandbar, backwater, and marsh habitats found here are rare and threatened in the Missouri River system. The tallgrass prairie is interrupted by rich riparian vegetation, including galleries of cottonwoods extending 1 mi from the river in some places. The rare pallid sturgeon, blue sucker, sicklefish chub, and paddlefish may survive, and the endangered whooping crane, interior least tern, and peregrine falcon live here. Just downstream is 1 of the 2 largest populations of wintering bald eagles in the lower 48 states. Many historic sites can be found, including five campsites of Lewis and Clark, earthlodge sites covering up to 400 acres and dating from A.D. 1500–1650, burial mounds as old as A.D. 1, and a pioneer cabin. Recreation includes canoeing, other boating, fishing, hunting, and camping at Niobrara State Park.

Separated from the upper reach by a reservoir, the lower reach passes broadly through farmland and ranchland and past several bluffs, many islands, and some surviving riparian plant communities. Though the banks have been stabilized, the river is used for canoeing, riverside camping, and fishing. This case is unusual in being a private-land river designated without an official river study. The National Park Service entered into a cooperative agreement with the Army Corps of Engineers because it already had a presence on the river. The designation authorized structural bank stabilization work by the corps in return for donations of protective easements, but the corps has constructed no new stabilization structures since the designation. A revised management plan was being prepared in 1992.

Niobrara River, northern Nebraska, designated in 1991; 95 mi in 3 segments: 40 mi from Borman Bridge just south of Valentine to Chimney Creek, scenic classification; 30 mi from Rock Creek to Hwy. 137 bridge, scenic; 25 mi from the western boundary of Knox County to the mouth at the Missouri River, recreational.

Classification: scenic, 70 mi; recreational, 25 mi.

Designated tributaries: Verdigre Creek, 15 mi, north boundary of Verdigre to mouth at Niobrara River, recreational.

Total mileage: 110.

Administered by: NPS, Niobrara/Missouri National Scenic Riverways, P.O. Box 591, O'Neill, NE 68763.

Access: Fort Niobrara National Wildlife Refuge, Cornell Bridge and several other bridges east of Valentine, and other sites.

River difficulty: Class I with several short portages.

Other information: Stephen LeGreca, *Canoer's Guide: The Niobrara River, Cornell Dam to Norden Bridge* (1989).

One of only two national rivers in the Great Plains, the Niobrara is at a biological crossroads where five ecological zones host a wide diversity of plant, animal, and bird life.

The 400 mi long river serves as a major resting site on the midcontinent migratory flyway, and the upper portion of the designated reach is a popular canoeing river. The 67 ft high Smith Falls, formed by a tributary as it drops from bluffs to the Niobrara's flood plain, is Nebraska's highest.

This reach was imminently threatened by the Norden Dam and diversion project of the O'Neill Unit, fought in the 1970s and narrowly defeated, then deauthorized during the Carter administration. The Nature Conservancy then bought much of the land in the 19 mi reach that would have been impounded. Most riparian land remains in farms, the only federal ownership being the Fort Niobrara National Wildlife Refuge. Since it lacked long-term protection, conservationists pursued national river designation, which was enacted after several years of opposition by landowners. The National Park Service's management plan for this sensitive case of a private-land river will be an important step in either gaining support or facing protests of local residents.

The legislation omitted a 6 mi segment between the upper two reaches where a water project is proposed. In a unique arrangement, that segment will be designated in five years if funds are not authorized and appropriated for the project.

The 1991 legislation also called for study of a Niobrara–Buffalo Prairie National Park covering much of the reach designated as a scenic river, plus study of a national recreation area of the lower recreational-designated section and including the protected reach of the Missouri River below Fort Randall Dam.

NEW HAMPSHIRE
1 river, 4 rivers and tributaries, 14.5 mi

Wildcat River, central New Hampshire, designated in 1988; 9 mi, source to Ellis River.
Classification: scenic, 8 mi; recreational, 1 mi.
Designated tributaries:
    Bog Brook, 1.5 mi, scenic classification.
    Great Brook, Whitney's Pond Bridge to mouth, 1 mi, scenic.
    Wildcat Brook, 3 mi, scenic.
Total mileage: 14.5.
Administered by: White Mountain National Forest, 714 N. Main St., Laconia, NH 03247.

Access: Hwy. 16B, F.R. 233 near Jackson.
River difficulty: unrunnable.
Maps: White Mountain National Forest.

After flowing from the White Mountain National Forest, this small waterway plunges over a waterfall and series of ledges for 165 ft of drop—a centerpiece of the picturesque New England town of Jackson.

The Wildcat is one of the smallest rivers protected in the national rivers system, tumbling out of the White Mountains and over waterfalls. The river in Jackson is visited by residents daily and by thousands of tourists each year. Trails for hiking and skiing lead to the falls and the upper river, stocked with brook trout.

The designation resulted because a power company applied for a dam, diversion, and power plant at Jackson Falls. Steadfast local opposition led to interest in national river designation. At this stream the Park Service pioneered a new planning approach for river protection, encouraging full public participation at every step (see chapter 2). The river is uniquely administered by the Forest Service through a cooperative agreement with the town of Jackson.

NEW JERSEY
1 river, 35 mi of the Delaware River, shared with Pennsylvania

NEW MEXICO
5 rivers, 108.9 mi

Jemez River, East Fork, north-central New Mexico, designated in 1990; 11 mi, national forest boundary to Rio San Antonio.
Classification: wild, 4 mi; scenic, 5 mi; recreational, 2 mi.
Administered by: Santa Fe National Forest, Pinon Bldg., P.O. Box 1689, Santa Fe, NM 87504.
Access: Hwy. 4 at three crossings.
River difficulty: not run.
Maps: Santa Fe National Forest.

The East Fork Jemez originates in the Valles Caldera, which formed the Jemez Mountain complex, and then flows past the Valles Rhyolite cliffs and through green or golden meadows. Here are the southernmost Canadian dogwoods and the Jemez salamander, which is found only in the Jemez Mountains. The endangered peregrine falcon feeds in the canyon.

The river is less than a two hour drive from Albuquerque and Santa Fe and forms the heart of a popular recreation area in the Jemez Mountains. The canyon is used for fishing, swimming, hiking, rock climbing, and camping, with Las Conchas Campground located along the waterfront.

Pecos River, north-central New Mexico, designated in 1990; 20.5 mi, source to Terrerro.
Classification: wild, 13.5 mi; recreational, 7 mi.
Administered by: Santa Fe National Forest, Pinon Bldg., P.O. Box 1689, Santa Fe, NM 87504.
Access: Hwy. 63 from Terrerro north to the Pecos Wilderness boundary.
River difficulty: not run.
Maps: Santa Fe National Forest.

This uppermost reach of a historic river flows as a small stream from the Pecos Wilderness and through granite canyons, over a waterfall, and around scenic meadows surrounded by forests of spruce and aspen. It is one of New Mexico's most popular trout-fishing streams, also popular for hiking and hunting.

For much of its remaining 750 mi course the Pecos is dammed, totally diverted, and polluted with pesticides, farm waste, sewage, and oil.

Red River, north-central New Mexico, designated in 1968; 4 mi above the confluence with the Rio Grande.
Classification: wild.

See Rio Grande.

Rio Chama, north-central New Mexico, designated in 1988; 24.6 mi, El Vado Dam to Abiquiu Reservoir.
Classification: wild, 21.5 mi; scenic, 3.1 mi.
Administered by: BLM, 224 Cruz Alta Rd., Taos, NM 87571; Santa Fe National Forest, Pinon Bldg., P.O. Box 1689, Santa Fe, NM 87504.
Access: El Vado, west of Hwy. 84; Hwy. 96 west of Abiquiu.
River difficulty: Class II, III.
Maps: USGS.

A remote section of river through a canyon of red rock and pine forests, the Rio Chama is considered New Mexico's finest wilderness boating.

A gorge several hundred feet deep begins below El Vado Dam, carving through undulated mesas to a canyon 1,400 ft deep. Conifer forests cover half the area, in contrast with rock strata of red, white, and yellow. Wildlife include deer, bears, cougars, elk, turkeys, and bald eagles. Rainbow and brown trout thrive below the dam. Careful hikers may find historic homesteads and Indian ruins in the canyon and on mesas. Most of the land is publicly owned.

The entire reach offers whitewater without major hazards, runnable in the spring and on some summer weekends with dam releases. Fishing, hunting, and hiking are popular. This is one of the most manipulated rivers in terms of dam controls; controlled summer releases are made from El Vado Dam above, and there is periodic flooding of the lower 2 mi by Abiquiu Dam.

Rio Grande, north-central New Mexico, designated in 1968 (see also Texas, Rio Grande); 48.8 mi, Colorado–New Mexico border to Taos Junction Bridge.
Classification: wild, 47.8 mi; recreational, 1 mi.
Administered by: BLM, 224 Cruz Alta Rd., Taos, NM 87571; Carson National Forest, P.O. Box 558, Taos, NM 87571.
Access: Hwy. 378 west of Questa, Hwys. 577 west of Arroyo Hondo and 570 south of Taos.
River difficulty: Class II–V with an unrunnable waterfalls.
Other information: Doug Wheat, *The Floater's Guide to Colorado* (1983); BLM, *Rio Grande Wild River* (brochure).

One of the original national wild and scenic rivers, the lower 16 mi of the Rio Grande's designated reach churn in big rapids through a radically incised canyon called the Lower Box.

The gorge, a 200 ft incision in volcanic rock beginning at the Colorado border, deepens to 800 ft. Pinon pine, juniper, and occasional ponderosa pine and Douglas fir color benches and walls of the canyon, while many species of cacti and desert plants cling to the dry slopes. A variety of wildlife lives here. Springs pour cold water into the river and create prime habitat for brown and rainbow trout.

If water levels permit—and some years there is no season at all—the gorge is a destination trip for whitewater boaters. A Class II run is a scenic 24 mi float from the Lobatos Bridge in Colorado to the Lee Trail. From there to the Red River, a 12 mi section called the Upper Box includes Class III rapids for 5 mi followed by Class IV–V water for 7 mi with a waterfall. Below the Red River there are 10 mi of scenic Class II rapids. Then, from the Highway 150 bridge to Taos Junction Bridge, whitewater is Class III and possibly IV in the Lower Taos Box. Registration is required for the Lower Box. The trout and pike fisheries attract anglers to all accessible areas, especially to the rich waters below Big Arsenic Springs above the Red River. Hiking trails lead to the river in several sites, including the La Junta Trail to the Red River confluence. The Bureau of Land Management staffs a visitor center on Highway 378 south of Cerro, and the canyon includes picnicking and camping sites near roads. The John Dunn Bridge (Highway 150) is the only river-level crossing.

In 1959 the state created Rio Grande State Park, including 70 mi of the river, part of which was designated as the national river in 1968. The stream is now managed throughout this length by the BLM. An interstate agreement allows Colorado to divert virtually all the water if the downstream Elephant Butte Reservoir fills, which has occurred twice since its completion in 1936. Groundwater from spring flows in the protected reach maintain the river somewhat. About 85 percent of the gorge lands are publicly owned. Cows— as many as 200 have been counted at once—crowd the Labatos put-in area for the upper Rio Grande trip, but cattle have been removed from the designated section in New Mexico.

NEW YORK
1 river, 73.4 mi of the Delaware River, shared with Pennsylvania

NORTH CAROLINA
4 rivers, 40.7 mi, including 10 mi of the Chattooga River,
which flows into Georgia

Chattooga River, 10 mi. See Georgia, Chattooga River.

Horsepasture River, western North Carolina, designated in 1986; 4.2 mi,
Hwy. 281 to Jocassee Reservoir.
Classification: scenic, 3.6 mi; recreational, 0.6 mi.
Administered by: Nantahala National Forest, P.O. Box 2750, Asheville, NC
28802.
Access: Hwy. 64 to Hwy. 281 (Bohaynee Road).
River difficulty: not run.
Maps: Nantahala National Forest.
This scenic river is beloved for its waterfalls and wild Appalachian setting. It is one of the shortest designation in the national rivers system (though tributaries of other designated rivers are shorter).
Through a rocky gorge, lush with greenery, the Horsepasture drops 1,700 ft in 4 mi with five major waterfalls, including a 125 ft plunge as the river tumbles off the Blue Ridge escarpment. The Horsepasture ranks as one of the smallest national rivers in volume, averaging 100 cfs. The site has been a favorite of hikers, anglers, and picnickers and is considered one of the most scenic streams in North Carolina.

A private power company applied to dam the river and divert its flow from the falls in the early 1980s; opposition to this scheme led to the designation.

New River, northwest North Carolina, designated in 1976 (see also West Virginia, New River); 4.5 mi, confluence of North and South forks to Virginia state line.
Classification: scenic.
Total mileage of New River system in North Carolina: 26.5 mi. See New River, South Fork.

New River, South Fork, northwest North Carolina, designated in 1976; 22 mi, Dog Creek to mouth (contiguous with the main stem).
Classification: scenic.
Administered by: New River State Park, P.O. Box 48, Jefferson, NC 28640.
Access: Wagoner Rd. north of Hwy. 88, Hwy. 221 bridge, Allegheny County access area on the main stem north of 221 at Virginia state line.
River difficulty: Class I, II, with 2 portages at bridges.
Other information: Bob Benner, *Carolina Whitewater* (1977).

This gentle river wraps around verdant Appalachian mountainsides of forest and pasture and is possibly the second oldest river on earth.

Predating the ancient Appalachian Mountains, the New swings in broad meanders, a pattern remaining from when the landscape was flatter. Entrenched in its path, the river incised the mountains as they rose up around it. The Nile may be the only river older than this 317 mi long waterway, including its 60 mi long South Fork. The New has a wealth of natural values and was also recognized for its traditional rural landscape of farms dating to the Revolution. The area harbors 16 rare or endangered animals and 9 fish on the state list.

An excellent, easy canoeing river, the New is also a good fishery for smallmouth bass and muskellunge. New River State Park was developed with recreational facilities along the river.

Protection as a state scenic river was inadequate to halt a huge reservoir project in the 1970s, and after a concerted nationwide campaign, the New was added to the national system by the secretary of the interior at the governor's request. This was one of the classic dam fights in river conservation history and a prime example of protection saving an imminently threatened waterway. Management of the river—a state responsibility—has failed to prevent subdivisions, and the New was once again included among the most threatened rivers in the country (see chapter 5).

OHIO
6 rivers, 7 rivers and tributaries, 149 mi, including 1 river and 22 mi not in
the Wild and Scenic Rivers System

Cuyahoga River, northeast Ohio, designated in 1974; not in the Wild and
  Scenic Rivers System; 22 mi, Bath Road (7 mi south of I-80) to Rockside
  Road (11 mi north of I-80).
Classification: Cuyahoga Valley National Recreation Area.
Administered by: NPS, 15610 Vaughn Rd., Brecksville, OH 44141.
Access: roads throughout the park, headquarters on Hwy. 303.
River difficulty: Class I.
Maps: NPS, *Cuyahoga Valley* (brochure).
    Flowing through a pastoral landscape surrounded by farmland and cities,
the Cuyahoga is one of the most urban-oriented of the nationally protected
rivers.
    Quiet waters drift through wooded bottomlands and past bluffs bordered
by farms. Historic buildings have been restored, and remains of the Ohio and
Erie Canal run the length of the river, which afforded the shortest portage
between the Great Lakes and the Ohio River.
    This river park is an ideal recreation area for residents of nearby Akron and
Cleveland—4 million people within an hour's drive—and includes bike
paths, environmental education facilities, and picnic areas.
    The national recreation area was designated during a brief period of the
early 1970s when the National Park Service embraced a "parks to the people"
movement to provide recreation near urban centers. The river was seen as an
example of the potential for restoration. Acquisition prevented riverfront
acreage from being developed while suburbia encroached on all sides.

Little Beaver Creek, southeast Ohio, designated in 1975; 16 mi.
Classification: scenic.
Designated tributaries: West Fork, 4.5 mi, scenic classification.
    Middle Fork, 8 mi, scenic.
    North Fork, 4.5 mi, scenic.
Total mileage: 33.
Administered by: Ohio Dept. of Natural Resources, Fountain Square, Co-
  lumbus, OH 43224.
Access: Hwy. 170 near the mouth, town of Fredericktown, Clarkson Road
  (North Fork), Beaver Creek State Park (on Middle Fork south of
  Clarkson), and other sites.
River difficulty: Class I, II, with one Class IV rapid.

This small river flows with uncommon wildness through a farming, strip-mining, and rural landscape of hill-covered eastern Ohio.

With steep banks, wooded shores, and open valleys, the Little Beaver winds south through one of the wilder areas in Ohio, and its watershed supports 63 species of fish. The river marks the western edge of the Appalachian foothills. Lower reaches have carved a narrow valley with hemlock-shaded slopes, uncommon in this midwestern state. Below the historic village of Fredericktown the river flows through a remote reach ending in the industrial Ohio River valley. Remains of the Sandy and Beaver Canal can be seen along the banks. Most land in the corridor is privately owned. Toxic waste drainage has been a problem on some tributaries.

In the springtime runoff and after summer rains, this is one of the finest gentle canoeing rivers in its region. A difficult Class IV rapid lies just above the Fredericktown bridge. Anglers come for bluegills and stocked trout. Beaver Creek State Park offers recreational facilities with the river as its centerpiece.

Little Miami River, southwest Ohio, designated in 1973 and 1980; 94 mi, Hwy. 72 bridge at Clifton to mouth at Ohio River.
Classification: scenic, 17 mi; recreational, 75 mi.
Designated tributaries: Caesars Creek, 2 mi.
Total mileage: 94.
Administered by: Ohio Dept. of Natural Resources, Fountain Square, Columbus, OH 43224.
Access: many roads and parks upstream from Cincinnati.
River difficulty: Class I with 1 portage.
Other information: from Little Miami Inc., 3012 Section Rd., Cincinnati, OH 45237.

The first urban-area river in the National Wild and Scenic Rivers System, the Little Miami flows between sycamore-lined banks across southern Ohio.

The river became a model of local organizing success as Little Miami, Inc. gained cooperation at all levels of government. Ohio included the river in one of the nation's first state scenic river programs, then the governor requested national designation. With 3.5 million people within a half-hour drive the river is a riparian oasis through urbanizing farmlands, the designation ending only 6 mi from Cincinnati. Remains of old mill dams and other historic landmarks lie scattered along the route. Scores of archaeological sites exist, including 100 acres ringed by 3.5 mi of earthen walls on a bluff overlooking the river, preserved as Fort Ancient State Memorial. Parts of the corridor are threatened by a proposed interstate highway.

The Little Miami is canoeable all summer, with riffles and one portage. Seven liveries rent boats on the upper and middle reaches. As a model of railsto-trails conversion, an abandoned railroad has been replaced by a bicycle and hiking path for 42 mi.

OREGON
49 rivers, 58 rivers and tributaries, 1,820.1 mi, including 66.5 mi
of the Snake River shared with Idaho, and the North Fork
of the Smith, which flows into California.

For other information on many Oregon rivers, see Willamette Kayak and Canoe Club, *Soggy Sneakers: Guide to Oregon Rivers* (1986); resource assessments prepared by the federal agencies were used for the information presented here, as was Oregon Rivers Council, *Omnibus National Wild and Scenic River Bills* (1987).

Big Marsh Creek, central Oregon, designated in 1988; 15 mi, source to mouth at Crescent Creek.
Classification: recreational.
Administered by: Deschutes National Forest, 211 N.E. Revere, Bend, OR 97701.
Access: Hwy. 58 crosses Crescent Creek just below the mouth of Big Marsh Creek west of Crescent; F.R. 6020 and 6030.
River difficulty: Class I.
Maps: Deschutes National Forest.
A meandering stream through glaciated meadows, this important Deschutes tributary is being reclaimed from diversions and cattle grazing.
In 1946 the stream was diverted to drain the meadows for cattle. The Forest Service bought the marsh and in 1989 directed the creek back to its original channel to restore natural conditions, making this a good example of river restoration in the national rivers system. Beavers returned, and the potential for fish habitat is good. The upper reach lies in the Oregon Cascades National Recreation Area where Diamond Peak rises in the background. Bald eagles and as many as 200 elk feed here.
Canoeists paddle on a 2 mi reach below the marsh. A trail along its eastern edge gives visitors a chance to see birds and wildlife of the reclaimed wetland. About 88 percent of the stream frontage is publicly owned.

Blitzen River, South Fork, southeast Oregon, designated in 1988; 16.5 mi, source to mouth.
Classification: wild.
See Donner and Blitzen River.

Chetco River, southwest Oregon, designated in 1988; 44.5 mi, source to national forest boundary.
Classification: wild, 25.5 mi, source to wilderness boundary; scenic, 8 mi, to 1 mi above Eagle Creek; recreational, 11 mi, to national forest boundary.
Administered by: Siskiyou National Forest, 200 N.E. Greenfield Rd., P.O. Box 440, Grants Pass, OR 97526.
Access: Hwy. 101 to North Bank Chetco River Rd., F.R. 1376.
River difficulty: Class I, II in lower reaches below the South Fork. Class III–V above the South Fork.
Maps: Siskiyou National Forest.

Pristine headwaters and crystal-clear water make this one of the finer salmon and steelhead rivers on the West Coast.

The upper 25.5 miles of this 55 mi long river are in the Kalmiopsis Wilderness and drop from sparsely vegetated high country to old-growth forests and then to a thickly wooded valley. Along with towering Douglas fir are tanoak, madrone, and myrtle in a basin where precipitation averages 100 in. The outstanding fishery includes chinook salmon, coho salmon, steelhead, and some sea-run cutthroat trout. Spawning areas are vital to one of the most commercially viable fisheries off the Pacific coast. Wildlife include the spotted owl, marbled murrelet, black bear, Roosevelt elk, blacktail deer, cougar, river otter, northwestern pond turtle, and Del Norte salamander.

A Class I and II float can be taken for 9 mi from 0.5 mi above the South Fork at the Chetco Gorge Trailhead to Loeb State Park, runnable all summer. Fishing is excellent, and trails provide views of the river. The Chetco Gorge includes Class IV–V rapids; upper reaches of the river are Class III–IV.

Several areas near the river were clearcut in the past. Private land and cabins are found in the 11 mi below the designated reach, but water quality protection remains important—the river is the sole water source for the city of Brookings.

Clackamas River, northwest Oregon, designated in 1988; 47 mi, source at Big Spring to Big Cliff.
Classification: scenic, 20 mi; recreational, 27 mi.
Administered by: Mount Hood National Forest, 2955 N.W. Division St., Gresham, OR 97030.
Access: Hwy. 224 and F.R. 46 southeast of Estacada.
River difficulty: Class II–V, 1 portage.
Maps: Mount Hood National Forest.
Other information: John Garren, *Oregon River Tours* (1976).

One of the most important anadromous and trout fisheries in the Northwest, the Clackamas's excellent scenery, water quality, whitewater, old-growth forests, and wildlife lie within a one hour drive of Portland.

Dense forests and canyon walls alternate with open meadows in the upper river. Lower sections churn through a deep, forested canyon. Threatened and endangered plants survive here, as well as spotted owls, eagles, ospreys, bears, cougars, and coho salmon. The Big Bottom area of 9 mi above Cub Creek remains as a relatively undisturbed riverfront habitat. Geothermal vents heat the Austin Hot Springs along the river.

For 25 mi the Clackamas serves up challenging whitewater with one portage 0.5 mi below Alder Flat Campground. Boaters run in winter and spring, with summer runs possible on lower sections. An excellent trout, salmon, and steelhead fishery, the river can be enjoyed from many Forest Service campgrounds. The Riverside National Recreational Trail and other trails follow the river in several sections and lead to old-growth forests at Alder Flat.

Though some of the watershed has been clearcut, the basalt canyon remains scenic; 95 percent of the river corridor is national forest. Below the national river section, the Clackamas is included in the Oregon State Scenic Waterway System from River Mill Dam to Carver.

Crescent Creek, central Oregon, designated in 1988; 10 mi, Crescent Creek Dam to Hwy. 61 bridge.
Classification: recreational.
Administered by: Deschutes National Forest, 211 N.E. Revere, Bend, OR 97701.
Access: Hwys. 61, 58, and Cty. Rd. 61 parallel the river for 5 mi.
River difficulty: not run.
Maps: Deschutes National Forest.

Flowing past dramatically recent lava flows and between the cones of Royce Mountain and Odell Butte, Crescent Creek is known for its geology.

A gently flowing stream, the creek winds past 4 mi of private land with cabins and grazing, then through national forest in a marsh-filled valley. The North Black Rock Butte lava flow, only 6,000 years old, forms a 100 ft cliff before the river drops through a canyon 150 ft deep with old-growth ponderosa pine and other conifers. The creek sustains native reproducing rainbow trout, brown trout, and whitefish.

Recreation is limited to some fishing and to the Crescent Creek Campground east of Highway 58. Logjams prevent canoeing.

The entire 30 mi creek was originally proposed for designation, but 70 percent of the shoreline is privately owned. Logging, grazing, and irrigation withdrawals have degraded some sections, and a small hydroelectric plant was proposed.

Crooked River, central Oregon, designated in 1988; 15 mi in 2 sections: downstream from Bowman Dam for 8 mi; 7 mi beginning 0.5 mi below Hwy. 97.

Classification: recreational.

Administered by: BLM, 185 E. 4th St., P.O. Box 550, Prineville, OR 97754 (upper section); Ochoco National Forest, P.O. Box 490, Prineville, OR 97754 (lower section).

Access: upper reach, Hwy. 27 parallels the river for 8 mi below Prineville Reservoir; lower reach, downstream of Hwy. 97 bridge.

River difficulty: Class III–V with 1 portage.

The upper reach cuts through one of the most spectacular basalt canyons in Oregon with cliffs 600 ft high. The river includes excellent rainbow and Lahonton trout fisheries.

Experts run the whitewater only when spring runoff is sufficient. Highway 27 offers ample access for fishing and BLM camping areas. The Chimney Rock Recreation Site lies along the river. Bald eagles, peregrine falcons, and golden eagles nest near the river.

A middle section in the spectacular Smith Rock State Park is not designated. The lower section flows through rolling volcanic grassland and a basalt canyon, inaccessible except by whitewater boaters; access is very difficult even for them, with a portage over a dam upriver from the designated reach and a take-out that involves climbing out of a rugged canyon.

Round Butte Dam, just below the designated reach, was built after bitter controversy, and blocked salmon and steelhead from the Crooked, Metolius, and upper Deschutes rivers. The Crooked still has an excellent native rainbow trout fishery, but riparian destruction has limited fish habitat, and diversions from upstream dams deplete upper river flows.

Crooked River, North Fork, central Oregon, designated in 1988; 32.3 mi, source at Williams Prairie to 1 mi above the Crooked River.

Classification: wild, 11.1 mi; scenic, 9.5 mi; recreational, 11.7 mi.

Administered by: BLM, Prineville District, 185 E. 4th St., P.O. Box 550, Prineville, OR 97754.

Access: Post-Paulina Road east of Prineville to the lower river; F.R. 42 crosses the upper river.

River difficulty: not normally run.

Maps: Ochoco National Forest; BLM, Prineville District.

This remote river flows in a pristine canyon and is designated nearly from source to mouth.

Beginning in a series of prairies, the North Fork of the Crooked River winds for 13 mi through a wilderness study area and drops into a basalt canyon with cliffs up to 900 ft high. Plant life includes Douglas fir, ponderosa pine, and aspen, followed by juniper and sage on rolling hills. A favorite winter roosting area for bald eagles, the canyon is also winter range for large mammals.

Fishing and hunting are popular, and a Forest Service campground is located along the upper river. Public land accounts for 78 percent of the mileage.

Deschutes River, north-central Oregon, designated in 1988; 173.4 mi in 3
    sections: Wickiup Dam to Bend, 54.4 mi; Oden Falls near Hwy. 20 to
    Billy Chinook Reservoir, 19 mi; Pelton Reregulating Dam near Hwy. 26
    to Columbia River, 100 mi.
Classification: scenic, 30 mi; recreational, 143.4 mi.
Administered by: BLM, P.O. Box 550, Prineville, OR 97754; Deschutes
    National Forest, 211 N.E. Revere, Bend, OR 97701.
Access: Wickiup Dam; La Pine Recreation Area; Sunriver; Hwys. 126, 26,
    and 197; Macks Canyon Rd. along lower river; I-84 near the mouth; and
    many other sites.
River difficulty: Class I with several falls in the upper reach; Class II–IV in
    lower canyons, 1 portage.
Other information: John Garren, *Oregon River Tours* (1976).

One of the premier rivers of Oregon, the Deschutes has the fourth longest designated mileage outside Alaska and offers remote desert canyons, excellent fisheries, and whitewater. The river possesses all the values for which a river can be designated: fish, wildlife, scenery, recreation, and historic, cultural, and geologic interest.

At 252 mi, this is the second longest river flowing entirely within Oregon. The designation begins on the volcanic plain south of Bend, meandering past ponderosa pine and wet meadows but also including several falls and rapids. Some sections are developed with homes and recreational facilities, such as the resort community of Sunriver. Below Benbow Falls the Deschutes crosses remarkable lava flows unlike any other river landscape in the United States. Discharges from springs delay the river's peak; the Deschutes is one of few major rivers outside Alaska with a natural peak discharge in midsummer. The canyon deepens in middle reaches, and Sherar's Falls is an impassable drop where Indians dip net for salmon. The lower river includes wild canyons 0.5 mi deep and 12 major rapids.

The Deschutes is considered one of the best sport fisheries in the nation: rainbow trout, brown trout, Dolly Varden, and kokonee thrive in upper reaches, with salmon and steelhead below Pelton and Round Butte dams. Rock shelters, pictograph sites, and historic landmarks are found near the river. An unusual plant, the estes wormwood, occurs nowhere else in the world.

Several sections of the upper river are good for canoeing and rafting, with nearly 40,000 people floating per year, making this one of the most used rivers in the West. Several falls, a logjam, and rapids must be portaged to run the entire upper reach. A Class III rafting run is popular above Bend. The 13 mi section between Highway 26 and South Junction has only one major rapid. Class III water runs for 7 mi from Maupin to Sherar's Falls—an unrunnable cataract that separates lower river runs. One of the outstanding multiday whitewater trips in the Northwest, the lower 44 mi include four Class III rapids and excellent campsites where state park permits are required. The fishing here is world famous for steelhead. Campgrounds and trails for walking and biking are plentiful along upper reaches, where the large resort and second-home complex of Sunriver is centered on the river.

In a U.S. Supreme Court case, the state lost a battle against Portland General Electric Company, which built dams at Pelton and Round Butte, blocking anadromous runs from the upper river. Recent hydroelectric proposals were stopped by the national river designation. The upper river is sometimes totally dried up for irrigation storage at Wickiup Dam, decimating the fishery for 22 mi. About 89 percent of the upper river and 51 percent of the lower river flow through public lands.

Donner and Blitzen River, southeast Oregon, designated in 1988; 16.8 mi, confluence of South Fork Blitzen and Little Blitzen River to upstream boundary of Malheur National Wildlife Refuge.
Classification: wild.
Designated tributaries:
   Big Indian Creek, 10 mi, wild classification.
   Little Indian Creek, 3.7 mi, wild.
   Fish Creek, 13.3 mi, wild.
Total mileage: 43.8 (see Blitzen and Little Blitzen rivers).
Administered by: BLM, Hwy. 20-W, Hines, OR 97738.
Access: Hwy. 205 south of Frenchglen to gravel road; unimproved road east of Frenchglen to Mountain Loop Rd.
River difficulty: not run.
Maps: BLM, Burns District, south half.
   A unique river in many respects, the Blitzen flows from the high desert fault block of Steens Mountain through glaciated headwaters and distinctly rimmed canyons in a superlative wilderness setting.
   A desert oasis, the river drops over waterfalls and through majestic scenery of alternating meadows and canyons to the Malheur National Wildlife Refuge. The rare mottled sculpin survives in upper reaches. Native rainbow trout thrive, and the uncommon redband trout is found here. Hikers can discover the river and its branches by beginning at the Page Springs Campground near Frenchglen.
   Ironically, once the river enters the wildlife refuge the water is diverted for

pasture, and the stream nearly disappears. Biologists have begun studies to determine effects of the diversions on native trout in the rivers, which may have migrated to Malheur Lake in the past.

Eagle Creek, northeast Oregon, designated in 1988 (tributary to the Powder River); 27 mi, source to national forest boundary at Skull Creek.
Classification: wild, 4 mi; scenic, 6 mi; recreational, 17 mi.
Administered by: Wallowa-Whitman National Forest, P.O. Box 907, Baker, OR 97814.
Access: Hwy. 86 at Richland to F.R. 7735.
River difficulty: not normally run.
Maps: Wallowa-Whitman National Forest.

This 38 mi long river begins in glaciated valleys of the Wallowa Mountains, where snowmelt glistens over polished granite, then flows through a canyon with old-growth ponderosa pine and mountain meadows.

The upper 4 mi are in the Eagle Cap Wilderness Area; below, 5 mi remain roadless with some of the best native trout habitat in northeast Oregon. Turquoise pools alternate with rapids and waterfalls.

Scenic trails lead to the headwaters and through the roadless canyon. Easy road access brings many visitors to fish, hike, camp, and hunt for deer and elk.

About 78 percent of the designated reach is in public ownership. Before Hells Canyon Dam was constructed, salmon and steelhead spawned in Eagle Creek. Below the designated reach the creek is diverted for irrigation. Additional logging planned in the national forest headwaters could affect the flows and water quality, though all uses in and next to the corridor are required to be planned for protection of river values.

Elk River, southwest Oregon, designated in 1988; 17 mi, North and South forks confluence to fish hatchery.
Classification: recreational.
Administered by: Siskiyou National Forest, Powers, OR 97466; Oregon State Parks, 525 Trade St. S.E., Salem, OR 97310.
Access: Cty. Rd. 208 east of Port Orford, F.R. 5325.
River difficulty: Class IV.
Maps: Siskiyou National Forest.

With one of the most important runs of wild steelhead and salmon in Oregon—perhaps the finest for its size—the Elk is also stunningly beautiful with deep green pools, rock walls, and towering evergreens.

Most of the riverfront has old-growth timber remaining. In 1985 the Elk yielded 240,000 wild chinook salmon, 14,000 wild steelhead, and a major return of sea-run cutthroat trout, and that same year the river had one of the highest coho smelt densities in Oregon. The Elk River watershed is a major reason why the Siskiyou National Forest is the largest producer of native anadromous fish in the Northwest; it also harbors old-growth habitat for the spotted owl, marbled murrelet, and other wildlife.

A 6.5 mi kayak run from Slate Creek Bar to the hatchery involves Class IV rapids in winter and spring. Anglers use the river from roadside sites.

Several large blocks of forest near the river have been clearcut. Even though Forest Service studies found that logged tributaries were "heavily impacted by logging," the forest plan called for extensive clearcut logging in the basin of this 30 mi long river with another 8 mi on the North and South forks. A "model national process" convened agencies and interest groups to draft an ecologically sound watershed plan for this basin, which is 94 percent in public ownership.

Elk River, North Fork, southwest Oregon, designated in 1988; 2 mi above mouth at Elk River.
Classification: wild.
See Elk River.

Grande Ronde River, northeast Oregon, designated in 1988; 43.8 mi, Wallowa River to Washington state line.
Classification: wild, 26.4 mi; recreational, 17.4 mi.
Administered by: BLM, 100 Oregon St., Vale, OR 97918; Umatilla National Forest, 2517 S.W. Hailey Ave., Pendleton, OR 97801.
Access: Hwy. 80 at Minam, gravel road north of Minam or north of Elgin, Troy Rd. west of Hwy. 3, Hwy. 3 bridge (downstream from designated reach).
River difficulty: Class III.
Maps: BLM, Vale District; Umatilla National Forest.
Other information: John Garren, *Oregon River Tours* (1976).

This large tributary to the Snake River makes one of the best multiday river trips in Oregon with spectacular scenery.

Upper reaches in the Blue Mountains are forested with pines; lower sections are mainly grasslands in the 3,000 ft deep canyon with volcanic outcrops and vital winter range for 1,000 elk, for deer, and for mountain sheep. Otters, great gray owls, goshawks, and up to 80 bald eagles can be seen.

The river draws 6,000 floaters a year in drift boats, rafts, canoes, and kayaks, and can be run through mid July. A 2–5 day trip extends from Minam on the Wallowa River (8.5 mi upstream from the Grande Ronde) to Troy or Highway 3. Trout and steelhead fishing are excellent.

Irrigation, grazing, and logging heavily affect other reaches of this 150 mi long river. Although it was once one of Oregon's most respected salmon and steelhead streams, its fish populations were decimated by the lower Snake River dams; the legendary Grande Ronde coho salmon run was extinct in 1987. Additional dams were proposed for the designated reach before it was protected. About 66 percent of the frontage is public land.

Hood River, northern Oregon, designated in 1986; not in the Wild and Scenic Rivers System; 67 mi, source to mouth at the Columbia River.
Classification: hydroelectric dam prohibition.
Administered by: USFS, Columbia Gorge National Scenic Area, 902 Wasco Ave., Hood River, OR 97031.
Access: Tucker Rd. to Odell and Parkdale, Lolo Pass Rd. and Lost Lake Rd. to headwaters.
River difficulty: Class III, IV.
Maps: USGS; Mount Hood National Forest.

Rising on Mount Hood and with its source at the spectacular Lost Lake, this beautiful river drops through heavy rapids to the Columbia River.

During the rainy season and snowmelt, the river runs with continuous Class III rapids that become Class IV at higher flows. Access is available at Dee and at a bridge on the Tucker Road, for a run of 7.5 mi with large rapids 0.5 mi below Dee and above Tucker Park.

Hydroelectric projects are banned by the Columbia Gorge National Scenic Area legislation.

Illinois River, southwest Oregon, designated in 1984; 50.4 mi, Siskiyou National Forest boundary to mouth.
Classification: wild, 28.7 mi; scenic, 17.9 mi; receational, 3.8 mi.
Administered by: Siskiyou National Forest, P.O. Box 440, Grants Pass, OR 97526.
Access: Hwy. 199 at Selma to F.R. 3504, Oak Flat south of Rogue River Rd. (east of Gold Beach).
River difficulty: Class IV, V.
Maps: Siskiyou National Forest.

One of the preeminent whitewater challenges in the United States, this is also one of the pristine wilderness canyons.

The lucid water of the Illinois flows from the Siskiyou Mountains and through the Kalmiopsis Wilderness for 22 mi. Rapids here challenge the finest paddlers, and the trout and steelhead fishery is good. One hundred inches of rain and a variety of geology and soil types yield an abundance of plant species—over 1,400, including many that are rare. Bald eagles, osprey, otters, cougars, bears, and 20 species of fish make this their home. Largely devoid of topsoil, the area is easily eroded.

This extraordinary run is one of the ultimate trips for the serious whitewater boater. Difficult rapids, remoteness, cold water, fluctuating levels, and a short season add to the challenge of seeing this remarkable canyon. The 34 mi run can only be done in winter or spring; late April and early May is the best combination of water and weather. Flows have exploded from 1,800 to 8,000 cfs in one short storm, posing extreme hazards. The final 4 mi above the Rogue are a fine Class II, road-accessible section. Fishing is done at the few access points or from rafts. A trail for summer backpackers reaches the cool relief of the river at Pine Flat and below Collier Creek.

Before designation, the Buzzard's Roost hydroelectric dam was proposed above Oak Flat. Logging continues to pose acute threats to the exceptional water quality, and Friends of the Illinois River has lobbied to add another 7 mi of the river and 100,000 acres to the wilderness area.

Imnaha River, northeast Oregon, designated in 1988; 68 mi, source at South and North forks confluence to mouth.
Classification: wild, 6 mi; scenic, 4 mi; recreational, 58 mi.
Total mileage of designated Imnaha system: 77 (see South Fork).
Administered by: Wallowa-Whitman National Forest, P.O. Box 907, Baker, OR 97814.
Access: F.R. 39 east of Joseph, F.R. 3960 parallels the river.
River difficulty: Class III with some sections unknown.

This gem of the greater Northwest is exceptionally scenic with outstanding wilderness, fish, and wildlife. Little known, the Imnaha River is one of the longer rivers designated from source to mouth.

Bursting from the Eagle Cap Wilderness in the Wallowa Mountains, the South Fork flows through a glaciated canyon surrounded by crags of limestone, granite, and basalt, then past old-growth conifers and lush meadows. The main stem drops through dense forests and a chaos of logjams, then into mountain ranch country of ponderosa pine and grasslands, and finally into deeply darkened canyons of basalt, remote and scenic. The last 5 mi are a roadless wonderland of cliffs and rock formations ending in the heart of Hells Canyon of the Snake River. Most of the river lies in the Hells Canyon National Recreation Area.

The Imnaha is an outstanding steelhead and trout stream and has one of the better surviving runs of chinook salmon in the vast Snake River basin. This is the uppermost major tributary to the Snake River accessible to anadromous fish. A haven for wintering wildlife, the canyon hosts bighorn sheep, elk, and deer. Chief Joseph's band of Nez Perce wintered here.

Several whitewater runs are possible, though they do not appear in guidebooks. Upper reaches are riddled with logjams. Ranch owners adamantly ban access on middle reaches. The final 5 mi are a superb Class III whitewater run with tight, rocky moves, though the river ends in Hells Canyon, requiring that it be run to Heller Bar or that boats be picked up by a coordinated trip through Hells Canyon. Fishing is excellent, and much of the river is accessible by road, serving several Forest Service campgrounds. One spectacular trail climbs the South Fork to its headwaters; another proceeds along the lowest 5 mi of river to the depths of Hells Canyon. About 40 percent of the frontage is publicly owned; this is perhaps the most splendid river in the national system with so much private land. Forest Service logging proposals threaten the vital water quality and salmon habitat of some Imnaha tributaries.

Imnaha River, South Fork, northeast Oregon, designated in 1988; 9 mi, source to mouth at Imnaha River.
Classification: wild.
This is effectively an extension of the Imnaha River to its source. See Imnaha River.

John Day River, north-central Oregon, designated in 1988; 147.5 mi, Service Creek to Tumwater Falls.
Classification: recreational.
Administered by: BLM, P.O. Box 550, Prineville, OR 97754.
Access: Hwys. 206, 218, 19, and local roads.
River difficulty: Class I with several Class III and 1 Class IV rapids.
Maps: BLM, Prineville District.
Other information: John Garren, *Oregon River Tours* (1976).
This 275 mi long river is one of the longest mostly undammed rivers in the United States outside Alaska and the longest relatively free-flowing river in the lower Columbia basin, the only impoundment being the lower miles flooded by John Day Dam on the Columbia. The John Day offers one of the longest canoe trips in the West.

Colorful, undeveloped desert canyons 1,000 ft deep in Columbia River basalt formations account for much of the mileage, interspersed with dry ranchland in several reaches, including those at Twickenham and Clarno. An important tributary to Columbia River steelhead and salmon, the John Day remains one of the largest wild anadromous streams in the Columbia system and a good bass fishery. Bald eagles, peregrine falcons, bighorn sheep, cougars, bobcats, and other wildlife live here. The river flows through three wilderness study areas between Butte Creek and Cottonwood Branch, recommended by the Bureau of Land Management as suitable for wilderness designation.

A favorite for canoeing and easy rafting, the 114 mi reach from Service Creek at Highway 19 to Cottonwood Bridge on Highway 206 runs with enough water from April to June and involves three rapids, including one

Class IV drop just downstream from Clarno. In the isolated Clarno-to-Cottonwood reach, rattlesnakes are a hazard, water must be carried, and private property should be respected. During summer, flows are reduced to a trickle. In 1984, 3,000 people floated the river.

As good as it is, the John Day is nothing like what it once was and offers only a hint of its potential value. Grazing, irrigation withdrawals, dredge mining, logging, and the Columbia River dams have taken a grim toll. Shorelines of the designated reach are 44 percent public land. If the missing links of mileage between either the South Fork or North Fork and the John Day were designated, this would be the longest protected river outside Alaska.

John Day River, North Fork, north-central Oregon, designated in 1988; 54.1 mi, source to Camas Creek near Dale.

Classification: wild, 27.8 mi; scenic, 10.5 mi; recreational, 15.8 mi.

Administered by: Umatilla National Forest, 2517 S.W. Hailey Ave., Pendleton, OR 97801; Wallowa-Whitman National Forest, P.O. Box 907, Baker, OR 97814.

Access: Hwy. 395, forest roads.

River difficulty: not normally run. Class II–III in sections below the designated reach.

Maps: Umatilla and Wallowa-Whitman national forests.

The North Fork of the John Day supports the largest population of spring chinook salmon and summer steelhead in the Columbia River system above Bonneville Dam.

Fed by snowmelt of the Blue Mountains, the North Fork rises in the North Fork John Day Wilderness and after 18 mi passes through rugged basalt canyons with ponderosa pine and Douglas fir in upper reaches and juniper and sage below. This fork carries twice the volume of the main stem of the John Day where the two meet.

At high flows in April and May a few kayakers negotiate the difficult rapids of this upper North Fork. Fishing is good, and swimming sites are excellent in summer. A trail follows along much of the river. Below the designated reach, a Class II–III run extends from Dale to Monument, runnable March through May, though reduced to a trickle by midsummer.

Many unprotected miles separate the upper North Fork from the designated reach of the main stem. About 72 percent of the designated reach is public land.

John Day River, South Fork, north-central Oregon, designated in 1988; 47 mi, Malheur National Forest to Smokey Creek.

Classification: recreational.

Administered by: BLM, P.O. Box 550, Prineville, OR 97754.
Access: Hwy. 26 at Dayville to a forest road that parallels the river.
River difficulty: not normally run.
Maps: BLM, Prineville District.

This river flows first through farmland and a gentle canyon that increases in ruggedness on the eastern side of the Ochoco Mountains. Large basalt outcrops and mixed vegetation of grasses, willows, juniper, ponderosa pine, and Douglas fir create scenery and wildlife habitat. A good fishery, the river tumbles over many small rapids and the 55 ft Izee Falls.

Camping and fishing are popular from many road-accessible sites. About 41 percent of the designated section is publicly owned.

Joseph Creek, northeast Oregon, designated in 1988; 8.6 mi, Joseph Creek Ranch to Wallowa-Whitman National Forest boundary.
Classification: wild.
Administered by: Wallowa-Whitman National Forest, P.O. Box 907, Baker, OR 97814.
Access: Hwy. 3, 28 mi north of Enterprise, to F.R. 46.
River difficulty: not run.
Maps: Wallowa-Whitman National Forest.

In a dramatic canyon of 2,000 ft depth, Joseph Creek rushes past primeval forests of ponderosa pine and shelters populations of native rainbow trout and steelhead.

By erosion, this wild and remote creek has exposed massive layers of basalt and myriad feeder dikes remaining from volcanic flows. Bald eagles, peregrine falcons, and Lewis's woodpeckers are found here, and the area provides winter range for elk, deer, bighorn sheep, and bears. Also rich in archaeological value, the stream is named for Chief Joseph, who may have been born downstream near the creek's confluence with the Grande Ronde. Beyond the designated reach, mostly in public ownership, scattered ranches blend with the natural scenery of this exceptional 49 mi long stream.

A rough trail parallels much of this section. Some hiking, fishing, and hunting is done.

Little Blitzen River, southeast Oregon, designated in 1988; 12.5 mi, source to mouth.
Classification: wild.
See Donner and Blitzen River.

Little Deschutes River, central Oregon, designated in 1988; 12 mi, source to a point 1 mi above Hwy. 58.
Classification: recreational.

Administered by: Deschutes National Forest, 211 N.E. Revere, Bend, OR 97701.

Access: Hwy. 58 (1 mi below designated reach).

River difficulty: not run.

Maps: Deschutes National Forest.

This small river cuts through the 1,500 ft deep Little Deschutes Canyon with steep walls and an uncommonly flat valley floor, the banks composed of an unusual tight sod.

Here glaciers carved their longest and deepest canyon on the east flank of the Oregon Cascades. The unique flat floor is due to sediment dropped by the river. Small brook and brown trout reproduce naturally. Roosevelt elk, deer, cougars, and bears are among the animals that live along this river, which sees very little recreational use.

Intensive grazing by cattle in the riparian zone has reduced shrubs and plant cover and may have led to bank erosion and loss of fish habitat.

Lostine River, northeast Oregon, designated in 1988; 16 mi, source to Wallowa-Whitman National Forest boundary.

Classification: wild, 5 mi; recreational, 11 mi.

Administered by: Wallowa-Whitman National Forest, P.O. Box 907, Baker, OR 97814.

Access: Hwy. 82 to F.R. 8210 south of Lostine.

River difficulty: not run.

Maps: Wallowa-Whitman National Forest.

Rising in the Eagle Cap Wilderness, this startlingly scenic river flows through a U-shaped glacial valley, then with steep canyon walls at 7,000 ft and across brilliant meadows surrounded by crags of granite, then through dense forests in lower sections.

With 97 percent of the corridor in public ownership, the only private land is Lapover Ranch, which was a summer home of Justice William O. Douglas. Wild salmon and steelhead spawn in this important Grande Ronde tributary. Bears, deer, elk, bobcats, and cougars do well here, as did bighorn sheep that were occasionally seen from the road until a virus passed by domestic sheep reduced the herd in 1987.

Hiking, camping, horseback riding, and fishing are popular in this spectacular, easily accessible area. The entire river runs 31 mi.

Malheur River, east-central Oregon, designated in 1988; 12 mi, Malheur National Forest boundary below Bosonberg Creek to lower national forest boundary.

Classification: wild, 7 mi; scenic, 5 mi.

Administered by: Malheur National Forest, 139 N.E. Dayton St., John Day, OR 97845.

Access: Hwy. 395 east of Silvies to F.R. 902 and 147 below Bosonberg Creek, and F.R. 1651 at Malheur Ford.

River difficulty: Class I, II.

Maps: Malheur National Forest.

The river begins in a wide valley with rolling hills, descends to a narrow gorge with ponderosa pine, sage, and grasses, then drops into a canyon of 300–1,000 ft depth with hulking basalt outcrops and diverse plant life. Native redband trout and stocked rainbow and brook trout are here, as well as the uncommon bull trout. Cougars, otters, deer, pronghorn, elk, and bears can be seen.

The Malheur River National Recreation Trail parallels the waterway for 6 mi below Malheur Ford with scenic views for much of the length, serving hikers, horseback riders, and anglers. Boaters only occasionally run the river during spring runoff from April to June, and logjams are a hazard.

Before Warm Springs Dam was built in 1919, chinook salmon and steelhead spawned in the river. The entire reach is public land.

Malheur River, North Fork, east-central Oregon, designated in 1988; 22.9 mi, source to Malheur National Forest boundary.

Classification: scenic.

Access: Hwy. 26 to south of Prairie City and to F.R. 1870 and 1675.

River difficulty: Class I, II.

Maps: Malheur National Forest.

This mostly undisturbed river offers exemplary scenery of rolling hills, large ponderosa pines, and a basalt canyon.

With headwaters in the Blue Mountains at 8,000 ft, the North Fork travels through volcanic hills with thick stands of lodgepole pine, mixed conifers, and grassy meadows. The lower section runs through a 750 ft deep basalt canyon with large ponderosa pines, larch, and Douglas fir. Grazing and logging have affected some areas, but the corridor is mostly undisturbed. The river supports native redband, rainbow, and the rare bull trout, which has been in decline for 20 years. Wildlife includes cougars, badgers, beavers, ospreys, elk, deer, bears, and pileated woodpeckers.

Paddlers only occasionally run the river during spring runoff; logjams and fences are hazards. Fishing for stocked trout, camping, hiking, and hunting are recreational pursuits. The North Fork Malheur Trail follows the river partway through the corridor.

The river supported chinook salmon and steelhead until Agency Dam was built in 1935. The entire reach is on national forest land.

McKenzie River, west-central Oregon, designated in 1988; 12.7 mi, source at Clear Lake to Scott Creek.
Classification: recreational.
Administered by: Willamette National Forest, P.O. Box 10607, Eugene, OR 97440.
Access: Hwy. 126 parallels the river.
River difficulty: not normally run above Olallie Campground.
Maps: Willamette National Forest.

Only the upper 14 percent of this great Oregon river is in the National Wild and Scenic Rivers System, including rapid water through dense conifers.

Clear Lake, the McKenzie's source, is the result of a 3,000-year-old lava flow that drowned a forest, the remains of which can amazingly still be seen in the preserving and transparent waters of the lake. The river then rushes off the slopes of the Cascades, through a deep green forest of Douglas fir, western hemlock, and other conifers to the upper McKenzie hydroelectric complex of the Eugene Water and Electric Board. Elk, pine martens, bald eagles, and spotted owls live here.

The McKenzie River National Recreation Trail closely follows the upper river. Below Olallie Campground, outside the designated reach, the McKenzie is one of the most popular whitewater rivers in Oregon and the Northwest with six sections of Class II and III water, rich in northwestern river tradition.

Metolius River, central Oregon, designated in 1988; 28.6 mi, Deschutes National Forest southern boundary (below Metolius Springs) to Billy Chinook Reservoir.
Classification: scenic, 17.1 mi; recreational, 11.5 mi.
Administered by: Deschutes National Forest, 211 N.E. Revere, Bend, OR 97701.
Access: Hwy. 20 west of Sisters to Cty. Rd. 14 and F.R. 14, Metolius River Rd. west of Madras.
River difficulty: Class III, IV.
Maps: Deschutes National Forest.

One of the largest spring-fed rivers in the United States, the Metolius is unique in water quality, rapids, and wilderness.

Bordered by old-growth ponderosa pine, the river flows through a scenic kaleidoscope beneath the sky-piercing Mount Jefferson and along the Green Ridge Fault. Springs in the upper 5 mi fill the river with water at a constant 45–54 degree temperature and run at a constant pace all year—one of the steadiest hydrographs known. The water quality is singular, with aquamarine pools and white rapids. Kokanee salmon migrate up from Billy Chinook Reservoir. Beavers, otters, goshawks, and bald eagles are residents.

A difficult whitewater run is prized by kayakers and rafters, and the upper river is heavily used with 12 campgrounds, summer homes, and 6 resorts, totaling 122,000 recreation days a year. On this legendary trout-fishing river, the state set one section aside for fly fishing in 1939.

The upper river is almost entirely in national forest land, some of it logged while other timber sales are planned but doggedly opposed. The lower river flows through the Warm Springs Indian Reservation.

Minam River, northeast Oregon, designated in 1988; 39 mi, source at Minam Lake to Eagle Cap Wilderness boundary.
Classification: wild.
Administered by: Wallowa-Whitman National Forest, P.O. Box 907, Baker, OR 97814.
Access: F.R. 6220 east of Cove to Moss Springs Campground.
River difficulty: not normally run.
Maps: Wallowa-Whitman National Forest.

The Minam is the only national river reach outside Alaska entirely within designated wilderness, and the basin is one of few that are nearly untouched in the state, though temporary splash dams were historically built on the lower one-third of the river.

Crystal-clear water begins its drop from 7,000 ft peaks of the Wallowa Mountains, passes rugged outcrops of limestone and granite, winds around green meadows in a glacial valley, then courses through deep forests and old-growth ponderosa pine. Native rainbow trout, cutthroat trout, and bull trout do well here, and chinook salmon and steelhead survive. Bald eagles, elk, cougars, bears, and other wildlife thrive. The river was included in Oregon's six original state scenic waterways and appears in the writings of Justice William O. Douglas, who had a home in the area.

Hiking, backpacking, horseback packing, fishing, and hunting are pursued here. Clients fly or hike to two private lodges.

Among the entire 50 mi of the Minam, only 8 mi have roads, all on Boise-Cascade Corporation land. Already a state-designated scenic waterway through this lower reach, the entire Minam is an ideal candidate for national designation from source to mouth.

Owyhee River, southeast Oregon, designated in 1984; 86 mi in 2 sections: 35 mi from Three Forks to China Gulch (4 mi above Rome); 51 mi from Crooked Creek (6 mi below Rome) to Owyhee Reservoir.
Classification: wild.
Administered by: BLM, 100 Oregon St., Vale, OR 97918.
Access: Hwy. 95 east of Jordan Valley and dirt road to Three Forks, Hwy. 95 at Rome, Leslie Gulch Rd. 44 mi north and west of Jordan Valley.

River difficulty: Class III–V.
Maps: BLM, Vale District.
Other information: John Garren, *Oregon River Tours* (1976); BLM, *Owyhee River Boating Guide.*

The Three Forks reach of the upper Owyhee is one of the least accessible rivers run in Oregon.

This upper section plunges through a desert canyon 1,250 ft deep with no development or access for 35 mi. The section below Rome is also isolated, with little access for the entire 67 mi run where remarkable cliff faces and geologic curiosities abound, including Chalk Basin and Lambert Rocks, hot springs, and basalt formations in the 1,350 ft deep canyon. Bighorn sheep, many raptors, and petroglyphs can be seen.

The Three Forks–Rome trip includes several Class IV rapids and possible Class V drops, and portages are likely in the boating season of March–May. Roads are rough to Three Forks, and rattlesnakes are plentiful. The section below Rome is the most popular, with floating normally possible from March to June. This lower section is mostly Class II–III with an 8 mi row across Owyhee Reservoir to the take-out. The remains of Morcum Dam, a rock weir 39 mi below Rome, is a hazard at low water. Below 1,000 cfs the Owyhee becomes exceedingly difficult, though possible in kayaks—with many portages—down to 300 cfs.

Owyhee River, North Fork, southeast Oregon, designated in 1988; 9.6 mi, Idaho-Oregon state line to mouth at Three Forks.
Classification: wild.
Access: gravel road southeast of Jordan Valley to North Fork crossing, Three Forks Rd. to mouth of the North Fork (see Owyhee River).
River difficulty: Class III, IV, not normally run.
Maps: BLM, Vale District.

This small desert river pierces an incised canyon in the high desert plateau of Oregon. Markedly remote, the river is rarely visited and includes habitat for bald eagles, bighorn sheep, rainbow trout, smallmouth bass, and catfish. About 75 percent of the corridor is public land.

The river can be kayaked for 15 mi from North Fork Crossing to Three Forks during a very short season in the spring. No trails exist, but the stream can be hiked in low flows with great difficulty.

The Air Force plans an extensive new bombing range in the desert of southwest Idaho near North Fork headwaters—a proposal being fought by Oregon and Idaho conservationists and by ranchers because of its impacts on wildlife, ranching, and the natural flavor of one of America's least touched regions outside Alaska. The Committee for Idaho's High Desert proposed that 1.2 million acres be set aside as wilderness.

Owyhee River, South Fork, southeast Oregon, designated in 1984; 24 mi, Idaho-Oregon state line to Three Forks.
Classification: wild.
Access: 4-wheel dirt road near the Idaho-Nevada line west of Owyhee, Nevada.
River difficulty: Class III with IV–V below the East Fork and 1 portage likely.
Other information: BLM, *Owyhee River Boating Guide.*

This wilderness canyon is incised 1,000 ft into a plateau that lies beneath 8,000 ft mountain summits. Indian petroglyphs, bighorn sheep, golden eagles, native redband trout, and intriguing geology mark this and other tributary canyons of the Owyhee.

Visitors are not likely to see other parties during a river trip here, since trips are limited by a short April–May season when weather can be either hot or snowy, by four-wheel-drive access roads, by dens of rattlesnakes, and by several steep rapids often requiring portage. During low water, hikers can use animal trails and wade in the streambed.

Owyhee River, West Little Owyhee River, southeast Oregon, designated in 1988; 57.6 mi, source to mouth.
Classification: wild.
Access: gravel road off Hwy. 95 beginning 14 mi north of McDermott and running to Anderson Crossing Rd., then reaching the river.
River difficulty: not run.
Maps: BLM, Vale District.

One of the longer rivers designated from source to mouth, the West Little Owyhee is exceptional in having wild classification for the entire length. From Anderson Crossing to the mouth makes an interesting but very difficult and dry 36 mi backpacking trip.

In a deeply incised canyon with varied rock formations, the tiny river has vegetation of rare quality because the canyon walls have prevented grazing of livestock. Bighorn sheep and several species of raptors thrive. Nearly all of the basin is managed as a wilderness study area. The river offers scenery, archaeological sites, and opportunities for canyon backpacking along some of the least accessible and least visited river frontage in 49 states.

Powder River, northeast Oregon, designated in 1988; 11.7 mi, Thief Valley Dam to Hwy. 203 bridge.
Classification: scenic.
Administered by: BLM, 100 Oregon St., Vale, OR 97918.
Access: Hwy. 237 to county roads east of North Powder, Hwy. 203.

River difficulty: not normally run.
Maps: BLM, Vale District.

The Powder River Canyon, the only undeveloped reach left on the 130 mi long river, provides exceptional wildlife habitat and a native rainbow trout fishery.

This scenic canyon is critical habitat for mule deer and reintroduced pronghorn. Bald eagles feed on waterfowl that flock here in winter; prairie falcons and golden eagles nest on cliffs. Beavers, otters, and bobcats find the remoteness they need along this river, famous for large rainbow trout. Public land accounts for 81 percent of the reach. The river is completely diverted immediately below the designated reach in dry years.

Powder River, North Fork (North Powder River), northeast Oregon, designated in 1988; 6 mi, source to Wallowa-Whitman National Forest boundary.
Classification: scenic.
Administered by: Wallowa-Whitman National Forest, P.O. Box 907, Baker, OR 97814.
Access: unimproved roads east of the town of North Powder and east of Hwy. 30.
River difficulty: not normally run.
Maps: Wallowa-Whitman National Forest.

The North Fork of the Powder begins at 8,000 ft and flows past the glaciated peaks of Twin and Red mountains in the Elkhorn Range before dropping into forested terrain. Old-growth fir, lodgepole pine, Engelmann spruce, Douglas fir, and white fir decorate the riverfront and canyons near the center of the Twin Mountain Roadless Area. Native trout, elk, deer, and wildlife dependent on old growth live here. Hikers, hunters, and anglers visit the watershed. The entire section runs through public land.

In the 1980s irrigators proposed a new dam just below the protected reach of this 24 mi long river.

Quartzville Creek, west-central Oregon, designated in 1988; 9 mi, Willamette National Forest boundary to Green Peter Reservoir.
Classification: recreational.
Administered by: BLM, 1717 Fabry Road S.E., Salem, OR 97306.
Access: Quartzville Rd. off Hwy. 20 near Sweet Home.
River difficulty: Class IV.
Maps: BLM, Salem District.

A rapid stream of intense whitewater, Quartzville Creek flows through lush, low elevation forests of the Cascades. The woodland environment is home to Roosevelt elk, blacktail deer, and myriad forest species. The creek produces winter steelhead and native rainbow trout.

Close to the Willamette Valley and with easy road access, Quartzville Creek sees heavy use by anglers and campers and is growing in appeal to expert kayakers during high flows.

Much of the creek's Santiam River drainage has been dammed and logged. Immediately above this reach of the 27 mi long stream are 12 mi of national forest frontage deserving protection. Public land accounts for 59 percent of the designated section.

Roaring River, northwest Oregon, designated in 1988; 13.7 mi, source to mouth at Clackamas River.
Classification: wild, 13.5 mi; recreational, 0.2 mi.
Administered by: Mount Hood National Forest, 2955 N.W. Division St., Gresham, OR 97030.
Access: Hwy. 224 at mouth.
River difficulty: not run.
Maps: Mount Hood National Forest.

An archetypal wild river, the Roaring is undeveloped in its entirety with road access only at the mouth, and is among the prestigious group of rivers protected in their entire length.

Well named, the Roaring River drops from 4,000 to 1,000 ft—200 ft per mile from snowy Cascade slopes to old-growth fir and cedar. Skirting the flank of the Salmon-Huckleberry Wilderness, it evolves from a glacial valley to a V-shaped canyon with critical nesting sites for peregrine falcons, bald eagles, and spotted owls. The river creates spawning grounds for wild coho salmon, chinook salmon, steelhead, rainbow trout, and cutthroat trout.

A Forest Service campground marks the Roaring's confluence with the Clackamas River, and three Forest Service trails invite hikers to explore this textbook example of a wild river, all of it in public ownership.

The South Fork Roaring River is equally wild and eligible for national protection but undesignated for its 4 mi length.

Rogue River, southwest Oregon, designated in 1968 and 1988; 124.8 mi in 2 sections: Crater Lake National Park boundary to lower Rogue River National Forest boundary, 40.3 mi; Applegate River to Lobster Creek Bridge, 10 mi above the mouth of the river, 84.5 mi.
Classification: Upper Rogue: wild, 6.1 mi; scenic, 34.2 mi.
Classification: Lower Rogue: wild, 34 mi; scenic, 7.5 mi; recreational, 43 mi.
Administered by: Rogue River National Forest, P.O. Box 520, Medford, OR 97504 (upper river); BLM, 3040 Biddle Rd., Medford, OR 97504;

Siskiyou National Forest, P.O. Box 440, Grants Pass, OR 97526 (lower river).

Access: upper river, Hwys. 62 and 230 parallel some of the reach; lower river, roads to Merlin, Galice, Almeda, and Grave Creek. The Gold Beach–Agness road leads to lower sections.

River difficulty: upper, not run; lower, Class III with 2 Class IV rapids.

Maps: USFS, "The Rogue River, Wild and Scenic"; Rogue River and Siskiyou national forests.

Other information: John Garren, *Oregon River Tours* (1976).

The lower Rogue is one of the original national wild and scenic rivers and one of the classic wild river trips in America. The upper river is a wonderland of waterfalls, geologic phenomena, and old-growth forest.

The upper river is presumed to originate with the waters of Crater Lake, erupting from spring flows. The river later disappears underground and bursts out 200 ft away after churning through lava tubes. Thick stands of ancient forests and the translucent river harbor otters, elk, fishers, gray foxes, ringtail cats, rainbow trout, and cutthroat trout. Tourists in great numbers stop and camp along the river on their way to Crater Lake. Excellent trails follow the water's scenic route. A hydroelectric project, banned by the designation, had been proposed at the geologically unique Natural Bridge. Public land constitutes 99 percent of the upper river frontage.

After many intervening sections on this 210 mi long river, an 84 mi reach of the lower river is designated. In the upper 27 mi of this section the river flows past forest and farmland with mostly gentle currents and frequent highway access. Boaters of all types use this reach extensively, as do anglers and car campers. Conflicts and recreational demands led the Bureau of Land Management to seek funding for new facility development and recreational management here in 1990.

The lower portion of the reach designated in 1968 is one of the most sought-after river trips in the West for fishing and intermediate whitewater. BLM requires permits for a wilderness run of 35 mi featuring scenery of the Klamath Mountains, exciting rapids, pleasant summer and fall weather, wildlife including frequent sightings of bears, exceptional salmon and steelhead fishing, and ideal campsites. Historic sites include a cabin owned by writer Zane Grey. The forest is perhaps the greatest cross section of the plant kingdom on the Pacific coast. Douglas fir is found with ponderosa pine, sugar pine, white fir, and incense cedar. Red cedar, Port Orford cedar, and Pacific yew grow in wet areas, and the rare Brewer spruce and Lawson cypress can be seen. Hardwoods include Oregon white oak, California black oak, Pacific madrone, Oregon ash, black cottonwood, red alder, golden chinquapin, tanoak, Oregon myrtle, and big leaf maple. The river is world renowned for salmon up to 40 lb and steelhead up to 15 lb. Over 100,000 anadromous fish spawn in the basin each year.

Boaters circumvent Rainie Falls by bumping through a channel dynamited into bedrock as a fish ladder. Mule Creek Canyon, not as wide as the length of some rafts, is followed by Blossom Bar, a Class IV rapid. Several lodges along the river host river-traveling guests. Flows are adequate all summer and fall, and additional reaches above and below the wild section offer a total of 55 mi of whitewater boating. The lowest reach below Agness is mostly Class I in a nearly wild canyon, making an excellent two-day canoe voyage. Power boats—a big tourist business—are allowed below Blossom Bar. The Rogue River Trail of 40 mi presents one of the finer river-backpacking opportunities, especially in the cool seasons.

As one of the earliest wild and scenic rivers, the Rogue is a rare case where much land acquisition has followed designation: several million dollars was spent to protect stream frontage. Combating overuse and conflicts over camping space, the federal agencies instituted a permit system in 1978 limiting floating to 12,000 people a year, split evenly between commercial outfitters and private boaters.

Salmon River, northwest Oregon, designated in 1988; 33.5 mi, source to
   mouth at Sandy River.
Classification: wild, 15 mi; scenic, 4.8 mi; recreational, 13.7 mi.
Administered by: BLM, 1717 Fabry Road S.E., Salem, OR 97306;
   Mount Hood National Forest, 2955 N.W. Division St., Gresham, OR
   97030.
Access: Hwy. 26 near Zigzag and 2618 south of Zigzag, Timberline Lodge on
   Mount Hood.
River difficulty: not normally run.
Maps: BLM, Salem District; Mount Hood National Forest.

Called an "Oregon work of art" by the Oregon Rivers Council, the Salmon runs from the Palmer Glacier on Mount Hood to the Sandy River with little disturbance.

Sparse stands of noble fir, Douglas fir, and western hemlock speckle the glaciated headwaters area, followed by miles of deep forests where spotted owls live. The river flows in the Salmon-Huckleberry Wilderness for 8 mi and plunges over a magnificent set of six waterfalls up to 75 ft high. These separate the steelhead, chinook, and coho salmon from the headwaters fishery of cutthroat trout. The Barlow Road, part of the Oregon Trail, crosses the river, and Timberline Lodge sits 0.5 mi from the source. A popular fishery, the river can be seen from the Salmon River National Recreational Trail. Public land covers 82 percent of the frontage.

Sandy River, northwest Oregon, designated in 1988; 24.9 mi in 2 sections: 12.4 mi from the source to Mount Hood National Forest boundary, 12.5 mi from near Dodge Park to Dabney State Park.
Classification: wild, 4.5 mi; scenic, 3.8 mi; recreational, 16.6 mi.
Administered by: BLM, 1717 Fabry Road S.E. Salem, OR 97306; Mount Hood National Forest, 2955 N.W. Division St., Gresham, OR 97030.
Access: upper reach, Hwy. 26 to F.R. 18 (Lolo Pass Rd.); lower reach, Dodge Park via Ten Eych Rd. north of Sandy, Oxbow Park east of Hwy. 26, Dabney State Park off Stark St. south of Troutdale.
River difficulty: upper reach Class IV or V, lower reach Class I–II with 1 Class III rapid.
Maps: Mount Hood National Forest; BLM, Salem District.
Other information: John Garren, *Oregon River Tours* (1976).

One of the most used rivers in Oregon for recreation, the Sandy combines exquisite high country, a recreational gorge to which whitewater boaters flock, and superb runs of salmon and steelhead.

Beginning on the Sandy Glacier, 4.5 mi flow through the Mount Hood Wilderness, and the entire reach runs through public land with great scenic beauty that undergoes heavy use by campers and anglers. The lower gorge appears as a miniature version of the Columbia River Gorge and shelters spotted owls, otters, minks, martens, and cougars. One of the state's top producers of winter and summer steelhead, the Sandy also nurtures spring chinook, coho salmon, smelt, and native rainbow and cutthroat trout in the upper river. Three rare or endangered plants survive in the gorge.

The upper river has a Class IV or V whitewater run for expert paddlers. Only an hour's drive from 1 million people in the Portland area, the lower gorge is one of the most popular whitewater and fishing rivers in the Northwest, and a Class II run from Oxbow to Dabney Park draws crowds in the summer.

Population pressures have grown intense in the lower areas, and developers had proposed hydroelectric projects before the designation. Some local residents and the Oregon Rivers Council are working to have the middle section of the 75 mi long river designated in the National Wild and Scenic Rivers System.

Smith River, North Fork, southwest Oregon, designated in 1988 (see also California, Smith River, North Fork); 13 mi, source to Oregon-California line (source to mouth including the California portion is 26.5 mi).
Classification: wild, 6.5 mi; scenic, 6.5 mi.
Administered by: Siskiyou National Forest, 200 N.E. Greenfield Rd., Grants Pass, OR 97526.

Access: Hwy. 101 in California to Rowdy Creek Rd. to F.R. 4402, spur 206.
River difficulty: Class IV.
Maps: Siskiyou National Forest.
Other information: James Cassady and Fryar Calhoun, *California White Water* (1984).

One of the most extraordinary wild rivers protected from source to mouth, the North Fork of the Smith features emerald water that drops through intricate rapids and a deep green forest.

Beginning below Chetco Peak, half the reach flows through the Kalmiopsis Wilderness. Douglas fir and mixed conifers crowd the steep canyon. Water quality is renowned, supporting chinook salmon, coho salmon, steelhead, and sea-run cutthroat trout. The region is noted for endemic, unusual, and rare plant species.

Whitewater boaters revere this river as one of the finer Class IV wilderness runs anywhere. The North Fork is closed to fishing in order to provide spawning for the main stem Smith River fishery. The Sourdough Trail, reached from Forest Road 1107-220, passes through a botanical area and to the river. The Oregon segment of the Smith flows entirely through Siskiyou National Forest.

Snake River, northeast Oregon, designated in 1975; 66.5 mi.
See Idaho, Snake River.

Sprague River, North Fork, south-central Oregon, designated in 1988; 15 mi, River Spring to National Forest boundary.
Classification: scenic.
Administered by: Fremont National Forest, 524 North G St., Lakeview, OR 97630.
Access: Hwy. 140 at Quartz Mountain to F.R. 366, 348, and 337.
Maps: Fremont National Forest.

This unusually scenic river originates in high mountain meadows, cuts through a canyon of andesite lava 200 ft deep, then through sagebrush-blanketed hills. It flows at the edge of the Gearhart Mountain Wilderness and through the Gearhart Mountain Volcanic eruptive center. People fish for wild rainbow, brook, and brown trout.

Parts of the 34 mi long river have been logged to the waterline and heavily grazed. A section of the Sprague was deleted from protection at the last minute to allow a dam and diversion for hydroelectric power.

Squaw Creek, central Oregon, designated in 1988; 15.4 mi, source to a point 800 ft above McAllister Ditch.

Classification: wild, 6.6 mi; scenic, 8.8 mi.
Designated tributaries (all in the Three Sisters Wilderness):
    Squaw Creek, North Fork.
    Squaw Creek, South Fork.
    Squaw Creek, Soap Fork.
    Squaw Creek, Park Creek Fork.
    Park Creek, East Fork.
    Park Creek, West Fork.
Total mileage: 27.
Administered by: Deschutes National Forest, 211 N.E. Revere, Bend, OR 97701.
Access: Hwy. 126 at Sisters and south to forest roads including 1514600.
River difficulty: not run.
Maps: Deschutes National Forest.

With headwaters in the Three Sisters Wilderness, Squaw Creek and its tributaries begin as braided glacial streams, then flow through mature ponderosa pine forests and high desert country of juniper.

The numerous cascades include Squaw Creek Falls, reached by trail from Forest Road 1514600. At the headwaters, an unstable glacial moraine has impounded Carver Lake, where the designation allowed an exemption for a reinforcement structure to be built to protect the town of Sisters. Forest roads and paths lead to the river.

Sycan River, south-central Oregon, designated in 1988; 59 mi, source to Coyote Bucket at Fremont National Forest boundary.
Classification: scenic, 50.4 mi; recreational, 8.6 mi.
Administered by: Fremont National Forest, 524 North G St., Lakeview, OR 97630; Winema National Forest, 2819 Dahlia St., Klamath Falls, OR 97601.
Access: Hwy. 140 east of Klamath Falls to Cty. Rd. 1257 and F.R. 3312.
River difficulty: not normally run.
Maps: Fremont and Winema national forests.

The Sycan flows through a canyon with forests and stringer meadows, supplies the biologically rich Sycan Marsh, and drops through a canyon with old-growth ponderosa and lodgepole pines.

The marsh supports rare plant communities and 130 nesting bird species, including sandhill cranes, upland sandpipers, and bald eagles. The river hosts an abundance of wildlife and a native trout fishery. Fishing, hiking, and bird watching are done on public land, as well as some boating in the spring.

About 75 percent of the corridor is public land, with most of the remainder belonging to the Nature Conservancy, which bought the 23,600 acre marsh and leased much of it for ranching.

Umpqua River, North Fork, southwest Oregon, designated in 1988; 33.8 mi, Soda Spring Powerhouse (below Toketee Lake) to Rock Creek (above Idleyld Park).

Classification: recreational.

Administered by: Umpqua National Forest, P.O. Box 1008, Roseburg, OR 97470; BLM, 777 N.W. Garden Valley Blvd., Roseburg, OR 97470.

Access: Hwy. 138 parallels the river.

River difficulty: Class II, III.

Maps: Umpqua National Forest; BLM, Roseburg District.

An internationally renowned salmon and steelhead river, the North Umpqua has green and white beauty with old-growth forests and offers excellent paddling.

The summer steelhead run is one of the best on the West Coast; annual runs average 6,600 steelhead and 10,600 chinook salmon, 74 percent of them wild fish. Coho salmon, rainbow trout, and brown trout also live in the river. Declines, however, have resulted from intensive logging. Historic and archaeological sites can be seen along the river. Important for many species of wildlife, the river is bordered by four roadless areas and the Boulder Creek Wilderness.

The 106 mi long North Fork is easily reached by road and has been renowned among sport anglers since the 1930s. The combination of large steelhead and difficulty of wading near deep holes and steep banks makes this river one of the anglers' ultimate challenges. The North Umpqua is also a favorite of whitewater boaters who can travel the river all summer and fall. The emerald-green water, rock-filled rapids, and deeply forested shorelines are an uncommon blend on such an accessible river, the only distraction being a continuous stream of log trucks—several per minute in some years—coming down the canyon. The Steamboat Inn Resort is world famous.

Efforts to designate the river in the state and national rivers system in the 1970s and early 1980s were stymied by vehement local opposition centered in the timber industry, in spite of public ownership of 94 percent of the corridor. Since 1978, however, the river corridor has been managed under special Forest Service direction to protect river qualities. Logging of residual old-growth timber in the basin remains a contentious issue.

Wenaha River, northeast Oregon, designated in 1988; 21.6 mi, source at confluence of North and South forks to mouth.

Classification: wild, 18.7 mi; scenic, 2.7 mi; recreational, 0.2 mi.

Administered by: Umatilla National Forest, 2517 S.W. Hailey Ave., Pendleton, OR 97801.

Access: local roads near Troy, trails from F.R. 62 between Elgin and Troy.

River difficulty: not normally run.

Maps: Umatilla National Forest.

One of the wildest, least accessible rivers in the Northwest, the Wenaha is protected for its wilderness and fisheries.

From the Blue Mountains the river flows through the Wenaha-Tucannon Wilderness for all but its lower 6 mi. Prime habitat for bighorn sheep, bald eagles in winter, and many wildlife species, the river also offers some of Oregon's finest native rainbow and bull trout fishing and much of the remaining salmon and steelhead habitat in the Grande Ronde basin. The large flat at the mouth was an important Indian meeting place. Most of the river can be reached only on foot, so anglers, backpackers, and horseback riders mainly use the Wenaha. About 95 percent of the frontage is public land.

White River, north-central Oregon, designated in 1988; 46.5 mi, source to mouth at Deschutes River, but undesignated at one waterfall.

Classification: scenic, 24 mi; recreational, 22.5 mi.

Administered by: Mount Hood National Forest, 2955 N.W. Division St., Gresham, OR 97030; BLM, P.O. Box 550, Prineville, OR 97754.

Access: Hwy. 26 to Hwy. 35 to F.R. 48 to Barlow Campground, Hwy. 197 bridge.

River difficulty: Class III, IV.

Maps: Mount Hood National Forest; BLM, Prineville District.

Pristine for many of its miles, the White joins the Deschutes River for 92.5 continuous miles of national river.

Tumbling with white glacial flour off Mount Hood, the river courses through high glacial valleys, past evergreen forests, and into an enclosed canyon of the central Oregon volcanic plain. A series of waterfalls drops 100 ft below Tygh Valley. A fascinating array of plant life evolves from alpine forest to fir and pine, then to oak and cottonwood. Many wildlife species live here, and a native cutthroat trout fishery does well in lower reaches, which also serve as spawning habitat for salmon and steelhead. The historic Barlow Road, part of the Oregon Trail, passes nearby.

A magnificent Class IV kayak run extends for 18 mi from Barlow Crossing to the Victor Road bridge during the snowmelt season. From Victor Road to Tygh Valley, an 11 mi Class II or III run, likely including logjams, is considered one of the most beautiful runs in Oregon. Many people use the river for trout fishing and camping, and the Timberline Trail crosses the upper section.

Before designation, a permit had been granted for hydroelectric development on the lower river, and the Forest Service had planned timber sales. Public land covers all the Forest Service half of the river and 57 percent of the BLM portion.

Willamette River, North Fork of the Middle Fork, west-central Oregon, designated in 1988; 42.3 mi, Waldo Lake to Willamette National Forest boundary.

Classification: wild, 8.8 mi; scenic, 6.5 mi; recreational, 27 mi.

Administered by: Willamette National Forest, P.O. Box 10607, Eugene, OR 97440.

Access: Hwy. 58 to Hemlock to F.R. 19, which parallels the river.

River difficulty: Class IV, V.

Maps: Willamette National Forest.

The last bastion of wilderness in the systematically dammed and logged Willamette River basin, the North Fork combines outstanding habitat, fisheries, whitewater, and forest scenery. At the source, Waldo Lake is one of the purest lakes in the world.

Nearly all of this 44 mi long river is designated. The upper 12 mi remain roadless where the river cascades over 34 waterfalls in 6 mi. The middle section flows through a wide flood plain, and the lower 12 mi cut through a canyon 1,000 ft deep. Excellent habitat supports fishers, northern spotted owls, and bald eagles. Winter range is important for elk, deer, bears, and cougars. Several endangered plants survive in the canyon, and wild rainbow and cutthroat trout are managed for fly fishing only. Archaeological records of Indian travel and hunting date back 10,000 years.

A difficult kayaking run, 9 mi of the North Fork are considered one of Oregon's premier expert descents during the rainy season. People come to fish, camp, and hike along this river, which offers easy access within a two hour drive of two-thirds of the state's population. The Shale Ridge Trail follows the upper 9 mi.

River conservationists included the North Fork in the original State Scenic Waterway System to fight off a dam threat. All of the corridor is public land.

PENNSYLVANIA
2 rivers, 193.4 mi

Allegheny River, northwest Pennsylvania, designated in 1992; 85 mi, Kinzua Dam to Hwy. 6 bridge (7 mi), Irvine to Oil City (47 mi), Franklin to Emlenton (31 mi).

Classification: recreational.

Administered by: Allegheny National Forest, 222 Liberty St., P.O. Box 847, Warren, PA 16365.

Access: Hwys. 59 and 62 parallel the river from Kinzua Dam to Franklin; Hwy. 208 crosses at Emlenton; Bullion-Rockland Rd. crosses between Franklin and Emlenton.

River difficulty: Class I.

Maps: Allegheny National Forest, topo maps.

One of the larger protected rivers, the Allegheny had been considered for national river status since the inception of the system. It is one of the largest rivers in the national system flowing predominantly through private land. Lower reaches in July carry over 4,000 cfs.

With a gentle current, the river flows through Allegheny National Forest, around 109 islands between Kinzua Dam and Oil City, and past steep mountainsides with a wide diversity of northern hardwoods and other plant life. The fishery ranges from cold-water species below Kinzua Dam to warm-water fishes farther downstream. The more urban and developed reaches were omitted from the designation. Within the corridor, 34 of 394 wildlife species are designated as state endangered, threatened, or of special concern. Bald eagles feed along the river in winter. A prehistoric site, Indian God Rock, is listed on the National Register of Historic Landmarks.

The river is heavily used for fishing, canoeing, and other recreation. About 4,000 homes and summer cottages are located in the corridor.

Gravel dredging had been a chronic problem in one section; sewage discharges and an oil refinery at Emlenton have caused water quality problems in the past. Oil and gas drilling occurs throughout the corridor. The river is to be administered by the Forest Service with cooperative agreements with the state and county governments, including formal advisory councils.

Delaware River, northeast Pennsylvania, designated in 1978, shared with New York and New Jersey; 108.4 mi in 2 sections: 73.4 mi from the confluence of East and West branches below Hancock, New York, to Cherry Island near Sparrow Bush, New York; 35 mi through the Delaware Water Gap National Recreation Area (upper and lower reaches are separated by 5 mi of undesignated river).

Classification: scenic, 59 mi; recreational, 49.4 mi.

Administered by: NPS, P.O. Box C, Narrowsburg, NY 12764 (upper reach); NPS, Delaware Water Gap National Recreation Area, Bushkill, PA 18324 (lower reach).

Access: State Hwys. 191, 371, 652, 590, 434, 209, and many other sites.

River difficulty: Class I, II.

Maps: NPS, *Upper Delaware Map and Guide*; Delaware Water Gap National Recreation Area.

Other information: Walter Burmeister, *Appalachian Waters: The Delaware and Its Tributaries* (1974).

This section of the Delaware—long by eastern standards for a protected river—is mostly undeveloped and exceptional, offering scenic and recreational values within 215 miles of 50 million people. The Delaware is one of the largest undammed rivers outside Alaska.

Forming the boundary between Pennsylvania and New York and then between Pennsylvania and New Jersey, the river riffles past a broad flood plain between the Catskill Mountains to the east and Pocono Plateau to the west. Hardwood-blanketed slopes shelter diverse plant and animal life. Long pools and alternating gravel-bottomed riffles support smallmouth bass, walleye, American shad, and other fishes. One of the richest of the national rivers for its cultural landscape, the Delaware has shores dotted with old villages, farms, and historic sites.

The Delaware provides for one of the longest free-flowing canoe trips in the East (the entire river runs 330 mi, much of it boatable). Gentle water is broken by an exciting Class II rapid at Skinner's Falls. Plentiful accesses and campsites accommodate great numbers of people, and 26 canoe liveries can put a saturation quantity of 4,000 boats on the water at once. Fishing is popular throughout, along with hiking, camping, and picnicking, especially in the national recreation area.

The upper section was one of the study rivers in the original Wild and Scenic Rivers Act, and the lower section was designated in direct response to the threat of Tocks Island Dam—one of the path-breaking dam fights in conservation history. With 93 percent of the land in private ownership, the Delaware is one of the foremost examples of a national river within private land.

SOUTH CAROLINA
Chattooga River, 40 mi shared with Georgia

SOUTH DAKOTA
Missouri River, 98 mi shared with Nebraska

TENNESSEE
3 rivers, 7 rivers and tributaries, 98 mi, including 1 river and 53 mi not in the Wild and Scenic Rivers System

Cumberland River, Big South Fork, northeast Tennessee, designated in 1974, also in Kentucky; not in the Wild and Scenic Rivers System; 25 mi, source to Kentucky state line (another 20 mi in Kentucky are designated to the backwater of Cumberland Reservoir).
Classification: national river and national recreation area.

Designated tributaries:
  Clear Fork, 20 mi.
  New River, 8 mi.
Total mileage: 53, plus 20 additional miles in Kentucky.
Administered by: NPS, Rt. 3, Box 401, Oneida, TN 37841.
Access: Hwy. 27 at Oneida to Leatherwood Rd., Kentucky Hwy. 92, other
  sites in the national recreation area.
River difficulty: Class IV.
Maps: NPS, "Big South Fork National Recreation Area."
Other information: Bob Sehlinger and Bob Lantz, *Canoeing and Kayaking*
  Guide to the Streams of Tennessee, Vol. 1 (1983).

Draining one of the largest undeveloped areas of the East, the Big South
Fork and much of its basin in Tennessee and Kentucky are a national recreation area centered on the river.

The Big South Fork and its tributaries have cut gorges 500 ft deep into the
lush Cumberland Plateau, leaving sandstone outcrops and boulder-
congested rapids. This network of primitive Appalachian gorges is some of
the most rugged topography in the East. Biologists regard the flora, including
giant hardwoods, as some of the richest and most diverse in the nation. Three
endangered species—the Indiana bat, southern bald eagle, and southern red-
cockaded woodpecker—live here.

Whitewater boating is a highlight in spring and early summer. Hiking,
camping, and fishing for smallmouth bass, rock bass, and bream are popular.

Water quality has been threatened by coal mining and logging in the past,
and some threats continue. The Bureau of Outdoor Recreation recommended
wild river status for the Big South Fork in 1963, before the Wild and Scenic
Rivers System existed. In 1968 the Army Corps proposed Devil's Jump Dam
on the lower river in Kentucky for hydropower. Opposition led to the creation
of the national recreation area and management of the gorge as wilderness.

Emory River, southwest Tennessee, designated in 1976; 1 mi, mouth of
  Obed River to Nemo Bridge.
Classification: recreational.
Access: Nemo Bridge on Catoosa Rd. southwest of Wartburg.
  This short reach is continuous with the Obed River (see description below).

Obed River, southwest Tennessee, designated in 1976; 24 mi, western
  boundary of Catoosa Wildlife Management Area to Emory River.
Designated tributaries:
  Clear Creek, 18 mi, Morgan county line to Obed River, wild.
  Daddy's Creek, 2 mi, Morgan county line to Obed River, wild.
Total mileage: 44.

Total mileage designated in Obed system: 45 (includes Emory River).
Administered by: NPS and Tennessee Wildlife Resources Agency, P.O. Box 429, Wartburg, TN 37887.
Access: Obed River reached from Potters Ford east of Hwy. 4252, Obed Junction south of Hwy. 4252 west of Wartburg, Clear Creek at Barnett Bridge south of Hwy. 62, Jett Bridge on Hwy. 4252, Lilly Bridge south of Hwy. 62, Daddy's Creek at bridge north of Catoosa Rd.
River difficulty: Class II–IV.
Maps: NPS, "Emory River Watershed Map."
Other information: Monte Smith, *Paddler's Guide to the Obed/Emory Watershed;* NPS, *The Obed Wild and Scenic River* (brochure).

One of the most primitive and rugged river systems in the Appalachians and one of the least spoiled in the East, the Obed offers miles of wild gorges, whitewater, and a rich diversity of plant life.

The river has cut 500 ft deep into the Cumberland Plateau where 100 mi of gorges are undeveloped except for a few cabins. House-sized boulders and sandy beaches decorate the river. Trees include oak, pine, hickory, ash, beech, maple, poplar, hemlock, sycamore, birch, elm, and others. Bluegill, catfish, and three species of bass are sought by anglers, and the rare Cumberland Plateau musky is the southernmost muskellunge. Bald eagles, golden eagles, and red-cockaded woodpeckers live here. Water quality remains excellent in an area often fouled by acid mine drainage.

Paddling the technical, sandstone-filled whitewater in the early spring is the highlight of many canoeists' seasons. Boaters often run 10 mi of Class III–IV water from Obed Junction to Nemo and sometimes travel the 12 mi Class II pitch from Potter's Ford to Obed Junction and 9 mi of Class II–IV on Clear Creek. Fishing is done year-round. A campground is sited at Frozen Head State Park, and camping is allowed along the river.

Opposition to Nemo Dam in the 1960s led to inclusion of the Obed as one of the original wild and scenic study rivers. About half the recommended mileage was not designated because of opposition by the upstream congressional representative. The addition of unprotected reaches of the Obed, Clear Creek, and Daddy's Creek is sought by Tennessee conservationists to discourage strip mining and second-home development. About one-third of the national river shoreline is public land in a state wildlife area.

TEXAS
1 river, 191.2 mi

Rio Grande, southwest Texas, designated in 1978; 191.2 mi, above Mariscal Canyon to Terrell–Val Verde county line (about 20 mi above Amistad Reservoir).

Classification: wild, 95.2 mi; scenic, 96 mi.
Administered by: Big Bend National Park, Big Bend, TX 79834.
Access: Hwy. 385, access in Big Bend National Park, private ranch roads.
River difficulty: Class I, II in upper reaches, Class I–IV in lower canyons.
Maps: Big Bend National Park.
Other information: John Pearson, *River Guide to the Rio Grande*, 4 vols.
   (1982); Big Bend Natural History Association, Big Bend National Park,
   TX 79834.

The historic border river between the United States and Mexico flows through four major canyons and many miles of hauntingly wild and inaccessible desert. This is one of the ultimate desert canyon river trips in America and one of the most remote. The Rio Grande is the second longest national river outside Alaska.

In the heart of the Chihuahuan Desert, the upper section cuts through the 1,800 ft deep limestone canyons of Mariscal and Boquillas, a run of 30 mi. After traversing a broad flood plain, the Rio Grande narrows again into lower canyons, flowing for 40 mi 500–1,500 ft below the plateaus with hot springs scattered in several places. Martin Canyon follows, where walls along the river decrease to 50 ft in height, the whole voyage reminiscent of a small Grand Canyon. Riverfront vegetation includes willows, reeds, cane, tamarisk, seepwillows, acacias, and mesquites. The muddy water supports shiners, daces, longnose gar, and catfish. The endangered peregrine falcon nests in cliff faces. Important historic and archaeological sites can be found along the river.

Canoe trips of one day to two weeks are possible, and there are opportunities for winter boating. Adequate flows exist 76 percent of the time. Rocky overlooks and caves make fascinating hikes from the riverfront, but visitors should respect private property. The most popular canyon, Santa Elena with its Rockslide Rapid, lies above the national river reach. Permits are required for all floating. Fishing is limited by muddy water to catfish and some bass. Trails lead to the river in the Big Bend National Park.

Most of the water comes from the Rio Conchos River in Mexico, as irrigators divert the Rio Grande in Texas entirely (a treaty allows the United States to consume all of its water while requiring Mexico to deliver 350,000 acre-feet annually). The pesticide DDT from Mexico is a significant water quality problem, and cattle grazing on the south side of the river is not controlled.

All of the American side in Big Bend National Park is public land; 67 percent of the land on the 127 mi below the park is private. After designation and heated controversy, landowners drew up a plan that the National Park Service largely adopted. Instead of acquisition, the government is to negotiate use agreements with landowners.

WASHINGTON
10 rivers, 223.5 mi, including 2 rivers and 47 mi not in the
Wild and Scenic Rivers System

See Jeff Bennett, *A Guide to the Whitewater Rivers of Washington* (1991), for more information on all rivers.

Cascade River, northwest Washington, designated in 1978; 20 mi, source at North and South forks confluence to mouth.
Classification: scenic.
Administered by: Mount Baker–Snoqualmie National Forest, 2105 Hwy. 20, Sedro Woolley, WA 98284.
Access: Hwy. 20 to Marblemont bridge and Cascade River Rd.
River difficulty: Class V.
Maps: Mount Baker–Snoqualmie National Forest.

A spectacular river of glacial-green water, extreme rapids, and boulder gardens in a lush canyon with old-growth forests, the Cascade is designated from source to mouth either in the Glacier Peak Wilderness or as a national river.

An important spawning stream for anadromous fish, the Cascade was designated with the Skagit, which it joins at Marblemont for a continuous national river reach of 70 mi. In upper reaches, forested scenery with abundant old-growth trees is enjoyed by hikers. A very difficult kayak descent extends for 8 mi from Marble Creek Campground to the mouth in early summer. Massive clearcuts have been made on state and private land that adjoins the lower river. The designation precluded a hydroelectric proposal that had threatened the stream.

Cascade River, South Fork, northwest Washington, designated in 1978; 1 mi, Glacier Peak Wilderness to mouth.
Classification: scenic.
Access: Hwy. 120 to Marblemont bridge and Cascade River Rd., then to F.R. 1590.

With designated wilderness above the short national river reach, the South Fork's protection extends from source to mouth and on down the Cascade and Skagit rivers.

Klickitat River, south-central Washington, designated in 1986; 11 mi, Wheeler Creek, near Pitt, to mouth at Columbia River.
Classification: recreational.
Administered by: USFS, Columbia Gorge National Scenic Area, 902 Wasco Ave., Hood River, OR 97031.
Access: Hwy. 142 north of Lyle parallels the river.

River difficulty: Class II with 1 Class III rapid and 1 Class V gorge.
Maps: USGS.

With headwaters on Mount Adams, the second highest peak in the Cascades, the Klickitat flows through scenic forests and gorges 1,400 ft deep. Basalt outcrops form large cliffs as the river cuts its way toward the Columbia, including a bedrock gorge 40 ft deep and as little as 8 ft across. Each year, two different runs of steelhead, chinook salmon, and coho salmon spawn here. The Yakima Tribe depends on the chinook for subsistence; Indians dip net in the river. Exceptional values were found for fisheries, endangered plant and animal species, and winter range for deer.

Access is available at the Klickitat County park downstream from the Pitt Bridge, at a private site called Three Pines, at Dillacourt or Turkey Hole Road, and at several other sites. The scenic canyon is used for whitewater paddling above the gorge section. This and Oregon's Deschutes are the only rivers in the region runnable year-round in drift boats. The most popular boating and fishing areas of the 95 mi long Klickitat lie upriver from the designated reach in a section that has been studied for wild and scenic status, and also above the Yakima Indian Reservation. Boaters regard the excellent whitewater run of the upper river as the finest river scenery in central and eastern Washington. Residential development encroaches on the lower reach.

Little White Salmon River, south-central Washington, designated in 1986; not in the Wild and Scenic Rivers System; 18 mi, Willard National Fish Hatchery to Columbia River.
Classification: hydroelectric dam prohibition.
Administered by: USFS, Columbia Gorge National Scenic Area, 902 Wasco Ave., Hood River, OR 97031.
Access: Willard Rd. north of Hwy. 14.
River difficulty: not normally run.
Maps: Gifford Pinchot National Forest.

This small river in the volcanic mountains south of Mount Adams is protected from hydroelectric projects by the Columbia Gorge National Scenic Area.

Sauk River, northwest Washington, designated in 1978; 43 mi, Elliott Creek to mouth.
Classification: scenic.
Administered by: Mount Baker–Snoqualmie National Forest, 2105 Hwy. 20, Sedro Woolley, WA 98284.
Access: Rockport-Darrington Rd., F.R. 20 south of Darrington.
River difficulty: Class III.
Maps: Mount Baker–Snoqualmie National Forest.

Other information: Douglass A. North, *Washington Whitewater, Vol. 1* (1988).

The Sauk was designated with the Skagit and joins it as a critical spawning ground for anadromous fish.

The upper river includes cascades and boulder-riddled whitewater. Much of the river lies at least 0.25 mi from the road and remains remote in character. Breathtaking views show clear, green water in front of forested shores and snowcapped peaks. The lower river, silty with glacial runoff, flows through a wide flood plain with views to distant glaciers.

An excellent paddling trip of 8.3 mi with two Class III rapids lies between Bedal Campground and White Chuck from May through July, though log-jams create a hazard. The middle Sauk between White Chuck and Darrington offers 10.3 mi of expert Class IV whitewater; it is considered among the most exciting and scenic river trips in Washington and is boatable from late April through July. Anglers flock here and use Forest Service campgrounds along both sections. Designation prohibited construction of a flood control and hydroelectric project that had been proposed on the lower Sauk. While spectacular stands of old-growth forests are seen throughout the reach, large tracts on the mountainsides are being clearcut.

Sauk River, North Fork, northwest Washington, designated in 1978; 8 mi, Glacier Peak Wilderness to mouth.
Classification: scenic.
Access: F.R. 20 south of F.R. 49 south of Darrington.
River difficulty: not run, includes waterfalls.
Maps: Mount Baker–Snoqualmie National Forest.

Combined with the Sauk and Skagit, to which it flows, the North Fork makes a continuous national river of 100 mi. The reach is well screened from the road and retains a wild character with towering old-growth forests, though many areas above the valley floor are being clearcut. The wilderness area above the designated reach includes one of the nation's finest riverfront trails through ancient forests. The North Fork falls is a cataract framed by virgin timber.

Skagit River, northwest Washington, designated in 1978; 58 mi, Bacon Creek (above Marblemount) to Sedro-Woolley pipeline.
Classification: recreational.
Administered by: Mount Baker–Snoqualmie National Forest, 21905 64th Ave. W., Mountlake Terrace, WA 98403.
Access: Hwy. 20 parallels the river.
River difficulty: Class I, II (Class III above the designated reach).
Maps: Mount Baker–Snoqualmie National Forest.

The Skagit provides for one of the richest anadromous fisheries in America and one of the largest winter populations of bald eagles outside Alaska.

This largest river draining to Puget Sound features a broad flood plain and densely forested slopes as it riffles westward, showing views of snowcapped Mount Baker and the North Cascades. Farmland, home sites, and small towns appear along middle and lower reaches. The river supports five salmon species (chinook, coho, pink, chum, and sockeye) and three seagoing varieties of trout (steelhead, Dolly Varden, and cutthroat) for 2.2 million fish per year in the early 1980s. It provides 30 percent of the anadromous fishery of Puget Sound. A large commercial industry depends on the Skagit, as do sport anglers and Indians. This was once the most productive steelhead river in Washington. On the flood plain of the middle river, up to 200 bald eagles winter in roosts along the shores.

This entire reach of the Skagit offers excellent, easy canoeing year-round— one of the longest free-flowing trips that can be taken on the West Coast. Class III rapids run above the designated reach from Goodell Creek to Copper Creek. The river is popular for steelhead fishing, and opportunities for bald eagle watching in the winter rank among the best in the country. Several campgrounds lie along the river.

The Skagit was one of the original rivers authorized for wild and scenic study in 1968, including the Cascade, South Fork Cascade, Sauk, North Fork Sauk, and Suiattle. Congress excluded the critical Skagit River reach from Copper Creek to Bacon Creek—the most scenic with excellent whitewater—because Seattle City Light proposed a dam. Congress likewise omitted the bottom reach, from Sedro Woolley to Mount Vernon, because of a proposed nuclear power plant and flood control levees planned for urban areas. Inclusion of that short additional mileage to Puget Sound would make the Sauk-Skagit one of the longest rivers protected from source to sea. Private land covers much of the river frontage. Recreational subdivisions and accelerated logging remain major threats to the river and to riparian habitat.

Suiattle River, northwest Washington, designated in 1978; 27.5 mi.
Classification: scenic.
Administered by: Mount Baker–Snoqualmie National Forest, 21905 64th
    Ave. W., Mountlake Terrace, WA 98403.
Access: F.R. 26 and 25 east of Rockport-Darrington Rd.
River difficulty: Class III.
Maps: Mount Baker–Snoqualmie National Forest.
Other information: Douglass A. North, *Washington Whitewater, Vol. 1*
    (1988).

With heavy, continuous whitewater, the Suiattle flows past old-growth forests on its way to the Sauk and Skagit rivers. From source to mouth it is protected as a national river or wilderness.

With excellent tributaries for anadromous fish spawning, the river sits back from nearby roads and the milky, glacial waterway retains a remote wildness.

A whitewater run of 12.7 mi includes two Class III rapids from Rat Trap to Sauk River Bridge in July and August. It is considered one of the best wilderness river trips in western Washington and presents no signs of civilization except for clearcuts on mountains above. Logjams may clog the rapids and can be counted on as an extreme hazard above this section. Fishing is popular and Forest Service campgrounds lie along the river. The designation precluded several hydroelectric dam proposals.

White Salmon River, south-central Washington, designated in 1986; 8 mi, Gilmer Creek at BZ Corner to Buck Creek at Northwestern Lake inlet.
Classification: scenic.
Administered by: USFS, Columbia Gorge National Scenic Area, 902 Wasco Ave., Hood River, OR 97031.
Access: Hwy. 141 north of Bingen.
River difficulty: Class IV with 1 Class V rapid.
Other information: USFS, *White Salmon River User Guide* (brochure).

The White Salmon churns through an astonishing basalt gorge, cut narrow and deep with cascading rapids and rock gardens of ferns and other plant life clinging to damp canyon walls.

An 11 mi reach is the longest vertical-wall gorge in the lower Columbia region, and the river features caves, falls, and springs. Unique, reliable flows are a result of late glacial runoff and spring discharges. Beyond the gorge walls lie pine, fir, and Oregon white oak forests in a transition zone joining marine and continental climates. Deer, turkeys, and bald eagles range here in winter. A good resident population of rainbow and Dolly Varden trout thrive in the national river section, but anadromous fish have been blocked by Condit Dam since the early 1900s.

Skilled kayakers, rafters, and canoeists paddle here June through August on whitewater including occasional Class IV drops and Husum Falls, a Class V portage. A series of unrunnable falls lies upstream of the designated reach. Private put-in sites are available for a fee just upstream from BZ Corner and along Hwy. 141 below Husum Bridge (inquire at the Whitewater Market in Husum). Take-out is available above Husum Falls and at Northwestern Lake. Fishing pressure remains light because access to the basalt-walled gorge presents a formidable challenge.

Very little public land exists along the designated reach, yet local support was strong for designation because of a long-standing effort to defeat a chain of six hydroelectric dams on the 45 mi long White Salmon. The upper river, including remarkable scenery of Mount Adams, an expert whitewater run, and a good fishery, was studied for wild and scenic status.

Wind River, south-central Washington, designated in 1986; not in the Wild and Scenic Rivers System; 29 mi, source to mouth at Columbia River.
Classification: hydroelectric dam prohibition.
Administered by: USFS, Columbia Gorge National Scenic Area, 902 Wasco Ave., Hood River, OR 97031.
Access: Wind River Rd. parallels the river from Carson on Hwy. 14 to upper reaches.
River difficulty: not normally run.
Maps: Gifford Pinchot National Forest.

Flowing mostly through National Forest land in the volcanic mountains south of Mount Adams, this scenic river is protected from hydroelectric projects by the Columbia Gorge National Scenic Area legislation.

WEST VIRGINIA
4 rivers, 93 mi, 3 rivers and 82.5 mi not in the Wild and Scenic Rivers System

Bluestone River, southern West Virginia, designated in 1988; 10.5 mi, 2 mi above Summers and Mercer county line to Bluestone Reservoir.
Classification: scenic.
Administered by: NPS, 104 Main St., Glen Jean, WV 25846.
Access: Hwy. 20 south of Hinton, Pipestem and Bluestone state parks.
River difficulty: Class II–IV.
Maps: USGS.
Other information: Davidson, Eister, Davidson, *Wildwater West Virginia*, Vol. 2 (1985).

The lower Bluestone flows through a rugged valley with luxuriant vegetation. Hemlocks, rhododendron, and hardwoods crowd this lively river, bound within 500 ft high gorges and supporting nearly every warm-water fish species found in the state. Species of special concern include the southern bog lemming and Florida cooter. Much of the designated section cannot be reached by road. Two state parks and a state wildlife area border the river.

Exciting kayaking is possible during spring and after summer rains. Canoeists often favor Class I and II water above the designated reach, below Spanishburg. The Bluestone Public Hunting and Fishing Area is popular for warm-water fishing. Visitors find a wide range of recreational facilities at the two state parks; at Pipestem the River Trail, used by hikers and horseback riders, descends 1,000 ft.

Sixty miles of the 77 mi long river were studied for designation, and 25.5 mi qualified. Water quality, once poor, has improved slightly in recent years. Bluestone Dam, immediately downstream, could impound the lower 8 mi of the river if a maximum pool elevation is reached. With the Rio Chama and the lower Saint Croix, this is one of three national rivers subject to reservoir flooding by exceptions written into the specific legislation designating the rivers. National Park Service ownership accounts for 82 percent of the land along the designated reach, and a state park covers most of the rest.

Gauley River, southwest West Virginia, designated in 1988; not in the Wild
    and Scenic Rivers System; 26 mi, Summersville Dam to Swiss.
Classification: national recreation area.
Administered by: NPS, 104 Main St., Glen Jean, WV 25846.
Access: local roads south of Hwy. 39 west of Summersville, town of Swiss.
River difficulty: Class V, VI.
Maps: USGS.
Other information: Davidson, Eister, Davidson, *Wildwater West Virginia,*
    Vol. 2 (1985).

With the ultimate big rapids in the East, the Gauley is one of the preeminent whitewater rivers in the nation, flowing through a nearly undisturbed Appalachian gorge of sensational beauty. This is the only river studied for wild and scenic status but designated under another form of land protection.

Deep pools of clear water occasionally break the intensity of boulder-strewn miles of rapids. Only an unobtrusive railroad affects the natural scene in this canyon of rocky outcrops and palisades. Richly diverse plant life includes northern hardwoods, hemlocks, red spruce, and central hardwoods. Beavers, bears, and other wildlife can be seen. Living near the river are 29 reptiles and 37 amphibians. Within a 10 hour drive of 90 million people, the 108 mi long river has enormous recreational potential.

The 26 mi reach offers 100 major rapids, including at least 4 Class V and 1 Class VI drops, runnable when water is released from Summersville Dam in September and October. Seldom recognized are excellent opportunities for hiking and camping. The native warm-water fishery is depressed by cold releases from the dam.

The 1983 study of the Gauley for wild and scenic river status found the river and its tributaries the Cranberry and Meadow rivers eligible for designation. Opposition from rafting outfitters fearing too much regulation of their businesses halted protection, even though an Army Corps plan to divert the upper 3 mi for hydropower imminently threatened the river. The national recreation area status was devised to appeal to tourism and to gain protection of a larger land base, which was endangered by strip mining.

Meadow River, southwest West Virginia, designated in 1988; not in the Wild and Scenic Rivers System; 4.5 mi.
Classification: Gauley National Recreation Area.
This wild tributary to the Gauley offers extreme whitewater for expert paddlers in springtime runoff.

New River, southwest West Virginia, designated in 1978; not in the Wild and Scenic Rivers System; see also North Carolina, New River; 52 mi, Hinton to Fayetteville.
Classification: New River Gorge National River.
Administered by: NPS, 104 Main St., Glen Jean, WV 25846.
Access: Hwy. 20 at Hinton, Hwy. 41 at Prince, Hwy. 25 at Thurmond, Fayette Station Rd. east of Fayetteville; McKendree Rd. (gravel) parallels the river above Thurmond.
River difficulty: Class IV, also a Class II section.
Maps: NPS, "New River Gorge National River."
Other information: Davidson, Eister, Davidson, *Wildwater West Virginia*, Vol. 2 (1985).
The New River Gorge offers the biggest whitewater in the East, with flows of 5,000 to 25,000 cfs churning through 15 mi of difficult rapids and enormous waves and holes. Carving one of the most dramatic gorges in the Appalachians—as much as 1,200 ft deep—the river may be the second oldest in the world. Later joined by the Gauley River to form the Kanawha, this is the largest north-flowing drainage in the nation.

An incredibly varied fishery includes 58 species and is one of the most important warm-water fisheries in the state. Diverse hardwoods shelter many species of wildlife. At the height of the coal-mining era, more than 24 towns were built in the gorge; several remain, one of which, Hinton, has undertaken a revitalization project that recognizes the river as the town's economic backbone. The New River Gorge Bridge on Highway 19 is the longest single-span, steel-arch bridge in the world and the highest (876 ft) east of the Rocky Mountains.

The New River Gorge whitewater run is a 15 mi reach below Thurmond with 21 major rapids, some of them between house-sized boulders of sandstone, runnable all summer and fall. With 23 commercial outfitters and much private use, this is one of the most popular whitewater rivers in the nation. Sections below Hinton and Prince offer canoeable water, though high flows can produce Class III and IV rapids. The spectacular Sandstone Falls lies about 5 mi below Hinton. Fishing is popular in this reach. State parks nearby have camping, and thousands of climbers now flock to the long sandstone faces above the river. The New lies within 500 mi of nearly 65 percent of the U.S. population.

The national river designation was a response to state interest in promoting tourism and to some concerns about strip mining near the canyon. The designation differs from that of wild and scenic rivers by having more emphasis on recreational use, more facility development, larger appropriations, and a larger land base. Congress required the Army Corps to "facilitate protection of biological resources and recreational use of the national river" as it operates Bluestone Dam, just upstream.

WISCONSIN
3 rivers, 277 mi

Namekagon River, northwest Wisconsin, designated in 1968; 98 mi, dam impounding Lake Namekagon (near the source) to mouth.
Classification: scenic, 91.5 mi above and below Trego Lake (an impoundment); recreational, 6.5 mi (at Trego Lake).
Administered by: NPS, P.O. Box 708, Saint Croix Falls, WI 54024.
Access: Hwy. 63 parallels part of the river; Hwys. M east of Cable, K, 77, and many local roads and access points.
River difficulty: Class I.
Maps: USGS.
Other information: Bob and Jody Palzer, *Whitewater; Quietwater* (Evergreen Paddleways, Two Rivers, WI 54241); *Canoeing the Wild Rivers of Northwestern Wisconsin* (Northwest Canoe Trails, Inc., Shell Lake, WI 54871).

Though usually listed as part of the Saint Croix National Scenic Riverway, the Namekagon is the second longest designated river east of the Mississippi and the only one in the East protected essentially from source to mouth, though several low dams are included in the designated reach. This is also one of the longest national rivers for novice canoeists. Combined with the Saint Croix, nearly 200 continuous miles are included in the National Wild and Scenic Rivers System to Taylors Falls—the longest designated river reach outside Alaska.

The clear stream flows with a sandy or rocky bottom through slow meandering bends with thick willows, pines, and other vegetation, rich with fish and wildlife. While summer homes and other development have been built near some banks, most of the stream appears natural. The Namekagon is longer than the Saint Croix where the two meet.

All summer, canoeists paddle on all sections, especially the lower 65 mi from Hayward to the Saint Croix. Four low dams in upper and middle sections require portage. Anglers prefer the upper river above Hayward, which is managed as a trophy trout fishery. Visitors can find many access points and campgrounds.

One of the handful of rivers initially protected in the Wild and Scenic Rivers Act, the Namekagon is one of few streams designated that have dams. The river was a historic battleground between hydropower and fishing groups in the 1950s when the Federal Power Commission made its first ruling that a dam would not be licensed because of fishery values.

Saint Croix River, northwest Wisconsin, 103 mi designated in 1968, 27 mi in 1972, and 25 mi in 1976 (most mileage shared with Minnesota); 155 mi in 2 sections: Gordon Dam to Taylors Falls Dam; Taylors Falls Dam to mouth.

Classification: scenic, 100.6 mi; recreational, 54.4 mi.

Administered by: NPS, P.O. Box 708, Saint Croix Falls, WI 54024; lowest 25 mi: Minnesota Dept. of Natural Resources, Centennial Bldg., Saint Paul, MN 55155, and Wisconsin Dept. of Natural Resources, P.O. Box 450, Madison, WI 53701.

Access: information center at Hwy. 70 bridge, Hwy. 35, Hwy. 8 at Taylors Falls, Hwy. 243, and many other points.

River difficulty: Class I with a short section of easy Class II.

Other information: Bob and Jody Palzer, *Whitewater; Quietwater* (Evergreen Paddleways, Two Rivers, WI 54241); *Canoeing the Wild Rivers of Northwestern Wisconsin* (Northwest Canoe Trails, Inc., Shell Lake, WI 54871).

One of the first wild and scenic rivers, the Saint Croix is the longest in the East, and if the continuous mileage of the Namekagon and Saint Croix are counted as one river, it is even longer—252 mi from Namekagon headwaters to the mouth of the Saint Croix, though that mileage is interrupted by Taylors Falls Dam and by several other small impoundments on the Namekagon.

The upper 25 mi in Wisconsin flow through wooded wetland areas and rolling terrain. Below, the river riffles with many islands and easy rapids. Willows, hardwoods, and some pine shade flood plain terraces. One section offers an example of river reclamation where Nevers Dam was removed in 1955. A 60 ft high dam at Taylors Falls separates the upper and lower Saint Croix. Below there, the river flows through a scenic gorge with vertical rock sides, then through a broad valley with some development, including a power plant in lower reaches. Lock and Dam No. 3 on the Mississippi below the confluence impounds the lowest reach of the Saint Croix, though it is designated to the mouth. A wealth of plant life, wildlife, waterfowl, bald eagles, and other birds thrives along the river, which supports a diverse warm-water fishery and mussels in danger of extinction. Historic waterways, the Saint Croix and Brule River to the north were for many years a primary route between the Great Lakes and the Mississippi River; the first recorded Europeans to visit the valley arrived in 1680. State parks line some of the river frontage, including thousands of acres sold and donated to the government by the Northern States Power Company, which had once planned a hydroelectric dam for the upper river.

Only 75 mi from 2.5 million people, the river is popular for many kinds of recreation. The entire reach offers excellent canoeing with Class II rapids in the Kettle River area during higher flows of springtime. Twenty-one outfitters guide trips or rent canoes. Anglers use the river throughout, fishing especially for smallmouth bass. Power boaters and sail boaters cruise the lowest reaches. Many campgrounds are located along the river.

Wolf River, northeast Wisconsin, designated in 1968; 24 mi, Langlade-Menominee county line to Keshena Falls.
Classification: scenic.
Administered by: Menominee Indian Tribe of Wisconsin, P.O. Box 397, Keshena, WI 54135 (officially administered by NPS, but the Menominee Tribe owns the land).
Access: Menominee Tribe permission required.
River difficulty: Class III.
Other information: Bob and Jody Palzer, *Whitewater; Quietwater* (Evergreen Paddleways, Two Rivers, WI 54241) for nearby sections of the Wolf.

This section of the Wolf runs entirely through Indian land. The clear stream cascades through rock-walled gorges with mixed deciduous and coniferous forests.

This section of the 223 mi long Wolf is excellent cold-water habitat, every tributary in the upper river system sustaining a trout population. An exciting whitewater run involves several portages around waterfalls; during some years it has been run by an Indian-owned commercial rafting company. The tribe has closed the entire reach to public use. The Park Service tried unsuccessfully to work with the tribe to plan for recreational management.

In 1965 the Wisconsin legislature passed a law to preserve the scenic, wildlife, and recreational qualities of the Wolf, sometimes called Wisconsin's most beautiful river. This was one of the first rivers in the nation to be protected under a state scenic rivers program. Menominee Enterprises, a tribal company, agreed in 1966 to preserve the shorelines within 200 ft of the river. The Wolf is the only wild and scenic river not open to public use.

Paddlers and anglers frequently use a different 24 mi reach between the town of Lily and the Highway M bridge at Markton.

WYOMING
1 river, 20.5 mi

Clarks Fork of the Yellowstone, northwest Wyoming, designated in 1990; 20.5 mi, 1 mi below the Hwy. 296 crossing near Crandall Creek to mouth of the canyon.

Classification: wild.

Administered by: Shoshone National Forest, 1002 Road 11, Powell, WY 82435.

Access: F.R. 165, which ends near the river east of Cooke City, and Hwy. 119 (four-wheel-drive recommended). Views can be seen from Hwy. 296 at Dead Indian Pass and between Sunlight Creek and Reef Creek.

River difficulty: not run.

Maps: Shoshone National Forest.

The Clarks Fork can arguably be called the wildest river in the nation outside Alaska. Its canyon, one of the most spectacular anywhere, is virtually impassable on foot or by boat, but can be seen from trails on the canyon rim.

Crystal-clear water from the Beartooth Range northeast of Yellowstone flows through an upper canyon of 8 mi with 500 ft granite cliffs. The middle 8 mi constitute The Box, a phenomenal granite canyon with vertical walls towering 800 ft and with cascades and waterfalls. The lower canyon of 7 mi opens to a U shape from glacial erosion with slopes rising 4,000 ft above the river. Yucca and junipers grow on the canyon floor; Douglas fir shades the slopes above. Grizzly bears, mountain goats, elk, cutthroat trout, and other wildlife live in the area. Chief Joseph and his band of Nez Perce temporarily escaped the U.S. Army by fleeing through a portion of the canyon.

Though the river has been kayaked by expert teams of paddlers and rock climbers, it is essentially an unrunnable blizzard of whitewater and water-falls. Fishing is excellent, and the river can be reached at the upper and lower ends of the reach. Forest Service Trail No. 628 in the upper canyon follows the river for 4 mi and climbs to the spectacular north rim of The Box. The Lower Dead Indian Trail offers a view of The Box. Vehicles can reach the lower end of the reach for backcountry camping, hiking, and fishing via the unimproved Highway 292 and Forest Road 119—a rough, two-wheel track.

This section of the 120 mi long Clarks Fork is Wyoming's first national river, designated after much political opposition and after a 0.5 mi section was dropped from the lower end to allow for an irrigation dam. About 98 percent of the designated section is public land.

5

The Management Imperative

THE EXPECTATION OF QUALITY

Once a river has been designated and thereby protected from the dams, the hydropower turbines, and the channelization that may otherwise threaten the stream, what happens?

National river status creates the expectation that the river will be managed to retain its qualities. To achieve better management of recreation is one of the reasons rivers are designated. How do the agencies carry out this job? Some people believe that, once saved, the rivers are loved to death. Are they?

"A lot of people feel that because a river is in the system, it's safe," said Stanford Young, who was instrumental in establishing the wild and scenic program and later served as chief of National Park Service river programs in the Northwest. "That's not true. Unfortunately the fight has only begun." Jim Huddleston of the Park Service in San Francisco called management of some rivers "a coordination nightmare" involving road repairs, agricultural diversions, subdivision, tribal land development, and the gamut of land use activities.

This highly professionalized aspect of national rivers has been ignored by conservationists, who have been more concerned with getting rivers protected from the extinction threats, and by researchers, who are more attracted to ideas than to nuts-and-bolts issues. At times the bureaucracies themselves pay inadequate attention to river management, and some people often lack the time to reflect on or to analyze the aggregate of day-to-day decisions.

WHOSE JOB IS THIS?

Four federal agencies plus a few state and local governments manage the National Wild and Scenic Rivers System (see table). Mileage figures are derived from Forest Service data in Washington, DC, and vary slightly from some other measurements. The 15 rivers protected in alternate designations, such as national recreation areas, are not included in this list and are mostly managed by the National Park Service.

Federal agencies manage 84 percent of the wild and scenic rivers and 92 percent of the mileage in the system. California's north coast rivers were designated through Governor Brown's request, but agreements call for the state, the Forest Service, Bureau of Land Management, National Park Service, and tribes to manage reaches through their respective land.

One effect of designation can be consolidation of management; for the Middle Fork Salmon, one office assumes responsibilities formerly found at three national forests and seven ranger districts. The Forest

MANAGEMENT RESPONSIBILITY FOR NATIONAL WILD
AND SCENIC RIVERS

Managing Agency	Number of Rivers	Percentage of Rivers	Number of Miles	Percentage of Miles
U.S. Forest Service (USFS)	110	52%	4,312.5	41%
National Park Service (NPS)	36	17	2,264	21
Bureau of Land Management (BLM)	35	17	1,982	19
Fish and Wildlife Service	7	3	1,043	10
State agencies	31	15	750.7	7
Local agencies	2	1	(included with states)	
Indian tribes	3	1	65	1

Note: Percentages do not add up to 100 due to rounding.

Service and BLM split administration of some rivers based on shoreline ownership, including reaches as short as the 25-mile-long Rio Chama, which has 3 miles under the Forest Service. The Klamath, a complex example, is administered by the state, the Forest Service, BLM, National Park Service, and an Indian tribe. In effect, most of it is managed by the Forest Service, which is responsible for much of the shoreline mileage. Legislation may officially assign management to the Department of the Interior or Department of Agriculture; those offices later assign the work to a field agency, sometimes one in another department, such as Interior's recognition of the Forest Service at the Sandy River in Oregon.

States officially manage 750.7 miles on 31 rivers (13 river systems not counting tributaries). The Eel system in California alone accounts for 309 state miles. Maine and Ohio are most involved in actual management work. A giant on paper, California has considered its system "self-administering" and doesn't really do anything to manage it. The Forest Service has recommended a transfer of management from federal to state government on the lower Klickitat in Washington.

Local governments play a role that may grow. Sacramento County and California jointly manage the lower American; the state has the official responsibility, but the county assumes the practical duties on this urban river through the state capital. The Sandy River in Oregon is officially managed by the state, the Department of the Interior, and the counties of Multnomah and Clackamas. Under agreements with the Forest Service, the town of Jackson, New Hampshire, manages the private-land section of the Wildcat River, while along the Delaware, land use decisions are made by a conference of governments. In 1992 a study team considered Great Egg Harbor, a small river in New Jersey, for joint state and county management. In spite of precedents elsewhere, some federal officials resisted the county's role at Great Egg owing to fear that local government would be too difficult to oversee, and if it didn't perform, the federal government would stand powerless except for the repugnant possibility of forfeiture of designation. The local/national interface may be a moot point, considering that the federal government does very little anyway on rivers managed by others. The successful management and free rein of Ohio on the Little Miami and of Maine on the Allagash stand as good evidence of this.

On reservation land, Indian tribes manage three national rivers, two of them small reaches in northern California, along with the Wolf in Wisconsin, where after a fashion the Menominee practice the tightest program of all, allowing no public use of the river without special permission. Tribes and the Forest Service also jointly manage the Metolius in Oregon. The tribes generally take a low-key role, their official status as managers serving to make it clear that no federal agency is dictating what to do on the reservation.

The complex question of jurisdiction can be summarized by saying that the designated rivers are managed by the federal agency that owns the shorelines. States assume what management role they desire on rivers designated by governors' requests; local governments take the lead regarding private land, and Indian tribes retain autonomy through the reservations.

PLAYING BY THE RULES

No matter how professional, managers don't just do what they want on national rivers. Direction is found in the Wild and Scenic Rivers Act of 1968 and in "Guidelines for Eligibility, Classification and Management of River Areas," a set of federal regulations published in the *Federal Register* (September 7, 1982). The guidelines call for management plans on each stream to assure protection and provision of recreation and other uses that avoid degrading the river.

In principle, managing agencies accept existing land uses but evaluate new uses for compatibility. This is done by whatever jurisdiction applies—federal, state, or local. Regulation of private property emphatically remains a local government concern, influenced by state guidelines in rare cases where they exist.

Along some rivers agencies limit access or occasionally require permits under guidance that public use and access are to be distributed to serve people, protect values, and correct damage. Basic facilities may be provided, but major ones, such as newly developed campgrounds, are to be located outside the river corridor if possible.

Agricultural uses "should be similar in nature and intensity" to those at the time of designation. Logging is to "avoid adverse impacts on the river area values." On federal land, no logging is allowed along wild rivers; cutting with no "substantial effect" on the river is usually allowed along recreational rivers. The guidelines ban mining under new claims in wild river corridors through federal land; controlled mining with a minimal surface disturbance and with pollution safeguards can be allowed along scenic and recreational streams.

Water quality is to be maintained or improved to levels meeting federal or state standards. Water rights remain a state responsibility, yet a federal right for instream flow is reserved, perversely stated in the negative: designation "shall not be construed as a reservation of the waters of such streams for purposes other than those specified in this Act, or in quantities greater than necessary to accomplish those purposes."

Hunting and fishing remain unaffected and are regulated by state agencies. Motorboats are "generally permitted" but can be restricted to protect river values.

PLANS AND NO PLANS

Wild and scenic river studies, which had been completed for 50 percent of the designated rivers as of 1992, spell out much in the way of management, but they are not really management plans. The agencies draft separate documents as management plans, which are usually required within three years of designation. The Forest Service and BLM wrote plans for all the earlier rivers, the Rio Grande in New Mexico being the first. The Rogue River plan, one of the most complete, was done in 1972 and has been proposed for updating, as have the Middle Fork Salmon and some other plans. The Fish and Wildlife Service wrote no management plans for its Alaska rivers, designated in 1980, and exercises no special management provisions. The BLM in Alaska prepared plans for some of its rivers. No plan exists for the National Park Service's Noatak, although it is getting enough use to warrant one.

Plans are especially important on the glamour rivers that have abundant conflicts, such as the Salmon and Deschutes; on private-land rivers with residents to accommodate, such as the Skagit and Delaware; and on the more ecologically sensitive rivers, such as the Niobrara and Sheenjek.

Thick documents for some of California's north coast rivers were produced under contracts by consultants but never adopted by the state legislature and never pursued by an environmentally hostile administration following that of Governor Jerry Brown. For the Oregon rivers designated in 1988, the Forest Service and BLM plan to have the management plans completed in 1992. That is fast work compared with planning elsewhere, but in the meantime, Forest Service officials dumped soil contaminated with diesel fuel on the White River flood plain in 1990 without consideration of the river's protected status. After a complaint by the Oregon Rivers Council, the agency removed the soil—remedial action that might have been unnecessary had a plan—and the awareness it engenders—been in place.

The plans address the entire future of the river. How can the stream and its corridor be protected? What is the recreational carrying capacity, and how can use be contained to that level? What types of activity should be encouraged? Where are access and camping facilities best provided? How will conflicts between residents and visitors be resolved? Where should land or easements be bought? How much money and staff are needed? How can local government be encouraged to zone the riverfront for protection?

MONEY AND STAFF

The cost and staffing of river management varies from no money and no staff to investments such as seven summer and three year-round rangers on a budget exceeding $100,000 a year for the Allagash—no huge program. On the Missouri River in Montana, a staff of three full-time and two seasonal river rangers worked in 1980, but budget cutbacks soon forced a reduction of one-half—a typical cut in the 1980s. On the Gulkana in Alaska, BLM cut a staff of five seasonal rangers to two.

On the BLM reach of the Rogue in Oregon, seven full-time and four seasonal staff worked on river management in 1989, where nine full-time employees had worked in 1981. The agency requested an increase of 2 full-time and 11 part-time staff to cope just with the busy and neglected upper 27 miles of road-accessible frontage. One manager, five rangers at the two put-ins, and four boating rangers are employed on the Middle Fork of the Salmon in Idaho. Most of the national rivers, however, have no staff assigned solely to river work; recreation specialists fit river obligations into a larger program, and some of the more remote areas have no recreation specialist.

The costs of management rank among the lesser known facts regarding the national rivers system. For most rivers, no line item in the budget exists. None of the Forest Service rivers have line-item budgets; the money comes instead from recreation management or some other fund. The work is accounted for under other programs or, even more simply, it's not done at all. The opposite also happens: costs for generic recreational work can be attributed to river programs. For instance, at the Gulkana, BLM spends $30,000 a year, most of it at a road-accessible campground, and at the Delta River, it spends $18,000, including care of two campgrounds where boaters put in. The money would likely be spent regardless of the designations.

The classic wild and scenic rivers—the Rogue, Middle Fork Salmon, Selway, and Chattooga, for example—involve concerted management, and for most rivers, the subject is addressed in plans, some with elaborate detail. However, many of the streams simply and legitimately remain as they were. Agencies might improve access to a degree but tamper with little else. Little else may need doing. Some rivers, however, require attention they are not getting.

ACQUISITION AND LAND USE REGULATION

Land and easement acquisition poses a critical question in management plans. LuVerne Grussing, chair of the American River Management Society, an organization of professional managers, called acquisition "probably the most important management action along many designated rivers." He added that land exchanges are the most politically acceptable method to acquire property. Under this option, the federal government trades land that it already owns for tracts along the rivers having greater public value.

Some acquisitions or easements have resulted along many streams, rarely involving eminent domain. Along BLM's 47 mile portion of the Rogue, 166 scenic easements and 99 fee acquisitions were acquired for $7 million, one of the larger amounts of acquisition in the entire system.

The designation of some rivers included authorization to buy critical land or easements; for the Middle Fork Salmon, Congress earmarked $1.8 million for easements to prevent development on land, such as 80 acres owned by Holiday Inn. Another tract could have been a private country club for 500 members. The Forest Service's management plan called for eventual easements on all private land in the corridor. The original act and follow-up appropriations in 1973 brought the total for acquisition along the initial 12 rivers to $37.6 million. Along the Flathead, the Forest Service proposed acquisition of easements on all private land; as of 1982 Congress had appropriated $6.5 of $21 million needed for the job. At the Little Miami, $1 million from the state was matched by money from the federal Land and Water Conservation Fund, but $8.5 million was needed to protect 9,900 acres. Along the Chattooga, the Forest Service planned to buy all the private land it could from willing sellers. Along the Clearwater system in Idaho, the Forest Service acquired 146 easements for 3,700 acres. In 1986, $6 million was appropriated to buy land along two designated Michigan rivers—the largest amount assigned for one state. The Reagan administration cut land acquisition funds, but in contrast to many dry years, in 1988 Congress appropriated $35 million for acquisition for rivers and some other natural areas.

Along the Skagit and its designated tributaries in Washington, acquisition was urgently needed to halt enormous clearcuts. Congress authorized $16 million, but it was never appropriated. Thirteen years after designation, once much of the critical acreage had been clearcut, $1 million was appropriated in 1991.

To protect the national river corridors, many millions of dollars are needed to acquire critical parcels from willing sellers. Virtually all the rivers could benefit by public acquisition of flood plain, steep slope, or wetland areas, enhancing the river and avoiding the "taking" issue of regulation otherwise left to local governments. Funds have been available for only a minuscule part of the job, and the situation is not likely to change, at least not much. Costs of needed easements along 33 miles of the Little Beaver in Ohio were estimated at $5 million; little of it was ever made available.

Acquisition of open space is not necessarily required along many of the rivers, but most streams would benefit from more public land when the time is right for both seller and buyer. A benign, opportunistic, and realistic approach along this line could be pursued. Instead, federal agencies, pushed by the Office of Management and Budget, "force" decisions on acquisition during the designation debates, effectively killing national river proposals with cost estimates and an army of landowners who might have accepted the long-term prospect of selling acreage or easements if and when they wanted. But those people panic when they see their land identified in a report.

Land use regulations are addressed in management plans but are possible only through the local level of government, occasionally guided by states. In spite of incentives, such as the federal flood insurance program, local regulations are often manipulated by developers, landowners, bankers, and real estate agents who gain routine exemptions for pet projects. For example, state administration of the New River in North Carolina failed to prevent wholesale subdivision of the riverfront for recreational home sites. Land values increased fivefold, and the number of landowners increased threefold. The state Division of Parks and Recreation had requested $2 million for acquisition of many hundreds of acres in 1977—an adequate amount at the time—but the state assembly didn't appropriate the money. Meanwhile, attempts at regulation were shot down at the local level. In 1989, North Carolina spent $1.6 million to buy only 350 acres where developers were already excavating for a subdivision. A state budget crisis prevented further acquisition. The New was the first stream that American Rivers ever named on its most endangered rivers list because of a management deficiency *after* designation.

There was no easy solution to this problem, though Michigan and Minnesota effected state-mandated zoning at the local level. It's unclear what the federal government could have done about North Carolina's inability to buy land and the local government's unwillingness to zone. A better mobilized effort to protect rivers statewide and fund them through state channels may be the only possibility in many regions. Federal regulatory leverage is regarded as bureaucratic meddling, counterproductive for future designations, and toothless because its ultimate threat is simply to repeal designation, which wouldn't help the river at all. Federal funding for open space acquisition would certainly help but is unlikely at present.

LOGGING, GRAZING, AND MINING

With the old-growth forest issue at the forefront in the Northwest, timber management is a pivotal issue along some of the "woodland" wild and scenic rivers. Federal guidelines, refined by BLM in 1989 for its Oregon river plans (*Management Guidelines and Standards for National Wild and Scenic Rivers*), call for no logging in wild river corridors, "no substantial adverse effect" in scenic corridors, and logging under "standard restrictions" along recreational rivers. Direction in the Wild and Scenic Rivers Act is vague on this subject, and whether or not the guidelines will "protect and enhance the values which cause it [the river] to be included in said system," as the act says, is a good question. The act also states that "primary emphasis shall be given to protecting [the river's] esthetic, scenic, historic, archeologic, and scientific features." Critics argue that "standard restrictions" of the Forest Service and BLM have not adequately protected sensitive land elsewhere, and that using those standard prescriptions for designated recreational rivers is not good enough.

The Oregon rivers bill of 1988 named 1,442 miles of rivers and will reduce the allowable sale of timber by 7 million annual board feet on public land, less than 0.1 percent of the state's total annual cut. The Elk River provided a litmus test of wild and scenic status when conservation organizations in 1990 sued the Forest Service to halt two timber sales along the North Fork. The agency agreed to review harvest plans and sedimentation problems. "Designation focuses attention on the rivers," said Joe Higgins of the Pacific Northwest regional office in 1990. "The Forest Service is now sensitized to wild and scenic river values, and with that comes an interest in modifying timber management and improving fish habitat."

Logging procedures along Smith River tributaries in California were not satisfactory to the Smith River Alliance, which prevented cutting of some threatened frontage by overlaying national recreation area status on the wild and scenic river designation. Likewise, Friends of the River and the California Planning and Conservation League have expressed frustration in striving for better watershed management by the Forest Service on other northern California rivers including the South Fork of the Eel.

In the Tongass National Forest, local conservationists opposed wild and scenic enactments in 1990 out of fear that the Forest Service would use the designation as a weak substitute for wilderness status, which clearly bans logging. While the rivers issue indeed promised to add friction to a troublesome bill, it was unlikely that the Forest Service could "trade" protection in the public eye.

The outstanding national rivers of northern Washington illustrate another difficult shortcoming of the rivers system. Extraordinary old growth in the corridors of the Skagit, Cascade, and Sauk rivers has been heavily clearcut since designation. While cuts in the national forest tended to be small and fairly well screened in many cases, cutting on state and private land made eyesores out of entire mountainsides. State land on the otherwise exquisite Cascade River has been clearcut almost to the waterline. The Forest Service's management plan was not completed until five years after designation, and even then it offered little in the way of protection attempts aimed at the logging industry and state-owned land.

In most areas of the country, timber cutting is not a pivotal concern in the management of wild and scenic rivers. Most designated reaches are not classified wild, allowing give-and-take over logging, and other problems usually threaten rivers more. Riverfront zones, including those proposed along the Farmington in Connecticut, call for setbacks banning logging for at least 100 feet.

While cattle grazing has come under new controls after designation of some rivers, such as the Rio Grande in New Mexico, overgrazing continues essentially unaffected by some other wild and scenic designations. Some streams are more wild and scenic pastures than rivers. In a problem unique to the lower Rio Grande, cattle and horses that are free to roam in Mexico cross the river to overgraze and ruin habitat on the northern shore. Along the upper Missouri in 1990, cows preempted campsites, waded in the river without fencing or cowboys directing their movement, and toppled signs indicating where Lewis and Clark had camped. Legislation designating the Missouri allowed grazing to continue, though BLM's management plan stated that cattle would be controlled by fences at areas used by people. More important, cottonwoods, the climax of a once magnificent riparian forest along that river, stand dead and dying while cows eat or trample seedlings that might otherwise replace the old trees. Former

BLM scientist Hugh Harper, one of the agency's foremost range specialists, called the situation "pathetic." In 1992 BLM stated that it was attempting to get better control over the problem along the Missouri.

Grazing practices have long been a neglected area of management. With "riparian initiatives" by the BLM and Forest Service, there is even less excuse for grazing abuse on public land bordering the national rivers.

Mining is not often a problem in scenic river corridors, though industrial-scale gold mining, proposed on the Middle Fork of the Feather, was the subject of one of the first appeals by conservation groups regarding better management of a national river. In the 1970s an Arizona mining company was issued a permit to dredge a mile-long belt of gravel above Milsap Bar, in the heart of the national river reach. The forest supervisor had called the project not "controversial enough" to warrant an environmental impact statement. The Northern California Flyfishers and Friends of the River appealed and halted the dredging. In 1981 the chief of the Forest Service rejected the miner's application because of doubts about the "validity" of the claim.

Along the Fortymile River in Alaska, patented claims on state land lie in the riverbed itself. BLM, following the lead of state officials, administered wild and scenic rivers as though authority applied only to the corridor land and not to the river. The agency relied on water quality regulations of the Environmental Protection Agency (EPA) to control gold dredging, which is very destructive to the river, but the EPA initially did little owing to the politics of the state. Pressured by conservation groups in 1990, EPA threatened to fine a dredge operator $10,000 when his holding pond of silt was overtopped by the river. The situation was aggravated when one miner converted to the "New Zealand dredge," which excavated 2,000 cubic yards of riverbed a day instead of the abusive-enough 5 cubic yards excavated by conventional dredges. American Rivers, the Northern Alaska Environmental Center, and Sierra Club Legal Defense Fund protested, and EPA ruled against use of the new dredge.

Because of state landownership of stream bottoms—or the claim of ownership—ousting destructive mining from the very beds of national rivers in Alaska has turned out to be an onerous job. American Rivers challenged BLM to control the Fortymile River mining with right-of-way provisions and camping permits (required of miners living and operating along the river), which would quite likely be revoked in the case of anyone else doing comparable damage on a public-land campsite anywhere in the country. BLM officials reported in 1992 that the mining problem had been much reduced on the Fortymile and on Birch Creek, though its upper 12 miles were still plagued by mine-generated silt.

The mining problem in Alaska is affected by situations as subtle as whether or not BLM closed the boundary of the wild and scenic river at the upper and lower ends—a matter of a pencil line crossing the river on a map. With open-ended boundaries, as drawn, miners haul equipment in and gain access without restriction because they don't cross the "boundary" of the national river. The stream becomes their unregulated highway. Unsatisfied, the state sought a legal ruling of ownership of the riverbeds in order to allow even more mining with even less pollution abatement. Over 180,000 miles of waterways through federal and private land could theoretically be opened to dredgers, including streams in Denali National Park.

Elsewhere in the nation, strip mining and gravel dredging are important. Strip-mine proposals on the rim of the Youghiogheny gorge in Pennsylvania provided a reason to designate that river, one of the first streams studied for the national system, but owing to local and state opposition, the river was not included. One miner closed his stripping operation, which was permitted by the state, after the debate over his dragline eyesore escalated to a whole new level: the operator was literally shot at by an unknown person from the opposite side of the gorge.

More explicit than the Wild and Scenic Rivers Act, the Surface Mining Control and Reclamation Act of 1977 restricted coal mining on land within the boundaries of national wild and scenic rivers, providing solid protection for the few designated Appalachian streams, such as the Obed.

Gravel dredging poses the largest potential mining problem along rivers. The American Rivers Conservation Council won its first lawsuit in 1977 when it contested a gravel mine along the Middle Fork of the Clearwater. Conservation groups challenged the state of Pennsylvania in 1991 after it allowed a dredging operation alongside the Allegheny, a study river.

WATER RIGHTS

Water rights in national rivers are one of the most controversial issues facing river managers in the West. Wild and scenic rivers have implicit and explicit rights for maintenance of the natural river, but those rights usually remain undelineated because the practical threats of diverters drying up the rivers rarely arise. Troublesome diversions are largely a western phenomenon and typically lie on nondesignated reaches, usually below protected sections.

However, the John Day in Oregon is an instructive case because traditional irrigation withdrawals now cut flows to a trickle in summer. State scientists are studying the stream to determine minimum instream flows needed for retaining some aquatic life. Oregon law offers important guidance here: under the Diack decision in the Oregon courts, diverters must leave water in the river for fish, wildlife, and recreation. Few other western states grant such legitimacy to instream flows.

Irrigators oppose wild and scenic river proposals out of fear for their diversions. At the Snake River in Wyoming, ranchers helped to stonewall a designation proposal, though their minor and preexisting diversions would likely have been overlooked entirely, and state water law would assure their water supply even with increased attention to the river.

Wyoming Senator Malcolm Wallop habitually attached water rights disclaimers to wild and scenic river bills on principle, specifying that the designation not affect business as usual at the state level, which effectively means at the diverter's level. His riders have been amended or modified to allow the 1968 act's original language to stand in most cases, but the political machinations have consumed people's valuable time and energy in the cases of the Clarks Fork, Rio Chama, and Merced. For the Cache la Poudre in Colorado, language was added to prevent national river status from infringing on certain potential uses of the water.

The point of water rights is moot in many cases; many of the national rivers are in upper basin areas, unthreatened because the diversions occur below. Other cases will certainly be affected by the priority date of applications; a water right dated 1991 is virtually worthless anywhere in the West, though in some instances national river designations could highlight older, neglected federal rights, such as those attached to the creation of a national forest. These are the "federal reserved" water rights. In some rivers, such as the Gunnison in Colorado, a water right may be important regarding hydroelectric proposals that could dewater the proposed national river from sites above the designation. Even if weakening language on the Wallop model is attached to designations, its primary use would be in protecting irrigators and future irrigation potential; the Federal Energy Regulatory Commission and other federal agencies must still recognize wild and scenic river requirements apart from water rights when issuing hydropower licenses. This is one argument for designating rivers such as the Gunnison, even with water rights language that would not favor the river.

Water rights are sure to become a more troublesome issue as irrigators grow more fearful of having to share water supplies that have been unquestioned and unmonitored until modern times, as the importance of instream flows becomes more widely understood, and as river protection efforts move downstream to lowland rivers with superior wildlife habitat but intensified conflicts for water use.

Though change in the western states primarily comes through state policy, national river designations may be one of the fronts on which the new shape of western water law is hammered out. The law will no doubt continue to serve existing users but could also recognize other public values of water flowing in rivers.

RECREATION

Management plans on every designated river address recreation activity; in fact, management of recreation *is* river management in the minds of many. Typical needs are for trash pickup and disposal, prevention of trespass on private land, campsite location and care, road and trail maintenance, and safety. The budget and staff for national rivers mainly address recreational use. Local residents resent recreation—the plague of popularity—when they feel burdened by solid waste, crowded roads, and competition for emergency medical service. On the other hand, improved services in all these areas can follow river designation and benefit both visitors and residents alike.

The government agencies have amassed a fine record of manage-ment improvements at many of the national rivers. At the Saint Croix and Selway, national designation resulted in an excellent response to both a nearly urban recreational river and a wilderness river. Along the Chattooga, fights had broken out between groups competing for campsites, people littered irresponsibly, and campfire pits scarred shorelines. The management program following designation con-trolled these problems. Safety also improved: the Chattooga's annual death rate of four dropped to zero. Poorly located campsites and thoughtless scrambling up and down had caused streambank erosion along the Rogue and Saint Croix until better design, maintenance, and regulation corrected the problems. Along the Delaware, improved management of recreational problems followed the designation even as the federal presence ran a gantlet of local opposition.

Agencies build recreational improvements along national rivers, such as toilets, access ramps, picnic areas, and campgrounds. Along the Rogue, BLM in 1990 requested $32,000 for a new fishing access, with $2,500 a year for its maintenance; $15,000 for eight new toilets, to be maintained for $1,500 a year; and $28,500 for a boat ramp, requiring $2,200 a year. One new campground will cost $608,000 and $8,000 annually to keep up. Most of the well-used rivers now have improved access, though this would likely have happened with or without designation.

At the Rogue, recreational use has been the center of agency con-cern since the late 1960s; over the years, BLM installed 20 toilets, added minor facilities at 53 primitive campsites, improved 3 fishing access sites, and built 1 campground. Over 300,000 people use the designated reach (only 12,000 of them in the wild section, which has received most of the management attention). In 1990 the agency pro-posed new initiatives to cope with recreational problems of the 27-mile-long accessible upper reach and to capitalize on river recreation as a regional tourist attraction. These included planning drive-in campgrounds, float-in camps, interpretive sites, visitor centers, and effective law enforcement. Unlike old federal approaches charac-terized by planning in isolation, the BLM proposal called for coopera-tive agreements and joint planning, development, and management with counties, cities, and private businesses. These actions are likely harbingers of a national trend as agencies face the reality of booming growth in recreational use of readily accessible rivers.

The upper Rogue proposal is also unusual in its attempt to accommodate, if not encourage, more recreational use; management on other rivers has been limited to maintaining the status quo. While this may be appropriate and popular on the BLM's Rogue, the promotional aspect of the proposal would surely draw fire on many other national rivers where the philosophy and legal mandate have been to deal with what exists and not invite increased use.

A lack of public awareness was blamed for problems along the upper Missouri River, a situation partly resolved by stationing two rangers at access points to coach boaters and anglers about river etiquette. River rangers report similar success on other rivers.

Haggling between anglers and boaters occasionally happens on streams popular to both groups, degenerating in a few cases to rock-throwing battles. Along the Pere Marquette in Michigan, regulations are aimed to minimize conflicts by keeping canoeists off the water in early morning and late evening when fishing is prime.

On the national rivers and on others, concern grows that wildlife needs similar off-limits hours to allow for foraging. The Snake River in Grand Teton National Park, for example, serves an abundance of birds and riverine mammals, and research in 1989 for the Bureau of Reclamation showed that eagles are disturbed by people at feeding hours and by boaters or anglers who stop in critical areas. Waterfowl may be affected even more seriously. For several weeks after hatching, young ducks and geese are highly vulnerable, and boaters simply passing by can constitute a major threat. Regular boating or fishing traffic repeatedly scares wildlife from foraging sites and likely affects the ability to feed.

Among other goals, the Park Service seeks to protect wildlife by banning boating on all the rivers of Yellowstone. That model was abandoned at Yosemite, where the concessionaire's request for permission to rent rafts was granted. Mobs of tourists in rented rafts proceeded to clog the tiny Merced River. While the effects on wildlife may be less than they might be at Yellowstone, the effects on other people may be greater: visitors coming from all over the world to appreciate the sublime scenery of Yosemite Valley are confronted with a carnival scene.

Outside national park and refuge areas, wildlife has less chance of receiving recognition of any kind by regulation of human use, other than traditional fishing and hunting laws that deal with the direct taking of birds, animals, and fish. Even in a place such as Grand Teton National Park, restrictions for wildlife would arouse intense political hostility. The responsible agencies have undertaken little or no study of the effects of river recreation on wildlife, and such studies would be a good starting point in coping with this problem.

IS DESIGNATION TO BLAME?

Does designation of national rivers cause increased use? State river managers surveyed in 1975 thought that activity increased with formal designations. But ample evidence shows that increases occur on suitable rivers regardless of designation. Pennsylvania's lower Youghiogheny, which is not designated in any river system, had 5,000 paddlers in 1968 and 150,000 in 1983, making it the nation's most floated whitewater at the time. Virtually all of the most used rivers lack national designation: the Nantahala in North Carolina, Ocoee in Tennessee, Mohican in Ohio, South Fork American and Russian in California, Arkansas in Colorado, Salt in Arizona, and Snake River in Grand Teton National Park and in Alpine Canyon. In contrast, many of the national rivers gained little or no new popularity with designation, for example, the Little Beaver in Ohio. Floating increased on the Allagash, but comparable popularity affected the neighboring and undesignated Saint John. Floating on California's Tuolumne has increased and would have grown much more without regulations following designation, but use on the undesignated South Fork American exploded by comparison. Floating use on the Sheenjek in the Arctic National Wildlife Refuge increased from 190 people in 1984 to 461 in 1988, while use of the Kongakut—an undesignated but similar river also requiring air access in the same refuge—grew from 169 to 1,287 floaters in the same period. The lower Salmon River, undesignated and unregulated, received 12,000 boaters in 1991, far surpassing the Middle Fork, which had been more popular and would likely continue to be if it were not regulated as a wild and scenic river. The Deschutes in Oregon saw great increases in use before it was designated.

These examples suggest that designation generally causes little impact on amount of use; even when there is an impact, the effect may be small when compared with other factors, such as suitability for recreation, access, marketing by commercial outfitters, and media publicity (for example, the effect of the movie *Deliverance* on the Chattooga in the 1970s). Ultimately, as with the Middle Fork Salmon, post-designation regulations may be the only method to curb people pressure.

THE DIFFICULT DIVISION OF USE

On some public-land rivers that are both popular and limited in their carrying capacity, federal agencies require permits and limit the numbers of people running the rivers. For example, to preserve its unique character and to ensure an opportunity for a wild river trip without seeing other parties of boaters, the Forest Service regulates the Selway in Idaho more tightly than any other waterway: only one party per day is allowed to launch. As a result, the Selway remains a unique gem among the nation's rivers. Yet people are not denied access to the Selway: a trail parallels the river's length, an intense day's worth of unregulated whitewater lies above the wild river section, and there is a fine recreational float with road access below the wild river section. People's frustration in applying for Selway permits dozens of times and always being rejected could be remedied by switching to a permit system based on a waiting list, similar to the system used for the Grand Canyon.

Regulations typically restrict the parties of boaters to a reasonable number. On the Rogue, for example, BLM allows eight parties per day. On the Middle Fork Salmon, the Forest Service allows 7 groups a day with a maximum of 24 people in private parties and 30 in commercial groups, the trips being limited to 8 days. Congestion still occurs at put-ins, and visitors see many other parties as they float down the river, but the limits at least guard against traffic jams at rapids and other such problems. Friction over campsites is avoided by requiring visitors to reserve sites with a ranger before putting in. The Forest Service manages the river efficiently, allowing 10,000 people a year to have a good experience, yet the feeling of solitude is utterly gone: anyone sitting still for a day will see perhaps 175 people in 60 boats, and if you miss your reserved campsite, it's like looking for a motel on the Fourth of July weekend. Party sizes on regulated rivers are restricted to as low as 12 (the Allagash) and as high as 30 (the Middle Fork Salmon).

Permit systems on some popular western rivers predate national river designation, such as in Hells Canyon of the Snake River. Other requirements, including those on the Tuolumne, were instituted with increased management following designation. For some rivers, agencies require permits but have no limit on private use; the registration provides for information and safety only. Many of the best known "permit" rivers are not in the national rivers system at all, such as the Colorado in the Grand and Westwater canyons, and the Green in Lodore and Desolation canyons in Colorado and Utah. More river running and tighter control of permits have led to more off-season boating by those who want to avoid both the crowds and the permit hassle—flows and weather permitting.

Commercial rafting is banned from few rivers, and on almost none where an outfitting business is feasible. Outside the national rivers system there may be a few examples of these, such as the South Fork of the Salmon in Idaho. Federal agencies must approve commercial outfitters on any river flowing through public land, and the numbers of outfitters are often limited to what now exists, the big boom having occurred in the 1970s. On some rivers, such as the Chattooga and Rio Grande, commercial boating is subject to permit restrictions but private boating is not.

Regulations require commercial companies to meet standards for safety, guide training, and low-impact camping. On the Rogue River, BLM has 120 commercial outfitters of all types (floating, jet boating, fishing, and so forth) under permit and collects $90,000 a year in fees, ostensibly to cover administration and related facility costs, though the amount probably doesn't come close.

MOTORS

The issue of nonmotorized versus motorized use created a hotbed of conflict in Hells Canyon, where numbers of floaters were frozen at the 1973 level while jet boaters escaped regulation for another 18 years, their numbers increasing many times. The Forest Service had attempted to control motorboats, but the assistant secretary of agriculture during the Reagan administration ordered the agency to eliminate all proposed regulations. A compromise evolved through a consensus process in 1991, imposing limits on jet boats at roughly that year's level. Salmon River legislation in 1980 required that motorboat use be allowed to continue at no less than the 1978 level. Motorboats run the Rogue below Blossom Bar and below Grants Pass, where jet boats carrying 88 passengers maneuver with difficulty and create right-of-way problems with smaller boats.

Motorboaters routinely cruise on flatwater rivers of the national system, such as the Skagit, Missouri, and Delaware, with occasional restrictions on motor size (25 and 40 horsepower limits on two reaches of the Current, for example). Motors are banned from few rivers, perhaps from none that are suitable for motorized use.

The federal agencies allow motorboats and aircraft landings on virtually all the Alaskan rivers (some sections of the Alatna are restricted). No systematic study has been done and little consideration has been given to the fact that many more people now fly to Alaska's wilderness rivers and land anywhere pilots are able, which includes amazingly short and rocky gravel bars. The effect on wildlife is unknown but probably large, given the experience with grizzly bears, wolverines, wolves, and other vulnerable species elsewhere.

The Forest Service does not restrict flights at the many airstrips along Idaho's Salmon and its Middle Fork; on some days planes land every 15 minutes at the otherwise wild site of Indian Creek on the Middle Fork. People can fly into Moose Creek along the wilderness Selway, otherwise remote from motorized access. The policy has been to allow traditional motorized uses and not to restrict increases in their amounts, even if those increases substantially alter the character of the local environment.

MANAGEMENT AS AN ECOSYSTEM

The National Wild and Scenic Rivers System includes little authority to manage rivers above or below designated reaches, though water quality and instream flows from above are vital, and pollution regulations can be enforced in tandem with river designations. Where federal discharge permits are needed, a strong case can be made to consider the effects on downstream national river reaches. The federal Clean Water Act of 1987 directs states to recognize "outstanding resource waters," which are not to be degraded at all (most streams, in contrast, are assigned standards that allow for certain amounts of pollution).

Many wild and scenic rivers at the national or state levels are logical candidates for this superlative water quality designation but rarely enjoy recognition.

Efforts to designate tributaries to the Middle Fork of the Salmon as outstanding resource waters under state regulations failed in 1991 because of mining, logging, and grazing interests even in that sparsely used, premier basin of Idaho, leaving this gem of the National Wild and Scenic Rivers System without a state mandate to keep water quality even at current levels.

Water quality threats to national rivers abound. Several Oregon rivers, including the North Umpqua and Imnaha, lie below areas slated for clearcutting with its attendant watershed disruption. The salmon runs of the South Fork Trinity in California were threatened with extinction, yet the Forest Service's draft management plan did not prevent logging in the watershed outside the designated reach. This decision came under fire after an independent hydrologist found that the fisheries' problems stemmed partly from logging and related road building.

Heavy grazing above the designated reach undoubtedly affects the diminutive upper Rio Grande, with pesticides degrading the lower reach in Texas. The Salmon River in Idaho periodically runs brown with heavy runoff from mining districts far above the wild and scenic reach.

Conservationists have effectively used national river status as leverage against federal projects, such as an Army Corps of Engineers' plan in 1985 to dredge a section of the Salmon River above the protected reach. The flood-control channelization would have ripped out habitat and silted the river for miles.

Severe instream flow problems occur in some national rivers. These are now gaining more attention and promise to outpace even water quality as an issue in the West. Canal companies take virtually all of the upper and lower Rio Grande just above protected sections. Unscreened diversions kill salmon in the Salmon River, and irrigators divert water above the designated reaches of the Klamath and Middle Fork Feather. Irrigation, hydroelectric, or municipal diversions from upstream dams deplete flows in the Rio Chama, Deschutes, Trinity, and Eel.

Idaho Power Company's hydroelectric releases from Hells Canyon Dam create daily destructive flushes of water, scouring Snake River beaches and obliterating habitat in the national river below the dam in ways that may pose a worse problem than the notorious troubles of Glen Canyon Dam on the Colorado.

The middle Missouri is subject to fluctuations up to 4.5 feet daily and to seasonal manipulation, common below reservoirs. Water is held back in the spring and released in the fall, in a reversal of the natural pattern on which many plant and wildlife species depend.

Throughout the West, waters released from dams destroy river qualities through hydrologic effects: the reservoirs trap the silt and release clear water that erodes soil but deposits nothing. This imbalance leads to riverbed degradation, flood plain erosion, and biological devastation through the riparian corridor.

The management of existing dams, diversions, and water projects poses old and new threats to valuable rivers everywhere. Through the relicensing process mandated for private hydro dams, opportunities to reform reservoir management are many and can be leveraged by national river designations. American Rivers, for example, argued that the small, 1,200 kilowatt Trego project on the Namekagon River in Wisconsin should be retired when its license expires because it spans a national river. Far more common than removal of dams will be cases where minimum streamflows can be increased, damaging flushes from erratic peaking power releases can be reduced, and mitigation for lost fish and wildlife can be paid out of the hydroelectric profits made possible by destroying habitat years ago without compensation. National river status implicitly improves the chances for any of these reforms during hydropower relicensing.

Part of the New River Gorge legislation in 1978 required the Army Corps to cooperate with the national river by providing compatible releases from Bluestone Dam in West Virginia. This model of concern has been largely disregarded in other cases, though a revised flow regime for California's Trinity River shows progress, and reformed release schedules at Glen Canyon Dam, temporarily enacted in 1991, may open the way for reconsidered management of reservoir releases elsewhere.

Dams lie above many national river reaches, obviating the occasional argument, used in the Stanislaus debate in California, that upstream dams and altered flows disqualify rivers for designation. A few dams release flows that are accidentally convenient for boating—the Cache la Poudre, lower American, Rio Chama, and Tuolumne are examples—but good flows for boating don't necessarily mean good flows for the ecosystem overall. Hydropower releases at the upper Youghiogheny, a study river and Maryland state scenic river, make summer boating possible but result in a daily flush of exaggerated high and low levels, disruptive of aquatic ecosystems.

Far more common are the negative effects of upstream dams, which usually predate national river designations. Reservoirs on tributaries of the Delaware divert water to New York City and lower the river level. Trinity Dam diverted 90 percent of the Trinity's water, destroying an anadromous fishery on that northern California river, which is now in the national rivers system and has had diversion-related destruction reduced from 90 percent of the fishery to 70 percent.

The management of downstream reservoirs can impose even worse problems. On the Rio Chama and Bluestone River, lower ends of the designated reaches are periodically flooded. The Snake and Columbia dams reduce anadromous fisheries to a small fraction of their historic numbers, depleting what had been the finest salmon runs in the world on the Snake, Clearwater, Lochsa, Selway, Salmon, and Middle Fork Salmon. The same dams block large percentages of salmon and steelhead from the Rapid, Grande Ronde, Imnaha, Joseph Creek, Wenaha, Minam, and Lostine, all national rivers. In addition, dams block anadromous runs entirely on the Middle Fork Feather, North Fork American, Tuolumne, Merced, Metolius, Eagle Creek, Powder, North Powder, Malheur, North Malheur, Owyhee, North Owyhee, West Little Owyhee, and upper Deschutes and its tributaries. Columbia River dams below the mouth of the John Day bar many salmon from that fine waterway.

One example of an attempt to integrate management is the federal agencies' Salmon River Showcase Management effort in Idaho, designed to coordinate actions on all reaches of the river and its tributaries. This and other cases illustrate a growing awareness of rivers as ecosystems with management implications reaching beyond short designated pieces—a concern that may define much of the river protection movement of the future.

PIONEERS IN TENDING THE RIVERS

While the experience of land-managing agencies goes far back in regard to forests, wilderness, parks, and refuges, the deliberate and thoughtful management of rivers is new in many ways. Attempts to effectively cope with the recreational uses of protected waterways have evolved into a profession only during the past two decades. A river recreation conference sponsored by the Forest Service and other agencies in Minneapolis in 1977 marked the first major gathering of specialists to debate the present and probe the future of their profession. Since that time, what had looked like a thin slice of the resource pie has come to constitute a core of ecosystem management.

By trial and error, applied research, progressive thinking, and political intervention variously retarding and accelerating progress, management techniques have evolved and programs have become more attuned to real needs and to what works. In the future, agencies will likely pay more attention to conflicts between different kinds of recreation and place more importance on a consensus process. Guidelines such as the federal agencies' "Limits of Acceptable Change" will be employed, as was the case in Hells Canyon in 1991 to address thorny conflicts between motorized and nonmotorized boaters. Unfortunately, this approach often slights consideration of the ecosystem and its carrying capacity. The ability of managers to deal with people, disparate organizations, and agencies at all levels without compromising stewardship and congressional mandates for river conservation will be put to difficult tests.

As more rivers are safeguarded, as the traditional threats of dams and channelization fade and make way for new protection priorities, and as opposition to river designations persists, the effectiveness of management will be subject to many challenges. The agencies must perform well and deliver services if they are to maintain their credibility and if river protection is to stride forward. The importance of ecosystem management, reaching above and below designated reaches of streams, will become more apparent in the continuing efforts to keep these remnant gems of rivers as well-used showcases for generations to come.

A Wider Range of Protection

SEARCHING FOR AN ALTERNATIVE

With only 0.3 percent of the nation's total stream mileage protected by legislation at the national level, conservationists recognized that there had better be some other means of saving waterways. Even if by some political miracle all the rivers already judged eligible were designated in the National Wild and Scenic Rivers System, the total would be only 1.8 percent of the nation's total stream mileage.

The chief alternate approach is state scenic rivers systems, adopted in 32 states. A degree of protection—though sometimes not much—is offered to 13,000 miles on 303 streams as of August 1992. "I think the most effective tools will be state river programs," said American Rivers director Kevin Coyle. "A lot of activities are best managed under state law. In Arizona and New Mexico, for example, the greatest threat to rivers is dewatering. This is best addressed by the states." Surveys by the River Network found that citizens' main concern is now land development on the shorelines—an issue that the states, through local governments, are best able to approach.

The Brule became the first state-protected river when Wisconsin banned hydropower dams in 1905; it was followed by the Flambeau in 1908. For reasons of scenery and recreation, the Oregon legislature denied water diversions from certain streams and waterfalls in 1915 and stopped dams that would interfere with salmon on the Rogue. Minnesota bought easements in 1919 to halt subdivisions along a 150 mile section of river. To save steelhead, California banned dams on the Klamath in 1924. To save salmon, Washington passed a law to prohibit dams in parts of the Columbia basin, but the Federal Power Commission overruled the state on the Cowlitz River.

Wisconsin, once again, enacted the first system of scenic rivers in the nation with its 1965 designation of the Pine, Popple, and Pike rivers to prevent development and reserve waters for recreational use. Though it did not establish a scenic rivers system, Montana the same year named rivers that would be emphasized for recreational use; it had already instituted the blue ribbon title for good trout streams. Maine legislated the Allagash Wilderness Waterway in 1963. In 1968, Ohio, Tennessee, and Maryland initiated scenic rivers programs, followed by other states.

A few states saw their programs as an alternative to unwelcome federal intervention and offered state designation more as a politically acceptable alternative than as a serious attempt at stewardship. Others saw state involvement as a way of widening protection opportunities by nurturing local political support, avoiding the ruinous fear of the federal government. It would also expand the numbers and types of rivers that could be protected to include more pastoral, recreational, and urban waterways involving private land and not likely to be nationally designated. "People are skeptical of the federal government," said Frank Sherman, in charge of state river studies for the Idaho Department of Water Resources. "Some perceive national designation as a lock-up, and other people don't think it's aggressive enough."

A larger theme of decentralizing the government's role in domestic matters supported the state scenic rivers systems, which thrived in the antifederal era coming after 1973. Foreseeing the trend and in fact helping create it, the federal Wild and Scenic Rivers Act of 1968 directed the National Park Service to "encourage and assist" in the establishment of state systems. Former interior secretary Stewart Udall recalled, "Within about four years of the federal Act, many states had passed their own rivers bills, and nothing pleased me more."

Some of the states have taken vital action for river conservation. California put 4,006 miles of waterways in a state system, banning Dos Rios Dam on the Middle Fork of the Eel in 1972 (the protected mileage on many small streams in that system was later reduced). Pennsylvania included Stony Creek as one of its initial scenic waterways, nailing shut the coffin of a utility company's pumped storage proposal. North Carolina designated the New River in 1974 expressly to halt the Blue Ridge hydroelectric complex. South Carolina protected the Saluda, and Virginia designated the James, both threatened by water projects. In a major river conservation breakthrough, Idaho established a system of protected waterways and included two spectacular rivers—the North and South forks of the Payette, which were threatened by hydroelectric plans. Indiana designated Wildcat Creek, closing the door on Lafayette Dam, once one of the hottest water battles in the Midwest.

States added a few urban rivers with intense recreational or developmental pressures: the James through Richmond, Virginia; the Saluda through Columbia, South Carolina; and the Schuylkill above Philadelphia. Like many of the national river designations on public land, the state listings often exclude the critically threatened rivers and include the less controversial.

None of the state programs offers the degree of protection of federal designation, but that misses the point: There *is* no federal action in many states and along many rivers because of local and state animosity toward higher government.

THE ROLE OF THE STATES

Effectiveness of state approaches varies from toothless lists to state-level bans on dams and mandatory zoning. These programs offer at least minimal defense against water developments. Many fail to prohibit dams but implicitly turn them away with language about "protecting the values for which the river was designated."

American Rivers promotes a model state program of nine points: (1) a policy statement; (2) a list of rivers; (3) a selection method based on an inventory; (4) a nondegradation clause barring dams and other damaging actions; (5) a consistency provision requiring all state agencies to comply; (6) identification of a lead agency with full-time staff;

(7) authority to protect land; (8) coordination of related programs; and (9) emphasis on public participation.

Some states require that zoning at the local level (county, town, or

STATE SCENIC RIVERS SYSTEMS

State	Date	Number of Rivers	Miles of Rivers	Status of State Inventory
Alaska	1987	6	350	none
Arkansas	1979	4	250	ongoing
California	1972	8 (major)	1,365	none
Connecticut	1984	0	0	ongoing
Florida	1972	1	5	final for 50 rivers
Georgia	1969	4	74	none
Idaho	1988	13 (major)	581	final
Indiana	1973	3	108	none
Iowa	1984	5	315	none
Kentucky	1972	9	114	final
Louisiana	1970	47	1,260	final for 48 rivers
Maine	1983	18	1,500	final
Maryland	1968	9	441	ongoing
Massachusetts	1971	4	86	none
Michigan	1970	14	1,698	none
Minnesota	1973	8	955	final
New Hampshire	1988	4	120	final for some rivers
New Jersey	1977	1	14	none
New York	1972	55	1,248	ongoing
North Carolina	1971	3	142	none
Ohio	1968	10	629	final
Oklahoma	1977	5	151	none
Oregon	1969	17	580	final
Pennsylvania	1972	10	393	final
South Carolina	1974	1	5	final
South Dakota	1972	0	0	none
Tennessee	1968	10	318	ongoing
Vermont	1987	0	0	final
Virginia	1970	15	169	none
Washington	1977	4	74	final
West Virginia	1969	5	236	ongoing
Wisconsin	1965	10	371	none
Total (32 states)		303	13,552	final for 13 states

township) meet state guidelines for at least a modicum of river protection. Ideally, local governments zone flood plains as open space, require setbacks of at least 100 feet from the river, limit subdivision of farmland to low density, and code wetlands and steep slopes as off limits to new building—measures that any good zoning ordinance should include. Many of the laws encourage local zoning with no state requirements, but ten systems allow the state to assume implementation of a conservation plan if local governments fail. Shoreland zoning can require modest setbacks from streams statewide in Oregon, Vermont, Wisconsin, Minnesota, Maine, and Washington, and this offers a good alternative to scenic rivers programs. Unfortunately some setbacks are as little as 40 feet.

Many states fail to promote land use regulation in the face of unwilling municipalities. Local officials are often swayed by developers and by opportunities to sell land. And funds for the alternative—easements or acquisition—are generally nonexistent.

Flood plain management is the most effective and widespread program of land use regulation helping rivers. It is already required in many states, is fueled by economic and regulatory incentives, seeks taxpayer savings by avoiding flood damage, and preserves open space along bottomlands. About 85 percent of the communities in the nation adopted flood plain regulations, since such regulations are required for federally subsidized insurance to be available to existing flood plain homeowners. Too often the regulations simply require "flood proofing," accomplished by raising the building on fill, which can be quite damaging to riverine ecosystems. Also the program does not apply to land beyond the flood zone.

Only about half the state scenic river laws include regulations on logging or mining. In a Forest Practices Act, California adopted important state standards for timber management on private land, and Pennsylvania and Vermont regulate strip mining in river corridors. All of these programs are reinforced by state scenic river designations.

More important than it might sound, good state rivers systems require consistency among agencies so that highway departments, environmental divisions, bureaus of forestry, and departments of water resources act in concert. The consistent use of water quality laws, fish and wildlife regulations, incentives for flood plain management, soil erosion controls, and wetlands restrictions goes far toward ensuring wise management of rivers.

Essential to success is an aggressive program of citizen participation throughout the processes of inventory, study, selection, and designation. Advisory committees for individual rivers and for the statewide systems are important. Citizen involvement may absorb the lion's share of the budget for state rivers administration. The ability to deal with the public is one of the most important skills of managers in scenic rivers programs.

TAKING INVENTORY

An inventory of rivers is the place to begin—the logical first step for states interested in developing a system of wild and scenic rivers or otherwise protecting their waterways. These listings make possible a comprehensive view and an orderly program. They dramatize the need for action, build a constituency by involving disparate interests early, and aid states in all manner of related resource decisions. All streams can be surveyed and ranked for their natural and recreational qualities. The final lists do not seek to protect all rivers; in fact, only small percentages survive to the final cuts. Inventories help guide developers to locations where they can invest with the least conflict. Thus, states justify inventories as a tool for "efficient" development.

Pennsylvania conducted one of the first state river inventories in 1977. From that list, an advisory council selected candidates for wild and scenic status when local politics supported it. The inventory is being updated in 1992. A Connecticut inventory in 1992 drew on experience elsewhere and enlisted an active committee concerned with a wide range of resource values.

Since the early 1980s, American Rivers has been a catalyst for many inventories. Inventories typically require several years to complete and are often guided by technical assistance staff of the National Park Service. Researchers scan topographic maps, review literature and river studies, subsume stream classifications by fisheries agencies, read boating guides, solicit information from state agencies, incorporate public ideas, and examine the rivers firsthand. In addition, questionnaires may appear in fish and wildlife agency magazines, seeking input from interested individuals.

The "Maine Rivers List" set a state-of-the-art example as one of the early inventories. Encouraged by Glenn Eugster of the Interior

Department, Drew Parkin, a student in planning in the late 1970s, authored the analysis, which may be the most influential master's thesis ever done for river protection. This compilation of outstanding rivers led in 1983 to an executive declaration by the governor for protection of 18 rivers and 1,500 miles out of the state's total of 32,000. The order bans dams and protects 700 shoreline miles from incompatible development. This single administrative action safeguarded 3 percent of the state's rivers, an achievement for which Governor Joseph Brennan won the river conservationist of the year award from American Rivers in 1982. State lawmakers proceeded to fortify the policy with laborious amendments to 22 state statutes. As is so often the case, the legislature rejected the two most threatened segments—on the West Branch Penobscot and the Saint John—where dams were proposed (the dams were later dropped for economic and political reasons). Inventories have not usually led to such sweeping and immediate protection; rather, they often result in a farm list of rivers for scenic designation, as in the Pennsylvania model, which has led to a steady growth of protected rivers during the past 15 years.

THE BEST PROGRAMS

Several states stand out among those that have rivers systems. The largest numbers of designated streams are in New York (55) and Louisiana (47). New York, however, had already protected most of its rivers somewhat with the Adirondack Park constitutional amendment. Louisiana limited its program's authority and seeks mainly to avoid channelization and pollution. It staffed the office with only one part-time employee. The California program includes significant rivers and once halted imminent dam proposals, but officials consider their program "self-administering" and simply allow other state laws and the federal agencies to function, assuming that the state Forest Practices Act will cover waterfront logging provisions. The states with the largest mileage of protected rivers are Michigan (1,698), Maine (1,500), California (1,365), Louisiana (1,260), and New York (1,248).

Michigan, with 1,698 miles, may have the strongest program, including authority to enforce land use guidelines. The state gathers local input before designation, then allows one year for local governments to meet state guidelines. If they don't, the state assumes the zoning job in a 400-foot-wide belt from the water's edge. The program has enjoyed surprising popularity in balancing state and local interests. Michigan can prohibit logging and mining, and related state programs must be consistent with scenic river goals.

Minnesota's program gained a reputation for effectiveness through strong public information and participation efforts. Program staff visited all landowners individually when designations were being considered. The state operates the program in tandem with a boating system of 1,500 miles, flood plain management, and shoreline regulations. Minnesota may zone riverfronts if counties fail to do so.

Ohio has tapped citizen participation at all levels. Local governments nominate rivers with resolutions of support, advisory committees draft management plans, and a state coordinator from the area is hired by the state to implement the plan by encouraging land use regulations by municipalities. Designation bans strip mining within 1,000 feet of the rivers.

A state initiative thought up and organized by boaters Bob Potter and Bob Peirce was the start of the Oregon system. In 1969 voters named six streams and established a unique program. The state agency reviews major land use changes in the corridors, and if a conflict with scenic values occurs, the state negotiates to bring the development into compliance with guidelines. Failing this, the state may buy the land through eminent domain, but only two parcels have ever been condemned. Designation bans mining and water projects except small diversions. Local zoning and a state forestry law regulate logging, though these did not prevent cutting along the banks of the North Umpqua. In 1988, the state's voters passed another initiative adding 11 rivers to the program.

Washington designated a large part of the exquisite Skykomish River system, but few streams were added after that because of local animosity to government. The state manager Steve Starlund instead cultivated support through cooperative strategies with local municipalities involving no designation at all. This approach lacks federal and state authority to stop dams or large projects but deals more effectively with the touchy questions of land use.

After several attempts, Idaho passed a rivers program as part of a larger water planning package ordering that six rivers be studied by the Department of Water Resources. In 1991 the legislature confirmed protection for several important rivers, parts of the Payette, Boise, and Priest systems. This state with superlative rivers showed signs of building an effective river protection program. Studies of the intricate, unique, and troubled middle Snake River continued. Up for consideration in 1992, the legendary trout waters of the Henry's Fork of the Snake drew fire from a powerfully entrenched statewide water lobby that had little to lose by designating that great trout stream but resisted, apparently out of fear that river protection in Idaho could become a habit if other streams follow the model of the Payette, Boise, and Priest.

THE TENACIOUS HYDROPOWER THREAT

The chief drawback to state scenic river systems is a serious one: they haven't stopped hydropower dams licensed by the Federal Energy Regulatory Commission (FERC). North Carolina designated the New River to halt the Blue Ridge Project, but courts ruled that FERC could issue a license for the dam; only national designation saved the river.

In California, the state fought a hydropower dam on the South Fork of the Yuba River where a FERC license would have granted a private developer authority to condemn state parkland. The permit has lapsed, but the outstanding river still lacks protection, which is now being sought by the South Yuba River Citizens League. For the Klamath River in Oregon, state designation through a 1988 initiative failed to impress FERC. A dam proposal was stopped—perhaps only temporarily—by the state's refusal to grant the city of Klamath Falls a water quality permit for the hydroelectric project. In the mid 1980s the Virginia scenic rivers system faced six FERC applications on designated rivers.

A case in California confirmed the weakness of the states in this regard. Supported by every other state, California in 1989 sought to gain precedence over FERC in a hydropower permit at Rock Creek, but it failed in the U.S. Supreme Court. Ironically, it remains unclear which outcome would have been best for rivers. FERC, evolving somewhat with federal reforms, has taken at least a minimal river protection role, while many western states have taken none. In the case of Milner Dam on the Snake River, for example, FERC forced an improved instream flow over initial state resistance.

In addition to hydropower, other threats loom over the states' authority. New Mexico protected the Rio Chama in 1977, but the Army Corps of Engineers temporarily flooded lower reaches anyway, precipitating a fruitless lawsuit by the state, which ultimately sought national river designation for reinforcement.

Legislation proposed in 1983 by Senator David Durenberger of Minnesota required FERC to recognize state scenic rivers and rivers with similar status, but the bill died, as did a similar one in 1988. Amending the Federal Power Act in 1986, the Electric Consumers Protection Act ordered FERC to consider state designations and fish and wildlife reviews but fell short of mandating recognition of state scenic rivers. A bill again proposed in 1992 would recognize state authority.

National wild and scenic designation remains the best and often the only reliable tool to fend off hydropower projects and federal actions damaging to rivers.

THE BRIDGE TO PERMANENCE

Under section 2(a)(ii) of the Wild and Scenic Rivers Act of 1968, governors may request national designation by the secretary of the interior for state-protected rivers, a procedure that had been followed for 13 major river systems as of 1992. An environmental statement involving substantial documentation and assessment may be required along with the governor's request.

The low level of federal involvement in these state-administered, national rivers lends little credence to abiding fears that the federal overlay will bring a heavy federal presence, but the fear persists anyway. Few rivers have been named under this protection option. Beyond antifederal rhetoric, an underlying truth is that many governors and state legislators don't want their rivers to be saved, a fear couched in terms of "losing local control." Some California lawmakers were influenced by southern California water interests that fought federal designation of state scenic rivers because water supply projects might some day be desired; others were swayed by logging companies and northern counties that opposed protection out of fear of restricted timber cuts. The public argument of all the opposition groups was that the federal government shouldn't tell California what to do.

For the Suwannee River in Florida, the upper Iowa, and 20 national wild and scenic study rivers in all, federal agencies recommended state designation with perhaps a later upgrading to national protection, but the states have not responded, ostensibly because of concern over acquisition and administration costs. Some states believe that the federal overlay of protection offers no advantage. Administration, in fact, must be undertaken "without cost" to the federal government, yet nationally designated rivers are typically higher on priority lists for related federal support, such as the Land and Water Conservation Fund and programs for mine and toxic waste reclamation, water quality, and fish and wildlife enhancement. Maine, for example, received $1.5 million in matching funds for land acquisition at the Allagash, and Ohio received $1 million for the Little Miami.

Federal agencies many times passed the controversial rivers on to the states, knowing full well what would happen: nothing. This difficult dilemma pits the planner's professional judgment on conservation needs against political pressure. There is no doubt that state initiative is often appropriate because federal legislation would stall without support, but in other cases, waiving the river to state interests is the kiss of death for protection. The exemplary Sierra Nevada rivers—the Tuolumne, Kings, Kern, and Merced—might not have been designated if the decision had been left to California during the 1980s.

An inherent bias against federal involvement resides not only among local citizens but also within state governments. The Allagash—the first state river added to the national system—will likely be Maine's last. That state opposed federal protection for the West Branch of the Penobscot when Great Northern Paper Company planned a dam in the mid 1980s. Pennsylvania in the 1970s stonewalled designation of five streams—the largest block of study rivers in the original National Wild and Scenic Rivers Act.

Ideal candidates for federal protection at the states' request include 49 Adirondack Park rivers of 1,238 miles in New York, located deep in the preservation heritage of that region but eyed covetously by hydropower developers. Idaho rivers under state designation or study are clearly national gems where much of the riverbank mileage is federal land, but where hydropower threats persist against a waffling state legislature, which attached language to state designations attempting to bar the governor from requesting national river status.

FALLING SHORT

That rivers are sometimes easier to designate in a state system also means that they're easier to withdraw. In 1983 Tennessee withdrew 42 miles of the Collins River. Oklahoma rescinded protection of the Baron Fork River, and after communities buying cheap water pressured legislators, it also rescinded state protection for part of Lee Creek to allow for a dam and for lower water quality standards. Iowa cut protection for 80 miles of the upper Iowa River when it replaced its entire rivers act with an inventory-based system in 1984.

The most dramatic reduction was made by California, which in 1982 rescinded protection for many of the Smith River tributaries, about 2,700 miles in all. Included was Hardscrabble Creek, where three dams were to be built for a nickel mine (the stream was later protected in federal national recreation area legislation). In California, over 50 percent of the population lives in the southern 20 percent of the state, where lawmakers naturally favored water transfers from north to south. Their rumblings of discontent over state scenic river protection created the urgency to designate the northern California state scenic rivers in the national system in 1980 and to avoid their deletion from the state system by a simple majority vote at the state capitol.

The Indiana senate voted to deauthorize the entire state rivers system over a backyard argument about channelization in a tributary of the designated Cedar Creek; opposing sides compromised, however, and the system remains.

To prevent the undoing of protection, river supporters need to exercise constant vigilance against fast moves in late-hour sessions. This watch-dog job is more difficult to do at the state than national level where actions are monitored more closely.

By design, some state systems are weak in stopping dams and water projects—some states don't *want* to stop them. The Army Corps was permitted to dredge a channel in Louisiana's West Branch Pearl River. Kentucky authorized seasonal inundation of the North Fork of the Red River by a now defunct Corps proposal that was one of the highlights of the dam-fighting era of the 1970s.

Every government agency says that insufficient funds are a problem, but the state rivers really are poorly funded: no money was budgeted in 22 of the 32 states in 1984. The only ones allocating more than $100,000 in 1983—a time when programs tended to be strong— were Minnesota, Ohio, Oklahoma, and Pennsylvania. A few of the larger programs brought the average of the 10 budgeted states up to $125,000.

Most states allocate only one employee to river conservation. With that level of staffing in mind, it may be interesting to note here that there are 90,000 miles of streams in Oregon, 80,000 in Texas, 70,000 in New York, 45,000 in Pennsylvania, 43,900 in Ohio, 40,600 in Alabama, 40,000 in Kentucky, and so forth. Exceptions to the lonely staffers in the mid 1980s were Minnesota, which had 17 workers, Oklahoma with 5, and Pennsylvania and Ohio with 6 each. All of these have since been reduced. About 60 people worked on state river programs nationwide. The National Association for State and Local River Conservation Programs involves the managers and brings the states together to share knowledge and pool resources.

Land and easement acquisition are rarely practiced among the state programs. The more successful ones avoid the authority to condemn land—almost never used, anywhere, but nonetheless regarded by landowners as an ever present threat. Those programs without condemnation authority have found that support comes easier and operations go more smoothly.

As with the national system, the leading problem is that so few state scenic rivers have been designated. Researcher Curtis Alling of Texas A & M University reported in 1977 that key problems were opposition by local communities along private-land rivers, poor administrative support from high levels of government, unorganized constituents, and competition by industry, utilities, and real estate developers—an accurate but discouraging list of difficulties. Alling recommended local community action with state guidance.

In California, Friends of the River succeeded far better in lobbying Congress for federal designations than in getting the state to expand its own system. "The water development interests are stronger in Sacramento than they are in Washington," said conservation director Steve Evans. More bluntly, political observers say it's always easier for developers to buy a state legislator than a national one. After the original designations in 1972, nothing was added to the California system until 1989 with passage of the West Carson and East Walker rivers. The state dropped its proposal for the eminently qualified McCloud River because one landowner, which happened to be the wealthy Hearst family, objected.

Some states have no scenic rivers system at all. This group includes such riparian gifted landscapes as Mississippi, Alabama, Montana, and Colorado. Under fire from landowner groups and the farm bureau, Missouri voters in 1990 rejected a state program even though it specified that local residents write the management plans.

The state response to rivers is poor relative to their record on endangered species legislation, for which all states but two have adopted cooperative agreements. But relative to their record on wilderness legislation, which only a few states have enacted, the state response to rivers is good.

State river programs tend to be marked by insufficient citizen support in the absence of immediate threats by forces from beyond the local area. But Suzi Wilkins, director of American Rivers's state programs, cautioned, "For most rivers, slow, gradual changes are the problem: land use changes that threaten the river with erosion, sedimentation, and runoff; septic discharges near the river; and visual quality lost to developments with no screening. This kind of growth and cumulative impact on the rivers is much harder to get people involved in, yet it's as important as the massive threats." People more easily perceive a crisis as a need for national river designation, but the ordinary changes, if people once realized their importance, could become the driving force for state protection.

OTHER WAYS OF SAVING RIVERS

Even state river programs imply "too much government" in the minds of some people, leading to local options for protection.

At the upper end of the nation's 2,300 mile, largest river, the Mississippi Headwaters Board helps guide land use policy. The board represents eight Minnesota counties and is the most powerful multi-county agency authorized by a state to guide land use along a river. Established in 1980 as an alternative to national river designation, the board receives half its funding from the state and half from the counties and can override local zoning that fails to comply with a state-approved plan. The board coordinates acquisition of scenic easements and management of recreation along 400 miles of the Mississippi—the longest protected reach in the United States.

The Saco River Commission in Maine consists of 22 communities authorized by the state to adopt guidelines affecting land use in a 1,000-foot-wide belt up and down the river. The guidelines feature 100 foot setbacks from the water, open space on the flood plain, and standards for logging within 250 feet of the river. A similar commission governs the Connecticut River in Connecticut.

Indiana and Connecticut authorized river conservation commissions of two or more municipalities to regulate land use. Avoiding the regulatory approach, local efforts of the Nashua River Greenway in Massachusetts have secured scenic easements to 6,000 acres along 37 miles since 1966.

In the upper Colorado basin, the Nature Conservancy has launched a Rivers of the Rockies program to protect the ecosystems of the Yampa, White, Gunnison, San Miguel, and Dolores rivers through private and voluntary actions regarding water rights, land acquisition, and coordination of managing authorities.

At Montana's Blackfoot River, ranchers and timber companies (Champion International and two ranchers own 75 percent of the frontage), county planners, the state, Trout Unlimited, and citizens formed a coalition for planning and riverfront protection. Landowners allowed recreation on their property, and state agencies maintained the sites. The Nature Conservancy bought $20,000 worth of easements where full acquisition of the land in fee would have cost $15 million. The Blackfoot, Mississippi, and other experiences differ perhaps little from what would have occurred with national or state wild and scenic river status, but in these regions, as in many, "wild river" is not a popular term and "scenic" isn't much better.

At an even more local level, a 1981 Oregon law enabled individuals to receive property tax reductions if they set aside riparian acreage as fish and wildlife habitat, one of the most significant enticements for private river conservation anywhere. Unfortunately, the program has not been widely used.

At a multistate level, the Northwest Power Planning Council put together a Protected Areas Program, adopted in 1988. It identified 44,000 miles on about 5,897 streams in the Pacific Northwest for their fish and wildlife values (the region has 250,000 miles of streams in all).

This is the largest single action ever taken to protect specific stream mileage in the nation. The list, drafted principally by fish and game agencies and adopted after rigorous public review, denies nonconforming hydroprojects the privilege of using the Bonneville Power Administration's power lines, which form the region's grid. Regarded as part of a comprehensive plan, the Protected Areas List must be considered by FERC as it processes hydropower licenses. Time will tell if the federal agency will respect the council's rule, but FERC's locked-in approval of the Salt Caves project on the Klamath does not bode well for the difficult cases.

The National Park Service's technical assistance program reaches out to scores of additional rivers nationwide, advising state and local governments and citizens on protection techniques. With direction by Chris Brown in Washington, DC, the program expanded in 1992 to 58 staff members in 12 field offices. These offices handle 100 projects, including urban riverfront plans, greenway corridor promotion, and statewide river assessments. In 1992, a 60 percent budget increase to $8 million was proposed by the administration, enabling substantial growth, especially for greenway development along urban rivers. The program has produced the *River Conservation Directory*, the *Handbook of State Rivers Conservation Programs*, and the *Economics of Greenways*. Chris Brown foresaw a broad agenda that could ultimately affect 5,000 rivers through assistance to all levels of government and to mobilized citizens.

NATIONAL PARKS AND WILDERNESS

A discussion of river protection would not be complete without recognition of the national parks and wilderness areas, which hold many rivers, their exact number and mileage unknown. Though not explicitly protected, rivers in the parks enjoy effective security from development. Conservationists overturned the Hetch Hetchy precedent of building major dams in national parks at Devil's Postpile in 1911, Yellowstone Lake in 1922, the Bechler and Falls rivers in Yellowstone National Park in 1927, the Glacier View and Smoky Range sites on the North Fork Flathead in the 1940s and 1950s, and the Kings River in the 1920s and 1940s, leading to the rejection of Echo Park Dam on the Green River in Dinosaur National Monument in 1956. While scores of dams have been built in national parks, including the five-mile-long Sherburne Reservoir on Swiftcurrent Creek in Glacier National Park and a hydroelectric dam within Yosemite Valley, river developments in parks have usually been small and obscure. The trend has turned away from even those.

Hundreds of outstanding natural rivers flow at least partly through national parks and monuments. Among these are the Oconaluftee River in Great Smoky Mountains National Park; Big Thompson in Rocky Mountain; Gunnison in Black Canyon of the Gunnison; Green in Canyonlands; Yampa in Dinosaur; Virgin in Zion; Colorado in Canyonlands and Grand Canyon; Snake in Grand Teton; White and Nisqually in Mount Rainier; Kaweah in Sequoia; Copper in Wrangell–Saint Elias; Alsek in Glacier Bay; Toklat in Denali; and the Yellowstone, Firehole, Gardiner, and Madison in Yellowstone National Park.

America has over 500 wilderness areas, comprising over 90 million acres. Like the national parks, these include hundreds of wild rivers, most of them small. Congress has protected wilderness better than any other kind of natural area, though a loophole in the Wilderness Act allows water development if approved by the president. This threat surfaced in the 1970s on Colorado River tributaries in the Eagles Nest Wilderness, where the Denver Water Board planned to dam, divert, and tunnel Gore Creek, Piney Creek, and other streams from their westward flow to the east side of the Rockies. No president has invoked the exemption, however, and it thus far poses little threat to wilderness area rivers.

WIDE BUT NOT WIDE ENOUGH

This wider range of protection—the state scenic rivers systems, local formulas, and other means of safeguarding rivers—fails to offer the defense provided by national designation but more than doubles the mileage of protected rivers in the United States. Even so, that represents only 0.6 percent of America's total stream miles. How can people extend protection to more rivers? What is the unfinished agenda for river conservation in America?

The Unfinished Agenda

RIVERS THAT WAIT

Is a fraction of 1 percent of all the nation's rivers enough for the heritage of a people whose identity was shaped by a wild and supremely beautiful continent? Is it enough for the spirits of a people whose whole national character is one of individualism and freedom yet is also rooted in a new land with abundant fruits and pleasures, turbulent challenges and serene comforts, all so fittingly represented by free-flowing rivers?

How can more rivers be protected? Chapter 3 probed the ways in which the movement for rivers might grow, and Chapter 6 addressed the crucial role of state and local governments. It is important to note also that people can guide the fate of streams everywhere without national, state, or local designations by using water quality regulations, flood plain management, streamside and open space zoning, greenway planning, fish and wildlife enhancement, and land trust acquisition. But national rivers and the extra security afforded them are the topic of this book, so this final chapter examines a future for the rivers that await greater protection.

STUDY RIVERS

As a cornerstone to many future designations, the Wild and Scenic Rivers Act includes a study category of rivers authorized for deliberation by Congress. Before the public-land river bills of the late 1980s, authorization of a study river was considered a prerequisite to protection.

No one randomly threw the study rivers out on the table, as might be implied by the fact that "study" was needed. Most were selected through a rigorous process, chosen from larger lists of rivers known to be excellent. Some names came up because of local supporters, usually responding to a hydropower threat, who convinced a congressional member of the river's importance. The study process, then, is largely a political one of seeing what people think, of testing the opinionated waters, of examining reviews by competing agencies, of compromising with conflicting interests. More cynically, designation for study allows congressional members to take some action but not much; they can, for a time, pacify both sides of the debate, as was no doubt the strategy in cases such as the Tuolumne, though it was later designated.

Many of the study rivers sailed straight into the doldrums. As of August 1992, Congress had authorized 132 studies (not counting minor tributaries). Portions of 34 study rivers had been designated, though the segments often represented a small fraction of what had been studied, found eligible, and recommended by agency planners.

The agencies found eight of the study rivers ineligible, many under dubious rationale. Pennsylvania's Clarion, for example, was rejected because of pollution, a questionable judgment even in the late 1960s, yet the water quality of this picturesque river has undeniably improved and no longer encumbers even the fussiest debate about eligibility. Ironically, delaying national designation may have been the best thing in this case, as the Army Corps' Saint Petersburg Dam died of its own weight. The federal government's rapid exit allowed the Western Pennsylvania Conservancy to pursue an acquisition program without the strife and polarization that designation might have fed. In 1992 the Clarion was authorized for a second wild and scenic study. Part of the Allegheny in Pennsylvania was ineligible, but another part was designated in 1992.

Aside from the 8 "ineligible" rivers, agencies did not recommend designation of 36 study rivers, largely for political reasons. Some of these proposals were known to lack the essential support for the journey through Congress; others were killed by administration officials and policies aggressively opposing protection and never giving Congress a chance to decide otherwise. Among those unrecommended rivers, the federal agencies called for state designation of 20, a few of which were acted on by states; 3 were eventually added to the national system at the governors' requests. Other levels of government protected several of the study rivers, such as the upper Mississippi. Congress failed to act on 13 study rivers that agencies had recommended. In August 1992, 42 studies were planned or under way, including those for the Sheenjek and Squirrel in Alaska, and Yampa-Green in Colorado and Utah, which had been under study for many years and were no longer considered active.

Even when designation efforts died, benefits often sprouted out of the process. After a stormy study lacking political support in the 1970s, agencies and residents along Pine Creek in Pennsylvania dug in to accomplish much of the protection job anyway. Pushed by local conservation groups, the state Bureau of Forestry acquired some of the critical open space and designated a Pennsylvania version of wilderness on choice state forest tracts along the river, including Miller Run and three other wild tributaries. With county help, townships zoned the flood plain. Dumps were closed and solid waste collection begun. The state improved access areas to alleviate trespassing, and a Pine Creek Task Force of state agencies, local governments, and citizen organizations met regularly for five years to accelerate water quality and other improvements, resulting in better on-site sewage systems and reclamation of mine drainage. The river remains undesignated.

The list of undesignated study rivers is one of the finer lists of rivers in America:

ALABAMA

Cahaba, not qualified according to the reporting agency
Escatawpa (also in Mississippi), state designation recommended
Soldier Creek, not qualified

ALASKA

Coleville, not recommended
Etivluk-Nigu, not recommended
Kanektok, not recommended
Kisaralik, not recommended
Koyuk, not qualified
Melozitna, not qualified
Porcupine, not recommended
Sheenjek (lower), in study
Situk, not recommended
Squirrel, in study
Utukok, not recommended
Yukon (Ramparts section), not recommended

ARIZONA

Salt, not recommended
San Francisco, not recommended

CALIFORNIA

Little Sur River, in study
Lopez Creek, in study
Matilija Creek, in study
Piru Creek, in study
Sespe Creek, in study

COLORADO

Big Thompson, not recommended
Colorado (also in Utah), not recommended
Conejos, recommended
Dolores, recommended
Elk, recommended
Encampment, recommended
Gunnison, recommended
Los Pinos, recommended
Piedra, recommended
Yampa, no recommendation transmitted to the president

CONNECTICUT

Farmington (also in Massachusetts), in study
Housatonic, state designation recommended
Shepaug, state designation recommended

DELAWARE

White Clay Creek (also in Pennsylvania), in study

FLORIDA

Myakka, state designation recommended
Saint Mary's, in study
Suwannee, state designation recommended

GEORGIA

Ogeechee, state designation recommended

IDAHO

Bruneau, recommended
Moyie, not recommended
Priest, recommended
Snake (Asotin reach, also in Oregon, Washington), in study for the
second time

IOWA

Iowa, state designation recommended

KENTUCKY

Red, recommended

MAINE

Penobscot, state designation recommended

MASSACHUSETTS

Assabet, in study
Concord, in study
Sudbury, in study

MICHIGAN

Brule (also in Wisconsin), in study
Carp, in study
Little Manistee, in study
Ontonagon, in study
Paint, in study
Presque Isle, in study
Sturgeon (Hiawatha National Forest), in study
Sturgeon (Ottawa National Forest), in study
Tahquamenon, in study
White, in study
Whitefish, in study

MINNESOTA

Kettle, state designation recommended
Mississippi, recommended (now locally protected)

MISSOURI

Gasconade, state designation recommended

NEW HAMPSHIRE

Lamprey, in study
Merrimack, in study
Pemigewasset, in study

NEW JERSEY

Great Egg Harbor, in study
Manumuskin, in study
Maurice, in study
Menantico, in study

NEW YORK

Fish Creek, East Branch, state designation recommended

NORTH CAROLINA

Mills, in study

OHIO

Maumee, not qualified

OKLAHOMA

Illinois, state designation recommended

OREGON

Blue, in study
Chewaucan, in study
Malheur, North Fork, in study
McKenzie, South Fork, in study
Steamboat Creek, in study
Wallowa, in study

PENNSYLVANIA

Allegheny, lower, not qualified
Clarion, not qualified, but a new study was authorized in 1992
Mill Creek (Clarion tributary), in study
Pine Creek, state designation recommended
Youghiogheny, state designation recommended

TENNESSEE

Buffalo, state designation recommended
Nolichucky (also in North Carolina), not qualified but later recommended by the Forest Service

UTAH

Green (also in Colorado), no recommendation transmitted to the president

WASHINGTON

Columbia, in study
Klickitat, upper, state designation recommended
White Salmon, upper, recommended

WEST VIRGINIA

Birch, state designation recommended
Cacapon, state designation recommended
Greenbrier, state designation recommended

WISCONSIN

Wisconsin, state designation recommended

WYOMING

Snake, recommended
Sweetwater, not recommended

The Penobscot in Maine shines as a jewel of New England, beginning on the legendary slopes of Mount Katahdin, yet threatened by hydropower development in its lower reaches. The Maurice River in New Jersey holds hemispheric importance to migratory birds from many places, headed toward many destinations, which stop here in great numbers. Pine Creek carved one of the exquisite canyons of the Appalachians; downstream, private land is being developed along the river. The Youghiogheny is among the country's most popular whitewater rivers, a showcase of the East but with a history of strip-mine threats. The Cacapon in West Virginia emerges from a limestone cave; the Army Corps uncharacteristically recommended this as one of the first proposals for national river protection in 1963. A land of rivers, West Virginia also has the Greenbrier, one of the longest undammed rivers in the East.

The Suwannee in Georgia and Florida flows for 265 miles from Okefenokee Swamp to the Gulf of Mexico, one of the longest undammed rivers in the East. The Escatawpa in Alabama and Mississippi winds serenely with blackwater and white sand beaches. The Mississippi—466 miles of it—was the longest reach ever considered for river protection. The Illinois in Oklahoma, one of the finest Midwest rivers, offers abundant recreation opportunities.

The Colorado pounds through Westwater Canyon as one of the great river-running adventures in the West. The Snake River in Jackson Hole flows through a premier river-and-mountain landscape and then through a canyon with some of the West's most popular whitewater. A separate section below Hells Canyon is critical to endangered salmon and steelhead. The Bruneau cuts through a quintessential desert canyon, one of the wildest, most remote, and least visited in the nation. Though carefully considered, none of these rivers has been designated.

The study process became one of the disappointing aspects of the wild and scenic rivers program. Some studies required five to seven years; one took ten years. In 1978 the General Accounting Office (GAO) issued *Federal Protection and Preservation of Wild and Scenic Rivers Is Slow and Costly*, reporting that agencies took "an inordinate amount of time" to conduct a study. States did not participate, federal agencies depended too much on acquisition, and local land use controls were not pursued. Studies were variously delayed by poorly defined guidelines that required time-consuming interpretations of the act by inexperienced staff, and by long review periods and coordination sessions with states, local governments, and residents. The GAO fell silent regarding delays at the Office of Management and Budget, where administration officials in the 1980s cut proposed mileage, canceled agency recommendations, and eroded support and morale. Rivers finally receiving designation were grossly reduced: the Forest Service studied 165 miles of the Au Sable in Michigan, all of which arguably qualified for protection. The agency recommended 74 miles; the Office of Management and Budget approved 23. The Reagan administration then attached this gesture of conservation to a bill allowing states to dismantle the federal program by subtracting streams from the system at will (the bill failed but the chopped-down version of the Au Sable later passed). Out of 2,500 miles of study rivers considered in the dismal year of 1985, most of them eligible as national rivers, federal agencies recommended 337 miles and President Reagan approved 173.7.

Beginning in the mid 1980s, agencies bypassed full-blown studies for the public-land rivers and rather considered them during the ongoing land-planning process, which greatly streamlined the work. Still, Steve Whitney of the Wilderness Society and others complained, "The process is too slow. By fighting political battles river by river, segment by segment, tremendous numbers of valuable rivers will be lost before there is any chance for protection."

Owing to 1992 legislation, Michigan has 11 study rivers—the most under active consideration. Eight of them are extensions of reaches designated in 1992.

In Alaska, study rivers immediately vanished into a black hole of resource-exploiting politics. In spite of a three-year deadline, agencies accomplished little in the face of opposition from the state congressional delegation, which had seen the studies as a subtle way to thwart protection during debates over the Alaska Lands Act in the late 1970s. Alaska's study rivers include the remaining mileage of the superlative Sheenjek, the vital Porcupine, and a section of the Yukon that was the cause of one of the landmark dam fights in conservation history.

Colorado, with 10 study rivers, has only one designated stream, a poor record testifying to the force of old-guard, commodity-based politics inordinately persistent in the most urban state of the Rockies. Because the population there is by many other measures environmentally conscious, Colorado appears ripe for progress in river protection.

The smorgasbord of setbacks facing wild and scenic designations (discussed in chapter 3) materialized as full-blown problems on most study rivers: poor public information and participation; landowners' fear of condemnation; hostile presidential administrations in charge of the studies yet undermining them by scuttling recommendations; and the influence of hydropower entrepreneurs, real estate agents, miners, and loggers. The study process was so flawed and cumbersome that Glenn Eugster, a key participant in the Interior Department, abandoned faith in it and instituted the popular technical assistance program when the Heritage, Conservation and Recreation Service was formed from the old Bureau of Outdoor Recreation.

Yet the study rivers deserve protection somehow. Essential measures are to extend the temporary bans on federal developments, promote solutions through local government initiative, incorporate the rivers in state systems, and later add them to the national program if support grows.

In 1986 the General Accounting Office reported that state and local governments had initiated some kind of protection for 11 of 13 study rivers that had not been designated; this fact alone may justify study status and make all the agony worthwhile. No new water projects were built on the 13 reviewed rivers, though at least two serious threats were averted partly because of the study status. The GAO reported that the rivers "generally retained" their values, yet developments had "greatly degraded" wild and scenic values on several rivers: mining near the Suwannee, logging along the Youghiogheny, sewage discharges in Oklahoma's Illinois, and residential development on bluffs above the Wisconsin. The report overlooked the fact that the threats could arise again and that the GAO's time frame of one decade was absurdly short. If multiplied at the going rate over the next 100 years, the incremental changes on the unprotected rivers would render them basket cases of abuse.

Perhaps the most important task is to continue to revamp the study process on private-land rivers. The Wildcat River in New Hampshire may be a model for the future: Park Service planners facilitated a local effort and simply offered the added security of national protection (see chapter 3). The Farmington in Massachusetts, a larger river, followed that successful model, and one section of it may be designated. Even larger, the upper Allegheny, under study since 1975, received support from the Pennsylvania delegation and was designated in 1992 following the successful model of intensive local involvement.

Resolving problems of study rivers is essential because, in spite of private-land problems and criticism of studies, more rivers continue to be added to this category. The number of studies under way in 1992 was the highest ever.

Over the years, study legislation was introduced for additional rivers but for one reason or another didn't pass. These are streams that could easily come up again for consideration:

California: San Joaquin
Connecticut: Salmon
Florida: Saint Lucie and Oklawaha
Georgia: Satilla
Idaho: Box Canyon Creek
Indiana: Big Pine
Kansas and Oklahoma: Cimarron
Maine: Sheepscott
Massachusetts: Parker
Nebraska: Dismal
North Carolina and Virginia: Dan
South Carolina: Little Pee Dee
Tennessee: Caney Fork
Texas: Brazos
Washington: Hoh, Dosewallips, and Quillayute
West Virginia: Shavers Fork

In addition, the Interior Department in 1974 recommended study of two truly significant sections of river: 100 miles of the Snake from Yellowstone to Palisades Reservoir in Wyoming (excepting Jackson Dam), and all of the White River in Colorado and Utah. Only a portion of that Snake River reach was actually studied.

In 1992, Representative Peter Kostmayer introduced a bill to name 25 study segments in Pennsylvania, a water-rich state with more study rivers in the original Wild and Scenic Rivers Act than any other state but not a lot of luck in securing designations.

An extension of the moratoriums on development, renewed designation efforts under new models of public participation and leadership by community members, and alternate forms of protection including state designation are all avenues that could be pursued. The study rivers are simply too good to be lost and forgotten. The coming era of river protection should prevent their abandonment and safeguard them with a new conservation interest lacking the fatal threat of eminent domain.

THE NATIONWIDE RIVERS INVENTORY

The first designation of rivers in the national system resulted from professional surveys by Interior Department and Forest Service planners, the willingness of federal agencies (with direction from the top) to have a few rivers designated, and the political will of some powerful congressional members. Rivers were then added when local conservationists, residents, American Rivers, and occasionally the big conservation groups unearthed congressional support for them. While eligibility guidelines existed, they were justifiably broad, and most reasonable choices of flowing water seemed to have at least one "outstandingly remarkable" value. In effect, any river with congressional votes met the eligibility criteria.

The study rivers were clearly destined for evaluation, good or bad, and Interior Secretary Walter Hickel (with concurrence from the secretary of agriculture) in 1970 also approved a 5(d) list of 65 rivers (47 not counting tributaries) named under that section of the act for wild and scenic "consideration" by federal agencies and for potential addition to the system. In effect, this was a farm club of rivers that supporters hoped would graduate to the study phase. No other specific 5(d) list has been authorized by the secretaries of interior and agriculture. The rivers included the following:

Alaska: Birch Creek, Chatanika, Chitna, Delta, Fortymile and its major tributaries, Gulkana, Middle Fork Gulkana, West Fork Gulkana

California: Kern, Klamath, Russian, Sacramento, Smith, North Fork Smith, Middle Fork Smith, South Fork Smith, Tuolumne

Florida: Wacissa

Idaho: Henry's Fork, Snake (Hells Canyon, also in Oregon)

Iowa: Wapsipinicon

Louisiana: Tangipahoa (also in Mississippi)

Maryland: Pocomoke

Michigan: Au Sable, Manistee, Pine

Minnesota: Big Fork

Missouri: North Fork White

Montana: Blackfoot, Madison, Yellowstone

Nebraska: Niobrara

New Jersey: Mullica, Wading, Bass

New York: Beaverkill, Hudson

North Dakota: Little Missouri

Oregon: Deschutes, Grande Ronde, Granite Creek, Imnaha, John Day, North Fork John Day, Minam, Wallowa, Wenaha

Texas: Guadalupe

Utah: Escalante

Virginia: Rapidan, Rappahannock, Shenandoah

Washington: Chiwawa, Columbia, Wenatchee, White

West Virginia: Cacapon, Shenandoah

Wisconsin: South Fork Flambeau, Pine, Popple, Wolf

Wyoming: Green, Gros Ventre, Snake, Wind

Parts of 24 of these rivers were later designated.

While Hickel's list was a good one, nothing even remotely comprehensive had been drawn up since Interior Department planners had screened an initial inventory of 650 rivers for the original Wild and Scenic Rivers Act (a list that has been lost, ironically, to "water damage" at Interior's storage facility). As separate efforts, the Fish and Wildlife Service, Environmental Protection Agency, and some western states evaluated streams and prepared maps identifying high quality rivers for 12 states in the early 1970s. River basin commissions in the 1970s likewise recommended waterways for protection (most of those commissions were later disbanded).

The idea of a nationwide inventory probably began with Bob Baker, southeast regional director of the Bureau of Outdoor Recreation in the early 1970s, who had worked with William Penn Mott in the California state parks system when a statewide inventory for parkland was completed. Interior Department officials who were for a time sympathetic to the rivers program soon saw an inventory of eligible rivers as a way of meeting the 5(d) requirement that federal agencies consider additional rivers. Further interest surfaced at two opposite poles: first, enthusiasts who thought a list of all potentially eligible rivers would be helpful in advancing streams toward designation wanted a large list; second, critics fearing that river protection might be endless wanted a small list.

The Interior Department, with James Watt as director of the Bureau of Outdoor Recreation, proceeded with the inventory, trying to determine what the least amount of protection should be. In the late 1970s work began in the East and moved westward, and the study's name was changed from the cryptic "minimum system" study to the Nationwide Rivers Inventory (NRI). Regional offices of the Heritage, Conservation and Recreation Service (HCRS, the successor to the Bureau of Outdoor Recreation) evaluated rivers using criteria for accessibility, development, dams, recreation, fisheries, wildlife, geology, and historic, cultural, and archaeological values. The state of Montana objected to the project, and HCRS complied with requests that the federal government not consider the state's 20,500 miles of streams, not even those on federal land. Alaska, with 365,000 miles of streams that are virtually all unofficially eligible as wild and scenic rivers, was at first excluded from the inventory, but was added later. The rest of the country was included.

The inventory eventually selected 1,524 segments of 61,700 miles—only 1.8 percent of the nation's total stream mileage but still six times the size of the national rivers system in 1992. About 36 percent of the mileage lies in the East. In California alone, 3,062 miles were listed. Michigan had 3,026 miles, and Georgia, 2,973. Oregon and Washington should probably have been close to the top of the list, but the Western Region listed only the top 15 to 20 percent of eligible rivers on the inventory.

Even a sketchy examination revealed hundreds of waterways that could be added to the inventory. Forest Service officials—even some who were personally annoyed at the prospects—routinely found double or more the NRI mileage as eligible rivers in their forests (if the inventory had not been discontinued in 1982 it would be more complete). Most recreational rivers were not counted if they had ample access. Holes in the data notwithstanding, the main point was that a list had been drawn up with reasonably standard criteria and had identified a conservative agenda nationwide. The 1978 Nationwide Outdoor Recreation Plan by the Heritage, Conservation and Recreation Service meanwhile had supported the inventory by calling for federal agency cooperation, prompt consideration of rivers for the Wild and Scenic Rivers System, and "natural resource waters" status under the Clean Water Act for all inventory rivers.

At HCRS Bern Collins, caretaker of the inventory, crafted model directions for the rivers based on wetlands efforts, having no idea what opportunities might await the list housed in his office. When President Carter, a rivers enthusiast since his days as governor of Georgia, prepared an environmental message in 1979, HCRS assistant director Meg McGuire offered to contribute a statement on river conservation. She went to Collins, who rephrased his policy-in-waiting to say that federal agencies must consider the inventory in all decisions and that they should evaluate rivers and recommend suitable reaches for national designation during land-planning efforts.

In a landmark decision—the most far-reaching for rivers since President Johnson proposed the original Wild and Scenic Rivers Act—Jimmy Carter announced in his message on the environment that the Wild and Scenic Rivers System needed to be strengthened. Federal agencies, he said, were to avoid or mitigate actions that could foreclose wild and scenic eligibility on rivers in the inventory. Agencies were required to consult with HCRS about conflicts. Even though Reagan officials later ignored the directive and FERC only lackadaisically recognized it, Carter's order set into motion the evaluation of thousands of rivers by all federal land management agencies. This was the precipitating event in the advances of the 1980s regarding rivers through public land and in the focus of federal protection in the 1990s.

Beyond all this the inventory, published in 1982, proved useful in unexpected ways. Collins and regional Park Service staff consulted the list almost daily in reviews of federal activities, including hydropower permits; in 1990 alone the Park Service, inheriting the job from HCRS, reviewed over 30 projects on inventory rivers under section 404 of the Water Quality Act. Status on the inventory added weight to any other protection efforts for a particular river and legitimized local initiatives to save streams. The FERC eventually came to regard the list as a comprehensive plan, elevating it to status that must be recognized in any hydropower application, though no licenses have been denied solely because of inclusion on the inventory. Hoping to close an information gap, the Park Service in 1982 began a listing of important urban rivers in the East, an addendum variously pursued and then forgotten, still uncompleted. Park Service staff proposed an inventory update to add hundreds of streams that had been missed the first time around, and to include at a minimum all rivers determined by the Forest Service and BLM to be eligible in their land management plans.

In a similar vein, American Rivers published an Outstanding Rivers List incorporating the inventory and other rivers. Included were outstanding whitewater rivers listed by the American Whitewater Affiliation, "priority aquatic sites for biological diversity conservation" listed by the Nature Conservancy, and other sets of rivers. Altogether the American Rivers list included 11,000 entries of 300,000 miles, or 22 percent of the total stream mileage in America—the most complete compendium of quality rivers ever drawn up.

Bern Collins argued that beyond the inventory update, a nation-wide assessment of rivers could do much to focus attention on the plight of free-flowing water, much as wetlands research in the early 1980s and the National Wetlands Assessment had galvanized support for that critical habitat. An ongoing assessment could monitor changes so that everyone would have a better idea of what's really happening to rivers in America. Now, nobody knows.

Even in an expanded form, the inventory might include only 5 percent of the stream mileage. Though that exceeds even the wildest expectations for national river designation, 1 mile in 20 seems an immoderately modest goal when fashioning a future out of all rivers for all generations to come.

RIVERS ON PUBLIC LAND

Diverse, vital, unspoiled rivers flowing through federal land present the greatest opportunity for new advances in the protected river estate of America. Thousands of streams meet eligibility standards for national status, and reserving these is the most politically painless form of preservation (see chapter 3).

Landmark administrative rulings now call on the federal agencies to consider their rivers' eligibility for the wild and scenic system. The Forest Service found 100 segments in Oregon alone, beyond the rivers designated there in 1988. In Idaho, 25 rivers were found eligible (the final number should probably be much higher). A West Virginia proposal included 12 national forest rivers. American Rivers and a statewide coalition in Arizona sought preservation for 1,700 miles on 40 streams.

Alaska is a paradise of public-land rivers, including the Situk, one of the finest steelhead streams in the nation. Flowing amid marketable old-growth timber and with Natives who preferred to develop their own management plan, this river was found "not suitable" by Tongass National Forest officials. In that largest national forest in the nation, 112 rivers qualified for wild and scenic status; the Forest Service recommended 24, about half of them already in wilderness. Also in the Tongass, the lower Stikine flows as one of the great wild rivers of North America, the "100 mile long Yosemite," according to John Muir. Canadian dam and mine proposals threaten the upper Stikine, and commercial fishing threatens lower reaches of this northern artery. Alaska's Tazimina River is one of the most important sockeye salmon streams flowing to the rich Bristol Bay, but it is vulnerable to hydroelectric dams. The Kongakut on the north slope needs better recreational management, and its Arctic National Wildlife Refuge needs permanent protection instead of the current open-door consideration for oil and gas drilling.

In Washington state, the Forest Service found 107 rivers eligible and recommended 53. In 1991, the Northwest Rivers Council, Sierra Club, and other groups made their case for designation of 87 rivers in a comprehensive catalogue of these splendid waterways—the finest documentation of an omnibus rivers proposal ever put together. The streams include such notables as the Elwah of epic salmon spawning grounds, where a large dam may be removed to restore the fishery; the upper Skagit, omitted from earlier designation because of a dam threat; Big Beaver Creek, with remarkable old-growth forests once slated for flooding by a raised Ross Dam; the Carbon and White as they crash off Mount Rainier; the Methow and Wenatchee of the idyllic east Cascades; the Green, a playground for Seattle; the Toutle, beneath stark volcanism of Mount Saint Helens; and the Snake River just below Hells Canyon and ecologically a part of it.

Not to be outdone, Friends of the River in California sought national designation for 100 rivers out of 143 that the Forest Service and BLM had thus far deemed eligible. Included were 19 tributaries to the Klamath, which would elevate it to a highly protected river system, neighboring the Smith with its abundance of similarly designated tributaries. In the agricultural Sacramento Valley, BLM found 25 miles of the Sacramento River eligible because of habitat for endangered salmon—a significant finding considering the development and resource competition along the waterway. The brilliant Yuba, subject of many hydropower proposals, met eligibility requirements. The Forest Service recommended a 29 mile reach of the North Fork Stanislaus, where another in a long line of power projects was on the boards. Federal agencies recommended an important 8.5 mile extension to the Merced wild and scenic river, and the Forest Service finally admitted the eligibility of the critical 11 miles of the Kings, given "special management" but not national river status in 1987. Even in southern California, the Forest Service found nine streams eligible in the San Bernardino National Forest. The agency, however, did not recommend choice but threatened reaches that Friends of the River supported on the North Fork Mokelumne, Clavey, and Cosumnes rivers. If this doggedly determined and talented organization delivers as it has in the past, Friends of the Rivers' 100 Rivers campaign could yield one of the most monumental advances ever for river protection.

Wilderness areas harbor some of the recommended mileages of public-land rivers, and additional segments will be found in national parks. For status and symbolism, it once made sense to designate those premier, already protected rivers, but conservationists have succeeded in the "numbers game" of adding streams and mileage to the rivers system. To pad that mileage with unnecessary protective overlays is no longer needed as proof of success. While marginal reasons support the designation of any river—for instance, wilderness streams could be developed by presidential exemption or by hydropower variances within specific wilderness legislation, and national park rivers could be crowded with tourist clutter—those reasons generally lack urgency today. Bulking up the system with twice-saved rivers can be counterproductive, handing opponents the numbers to argue that enough is enough.

The nonwilderness national forest and BLM rivers, however, remain vulnerable, subject to hydropower dam proposals that often elicit agreeable responses from the agencies in charge of stewardship of the land. Subsidized logging, subsidized grazing, subsidized mining, and subsidized road building have taken clear precedence over the health of streams on most public property. National designation firmly protects rivers instead of abandoning them to an acquisitive brand of politics fueled by commodity spokespeople who move efficiently in the halls of Congress and at the upper levels of the bureaucracies.

RIVERS ON BORROWED TIME

Although the era of big dam building has ended, the era of river destruction has not, and neither have all the big dam plans. Auburn Dam poses the largest single threat to de facto wild and scenic rivers in America: it could flood 48 wild canyon miles of the American River's North and Middle forks in California. Friends of the River, the Planning and Conservation League, and local groups are lobbying for a national recreation area instead, strategically appealing to a recreation-based economy, something that wild and scenic status does not overtly do.

With the economic backing that power sales generate, utilities, entrepreneurs, and municipalities continue to propose hundreds of hydroelectric dams. The Klamath in Oregon, Clavey in California, Gunnison in Colorado, and Penobscot in Maine have been threatened and threatened again. When power prices go up—they've declined relative to inflation for many years—an intensified threat will press upon rivers wherever water plunges downhill.

Cities and states will again plot for water supply dams to slake the thirst of desert and poorly planned areas of growth, such as those in central Arizona and even suburban Seattle. Water conservation and conversion of unsuitable irrigated farmland can meet many needs for many years, but the threats will nonetheless rear up where suppliers cling to an outdated bias for new development as preferable to careful management, and where growth pressures exceed the ability to make do with existing reserves.

Though uncommon by past standards, flood control proposals continue; for instance, that is the major threat to the Greenbrier, one of the longest free-flowing rivers remaining in the East. Flood control is likewise the current "justification" for Auburn Dam.

A proposed British Columbia copper mine endangers Alaska's enormous, superlative, perfectly wild Alsek River. Highway expansion in Alpine Canyon of the Snake River, a national study river south of Jackson Hole, could turn that intensely popular whitewater canyon of the Rockies to alternate piles of cut and fill. The enriched, biologically vital swamp rivers of Louisiana, notwithstanding the urgency of wetlands preservation, are still being dredged and channeled. The national rivers system offers a fundamental tool to avert all of these intrusions to the remaining natural rivers.

Threats to rivers have always engendered the strongest motivation to add mileage to the national rivers system. If opposition to new protection increases and jeopardizes growth of the rivers program, the federally related threats, such as hydroelectric dams, will remain the convincing reason to designate more rivers. In this minimalist scenario, the future list of national rivers may be identical to the list of explicitly threatened rivers.

THE HEART OF THE ECOSYSTEM

Selection of rivers to be saved has had little to do with any systematic view of ecosystems or the vital matters of life and death for entire species. Likewise, and related to this, many of the nation's 80 physiographic provinces lack a designated river. Just as protection emphasis has variously focused on wildness, recreation, scenery, and threats, it could turn to critical habitats, a shift supported by endangered species efforts that have given rise to broader ecosystem concerns.

Endangered species depend unequivocally on rivers. The sockeye and other runs of salmon in the Snake River, the humpback chub in the San Juan, Green, and Colorado, and scores of other species balance at the edge of extinction. Bald eagles, peregrine falcons, and many other endangered species require river corridor protection for survival. Far more water-dependent species are in trouble than terrestrial ones.

A review of the nation's rivers to find gaps in protected riverine ecosystems would reveal serious shortcomings in the estate of saved rivers. A few streams where ecological concerns are highlighted are the Snake and Salmon in Idaho for anadromous fisheries, the Chilkat in Alaska and Hoh in Washington for bald eagles, the Platte in Nebraska for waterfowl traveling the midcontinent flyway, the Blackwater in West Virginia for the largest muskeg bog in the Appalachians, and the Appalachicola in Florida for southern blackwater and hardwood swamps, which have been reduced from 50 million to less than 3 million acres throughout the country. Legislation in 1992 intended to protect some areas of old-growth forests would secure the ecosystem integrity of many streams through ancient forests in Washington, Oregon, and California, most of them eligible or recommended for national river designation by the Forest Service.

In 1991, American Rivers announced a five-year program emphasizing the protection of river systems, not just segments, and stressing the importance of marine life, wetlands, endangered species, and biological diversity. "We realized we were not saving rivers; we were saving places," said Scootch Pankonin, vice chair for the group. "Now it's time to look at the job of protecting river systems." In keeping with the goal, the organization named the Snake and Columbia rivers the most endangered in 1992, citing an American Fisheries Society study that found 214 of the system's native fish and anadromous fish runs to be endangered, threatened, or imperiled.

The need for ecosystem management is clearly realized, but the prospect of actually succeeding is fogged by the failures at far less ambitious attempts in the past. In the face of stern resistance to even 100 foot setbacks or flood plain zoning, the expanded task is daunting, inevitably involving the whole range of protection techniques: water quality laws, water rights for instream flows, land use regulation, land acquisition, public facility planning, and wild and scenic designations.

LANDMARK RIVERS

Stretching across great expanses of a great landscape, surviving with epic sections intact after a century of development elsewhere, some rivers still flow as American landmarks.

The most galvanizing prospect for the national rivers system might be to add the Colorado River as it cuts through the most symbolic of all canyons. No section of the river—one of the six great waterways draining the Rockies—is included in the national rivers system, and in spite of national park status, the Grand Canyon suffers constant degradation by the erosive hydropower flushes from Glen Canyon Dam. Unlike most national park rivers, this one is not adequately protected.

The 1,056-mile-long Snake River—the second largest on the West Coast, after the Columbia, and two and a half times the volume of the Colorado—serves up one of the most varied and fascinating riverine systems on the continent. A 100 mile reach from the headwaters in Yellowstone to Palisades Reservoir excepting only Jackson Reservoir (the largest intrusion in any national park) would incorporate one of America's five largest roadless regions, the quintessential river-and-mountain landscape through Jackson Hole, the Rocky Mountains' finest high elevation riparian belt, the most floated river in the national park system, and one of the Rockies' two most popular whitewater runs. A classic among American rivers, the upper Snake is threatened and abused yet capable of recovery.

The Salmon River in Idaho, the nation's longest undammed stream outside Alaska, offers a kaleidoscope of mountain scenery and vital anadromous fish habitat, every bit of it suitable for protection from top to bottom, 420 miles. Although 237 miles were studied, only 125 were designated in 1980.

The Yellowstone in Wyoming and Montana, an idyllic wild and scenic river in upper reaches, runs for 670 miles from the first national park to the Missouri with only four diversion dams in lower reaches blocking the flow.

Alaska's Susitna, America's fifteenth largest river, slices through a thunderously roaring canyon that was threatened in the 1970s with damming. The Yukon, the third longest river in the United States, flows the whole way across Alaska where virtually every mile remains wild, vital to Indians and Innuit, and with continental significance to fish, wildlife, and waterfowl. It's fine to have the Horsepasture River of 4.2 miles in the national rivers system, but what of this howlingly wild reach of water, 1,980 miles long counting its upper reaches in Canada? To safeguard the Yukon today would be like designating as wild and scenic the whole Mississippi, the whole Columbia, or the whole Saint Lawrence in the year 1750, and it is reasonable to do this: national river status would preclude nothing that is existing or planned.

The Green River, from Flaming Gorge Dam to Lake Powell behind Glen Canyon Dam, survives as one of the nation's longest sections of runnable, free-flowing water outside Alaska, 407 miles traversing remote canyons and ranchland of the Utah desert. Within this reach, Desolation Canyon is one of the longest sections of river flowing through wild country with no roads or development (the Grand Canyon and Rio Grande have longer undeveloped reaches). Two other long runnable sections in the United States are the nearby Yampa-Green and White-Green combinations of 462 and 391 miles respectively.

Only one reach of the Columbia—the largest river on the West Coast and the fourth largest in volume in America—escapes without dams, a 51-mile-long section below Priest Rapids Dam now under wild and scenic study.

The Potomac, with remarkable forks through Appalachian country of jumbled topography, mountain farms, and rural villages, swells as a giant of the East, a vital source for the Chesapeake Bay, and a backdrop to the nation's identity at Washington, DC, and Mount Vernon. A 1975 bill to create a Potomac National River with a greenway for 100 miles from Cumberland to Washington failed, but perhaps the time will come once again to recognize a most symbolic river. The Hudson, surviving its dam threats of the 1950s, continues to flow with wildness and whitewater from an Adirondack stronghold in upstate New York.

The Suwannee may be the archetypal river of the Deep South and is the only remaining unprotected river from the original list of national river priorities in the early 1960s.

In the mid 1980s, National Park Service director William Penn Mott suggested that a complete river system be made a national park as a model of stewardship (47 rivers and another 46 diminutive tributaries are designated as national rivers from source to mouth, some of them quite small). A systematic search found 150 rivers worth considering. California's Smith, with its entire length and most of its tributaries already designated, was the obvious candidate, but Park Service planners looked further with hopes of political support. Among many possibilities were the Big Two Hearted made famous by Ernest Hemingway in Michigan and the Blackwater River on Maryland's eastern shore. The idea faded, perhaps doomed from the beginning by the ambitiousness of the concept and a presidential administration ideologically opposed to expansion of the park system.

The landmark rivers for now lie beyond political grasp, yet the importance, imagination, and symbolism attached to them dramatize the central role of rivers in American geography. For some of these streams, only a minor shift in politics would be needed; only one member of the House of Representatives is elected from Wyoming, for example. Alaska has one representative, Idaho has only two, and it is not out of the question that a changing electorate will someday vote a river conservationist into office. As the rivers movement matures, perhaps some of these magnificent waterways will receive protection to match their scale on the map of America.

THE NEEDS OF THE FUTURE

The river conservation movement bustles with possibilities. Congressional bills in the early 1990s would designate the threatened Klamath in Oregon. If all the legislation in the works in 1992 were to pass, the system would grow by 3,000 miles. New interest has arisen in the Southeast, where economic prosperity has perhaps given birth to a protection mentality, and in New England, where improved water quality led to recognition of a traditional regional belief that rivers are important to economy and to culture.

Renewed efforts could protect the study rivers, the Nationwide Rivers Inventory, the federal-land rivers, the threatened rivers, and streams that underpin vital ecosystems. Perhaps rivers of truly landmark stature will someday be recognized.

To be effective, river conservationists must form coalitions with allies of many kinds. People who fish and boat are an obvious core of support, but *everybody* enjoys rivers. The coalitions can include civic organizations that recognize the importance of the river to community identity, homeowners and agricultural groups that know the importance of open space in their surroundings, urban dwellers along with rural residents and irrigators for whom water quality is a concern, reform-minded leaders who strive for efficient use of land and the economic savings that come with flood plain management, and recreational groups that favor the riverfront for hiking, biking, running, and riding trails—activities that constitute one-third of all recreation in, for example, a state as recreation-oriented as California.

Chris Brown of the National Park Service, one of the key spokespeople for rivers nationwide, identified four pillars on which river conservation stands: American Rivers as the central lobbying organization; the federal government with the national rivers program and technical assistance; the state scenic rivers and related programs; and most of all, the grass roots in state, regional, and local groups, over 1,000 of them working on their rivers. Brown said, "The health of all is essential for progress, and the only really protected river is one with a vigilant organization looking after it."

Who opposes wild and scenic river protection? The National Inholders Association is perhaps the only organization that categorically fights designations, though the National Hydropower Association would come close. The latter's director, Elaine Evans, derides river supporters as "yuppies and elitists" for opposing private hydropower plans. Other opponents have included some landowners in small communities, chambers of commerce, the timber industry in the Northwest, and miners in Alaska, though none has represented an organized front or opposed river conservation across the board.

The resistance to national river designations grew as the movement for protection grew. Even with careful work on studies such as the Farmington in Connecticut, and even where national forest rivers flow as gems of an already public estate, resistance rears up and halts all but the strongest commitments. At those times, it seems that the Craighead brothers' "positive alternative" to constantly fighting rearguard battles is an illusion, a good idea that failed. In fact, it sometimes seems that fighting the threats as they come up is the only tenable course, ironically receiving frequent support from people who had opposed preventive measures that would have precluded new dams and diversions.

The confounding reality is that much of the resistance to protecting rivers is based on misunderstanding, the correction of which is so easily addressed but so unwillingly heard. Every attempt to designate a river is unnecessarily thrown into the pit of jurisdiction battles over land use. Those who would save a river are absurdly forced to confront fundamental principles of individual rights in America, when what they are fighting for is the survival of the America that made individual rights possible.

Given the perceived importance of such irrelevant arguments, and with little likelihood of winning the rhetorical battles in the forums where they are typically held, it's amazing that river conservation goes *anywhere*. Recognizing that designation attempts have lost too many of the contests against misunderstanding, American Rivers in 1991 did not give up but nonetheless identified the need for "new strategies and tools for rivers flowing through private lands."

With those discouraging words, some perspective on the question of success is in order. History shows that tenacious opposition has almost *always* surfaced, dating back to hearings on the original 1968 Wild and Scenic Rivers Act, yet much protection was accomplished anyway. And counter to daily pessimism, the rivers program compares well with the other federal natural area efforts (see chapter 3).

But river supporters should expect difficulties because the national rivers system seeks more than the parks, wilderness, and refuge programs ever sought. The rivers program accepts private land and the status quo, depends on watershed management above and below the limited reaches, and confronts the host of forces for change—land development, dams, channelization, diversions, logging, mining, and roads—not in "wastelands" but in prime areas for these activities.

Even more significant, the rivers program is a bridge from the efforts to protect isolated tracts, such as parks, to an expanded and voluntary stewardship for watersheds and ecosystems. *Of course* the resistance is strong. In a nation largely rejecting the pursuit of a land ethic, the rivers program is a bellwether attempt to adopt that stewardship outlook, still focused on particular places but going beyond the traditional public estate of federal land.

Though it simplifies the approach, the national rivers system can alternately be regarded as a public land designation or as a broader and generic form of land and water reform. The program is clearly successful in the first category. The difficulties with the second category are formidable, but that might be expected in a nation that so often rejects land use and ecosystem management when the decisions are tough. As society's outlook on the environment necessarily evolves toward one of more care, sustainability, and stewardship for future generations, the rivers program may both lead the way and benefit from the shifts in conventional wisdom.

National river movements can recognize not only wild and scenic aspects but also recreational and cultural values, and can expand protection to serve masses of people. Along with this, river reclamation challenges the imagination; many damaged and destroyed rivers can be put back to the way they were or at least to a level that permits use and enjoyment. People see the results on waterways that were fetid with pollution 20 years ago but are cleaner today, such as the Potomac, Cuyahoga, and Willamette. The possibilities are endless: reclaiming ripped-up shorelines, restoring flows where diversions now squander runoff unnecessarily, dismantling dams that have grown useless and dangerous with age. Some of these reclaimed rivers, such as the Elwha in Washington where dams might be removed, or the upper West Branch of the Susquehanna in Pennsylvania, where acid mine drainage is being reduced, could be nationally designated as models of society's search for the lost wonders of America.

Private and nonprofit conservancies can acquire land more easily than the government can, and they can protect it with less ire from local residents. In this form and without condemnation of homes or farms, acquisition of the most critical riverfronts can save the vestige of native landscape that graces our valleys in the 1990s but won't much longer without aggressive stewardship.

To manage the rivers as ecosystems becomes increasingly critical to the survival of these watery threads of life and to the health and existence of all creatures dependent on the flow. River management can look beyond the backyard of parochial concerns and toward whole watersheds to gain effectiveness in saving meaningful landscapes. Water quality, releases from reservoirs, logging in headwaters, and the whole package of impacts on earth are being reconsidered for what they do to rivers. Much of this lies outside the bounds of national river designations, which becomes one of the strongest points of this conclusion: the Wild and Scenic Rivers System is limited in the number of rivers and the shortness of the sections that are designated. Though they are not the subject of this book, many other approaches are vital.

FLOWING FREE

The national rivers system has proven its value: dams have been stopped, shorelines protected, and recreational management improved. Landowners along rivers designated in the past 20 years have seen little to fear; in fact, the program delivers the rural refuge that many people desire. This is one of the least expensive endeavors for natural area protection.

We've learned to involve local residents from the beginning of a proposal, to consider all values of a natural river, to avoid eminent domain and the polarization of landowners; we've learned to pursue the finest threatened streams before it's too late, and to effectively manage these places after they've been designated. Now we just need to practice what we've learned.

The national rivers system may be the natural areas program of the future, the pioneer in coping with the difficult conflicts between existing development and the protection of what is left. Since the early 1900s when legislation was passed to dam, channelize, and promote building along rivers, hundreds of laws have speeded development. In 1968 the Wild and Scenic Rivers Act was passed to favor the rivers for their natural qualities. A promise of balanced use of water has become a central aspect of conservation and the environmental movement, but balance has not yet been achieved.

Through reformed thinking and progressive action that saves rivers while recognizing the complexities of life and the needs of people, the national rivers can stand boldly for a new stewardship of the earth.

Sources

CHAPTER 2. THE LEGACY OF PROTECTION

American Rivers Conservation Council and American Rivers, Inc. Newsletters, 1974–92.

Olson, Kent W. *Natural Rivers and the Public Trust.* Washington, DC: American Rivers, 1988. Booklet.

Palmer, Tim. *Endangered Rivers and the Conservation Movement.* Berkeley: University of California Press, 1986. Contains information on additional sources.

Tarlock, Dan. "Preservation of Scenic Rivers." *Kentucky Law Journal* 55 (1967).

U.S. Congress. *The Wild and Scenic Rivers Act Through September 30, 1990.* A composite of the act and its amendments prepared by the U.S. Department of the Interior, National Park Service, Park Planning and Protection Division, Washington, DC.

U.S. House of Representatives. *Providing for a National Scenic Rivers System, and for Other Purposes.* 90th Cong., 2d Sess., Report No. 1623, July 3, 1968.

U.S. Senate. *National Wild and Scenic Rivers System.* 90th Cong., 1st Sess., Report No. 491, August 4, 1967.

Watanabe, Anne. *Two Decades of River Protection.* Washington, DC: American Rivers, 1988. Unpublished paper.

INTERVIEWS

Brent Blackwelder, American Rivers, Washington, DC

David Bolling, Friends of the River, San Francisco

Stewart Brandborg, Wilderness Society, Washington, DC

Christopher Brown, American Rivers and National Park Service, Washington, DC

Howard Brown, American Rivers, Washington, DC

Al Buck, Bureau of Outdoor Recreation, Washington, DC

Chuck Clusen, chair, American Rivers, Washington, DC

Bern Collins, National Park Service, Washington, DC

Kevin Coyle, American Rivers, Washington, DC

Frank Craighead, wildlife biologist, Moose, WY

John Craighead, wildlife biologist, Missoula

Dale Crane, staff, House Interior and Insular Affairs Committee, Washington, DC

Bob Doppelt, Oregon Rivers Council, Eugene

Paul Bruce Dowling, America the Beautiful Fund, Washington, DC

Mark Dubois, Friends of the River and World Wise, Sacramento

Bob Eastman, National Park Service, Washington, DC

Glenn Eugster, National Park Service, Philadelphia

Brock Evans, National Audubon Society, Washington, DC

Mike Fremont, Rivers Unlimited, Ohio, Cincinnati

Donn Furman, Committee to Save the Kings River, Fresno

John Haubert, National Park Service, Washington, DC

Jack Hession, Sierra Club, Anchorage

John Kauffmann, National Park Service, Washington, DC

Deen Lundeen, Forest Service, Washington, DC

Michael McCloskey, Sierra Club, San Francisco

Jerry Meral, Planning and Conservation League, Sacramento

Pat Munoz, American Rivers, Washington, DC

Gaylord Nelson, Senate and Wilderness Society, Washington, DC

Kent Olson, American Rivers, Washington, DC

Bill Painter, American Rivers, Washington, DC

Scootch Pankonin, vice-chair, American Rivers, Washington, DC

Ted Schad, staff, Select Senate Committee on National Water Resources, Washington, DC

Larry Stevens, Outdoor Recreation Resources Review Commission, Washington, DC

Ron Stork, Merced Canyon Committee, Sacramento

Ted Swem, National Park Service, Washington, DC

Stewart Udall, Secretary of the Interior, Phoenix
Stanford Young, National Park Service, Seattle

CHAPTER 3. A MALLEABLE SYSTEM

Brown, Christopher, Peter Carlson, and Robert Emeritz, eds. *Winning Strategies for Rivers: Proceedings of the Tenth Annual National Conference on Rivers*. Washington, DC: American Rivers Conservation Council, 1985.

Coyle, Kevin. *The American Rivers Guide to Wild and Scenic River Designation*. Washington, DC: American Rivers, 1988. Looseleaf booklet.

Coyle, Kevin. *Ten Benefits of National Wild and Scenic Rivers Designation to Landowners and Other Local Residents*. Washington, DC: American Rivers, 1990. Unpublished paper.

Diamant, Rolf, Glenn Eugster, and Christopher J. Duerksen. *A Citizen's Guide to River Conservation*. Washington, DC: Conservation Foundation, 1984.

Palmer, Tim. *Endangered Rivers and the Conservation Movement*. Berkeley: University of California Press, 1986.

Palmer, Tim. "A Time for Rivers." *Wilderness* (Fall 1984).

River Conservation Fund. *Flowing Free, A Citizen's Guide for Protection of Wild and Scenic Rivers*. Washington, DC: River Conservation Fund, 1977.

U.S. Department of the Interior. "National Wild and Scenic Rivers System: Final Revised Guidelines for Eligibility, Classification and Management of River Areas." *Federal Register*, September 7, 1982.

U.S. Department of the Interior, National Park Service. *Riverwork Book*. Washington, DC: National Park Service, 1986.

Utter, Jack G., and John D. Schultz. *A Handbook on the Wild and Scenic Rivers Act*. Missoula: University of Montana School of Forestry, 1976. Booklet.

van der Leeden, Frits, Fred L. Troise, and David Keith Todd. *The Water Encyclopedia*. Chelsea, MI: Lewis Publishers, 1990.

Watanabe, Anne. *Two Decades of River Protection*. Washington, DC: American Rivers, November 1988. Unpublished paper.

INTERVIEWS

Pope Barrow, American Whitewater Affiliation, Washington, DC
Barry Beasley, state river manager, South Carolina, Columbia
Chris Brown, National Park Service, Washington, DC
Dennis Canty, National Park Service, Seattle

Tom Cassidy, American Rivers, Washington, DC
Noreen Clough, Fish and Wildlife Service, Washington, DC
Chuck Clusen, chair, American Rivers, Washington, DC
Kevin Coyle, American Rivers, Washington, DC
John Craighead, wildlife biologist, Missoula
Rolf Diamant, National Park Service, Boston
Bob Dreher, Sierra Club Legal Defense Fund, Washington, DC
Bob Eastman, National Park Service, Washington, DC
Steve Evans, Friends of the River, Sacramento
John Haubert, National Park Service, Washington, DC
Jack Hession, Sierra Club, Anchorage
Chuck Hoffman, resource consultant, Silver Spring, MD
Phil Huffman, National Park Service, Boston
Denver James, Forest Service, Washington, DC
Will Kriz, National Park Service, Washington, DC
Tom Lennon, Forest Service, Washington, DC
Deen Lundeen, Forest Service, Washington, DC
Gary Marsh, Bureau of Land Management, Washington, DC
Ken Myers, Forest Service, Washington, DC
Beth Norcross, American Rivers, Washington, DC
Doug North, Northwest Rivers Council, Seattle
Kent Olson, American Rivers, Washington, DC
Ed Pembleton, National Audubon Society, Washington, DC
F. Dale Robertson, Forest Service, Washington, DC
Debbie Sease, Sierra Club, Washington, DC
John Turner, Fish and Wildlife Service, Washington, DC
Steve Whitney, Wilderness Society, Washington, DC
Jamie Williams, National Park Service, Boston

CHAPTER 4. THE CAST OF RIVERS

U.S. Department of Agriculture and Department of the Interior. *National Wild and Scenic Rivers System, December 1990.* Washington: Department of Agriculture and Department of the Interior, 1990. Map and short descriptions.

Additional information for the river listings came from many sources, including U.S. Department of Agriculture and Department of the Interior, wild and scenic river studies for many of the individual rivers. See also Ronald Ziegler, *The Whole Water Reference for Paddlers* (Kirkland, WA: Canoe America Associates, 1991), which lists guidebooks for many rivers.

For river-running guidebooks, see the sources and maps listed with each river. Reports, notes, and maps are filed with the various agencies, with American Rivers, and with regional, state, and local river conservation groups. Staff from the administering agencies were interviewed for some of the rivers, and nearly all river descriptions were reviewed by staff in the field offices, whose information often reflected an updated version of older, printed reports.

CHAPTER 5. THE MANAGEMENT IMPERATIVE

American River Management Society. *River Information Digest*. Littleton, CO: American River Management Society, 1992.

Echeverria, John, Pope Barrow, and Richard Roos-Collins. *Rivers at Risk*. Washington, DC: Island Press, 1989.

Louisiana State University, Department of Landscape Architecture. *1977 Scenic Rivers Symposium*. Baton Rouge: LSU, Department of Landscape Architecture, 1977.

Schafer, Thomas G. *Management Alternatives for the Improvement of Canoeing Opportunities and the Resolution of Problems Relating to the Recreational Use of Rivers*. Technical Report 5. Columbus: Ohio Department of Natural Resources, 1975.

Shelby, Bo, and Mark Danley. *Allocating River Use*. Corvallis: Oregon State University School of Forestry, 1979.

U.S. Department of Agriculture, Forest Service, North Central Forest Experiment Station. *Proceedings: River Recreation Management and Research Symposium*. Saint Paul, MN: Forest Service, 1977.

U.S. Department of the Interior and Department of Agriculture. "National Wild and Scenic Rivers System: Final Revised Guidelines for Eligibility, Classification and Management of River Areas." *Federal Register*, September 7, 1982.

U.S. Department of the Interior, Bureau of Land Management. *Management Guidelines and Standards for National Wild and Scenic Rivers, Oregon and Washington*. Washington, DC: Bureau of Land Management, December, 1989. Unpublished paper.

U.S. Department of the Interior, Bureau of Land Management. *Wild and Scenic River Manual*. Washington, DC: Bureau of Land Management, 1992.

U.S. Department of the Interior, Bureau of Land Management, Medford District. *Management of the Wild and Scenic Rogue River, Needs and Opportunities*. Medford, OR: Bureau of Land Management, 1989. Unpublished paper.

Management plans were consulted for many rivers including the following (see chapter 4 for addresses of agencies for each river): Allagash, ME; American, North Fork, CA; Chattooga, GA; Clearwater, Middle Fork, ID; Delaware, PA; Delta, AK; Flathead, MT; Klickitat, WA; Missouri, MT; New, NC; Obed, TN; Oregon rivers designated in 1988, management guidelines for many rivers; Owyhee, OR; Pere Marquette, MI; Rio Grande, NM; Rogue, OR; Salmon, Middle Fork, ID; Smith, CA; Van Duzen, CA; White Salmon, WA; Wildcat, NH.

INTERVIEWS

Ted Anderson, Challis National Forest, Challis, ID
Norm Ando, Bridger-Teton National Forest, Jackson, WY
Cliff Blake, Forest Service, Ogden, UT
Chris Brown, National Park Service, Washington, DC
Tom Cassidy, American Rivers, Washington, DC
Kevin Coyle, American Rivers, Washington, DC
Rolf Diamant, National Park Service, Boston
Bob Dreher, Sierra Club Legal Defense Fund, Washington, DC
Tom Edgerton, Arctic National Wildlife Refuge, Fairbanks
Don Fox, Yosemite National Park, CA
Marshall Gingery, Grand Teton National Park, WY
Hugh Harper, river guide and wildlife biologist, Boise
Mike Hart, river ranger, Desolation Canyon, UT
John Haubert, National Park Service, Washington, DC
Joe Higgins, Forest Service, Portland, OR
Brian Huddleston, National Park Service, San Francisco
Tom Lennon, Forest Service, Washington, DC
Deen Lundeen, Forest Service, Washington, DC
Gary Marsh, Bureau of Land Management, Washington, DC
Douglass North, Northwest Rivers Council, Seattle
F. Dale Robertson, Forest Service, Washington, DC
Arthur Seamans, Hells Canyon National Recreation Area, Lewiston, ID
Ron Stork, Friends of the River, Sacramento
Brian Stout, Bridger-Teton National Forest, Jackson, WY
John Turner, Fish and Wildlife Service, Washington, DC
Grant Werschkull, former Rogue River ranger, resource consultant, Sacramento
Stanford Young, National Park Service, Seattle

CHAPTER 6. A WIDER RANGE OF PROTECTION

Alling, Curtis Edwin. *An Identification and Analysis of the Critical Obstacles Encountered in the Creation of State Natural Rivers Programs.* College Station: Texas A & M University, Department of Recreation and Parks, 1977. Thesis.

Foreman, Dave, and Howie Wolke. *The Big Outside.* Tucson: Ned Ludd Books, 1989.

Hoffman, Robert C., and Keith Fletcher. *America's Rivers: An Assessment of State River Conservation Programs.* Washington, DC: River Conservation Fund, 1984.

Morrison, Charles C. *State Wild and Scenic River Programs.* Albany: New York State Department of Environmental Conservation, 1983.

Northern Resources Alliance of Minnesota. *25 by 96 Initiative.* International Falls: Northern Resources Alliance of Minnesota, 1990.

U.S. Department of the Interior, Bureau of Outdoor Recreation, *Outdoor Recreation Action* (Spring 1977). Entire issue.

INTERVIEWS

Barry Beasley, scenic rivers manager, Columbia, SC
Rich Bowers, National Association for State River Conservation Programs, Washington, DC
Chris Brown, National Park Service, Washington, DC
Dennis Canty, National Park Service, Seattle
Doug Carter, scenic river manager, Lansing, MI
Kevin Coyle, American Rivers, Washington, DC
Ed Crouse, Federal Energy Regulatory Commission, Washington, DC
Bob Doppelt, Oregon Rivers Council, Eugene
Glenn Eugster, Environmental Protection Agency, Washington, DC
Steve Evans, Friends of the River, Sacramento
Roger Fickes, scenic rivers manager, Harrisburg, PA
Ed Fite, scenic rivers manager, Tulsa, OK
John Haubert, National Park Service, Washington, DC
Chuck Hoffman, resource consultant, Washington, DC
Ann Miles, Federal Energy Regulatory Commission, Washington, DC
Charles Morrison, New York Department of Environmental Conservation, Albany
Sandie Nelson, Northwest Rivers Council, Seattle
Larry Ostrovsky, Alaska Department of Natural Resources, Juneau
Peter Pacquet, Northwest Power Planning Council, Portland, OR

Derek Richerson, scenic rivers manager, Annapolis, MD
Frank Sherman, Idaho Department of Water Resources, Boise
Steve Starlund, scenic river manager, Olympia, WA
Suzi Wilkins, American Rivers, Washington, DC
Wendy Wilson, Idaho Rivers United, Boise
Stanford Young, National Park Service, Seattle

CHAPTER 7. THE UNFINISHED AGENDA

Northwest Rivers Council et al. *Washington State Wild and Scenic Rivers Proposal.* Seattle: Northwest Rivers Council, 1991.

U.S. Department of the Interior, Bureau of Outdoor Recreation. *Outdoor Recreation Action* (Spring 1977). Entire issue.

U.S. Department of the Interior, National Park Service. *Nationwide Rivers Inventory.* Washington, DC: National Park Service, 1982.

U.S. General Accounting Office. *Wild and Scenic Rivers, Certain Rivers Not in National System Generally Retain Original Values.* Washington, DC: General Accounting Office, December 1986.

Watanabe, Anne. *Two Decades of River Protection.* Washington, DC: American Rivers, 1988. Unpublished paper.

INTERVIEWS

Chris Brown, National Park Service, Washington, DC
Bern Collins, National Park Service, Washington, DC
Kevin Coyle, American Rivers, Washington, DC
Ed Crouse, Federal Energy Regulatory Commission, Washington, DC
Doug Finlayson, Northwest Rivers Council, Seattle
John Haubert, National Park Service, Washington, DC
Jack Hession, Sierra Club, Anchorage
Beth Norcross, American Rivers, Washington, DC
Scootch Pankonin, vice-chair, American Rivers, Washington, DC
Claude Terry, resource consultant, Atlanta
Steve Whitney, Wilderness Society, Washington, DC
Suzi Wilkins, American Rivers, Washington, DC

Agencies and Organizations Involved in River Protection

FEDERAL AGENCIES

Bureau of Land Management, Interior Building, 18th and C Sts., N.W., Washington, DC 20240.
National Park Service, P.O. Box 37127, Washington, DC 20013.
U.S. Forest Service, P.O. Box 96090, Washington, DC 20090.

See addresses for each national river, listed in chapter 4.

STAGE AGENCIES

Write to National Association for State and Local River Conservation Programs, 801 Pennsylvania Ave., S.E., Suite 302, Washington, DC 20003.

NATIONAL CONSERVATION ORGANIZATIONS

American Rivers, 801 Pennsylvania Ave., S.E., Suite 303, Washington, DC 20003.
American Whitewater Affiliation, 136 13th St., S.E., Washington, DC 20003.
The River Network, P.O. Box 8787, Portland, OR 97207.
Sierra Club, 730 Polk St., San Francisco, CA 94109.

Trout Unlimited, 501 Church St., N.E., Vienna, VA 22180.
The Wilderness Society, 1400 Eye St., N.W., Washington, DC 20005.

For addresses of hundreds of agencies and organizations involved in river conservation, see the *1990 River Conservation Directory*, available from National Park Service, Recreation Resources Assistance Division, P.O. Box 37127, Washington, DC 20013.

Acknowledgments

The Wild and Scenic Rivers of America depended heavily on interviews, and I'd like to thank everybody who took the time to talk with me. I appreciate the careful review of the manuscript by Ann Vileisis, an environmental historian and whitewater rafting instructor, and by Jamie Williams, a consultant on river planning and a western river naturalist and guide.

Invaluable reviews were made by several of the country's most knowledgeable people in this field: John Haubert of the National Park Service, Chris Brown of the National Park Service, Deen Lundeen of the Forest Service, and Kevin Coyle of American Rivers. Jerry Meral of the California Planning and Conservation League and David Bolling, formerly of Friends of the River—both extraordinarily talented professionals in river protection—also reviewed portions of the manuscript and provided insightful, expert advice. Gary Marsh and LuVerne Grussing of the Bureau of Land Management reviewed chapter 5.

All descriptions in chapter 4 were sent for checking to administering agency staff—79 different offices in all—and most of those managers took the time to read, correct, and comment on my copy that had been derived from government reports and other written sources that were not totally reliable or up to date. Authoritative sources often disagree on what is fact; I hope that my review process has minimized any error.

The work of Stanford Young, now retired from the National Park Service after an important career in this field, provided a valuable source of information.

American Rivers and its staff were generous in offering their files and office space while I did research in Washington, DC, during January 1991. Thanks also to Polly Dement of the American Rivers board for making a part of her home available to me while I worked in Washington. American Rivers provided me with a small grant to help cover my expenses while working on the book.

The Teton Science School near the Snake River in the mountains of Wyoming was an ideal setting with ideal company and encouragement for me to write parts of the manuscript. My thanks to Teton Science School director Jack Shea and to Phil Shephard and Ann Humphrey for use of their cabin while they enjoyed a honeymoon in a warmer climate. Mark Dubois, Sharon Negri, and Tevin Dubois provided extraordinary hospitality while I wrote a portion of the book in Sacramento.

Barbara Dean and the entire Island Press staff provided expert professional advice and partnership throughout the process and continued their remarkable dedication to books on the environment. Photographer Mark Anderman tirelessly printed my black and white photos as he has done for six other books over the past decade.

Reaching much further into my past, I'd like to thank Jerry Walls, a former employer and regional planner of great experience who encouraged my professional interest in this subject.

I'd especially like to offer thanks in memory of Peter W. Fletcher, a professor of forestry, a superb educator, a dedicated believer that thoughtful people can fight environmental destruction, and a truly fine human being who initiated me to the Wild and Scenic Rivers System and launched my career on rivers.

Index

About the Author

Tim Palmer has worked as a planner and writer on rivers and resource topics for twenty years and has explored rivers and mountains throughout North America. His six books include *Endangered Rivers and the Conservation Movement*, *The Sierra Nevada: A Mountain Journey*, and *The Snake River: Window to the West*.

Also Available from Island Press

Balancing on the Brink of Extinction: The Endangered Species Act and Lessons for the Future
Edited by Kathryn A. Kohm

Better Trout Habitat: A Guide to Stream Restoration and Management
By Christopher J. Hunter

Beyond 40 Percent: Record-Setting Recycling and Composting Programs
By The Institute for Local Self-Reliance

Coastal Alert: Ecosystems, Energy, and Offshore Oil Drilling
By Dwight Holing

Death in the Marsh
By Tom Harris

The Energy-Environment Connection
Edited by Jack M. Hollander

Farming in Nature's Image
By Judith Soule and Jon Piper

The Global Citizen
By Donella Meadows

Healthy Homes, Healthy Kids
By Joyce Schoemaker and Charity Vitale

Holistic Resource Management
By Allan Savory

Inside the Environmental Movement: Meeting the Leadership Challenge
By Donald Snow

Last Animals at the Zoo: How Mass Extinction Can Be Stopped
By Colin Tudge

Learning to Listen to the Land
Edited by Bill Willers

Lessons from Nature: Learning to Live Sustainably on the Earth
By Daniel D. Chiras

The Living Ocean: Understanding and Protecting Marine Biodiversity
By Boyce Thorne-Miller and John G. Catena

Making Things Happen
By Joan Wolfe

Media and the Environment
Edited by Craig LaMay and Everette E. Dennis

Nature Tourism: Managing for the Environment
Edited by Tensie Whelan

The New York Environment Book
By Eric A. Goldstein and Mark A. Izeman

Our Country, The Planet: Forging a Partnership for Survival
By Shridath Ramphal

Overtapped Oasis: Reform or Revolution for Western Water
By Marc Reisner and Sarah Bates

Population, Technology, and Lifestyle: The Transition to Sustainability
Edited by Robert Goodland, Herman E. Daly, and Salah El Serafy

Rain Forest in Your Kitchen: The Hidden Connection Between Extinction and Your Supermarket
By Martin Teitel

Rivers at Risk: The Concerned Citizen's Guide to Hydropower
By John D. Echeverria, Pope Barrow, and Richard Roos-Collins

The Sierra Nevada: A Mountain Journey
By Tim Palmer

The Snake River: Window to the West
By Tim Palmer

Taking Out the Trash: A No-Nonsense Guide to Recycling
By Jennifer Carless

Turning the Tide: Saving the Chesapeake Bay
By Tom Horton and William M. Eichbaum

Visions upon the Land: Man and Nature on the Western Range
By Karl Hess, Jr.

For a complete catalog of Island Press publications, please write:
Island Press, Box 7, Covelo, CA 95428, or call: 1-800-828-1302

Island Press
Board of Directors